D1561181

AMPHIBIANS AND REPTILES OF NORTHERN GUATEMALA, THE YUCATÁN, AND BELIZE

By Jonathan A. Campbell

University of Oklahoma Press
Norman

Also by Jonathan A. Campbell

(with W. W. Lamar) *The Venomous Reptiles of Latin America* (Ithaca, 1989)

Library of Congress Cataloging-in-Publication Data

Campbell, Jonathan A.
    Amphibians and reptiles of Northern Guatemala, the Yucatán, and Belize / by
Jonathan A. Campbell.
        p.   cm. — (Animal natural history series : v. 4)
    Includes bibliographical references (p.   ) and index.
    ISBN: 0–8061–3064–4 (cloth)

    1. Reptiles—Guatemala—Petén (Dept.) 2. Reptiles—Yucatán Peninsula. 3. Rep-
tiles—Belize. 4. Amphibians—Guatemala—Petén (Dept.) 5. Amphibians—Yucatán Peninsula. 6. Amphibians—Belize.
    I. Title. II. Series.
    QL656.G9C35   1998
    597.9'097281'2—dc21   96–13121
                                                                                  CIP

Amphibians and Reptiles of Northern Guatemala, the Yucatán, and Belize is Volume 4 in the Animal Natural History Series.

1 2 3 4 5 6 7 8 9 10

CONTENTS

ILLUSTRATIONS

PREFACE AND ACKNOWLEDGMENTS

Although the Department of Petén constitutes about the northern third of Guatemala, until comparatively recently no system of roads connected the region with the rest of Guatemala. Petén was, in many respects, a nearly autonomous region and terra incognita to most *capitalinos*. Other than via a few remote, unpaved airstrips, most of the region was inaccessible by means other than on foot, with a beast of burden, or by boat along the major rivers. Tropical forest marked by many scattered Mayan archaeological sites and an occasional rural village or *chiclero* camp characterized the flat lands and rolling hills of Petén. One of the most famous Mayan cities, Tikal, lies a short distance to the northeast of Lago Petén Itzá, the largest lake in the Yucatán Peninsula. Tikal and the area immediately surrounding it were declared a national park by the Guatemalan government in June 1955, when the biota

within the boundaries of this park were for the first time offered protection that has lasted to the present day.

I first visited Petén in the late 1950s when I was 12 years old. My family moved to Guatemala City the year before and we set about exploring many of Guatemala's varied landscapes. My father originally had arranged for a week's stay at Tikal, but at my constant haranguing, he finally made arrangements for me to stay on by myself for more than two months after our initial visit. The break for the school year had just begun and I suppose he thought it safer for an adolescent to spend time in Petén than to prowl the streets and back alley business establishments of Guatemala City.

Many of the ancient Mayan cities, including those of Tikal, Uaxactún, Nakún, Yaxjá, and Ceibal, were devoid of today's multitude of tourists when I eagerly explored them. I "discovered" the caves of Jobitzinaj, Actun Kan, and Najohnaj Coholtunich, which at that time were almost unknown to people outside the immediate region. Fishing was one of my favorite activities and my hook pulled in many a *pescado blanco (Petenia splendida)* and *mojarra (Cichlasoma* sp.) from the waters of Lago Petén Itzá and the Río de La Pasión. With my trusty two-cell flashlight, I spent warm nights patrolling the edges of Lago Petén Itzá, the Río Holmul, and numerous nameless aguadas in search of any living thing that caught my fancy—and I was rarely disappointed.

I came to know many of the local inhabitants, including the *chicleros* who roamed the forest in search of the zapote tree *(Achras zapota)*, on which they would gouge out diagonal slashes with their machetes to gather the sap that would become the chewing gum purchased mainly by North American and Japanense city dwellers. I was fascinated by their woodsmanship and lore of the forest. Many of their fantastic tales I subsequently came to realize were about as credible as those told to me in later life by my Texan friends, but it made little matter to me at the time. They were the stuff that stoked my imagination and I wanted to believe everything I heard.

Some of the chicleros' scourges made me their host. These included the *nigua*, a flea *(Tunga penetrans)*, the female of which burrows on the skin, usually around the toenails or into the sole of the foot, growing to about the size of a pea and pumping thousands of eggs out of a tiny opening to the outside. Throughout Latin America there is a rumor, unfounded I believe, that the nigua bites only pigs and gringos; but they did seem to have a predilection for my fair skin. Periodically, I also contracted a number of *colmoyotes* usually on the back of my neck. These botfly *(Dermatobia hominis)* larvae soon grow to a size where they cause discomfort as they move around in their subcutaneous environment. They are easily removed, however, by suffocation. Each has a tiny breathing tube which supplies it with air through an opening in the boil-like structure it causes. I was first shown by chicleros how to use dripping wax from a candle to cover the hole and kill its occupant so that it could more easily be extracted; subsequently, I have learned that vaseline or even sticky tape can accomplish the same purpose without causing the mild burn resulting from hot wax.

Today, my recollections of some of the events of that first trip to Petén are more vivid than many memories I have of graduate school some fifteen years later. My one great overriding passion was, and remains, wildlife, especially amphibians and reptiles. During this initial trip, I was able to see the fiery reflections of the eyes of Morelet's crocodiles in the beam of my flashlight; huge Central American river turtles feeding tranquilly on wild fruits that fell into the river from overhanging boughs; an ill-tempered boa constrictor removed unceremoniously from the chicken coop of the neighbors after it had feasted on the rooster that awakened the community every morning at 4:00 A.M., and, on several occasions, a fearsome *barba amarilla* stretched across my footpath. But mostly I saw myriad small frogs, lizards, and snakes of which I knew nothing—not even their names. Many of these had no common local name other than *rana*, *lagartija*, or *culebra*. I was determined to learn something about these animals. I have subsequently returned to Petén perhaps fifty times and have come to know much of the herpetofauna relatively well and to regard many of these species as old friends.

In boxes among the species accounts, I have described some of my personal experiences with these remarkable and fascinating animals, even though I have little doubt that these encounters mean more to me than to anyone else and probably suffer in the recounting. I have been urged by my wife and others who know me well to tell some of these tales. Perhaps they have tired of my relating these stories and think that if I put them to paper, that will be the end of it.

Edmund "Butch" D. Brodie, Jr., Joseph R. Mendelson III, Eric N. Smith, Manuel E. Acevedo, Mahmood Sasa, and Ron Savage were my able field companions at various times and at various places in Petén. I especially owe a debt of gratitude to my wife, Tanya G. Dowdey, who has accompanied me on many of my excursions to Petén over the last ten years and who has enjoyed the hunt for various herpetological *bichos* as much as I have. In 1995, Butch Brodie spent over a month with me waiting for the rains that seemed as if they would never come. I am grateful to Judy Brodie for her collecting prowess, which included the discovery of the *Diploglossus* illustrated in figure 111. For help in collecting specimens while I was away, I am indebted to Tomás Najar of San Antonio and to Rafael Antonio Gonzalez of El Remate. I thank Santiago Billy and Oscar Lara for information on crocodiles. Antonio Ozaeta Z., the director of the Centro Recreativo Petencito on Lago Petén Itzá, kindly allowed me to photograph specimens in his care; I will not soon forget the response of the nesting Morelet's crocodile upon my entering her enclosure. My good friends Haroldo García, Luis Savala, and Miguel Angel Vásquez were most helpful during my visits to the Parque Nacional Tikal and elsewhere in Petén. Haroldo García, in particular, accompanied me on a number of forays and always seemed to know where the best *tepezcuintle* (a large and delicious species of rodent) was being served. Mario Jolón, a student from the Universidad de San Carlos who was studying mammals at Tikal, was kind enough to share with me his interesting discovery of the shed barba amarilla skins that he found in the cheek pouches of spiny pocket mice. I thank the "iron man," Eduardo Cofiño, my host at Hotel Gringo Perdido on the northeastern shore of Lago Petén Itzá; unfortunately his effort to "whip me into shape" was a complete failure.

I am fortunate, indeed, in having a number of friends and colleagues who are talented photographers and who responded to my pleas for photographs. These people include David G. Barker, Butch Brodie, Courtney Conway, William E. Duellman, William W. Lamar, Julian C. Lee, Robert A. Lubeck, Mark A. Nelson, Louis Porras, Peter Rockstroh, Eric Smith, Peter J. Stafford, Richard C. Vogt, and John E. Werler. Their specific contributions are acknowledged in the photo credits at the back of the book. The illustrations that appear in figures 10–13 were rendered by the following persons: Greg Willis and Gretchen Bracher (anurans), E. Galaviz (turtles, courtesy of Gustavo Casas-Andreu), Ty Kubin (lizards), and Mike Jusko (snakes). Manuel Paredes Chub, Antonio Cruz, and Oscar Paz from the Alcaldía of El Estor, Guatemala, I thank for assistance in photographing several recalcitrant *Crocodylus acutus* individuals.

A number of people have been helpful to me in my efforts to accumulate information relevant to the herpetofauna of Petén; these include James R. Dixon, William Duellman, Darrel R. Frost, Harry W. Greene, John B. Iverson, Roy W. McDiarmid, John R. Meyer, Ron Nussbaum, Greg Schneider, John Simmons, the late L. C. Stuart, R. Wayne VanDevender, and Jens Vindum. Over the years, many persons in official positions with the Comisión Nacional del Medio Ambiente and the Comisión Nacional de Areas Protegidas have courteously and tolerantly attended to my many requests; these officials include Jorge Cabrera and Santiago Billy (1987–89), Andreas Lehnhoff (1989–91), Enma Díaz de Gordillo (1993–96), Otoniel Chacón (1995–96), Oscar Lara (1994–96), and Mygdalia García (1995–96). Daniel R. Formanowicz, Darrel Frost, Harry Greene, William Lamar, Mahmood Sasa, and Alejandro Solórzano all read portions of the manuscript. Butch Brodie Jr., Tanya Dowdey, Roy W. McDiamid, Joseph Mendelson, and Eric Smith took on the daunting task of reading the manuscript in its entirety. All made useful comments, for which I am grateful. Karin Castañeda, Eric Smith, and Ofelia Urrutia kindly helped with translation of the identification keys into Spanish. Eric Smith was especially helpful in my coining of vernacular names for some of the lesser known species of amphibians and reptiles and in collecting large numbers of snakes in eastern Guatemala. Karin Castañeda recorded data from a multitude of contorted museum specimens. It has been my good fortune to work with a skilled group of individuals from the University of Oklahoma Press and I am appreciative of their assistance and cooperation in seeing this manuscript through the tedious process of publication; especially, I wish to acknowledge the help of Sally E. Antrobus, Jo Ann Reece, Kimberly Wiar, and Karen C. Wieder.

Victor H. Hutchison ably served as the general editor of the Animal Natural History series and offered encouragement and help.

Some of the research on which this work is based was supported in part by the Texas Advanced Research Program Grant No. 003656-001 to me. While it is always a pleasure to acknowledge those who have assisted in such a project as the assembling of this book, because its beginning reaches back many years I have undoubtedly omitted people whose trails I have crossed to my benefit. To all of them, my heartfelt thanks.

AMPHIBIANS AND REPTILES OF NORTHERN GUATEMALA, THE YUCATÁN, AND BELIZE

INTRODUCTION

We have an innate desire to identify the animals we see. When one knows what an animal is, it is not as quickly forgotten, a new appreciation and interest is gained for the species, and it becomes a more significant experience for the person who finds and identifies it. The chief aim in this book is to help in the identification of the amphibians and reptiles inhabiting the Petén region of northern Guatemala and immediately adjoining areas. My intent has been to write a brief guide for a general audience, including biologists who are not herpetologists. Because most laypersons (and, if the truth be known, most professional herpetologists too) may prefer to identify the amphibians and reptiles they see using photographs or descriptions, individual species accounts and photographs of nearly all species covered make up the main body of this guide. In the appendices, I have also provided dichotomous identifica-

tion keys. A problem with such keys is that their use usually requires that the specimen be in hand, and I do not want to encourage collecting or disturbing these animals solely for the purpose of identifying them. Handling of most species of amphibians by knowledgeable biologists usually will do no damage, but many salamanders, frogs, and lizards are small and delicate and easily harmed by inexperienced persons. Also, many snakes bite and several species in Petén are dangerously venomous. Some species of turtles are also capable of delivering a severe bite.

When I first began to assemble the materials for this manuscript on Christmas day in 1994, I intended to include all of the species known from Tikal National Park southward to the vicinity of Flores. I soon found that these plans had a pernicious aspect because the ranges of many species not initially among those I would cover either closely approached my initial circumscribed area or possibly overlapped that area—their absence being nothing more than an artifact of collecting. Hence I began to include those species occurring in the savanna region to the south of Lago Petén Itzá and then increased the scope of my work all the way to the rainforest of Río de La Pasión. The general Petén biotic area has been described as encompassing all of northern Guatemala and Belize as well as the humid valleys and lower slopes of the mountain ranges of northern and eastern Guatemala. In this work I have come to include most of the species known from Petén and Belize, taking in the Maya Mountains. Therefore, the Petén region, as treated herein, extends northward and westward through much of the Yucatán Peninsula, includes all but the littoral zone of Belize, and extends southward to the foothills of Alta Verapaz, Lago de Izabal, and the Río Dulce. In all, this area encompasses over 60,000 km^2. I have omitted those species with essentially montane distributions that are restricted to elevations above the 600 m contour in the Verapaz highlands or the Sierra de Santa Cruz and those few species that are endemic to the northern portion of the Yucatán Peninsula. I have also omitted marine turtles and those few species essentially restricted to beach and island habitats.

Most of the larger or more conspicuous species of amphibians and reptiles in the Petén region have vernacular names, and these may vary from place to place. Many of the small, secretive species, however, have no common English or Spanish name. For these, I have employed names that have been used in other sources, such as Alvarez del Toro's *Los Reptiles de Chiapas*, and in some instances I have supplied names that I think are appropriate. Kekchí names for various groups are in widespread use in Guatemala: *al-al* for salamander, *amoch* for frog, *popó* for toad, and *cantí* or *can* for either snake or caecilian. Ultimately, of course, use of common names is a matter of whim and their acceptance is up to the users.

For members of the Petén herpetofauna, I have provided modest descriptions that should be sufficient to distinguish particular species. The natural history is poorly known for practically every species inhabiting Petén, but I have attempted to summarize the information available. This sometimes amounts to little more than my own casual observations. Most of the species of amphibians and reptiles in the Petén region are geographically widespread, and few are restricted to the area. Many species occur as far north as southern Veracruz, Mexico, and a few species range into the United States. Some Petén species have distributions that extend far southward into Central America and even into South America. Most species are illustrated with color figures. In selecting photographs, I have sought to obtain illustrations of specimens from the main area covered, namely Petén, Izabal, or Belize. In a few instances, I have had to use photographs of individuals from outside this area. The provenance of specimens is given in the appropriate figure caption.

The herpetofauna of the Petén region, as defined here, consists of a total of 160 species, including 2 caecilians, 6 salamanders, 36 frogs, 9 turtles, 36 lizards, 69 snakes, and 2 crocodilians.

A check mark (✔) with the Distribution detail indicates that the species has been recorded from Tikal National Park. Amphibians and reptiles known from within the confines of this park total 91 species, including 19 frogs, 5 turtles, 24 lizards, 41 snakes, and a single species each of salamander and crocodilian.

BRIEF HISTORY OF HERPETOLOGICAL EXPLORATION

Only fragmentary information is available for the Petén region in the herpetological volume by A. C. L. G. Günther comprising part of the English series *Biologia Centrali-Americana* (1885–1902) and in the tomes of the French counterpart, *Mission Scientifique au Mexique et dans l'Amérique Centrale* (Brocchi, 1881–83; A. Duméril, M. Bocourt, and F. Mocquard, 1870–1909), although various intrepid scientific explorers such as Godman, Morelet, and Salvin, associated either with the British Museum of Natural History in London or the Museum National d'Histoire Naturelle in Paris, collected in Petén, what is now Belize,

or various parts of the Yucatán Peninsula in Mexico. Since the time of these great exploration and collecting parties sent out by the English and the French, the Petén region of Guatemala has been visited by many biologists, and several large collections of amphibians and reptiles have been assembled. The earliest effort to ennumerate the region's herpetofauna systematically was that of L. C. Stuart (1934a), whose report was based primarily on material he obtained during his travels in 1933 through wooded areas between the city of Belize and La Libertad southwest of Lago Petén Itzá, and on material collected by Harry Malleis for the Biological Survey of Washington in 1923, originating mainly from within a 30 km radius of Flores. Stuart (1935a) then published an extensive report on the herpetofauna of the savanna regions of La Libertad and nearby areas. In that paper, he gave an updated list of the herpetofauna of Petén and a brief description of the landscape. Stuart (1937) reported on another collection from Petén, which contained mostly species previously known from the region but from different localities. In 1939, H. M. Smith and Rozella Smith assembled a collection of amphibians and reptiles at Piedras Negras in northwestern Petén; most of these specimens are currently in the United States National Museum. Stuart (1948, 1950) provided extensive documentation on the composition and biogeography of the amphibians and reptiles inhabiting the mountains of Alta Verapaz to the south of Petén. The herpetofauna of the forested areas around the ancient Mayan cities of Tikal and Uaxactún was studied by Stuart (1958). The first report on the amphibians and reptiles of a mesic southwestern portion of Petén was presented by Duellman (1963), who worked primarily at Chinajá.

Schmidt (1941) was the first to attempt to summarize the various species of amphibians and reptiles of Belize. Subsequently, Neill and Allen published a series of papers in the late 1950s and 1960s on the Belizean herpetofauna, the most important contributions being Neill and Allen (1959) and Neill (1965). Henderson and colleagues published a series of papers in the 1970s on various aspects of the biology of certain Belizean amphibians and reptiles and provided an updated checklist and key (Henderson and Hoevers, 1975). McCoy, between 1966 and 1990, published a series of papers dealing with the biology of individual taxa or on collections from Guatemala and Belize. Campbell and Vannini (1989) provided an updated list of species occurring in Petén and Belize. Meerman (1993) published a herpetofaunal checklist for the Shipstern Nature Reserve in Corozal District, and Stafford (1994) reported on a herpetofaunal collection from the Upper Raspaculo Basin. The anurans of Belize were described and illustrated by Meyer and Farneti-Foster (1996).

Most of the literature on Yucatán herpetology has been rather diffuse,

with numerous articles reporting on collections from the region, such as Gaige (1936) and Smith (1938) on the states of Yucatán and Campeche, Smith (1944) on Tabasco, Peters (1953) on Quintana Roo, and Duellman (1965) on the Yucatán Peninsula. Alvarez del Toro (1960) provided an interesting and readable account of the reptiles of Chiapas, which has undergone two subsequent revisions (1972, 1983). Lee (1980a) published an important paper on the herpetogeography of the Yucatán Peninsula, and most recently (Lee, 1996) has published a masterful monograph on the herpetofauna of the entire region.

THE ENVIRONMENT

Physiography and Geology

Most of the Petén region (fig. 1) is of low relief, with maximum elevations usually not exceeding 300 m and the dominant rocks being Miocene limestones. The area around Tikal lies mainly between 250 and 280 m and Uaxactún is at about 200 m. Several major river systems drain the Petén region of Guatemala. The Río San Pedro and Río de La Pasión drain the western portion of Petén and are major tributaries of the Río Usumacinta, which eventually flows into the Gulf of Mexico. The major rivers of eastern Petén are not as large as those to the west, but the Río Sarstún, Río Mopán, and Río Azul are permanent rivers that flow to the Caribbean. Although the immediate vicinities around Tikal and Uaxactún are close to the divide between the Río Azul and Río San Pedro systems, they lie entirely within the Río Azul Basin. Most of the streams in the north are intermittent, although some of the deeper water holes may retain water into the dry season. Many moderate-sized lakes occur in Petén, especially in the central and northwest portions of the region. These include Laguna Petexbatún near Sayaxché, Lagunas Perdida and El Repasto in the northwest, and Laguna Yaxjá in the east. Lago Petén Itzá is the largest body of water in Petén and has a surface area often cited as 567 km², although in recent years the lake has risen considerably, giving it a larger extent. In addition to many small lakes and lagoons, Petén is pockmarked with many thousands of small *aguadas,* which are depressions thought to be mostly limestone sinks. *Akalchés,* which are larger depressions in the landscape, are also present. Although some aguadas and akalchés may retain water all or much of the year, most are seasonal, filling up only during the wet season, when they become important habitat for various species of amphibians and reptiles.

Weather and Climate

All of the Petén region experiences an equitable, tropical climate with relatively warm temperatures throughout the year (fig. 2A). Most places in Petén experience their lowest temperatures in January and February, with monthly means of 20–23°C; the highest monthly means are experienced in April and May, commonly between 25 and 30°C. In the vicinity of Tikal-Uaxactún, the mean annual temperature is about 27°C, with a mean maximum of about 30°C occurring in April or May and a mean minimum of about 23°C in December or January. From about October to March the entire area is subject to northern cold fronts or *nortes* that may drop temperatures to as low as 15°C.

Rainfall is seasonal, most falling from May to December; January through April is the dry season (fig. 2B). The southern portion of the Petén region receives more rainfall than the northern part, and this gradual decrease in rainfall continues northward throughout the Yucatán Peninsula. To the south, at moderate elevations of the north-facing highlands of Alta Verapaz, as much as 5,000 mm of rain may fall at certain localities, whereas the northern end of the Yucatán Peninsula may receive less than 1,000 mm of precipitation per year. Around Tikal, about 1,600–1,800 mm of rain falls per year. As noted, the dry season extends from about January through April; however, some precipitation usually falls every month of the year. March has a mean of about 30–70 mm of rainfall and is the driest month; in September the area receives about 250–300 mm of precipitation and this is the wettest month, although rainfall in June is almost as high.

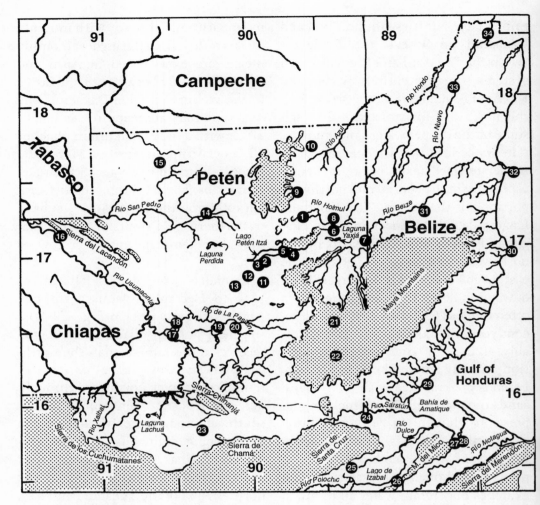

Fig. 1. Towns, archaeological sites, and topographic features of northern Guatemala and adjacent regions. Numbers represent the following localities: (1) Tikal, (2) Flores, (3) Santa Elena, (4) El Remate, (5) Gringo Perdido, (6) Yaxjá, (7) Melchor de Mencos, (8) Nakún, (9) Uaxactún, (10) Dos Lagunas, (11) San Francisco, (12) San Antonio, (13) La Libertad, (14) Paso Caballos, (15) Santa Amelia, (16) Piedras Negras, (17) Altar de Los Sacrificios, (18) El Porvenir, (19) Sayaxché, (20) El Ceibal, (21) Dolores, (22) Poptún, (23) Chisec, (24) Modesto Méndez, (25) El Estor, (26) Mariscos, (27) Puerto Santo Tomás, (28) Puerto Barrios, (29) Punta Gorda, (30) Stann Creek Town, (31) Belmopan, (32) Belize, (33) Orange Walk, and (34) Corozal.

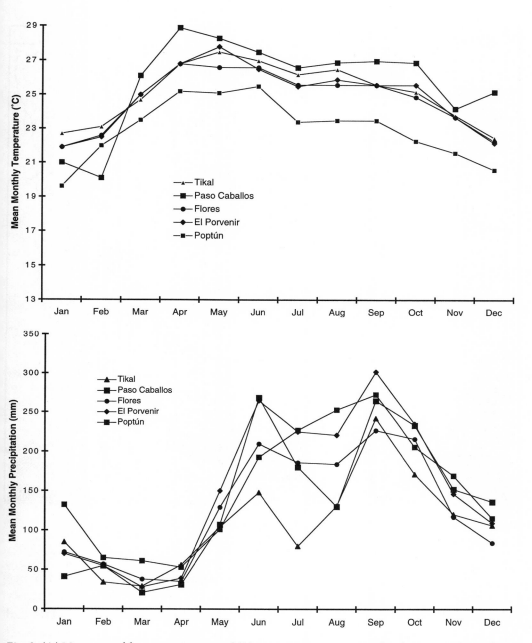

Fig. 2. (A) Mean monthly temperatures and (B) precipitation at various localities in Petén. Clima-tological data for Paso Caballos from Sapper (1932) for the years 1925–29; for Flores (airport), El Por-venir, and Poptún from INSIVUMEH (1992) for the years 1973–89, 1967–89, and 1977–89, respec-tively; and for Tikal from INSIVUMEH (1994) for the years 1988–94.

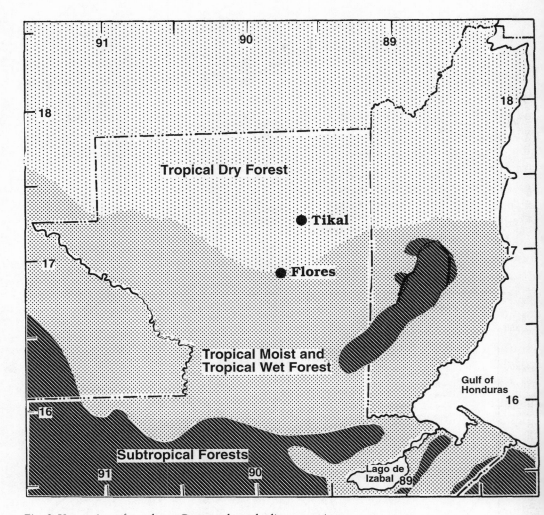

Fig. 3. Vegetation of northern Guatemala and adjacent regions.

Vegetation

Because of rainfall patterns, the forest of the southern Petén region tends to be lusher and wetter than that in the north (fig. 3). Overall, most of the forest covering Petén is transitional between the tropical moist forest of southern Petén–northern Alta Verapaz and the tropical dry forest of the northern portion of the Yucatán Peninsula, but a number of factors may influence vegetation, and forest type is highly variable throughout Petén. Tropical moist forest occurs from near sea level to about 600 m. In this type of forest the dry season extends for three to six months, depending on locality, and annual rainfall varies from about 2,000 to 5,000 mm. Tropical dry forest occurs at similar elevations to tropical moist forest but is subject to a harsh dry season of at least six months and receives less than 2,000 mm of rainfall per year. In the Maya Mountains and the ranges to the south of the Petén region, including the Sierra de Santa Cruz, the Montañas del Mico, the Sierra de Chamá, and the Sierra de Los Cuchumatanes, the windward slopes above 600 m are covered by subtropical wet forest and in protected valleys or on leeward slopes subtropical moist forest prevails. At elevations above 1,500 m, various lower montane forest formations (dry, moist, or wet) dominate the landscape. The forest immediately surrounding the Tikal-Uaxactún area has been classified as the Northern Petén Phytogeographic Province by Lundell (1937), who considered this forest to be quasi-rainforest, attaining a maximum height of about 50 m, being semideciduous in nature, and having the zapote (*Achrus zapota*) as the most conspicuous tree.

Much of the forest of central and northern Petén was classified as tropical dry forest by Holdridge, Lamb, and Mason (1950), who recognized "high forest" on the well-drained upland areas and "low forest" mostly in the akalchés or *bajos* (see figs. 4–6). The high forest contains different associations dominated by stands of tree genera such as *Achrus* (when the association is known as *zapotal*), *Brosimium* (the *ramonal*), *Swietenia* (*caobal*), and *Cedrela* (*cedral*). These trees attain huge size and provide a canopy that does not allow much light to penetrate to the forest floor. There is often a considerable amount of leaf litter, and little herbaceous growth occupies the forest floor. The low forest attains a height of only about 15–20 m, more light penetrates to the forest floor, and there is a dense undergrowth of herbaceous plants, shrubs, and palms. The dense understory is often so profuse that it forms almost an impenetrable thicket. Areas covered by low forest are often poorly drained and subject to flooding during the rainy season but become dried out during dry periods. Two primary associations are recognized in the low forest: the *escobal*, in which the escoba palm (*Cryosophila argentea*) and botán palm (*Sabal morrisiana*) are common, and the *tintal*, where the logwood tree (*Haematoxylum campechianum*) is predominant.

Open savanna habitats are scattered across central Petén, with large savannas occurring south of Lago Petén Itzá around La Libertad and San Francisco. These savannas are covered by species of short grasses, and short, scrubby trees, including nance (*Byrsonima crassifolia*), saba (*Curatella americana*), and the cocoyol palm (*Acrocomia mexicana*) are scattered throughout. Bush areas associated with these savannas represent secondary growth; this vegetation type is referred to as *acahual*. This is a dry type of forest dominated by bullhorn and other species of acacias, *Conostegia xalapensis*, *Vismia ferruginea*, and trees of the genera *Micronia*, *Metopium*, *Randia*, *Inga*, *Cecropia*, and *Bursera*. Dry savannas with

Fig. 4. Deep forest habitat within Tikal National Park, Petén, Guatemala. 11 June 1996. This habitat remains mesic over much of the year and is home to species such as *Eleutherodactylus rhodopis, Norops uniformis, Eumeces sumichrasti, Sphenomorphus cherriei, Coniophanes fissidens, Corytophanes cristatus, Imantodes cenchoa, Micrurus diastema, Pliocercus elapoides, Scaphiodontophis annulatus,* and *Atropoides nummifer.* The canopy is inhabited by *Norops biporcatus and Diploglossus rozellae.* JAC

Fig. 5. Advanced secondary growth forest within Tikal National Park, Petén, Guatemala. 10 March 1995. This low forest allows considerable penetration of sunlight and is subject to drying conditions during the dry season. *Norops bourgeaei, N. tropidonotus, Corytophanes hernandezii, Coleonyx elegans, Rhinoclemmys areolata, Leptophis ahaetulla, L. mexicanus, Oxybelis aeneus, Bothrops asper,* and *Porthidium nasutum* occur in this habitat. JAC

Fig. 6. Natural treefall within Tikal National Park, Petén, Guatemala. 20 July 1995. Many forest species may come to the edges of these forest gaps to bask or to lay their eggs. *Norops borgeaei, Eumeces sumichrasti, Ameiva undulata, Ninia sebae, Dryadophis melanolomus,* and *Lampropeltis triangulum* are commonly encountered in such situations. JAC

scattered nance and pine (*Pinus carib-aea*) occur around Poptún, Cahabón, and parts of the Sierra de Santa Cruz.

A series of hills extend across Petén both north and south of Lago Petén Itzá. These hills are covered by a thin layer of black calcareous soil. Forest covering these slopes varies according to slope, drainage, and exposure and is dominated by trees of the genera *Hirtella, Protium, Clusia, Rodeletia, Bursera, Eugenia, Swartzia,* and *Plume-ria.* The lower portions of these lime-stone hills or regions adjacent to them are characterized by large species of luguminose trees including *Enterolo-bium, Tipuana,* and *Schizolobium.* Trees in areas of primary forest may attain heights of 20–50 m, and epiphytes, palms, and strangler figs are common.

FINDING AMPHIBIANS AND REPTILES

Although the vast Mayan city of Tikal and the surrounding region was myste-riously vacated by its human inhabi-tants some 1,100 years ago, the true original inhabitants, many of which were probably well known and appre-ciated by the Mayas, are still there. The natural heritage of Petén is rich in amphibians and reptiles, with a great diversity of species representing many families. As do people currently living in the area, no doubt the Mayas had considerable respect for the venomous snakes on whose territories they trod, including the coral snake, jumping pitviper, rainforest hognosed pitviper,

and especially the barba amarilla and *cascabel* or Neotropical rattlesnake. Some species of reptiles graced Mayan tables and were an important source of protein; chief among these were proba-bly the Central American river turtle, the *jicotea* or Mesoamerican slider, Morelet's crocodile, the boa constric-tor, and in some places both green and black iguanas. Amphibians, because of their smaller size, were not usually eaten, but frogs nevertheless were im-portant to the Mayas as symbols of life-giving rain and fertility. Indeed, much of Mayan mythology involved various reptiles and amphibians; in Mayan cos-mology, for example, the very earth is the back of a huge crocodile.

Most people visiting the Petén re-gion arrive already interested in wild-life; if not, they have often developed an interest by the time they leave. Al-though birdwatchers have long recog-nized the biotic wealth of the area and a guide to the birds has been available for many years (Smithe, 1966), other groups of animals have been somewhat neglected. Birds are the most com-monly and easily observed group of vertebrates, but reptiles and amphib-ians do not lag far behind. Any visitor, whether hiking through the ruins of Tikal or along the nature trails of Cerro Cahui, is certain to see a number of agile lizards dart up trees and will probably also observe snakes slither across the path. With a little more dili-gence and patience, certain anurans and turtles are likely to be found by frequenting aquatic habitats (see figs.

Fig. 7. Aguada surrounded by low forest, east of Santa Elena, near Laguna Petenchel, Petén, Guatemala. 14 July 1995. This is habitat for *Bolitoglossa mexicana, Agalychnis callidryas, Basiliscus vittatus,* and many snake species. JAC

Fig 8. Aguada surrounded by secondary scrub, near old airfield at Tikal, Petén, Guatemala. 22 July 1995. A great number of species are found in this kind of habitat, including *Rhinophrynus dorsalis, Bufo marinus, B. valliceps, Scinax staufferi, Smilisca baudinii, Hypopachus variolosus, Rana berlandieri, Claudius angustatus, Kinosternon leucostomum, Basiliscus vittatus,* and *Drymobius margaritiferus.* JAC

Fig. 9. Laguna Yaxjá viewed from northeastern shore, Petén, Guatemala. 11 March 1995. The tropical evergreen forest surrounding this lake is at about its northernmost limit in the Yucatán Peninsula. In March of 1995, Central American river turtles *(Dermatemys mawii)* were seen in this lake and several adult Morelet's crocodiles *(Crocodylus moreletii)* hauled out almost daily on the beach of the small island Topoxté. *Thamnophis proximus* has a disjunct distribution in Petén but occurs along the shore of this lake. This forest provides habitat for such tree-loving species as *Laemanctus longipes, Spilotes pullatus,* and *Pseustes poecilonotus.* JAC

7–9). It may even be possible to observe the largest reptile in the region, Morelet's crocodile. For many years a large specimen lived in the reservoir at Tikal. Unfortunately, this individual became aggressive and eventually was removed. However, there were at least two small individuals in the Tikal aguada when I visited there in 1995 and 1996. Also, it is worth the effort to visit the small zoo, Petencito, located on the edge of Lago Petén Itzá and accessible by boat. This zoo usually has several crocodiles on display as well as a few larger snakes and other animals of the region.

There is no secret in knowing how to find amphibians and reptiles, but to be really successful, an understanding of when and where to look is critical. Some frogs (*Hyla microcephala*, *Scinax staufferi*, and *Hypopachus variolosus*), lizards (*Norops bourgeaei*, *N. sericeus*, *Eumeces schwartzei*), and snakes (*Ninia sebae*, *Oxybelis aeneus*) prefer open, nonforested habitat and are found only rarely in virgin forest. Conversely, many anoles (genus *Norops*) are found primarily in forested habitats. The lesser forest anole (*Norops uniformis*) is found in leaf litter or on low vegetation near the ground, usually in heavily shaded situations. The giant green anole (*N. biporcatus*) may occasionally descend to the ground or be found on tree trunks, but this species remains mostly in the canopy, and I have most often found individuals in areas where trees were being felled. One rainy night I was walking on a forest trail when I

observed a kinkajou (*Potos flavus*) in a tree some 50 m above the ground. As I was watching the kinkajou move directly above me, it dislodged a large male giant green anole, which fell squarely on my headlight. The long-legged anole (*N. capito*) is another deep forest lizard that may be found just about anywhere in virgin forest. I have found this species on the branches of low bushes, sitting on palm fronds at various heights, in leaf litter, and on trees of various sizes. Two other species of anoles, Bourgeau's anole (*N. bourgeaei*) and Rodriguez's anole (*N. rodriguezi*), may be encountered in virgin forest or in areas of secondary growth. Most frequently, Rodriguez's anole is seen sitting on the branches of low brushes and Bourgeau's anole on the trunks of moderate to large trees, especially those with buttressed roots.

Most species of lizards are diurnal, but a few are active only after dark. Most gecko species and the night lizards are nocturnal denizens of Petén. The turnip-tailed gecko (*Thecadactylus rapicaudus*) lives on the trunks of very large trees and comes out after dark to look for insects and other invertebrates. This species is also found in the dark interiors of abandoned human dwellings, including some of the ancient Mayan edifices. The Yucatán banded gecko (*Coleonyx elegans*) is terrestrial and is often observed scampering about on roads after dark. Other geckos in the area, the bark geckos (*Sphaerodactylus*), live under the loose or dead bark of trees but are also quick to invade houses and can commonly be seen on the walls of restaurants and *tiendas* at Tikal as well as in the villages around Lago Petén Itzá. Bark geckos may be active just about any time of day. The night lizards (*Lepidophyma*) are also active after dark, usually in limestone areas with numerous rocky outcroppings.

Some diurnal, terrestrial snakes are abundant. The speckled racer (*Drymobius margaritiferus*) is frequently seen along the edge of bodies of water as it forages for frogs. The Bronze-backed parrot snake (*Leptophis mexicanus*) also feeds heavily on frogs but is arboreal and often in bushes. However, the majority of snakes are noctural. The cat-eyed snakes (*Leptodeira*) are common species that are usually found after dark near water in pursuit of their favorite prey—frogs. These species may be found on the ground or in vegetation. The small-spotted cat-eyed snake (*L. polysticta*), in particular, tends to climb and I have observed this species at up to 10 m in trees along streams.

The leaf litter that accumulates on the floor of tropical forests is an especially important microhabitat for many amphibians and reptiles. It provides hiding places, reproductive sites, and foraging areas for many species such as leaf-litter frogs, anoles, skinks, earth snakes, and coffee snakes. Arboreal bromeliads provide ideal hiding places and moisture for many species, including leaf-frogs, Baudin's treefrog, the blue-spotted treefrog, common blunt-headed treesnake, and the snail-eaters.

Some reptiles spend much of their time living in the canopy or high in trees; these include Rozella's canopy lizard, the green iguana, the bird-eating treesnake, and the tiger treesnake.

Amphibians and, contrary to popular belief, even most reptiles are unable to withstand direct exposure to high daytime temperatures. When exposed to hot, dry conditions, even out of direct sunlight, most species will desiccate and die within a few minutes (in the case of small amphibians) to a few days (the larger reptiles). It is not surprising that many species of amphibians and reptiles tend to have a peak in their activity during the rainy season when conditions are more favorable. Frequent rains and temporary puddles and ponds provide the moisture necessary for survival and overcast days shield these animals from the direct rays of the sun. During the harshest part of the year, from about February to May in Petén, most amphibians burrow deep into the drying mud where they aestivate, conserving energy and moisture; others find refuge in the axils of bromeliads, in banana plant sheaths, or in the middle of large rotten logs located in sheltered, shaded parts of the forest. Many snakes, even arboreal species, seek their hiding places in deep crevices and abandoned mammal burrows and survive the dry season several feet underground.

The few studies on the feeding ecology of tropical snakes have revealed that most snakes tend to feed more frequently during the rainy season, which is the time that they are most active. Frog-eating snakes, in particular, tend to feed heavily during the rainy season and practically not at all during the dry season. Snakes that eat lizards also feed more frequently during the rainy season, but these snakes feed more frequently during the dry season than do the frogeaters. A few exceptions to this rainy season peak in activity are found among the aquatic snakes, such as the Middle American swamp snake, which is more frequently encountered along the shores of its aquatic habitat during the dry season. This apparent dry season activity, however, may be more a reflection of the habits of human observers and the restriction of these snakes to a smaller area of habitat than an actual increase in activity.

One of the easiest ways to see many snakes is on the road. If you are making a trip during the early morning hours, especially within an hour or so after dawn, you are likely to see snakes that were run over the previous evening. If you wait until midmorning, there will be far fewer because of scavengers such as vultures and caracaras, which learn to patrol roads. Anyone interested in acquiring knowledge about snakes may profit by stopping and examining dead specimens on the road. It is a good way to get close and see features that otherwise might not ever be noticed. Some notes of caution: remember that even "dead" snakes can sometimes bite and that vehicular traffic along Guatemalan roads is one of the greatest hazards of the region. When you are through,

leave the specimen on the road for the scavengers. It will probably be gone if you come back the same way later in the day.

Most species of amphibians and reptiles breed during the rainy season. It is during this period that large choruses of multiple species of frogs are heard. Most snakes and lizards have a breeding season that coincides with, or fecundity that increases during, the rainy season. Egg-laying species usually deposit their eggs during the early part of the rainy season, and live-bearers likewise give birth to their young at this time. Some species lay several clutches throughout the rainy season, and others may have an extended breeding season lasting many months. The young of amphibians and reptiles are not only more susceptible than adults to drying out but also are born or hatch with sufficient yolk reserves to last only a short time. Therefore it is critical that they actively seek out prey and acquire enough energy reserves to get them through the dry season. The effects of a rainy season that is several months late in coming, such as happened in 1995, probably take an important toll on many amphibian and reptile populations.

Even in the dry season, many species can be observed in or near permanent bodies of water. For example, on 14 March 1995, within a few minutes just before dark on a stroll along the edge of Laguna Petenchel, I saw two turtle species (*Dermatemys mawii* and *Trachemys scripta*), a Morelet's crocodile,

(*Crocodylus moreletii*), two kinds of toads (*Bufo marinus, B. valliceps*), a speckled racer (*Drymobius margaritiferus*), and a striped basilisk (*Basiliscus vittatus*). Other species that are active during the dry season include spiny lizards and several of the anoles.

Forest types are important in the distribution of animals. For example, some species of reptiles, such as the Yucatán whiptail (*Cnemidophorus angusticeps*), lizard killer (*Conophis lineatus*), and cantil (*Agkistrodon bilineatus*), are usually found in open savanna or low scrub and avoid deep forest. These open habitats are not continuous across the Petén, at least today, and the question of how these species came to be where they are often arises. There are at least three possible explanations. First, the habitats in which they live may have been more extensive and continuous at one time but subsequently became fragmented owing to changing climates or other factors. Second, perhaps these species were able to disperse through intervening and unfavorable habitats, eventually establishing populations at various outposts. Third, perhaps they were brought to some of their current locations by human agency. The second possibility is not widely regarded as a viable explanation with regard to Petén biogeography. The third explanation may have some merit, especially in relation to those few species of importance to indigenous human populations. There is little doubt that turtles especially, because of their durability and palatability, were transported by humans for long distances and sacrificed far from their original point of origin. However, in order to understand the disjunct distribution patterns of most amphibians and reptiles in the Petén, it is necessary to invoke vicariance as the most logical explanation. There is ample evidence that there have been alternating periods in which the climate has been both drier and wetter than that experienced in the region today. Current patterns of distribution also may have been affected by extensive Maya agriculture, which from about 500 B.C. to A.D. 900 greatly reduced the amount of virgin forest in Petén.

The Convention on International Trade in Endangered Species of Wild Fauna and Flora (CITES) strictly regulates the export of certain reptile species that occur in the Petén region; no amphibians occurring in the region are currently listed under the treaty's provision. Species are listed on two important appendices. Appendix I includes species threatened with extinction that are or may be affected by trade; both of the crocodilian species in Petén (*Crocodylus acutus* and *C. moreletii*) are on this list. Appendix II includes mostly species that, although not necessarily now threatened with extinction, may become so unless trade in specimens of such species is subject to strict regulation in order to avoid utilization incompatible with their survival. The Central American river turtle (*Dermatemys mawii*), green iguana (*Iguana iguana*), boa constrictor (*Boa constrictor*), and black mussurana (*Clelia clelia*) all appear on Appendix II.

While the spirit and goals of CITES are unquestionably noble, the sad fact is that in terms of conservation, CITES is a failure with regard to Guatemalan species simply because their declines result mainly from local consumption or utilization of these animals and from destruction of their habitats, not from international trade. Further, the placement of species such as the boa constrictor and black mussurana on the list is not based on sound scientific evidence. Green iguanas, once extremely plentiful over most of the Guatemalan lowlands, have now been severely depleted owing to local consumption and the deplorable exportation of vast numbers of juveniles for the pet trade; this species merits some form of protection. Regardless of whatever criticisms might be leveled against CITES, to date there have been no alternatives proposed and Guatemala is a signatory of this convention. Guatemalan law prohibits the collection, killing, or export of species listed on Appendices I or II without prior permission from the appropriate wildlife agency.

One final note—*all* species of amphibians and reptiles are protected by Guatemalan law, and the collection of these animals for scientific, personal, or commercial reasons without the proper permits is prohibited.

CHARACTERISTICS AND IDENTIFICATION

Besides the obvious differences in color pattern that distinguish various species of amphibians and reptiles, there are many morphological characteristics that are often useful in identifying species. Many of these are referred to as "key characteristics" because they are commonly employed in identification keys, as in the appendices here. Illustrations of some of these characteristics are provided in figures 10–13. Definitions for particular characteristics and for abbreviations used in this book may be found in the glossary. Appendix A is a key to groups of amphibians and reptiles of the Petén region; appendices B-F are keys for identification to species level.

Some species of amphibians and reptiles have distinctive color patterns or are uniformly colored, at least dorsally; others display a variety of patterns. Some of the more common terms describing patterns, again defined in the glossary, include punctated, mottled, banded, blotched, ringed, and striped. A ring is an element of color that completely encircles the body; because of the orientation of a ring around the long axis of the body, it is more appropriately considered to be long rather than wide, and its length is described in terms of the number of dorsal body scales it spans. Certain abbreviations for standard measurements are used throughout: TL refers to the total length of an animal from the tip of its snout to the tip of its tail, and SVL is the snout-vent length.

Caecilians are elongate, limbless amphibians that possess a number of grooves or annuli on their bodies; the total number of annuli is helpful in identification. Those annuli that completely encircle the body are referred to as primary annuli and those only partially encircling the body are called secondary annuli. The eyes of caecilians are tiny and lack eyelids, being located beneath skin or even bone. A sensory appendage, known as the tentacle, is located somewhat anterior to and below the level of the eye but posterior to the naris. The vent of caecilians is located so near the posterior terminus of the body that the tail is usually considered to be absent.

Salamanders have four limbs of about the same size and long tails. They also have a number of grooves on the sides of the body, referred to as costal grooves. All Guatemalan species of salamanders have eyelids. The vent in salamanders is longitudinal and the SVL is taken from the tip of the snout to the posterior edge of the vent. In regions rich in salamander species, identification can sometimes be difficult, requiring a close examination of foot structure, cranial osteology, shape of the nares, or even tongue morphology. There are few species of salamanders in the Petén region, however, and these are easily distinguished by size and color pattern.

Frogs and toads are "jumping" amphibians with hind limbs that are pro-portionally longer and stronger than the forelimbs. Anurans exhibit a variety of sizes, body shapes, and color patterns. Besides these obvious characteristics, features useful in distinguishing species are density and arrangement of tubercles, presence and shape of parotoid glands and cranial crests, structure of hands and feet (fig. 10), shape of pupil, and mating call.

Turtles are perhaps the most distinctive of vertebrates, and they are the only reptiles having a shell. Species may be distinguished by size and shape of the head, jaws, and shell, and the presence and arrangement of the epidermal scutes (lamellae) covering their shells (fig. 11).

Crocodilians are large aquatic reptiles with powerful jaws, thecodont teeth, a laterally compressed tail, and numerous osteoderms embedded in the skin. Only Morelet's crocodile is widespread in Petén, but the American crocodile probably occurs around the periphery of the region. These two species differ in snout shape and overall size attained. Morelet's crocodile may be found in a variety of habitats, including small aguadas and marshes, whereas the American crocodile is usually limited to the larger rivers.

All species of lizards occurring in the Petén region have both fore and hind limbs but vary considerably in the relative length of their limbs. Lizard species also differ from one another in the presence or absence of eyelids; the shape, size, and arrangement of scales on the body; head ornamenta-

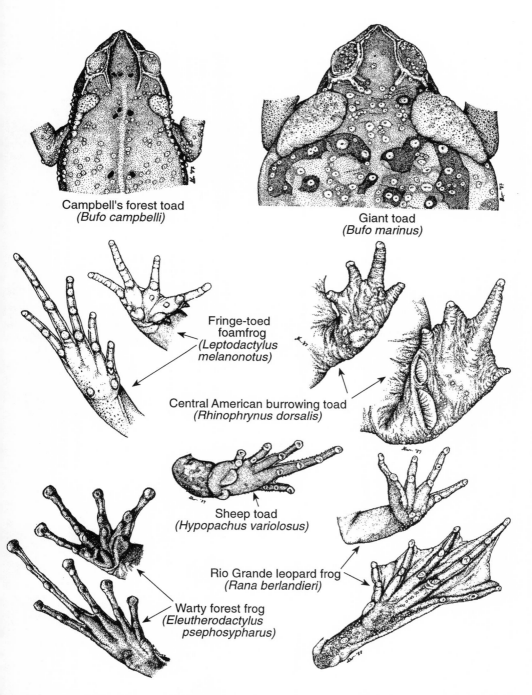

Campbell's forest toad
(Bufo campbelli)

Giant toad
(Bufo marinus)

Fringe-toed
foamfrog
*(Leptodactylus
melanonotus)*

Central American burrowing toad
(Rhinophrynus dorsalis)

Sheep toad
(Hypopachus variolosus)

Rio Grande leopard frog
(Rana berlandieri)

Warty forest frog
*(Eleutherodactylus
psephosypharus)*

Fig. 10. Variation of certain external morphological features of anurans occurring in Petén.

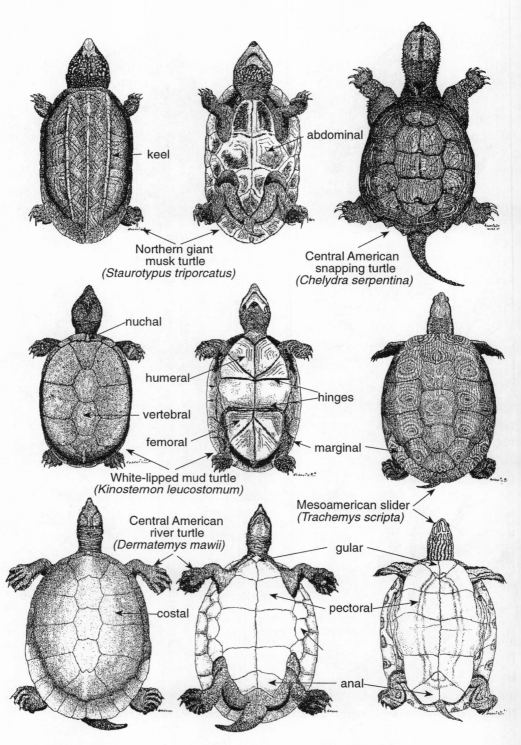

keel

abdominal

Northern giant
musk turtle
(Staurotypus triporcatus)

Central American
snapping turtle
(Chelydra serpentina)

nuchal

humeral

hinges

vertebral

femoral

marginal

White-lipped mud turtle
(Kinosternon leucostomum)

Mesoamerican slider
(Trachemys scripta)

Central American
river turtle
(Dermatemys mawii)

gular

pectoral

costal

anal

Fig. 11. Variation of the carapaces and plastra of different species of turtles.

tion such as crests or casques; presence and coloration of dewlaps; pupil shape; and presence of femoral pores (fig. 12).

Snakes are limbless squamates that are most easily identified by features of color pattern, body shape, and scalation, including the pattern of head scales or plates, the number of dorsal scale rows around the body, the presence of keeled versus smooth dorsal scales, whether the anal plate is single or divided into two scales, and the number of ventral, subcaudal, and temporal scales (fig. 13).

DECIMATION AND CONSERVATION

Since I first visited Petén in the late 1950s the region has changed profoundly. Much of the area has been cleared of its magnificent forest, and the places that have not been cleared have almost all been at least selectively logged. The human population has grown from about 15,000 in 1950 to its present 350,000. This tide of humanity has made unrealistic demands on the land and its biota. In the last two decades, Petén has lost over two-thirds of its forest. The clearing and burning has polluted the waters and air. In their relentless quest for flesh and skins, people have slaughtered the larger animals, reducing some species to numbers that no longer represent viable populations. As regards reptiles, it is shameful that so little foresight is employed. Species such as the Central American river turtle and Morelet's

crocodile—species that are still with us but have a precarious future—are not afforded the protection they deserve. Although my major concern is conservation of species for aesthetic and moral reasons, these species are good examples of animals that are already uniquely adapted to the region and that, if managed intelligently, could provide important future resources for people.

A huge tract of land including about the northern third of Petén (1.6 million hectares) has been designated as the Maya Biosphere Reserve. Unfortunately, the human population of this area is now increasing at an unprecedented 7 percent each year, leading to major deforestation. Besides slash-and-burn agriculture, logging and petroleum pipelines threaten this reserve.

If the wildlife and forests of Petén have been decimated, the lifestyles of the early human settlers, including some who were the descendants of the ancient Maya, have all but disappeared. These people, until recently, lived more or less in harmony with the abundant wildlife, at least in the sense that wildlife resources remained renewable. The people met with today in Petén, however—other than a very few old-timers—are not knowledgeable about the forest or schooled in its natural lore. Most are recent immigrants to the region who see no harm in fully exploiting any resource that comes their way, whether this means killing a deer out of season or digging up a crocodile nest.

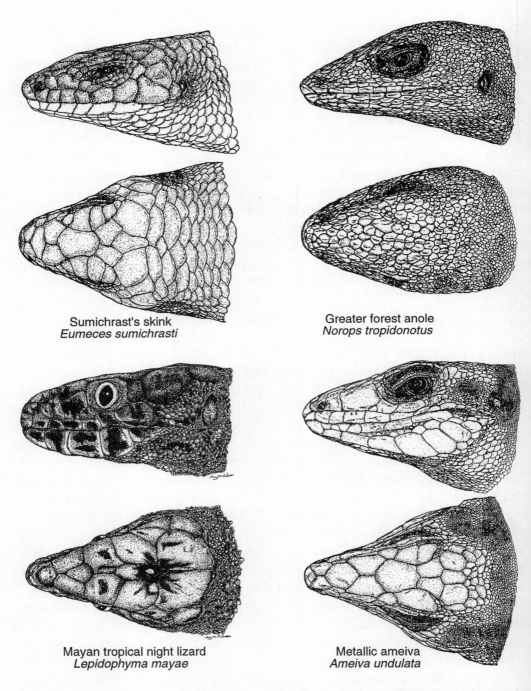

Sumichrast's skink
Eumeces sumichrasti

Greater forest anole
Norops tropidonotus

Mayan tropical night lizard
Lepidophyma mayae

Metallic ameiva
Ameiva undulata

Fig. 12. Lateral and dorsal aspects of heads of some lizards inhabiting the Petén region, showing diversity of head shape and scalation.

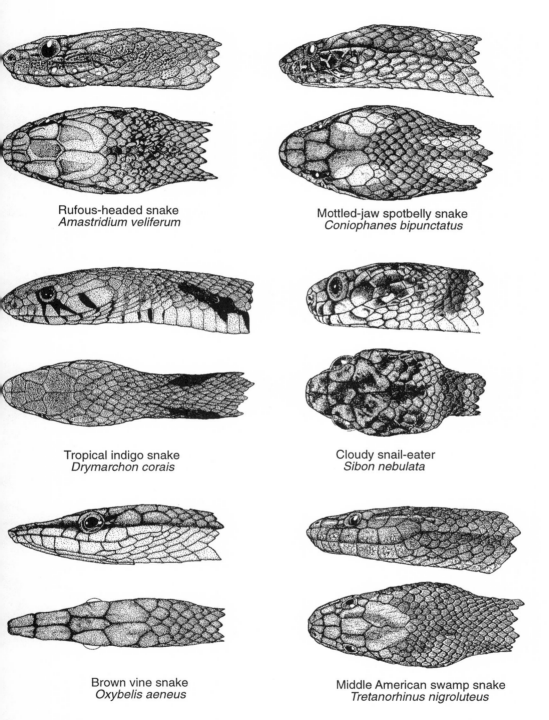

Rufous-headed snake
Amastridium veliferum

Mottled-jaw spotbelly snake
Coniophanes bipunctatus

Tropical indigo snake
Drymarchon corais

Cloudy snail-eater
Sibon nebulata

Brown vine snake
Oxybelis aeneus

Middle American swamp snake
Tretanorhinus nigroluteus

Fig. 13. Lateral and dorsal aspects of heads of some colubrid snakes inhabiting the Petén region, showing diversity of head shape and scalation.

The good news perhaps is that many species are remarkably resilient. Most of the smaller species of amphibians, lizards, and snakes are masters at avoiding human detection or at escaping once detected. Many kinds are what I refer to as deep forest species, requiring primary forest to survive. These species are adapted to the leaf litter of the relatively cool forest floor or to the unique conditions present in the canopy. As long as adequate patches of primary forest remain—and the continued existence of the Tikal National Park seems assured—then many of these species may also survive. Some amphibians and reptiles are adapted to open areas. These species were once probably rare or restricted in Petén, being confined to the savanna regions, the "canyons of light" provided by natural treefall, and other natural open areas. Today, some of these species are flourishing with the human-induced alterations to the habitat.

Part 1

AMPHIBIANS—ANFIBIOS

This diverse class of cold-blooded animals contains the caecilians, salamanders, and anurans (frogs and toads); all of these groups are represented in Guatemala. There are about 4,600 species of amphibians in the world, although new species are still being discovered, especially in the tropics. Unfortunately, the number of species going extinct may soon exceed the number being discovered, so the total number of living species known may go down (see "Harbingers of Environmental Degradation," page 58).

Amphibian skin is highly glandular and usually moist. Sometimes specialized skin glands produce toxic secretions that help guard against predators. Amphibians lack the epidermal scales that are so characteristic of reptiles. However, in one group of amphibians, the caecilians, many species, including both of the Guatemalan species, have dermal scales embedded in the skin. Most amphibians live near water or in damp environments. They are prone to rapid desiccation and are largely nocturnal. Most species are active mainly in the rainy season, and even then, chiefly during rainy nights. Amphibian eggs lack the leathery or calcareous shells of many reptile and all bird eggs. Amphibians are the only class of tetrapods to have a biphasic life cycle, one in which an egg hatches into a larva which then metamorphoses into the adult body type, but this sequence of life stages is not present in every species of amphibian. For example, all of the salamanders occurring in Petén and many of the frogs (genera *Eleutherodactylus* and *Syrrhophus*) lay eggs that undergo direct development and hatch into miniatures of the adult, forgoing the larval stage. The two species of caecilians in the region give birth to live young.

CAECILIANS—TAPALCUAS

The secretive, wormlike amphibians called caecilians occur in tropical southeastern Asia, Africa, Mexico, Central America, South America, and the Seychelles Islands in the Indian Ocean. These unusual animals lack limbs and possess many specializations for burrowing, including a rigid skull, eyes that are reduced to small dark spots under the skin (sometimes becoming pale after preservation) or under bone, and many annular grooves around the body. They also lack ear drums and middle ear cavities. In Guatemalan species, the tail is absent and the posterior end of the body is rounded. All species have internal fertilization and males have an intromittent copulatory organ. A protrusible, sensory tentacle is located between the levels of the eye and nostril. For some of the folklore surrounding caecilians, see "Unfounded Beliefs," page 31.

To distinguish the two species of caecilians occurring in the Petén region, see appendix B.

NEOTROPICAL CAECILIANS—CAECILIDOS NEOTROPICALES

FAMILY CAECILIIDAE

Amphibians are usually considered to be scaleless, and indeed they are devoid of the external epidermal scales so characteristic of reptiles. Not all amphibians lack scales however; most caecilians possess dermal scales, which are similar in their development to those of fishes. These scales are not visible externally but are embedded in the skin, especially beneath the folds of the posterior annuli. Species in the family Caeciliidae occur widely in the

American tropics from Mexico through Central America into South America. Members of this family are fossorial, have a rudimentary left lung, and lack a tail.

The species of caecilians inhabiting Guatemala all give birth to live, fully metamorphosed young. The plumbeous Central American caecilian (*Dermophis mexicanus*) has developed some remarkable adaptations for nurturing its young while they are still in the oviducts, and the same reproductive mode probably occurs in the mountain caecilian (*Gymnopis syntrema*); a close relative of the mountain caecilian is known to nurture its young in similar fashion. Embryos quickly exhaust their yolk stores and hatch from their egg membranes while still in the oviducts. Specialized epithelial cells line the oviduct and secrete a nutritive substance that is ingested by the developing young, allowing them to grow, develop, and eventually metamorphose within the oviducts. Developing young have unique spatula-shaped teeth with serrate crowns that function in scraping epithelial tissue and ingesting secretions from the lining of the oviduct. Fetal dentition is resorbed just before or immediately after birth.

To distinguish caecilians from salamanders, see appendix B.

Plumbeous Central American Caecilian—Tapalcua Grande de Costa
Dermophis mexicanus (Duméril and Bibron, 1841)
Fig. 14

Description.—This limbless amphibian resembles a large, dark earthworm. Mature individuals range from 300 to 600 mm in TL. The body of this species is relatively robust, the head is somewhat pointed in dorsal view, and the posterior end of the body is broadly rounded. The eyes are reduced to dark spots beneath the skin and a sensory tentacle is located about halfway between eye and nostril (slightly closer to the eye than to the nostril); the orbit is not roofed over by bone. The tentacular opening or foramen is in the anterior margin of maxillary bone. There is only one tooth row in each lower jaw, with teeth absent from the splenial ridge. The vent is almost at the terminus of the body, and there is no tail. There are 104–107 primary annuli and 51–72 secondary annuli, for a total of 155–179.

The dorsum of the head and body are gray-brown to powder gray. The sides of the head, chin, and throat are usually gray with the area around the tentacle paler and sometimes whitish. Ventrolaterally and ventrally the body is cream, pinkish, or silvery gray, except for the annular grooves which are dark gray, although the posterior part of the body near the vent tends to be smoky gray in color.

Natural History.—This species inhabits a wide variety of habitats including tropical dry and moist forest, subtropical wet forest, and even the pine-oak forest near Guatemala City. It is common in cattle pastures and coffee groves as well as primary forest.

Earthworms are the major prey of this caecilian, but it also feeds on termites and beetle larvae. There is a report of this caecilian having eaten several species of lizards (*Ameiva* and *Norops*), but whether these lizards were captured alive or scavenged is open to question.

Females reproduce biennially, and fertilization and presumably mating take place during the early rainy season in May and June. Females are pregnant for about 11 months and give birth in April and May. From 2 to 16 fully developed young are born during the rainy season and are 110–150 mm in TL.

Distribution.—The plumbeous Central American caecilian has not been taken within the Department of Petén, but it is widespread in Middle America, occurring on both the Atlantic and Pacific coasts of southern Mexico and various areas of Central America to Colombia. It is known from the lower Río Motagua valley of eastern Guate-mala and also from the Mexican state of Tabasco just to the northwest of the Petén region. Because of its secretive nature, it may well have been overlooked and yet prove to be a component of the Petén herpetofauna. In Guatemala, it occurs in wet soils of humid and subhumid habitats at elevations ranging from near sea level to about 1,500 m.

Remarks.—Other common names for this species include *tepulcuate* and *dos cabezas,* the latter name derived from the fact that the body is rounded at both ends, giving the appearance of two heads. Subspecies sometimes have been recognized: *Dermophis mexicanus mexicanus* from southern Veracruz, Tabasco, and northern Chiapas, Mexico, and from southeastern Oaxaca southward on Pacific slopes to Costa Rica and Panama, where it crosses over onto Caribbean slopes; and *D. m. clarkii* from the lower Río Motagua Valley of Guatemala and the Río Ulúa Valley of northwestern Honduras.

Unfounded Beliefs.—People tend to exaggerate or distort many attributes of various groups of animals, but perhaps none more so than reptiles and amphibians. Beliefs are often widely held and so deeply ingrained that no amount of logic or rational explanation is likely to change the mind of a believer. This was brought home to me many years ago when I almost got myself killed late one evening at a West Texas truck stop. I had politely, or so I thought, questioned the veracity of the existence of a ten-foot rattlesnake that was described to me by a weather-beaten old rancher. He finally spat out, "Listen here young feller, I saw the varmit with my own eyes! You callin' me a liar?" This challenge pretty much ended our conversation and subsequently I have learned to bite my tongue when listening to such tales, approvingly nodding my head.

As in other places that harbor a large number of amphibians and reptiles, in the Petén region many perfectly harmless animals are greatly feared. The most common attribute of these species is a shared human ignorance of their true nature. Often this ignorance stems from the secretive, nocturnal habits of the animals. Additional traits that seem further to engender human fear are relatively slow and deliberate movements, large heads that suggest a venomous bite, or something about the eyes that calls attention to them.

Particularly vulgar traits are attributed to the secretive caecilians, possibly owing to their body shape and coloration. Their vernacular name *tapalcua* is a polite rendition of *tapalculo*, which in turn is derived from a Spanish phrase that describes certain almost unspeakable acts thought to be performed by these animals. Briefly, there is a widely held belief that caecilians will spring out of the ground and enter the lower body orifices of unsuspecting people who are answering the call of nature. The fact that caecilians may be found in mounds of rotting vegetation probably does not help.

Salamanders, as well as some skinks, are widely referred to as *niños dormidos*, which can be translated in English as "sleeping children." I once thought this name must have its origin in salamanders being secretive and often immobile when encountered, giving the appearance that they may be sleeping, and that there was confusion over identity in that skinks may resemble salamanders to some viewers. Although this may be the case in places, it has been explained to me that these animals cause children to never wake from their sleep, and eventually to die. How salamanders and skinks accomplish this remarkable feat varies according to geographic locality and storyteller. In some instances, the mere act of the animal crawling across a sleeping child is enough to doom the child to oblivion; in other cases, the animal purportedly enters the child's mouth or the child is thought to be bitten.

Several harmless species of lizards are referred to as *escorpión*, a name also given to the venomous beaded lizard of western Mexico and the Motagua Valley of Guatemala. Again, it is perhaps no coincidence that, other than the secretive skinks, none of the diurnal lizards of the Petén are regarded by local inhabitants as being dangerous, but all species of nocturnal lizards are generally feared. Night lizards of the genus *Lepidophyma* lack eyelids, giving them a glassy stare, and they have sinister (to some) pointed heads. These lizards venture out from their rocky or forested retreats after dark and often are seen as shadowy figures moving at the edge of light cast by a dim campfire or flashlight. The Yucatán banded gecko (*Coleonyx elegans*) is brightly patterned and has a large head. It skitters along on the ground after dark and, when confronted, usually stands upright in a threatening way on stiff, extended limbs and menacingly waves its elevated tail back and forth. When further provoked, this lizard is also capable of vocalization and emits a catlike mewing sound. To a lesser extent than other lizards in Petén, the turnip-tailed gecko (*Thecadactylus rapicaudus*) is also thought to be venomous, although it is nevertheless often tolerated in human habitations. These lizards lack eyelids, are nocturnal, have large, flat heads, and are capable of amazing scansorial feats that make them good candidates for the *bicho peligroso* (dangerous critter) list.

Snakes, of course, are the most generally feared animals and most species are thought to be venomous. The false barba amarilla (*Xenodon*) and cat-eyed snakes (*Leptodeira*) are especially feared. I have tried to demonstrate to various people, by freely handling these snakes, that they are innocuous enough. The usual response I get is, "Oh yes, if they were to bite you, nothing would happen because you have a secret remedy. However, we do not have this medicine and we would die very quickly if we were to touch these snakes."

Mountain Caecilian—Tapalcua Pequeña de Montaña
Gymnopis syntrema (Cope, 1866)
Fig. 15

Description.—Because of its pinkish coloration, this small, slender species may be mistaken easily for an earthworm. It usually does not exceed 270–300 mm in TL. The head is rather pointed in dorsal view and the posterior end of the body is broadly rounded with practically no tail. Eyes are poorly developed and not obvious, being in life no more than small dark spots. The sensory tentacle is just in front of the eye, and the orbit is covered not only by skin but also by the squamosal bone. The tentacular foramen is located near the center of the maxillary bone. A single splenial tooth is on each ramus of the lower jaw so that there are two series of teeth (dentary and splenial). Mountain caecilians have 128–132 primary annuli and 63–93 secondary annuli for a total of 193–206.

The head and anterior part of the body are usually pink. Posterior to the head is a gradual suffusion of gray pigment that becomes darker over most of the body. The area around the vent is usually pink. In this species the annular grooves are pale pink or whitish. Some specimens have a mostly gray body with pinkish coloration confined to the lower surface of the head.

Natural History.—Little is known about this rare species. I have encountered it in tropical wet forest and in subtropical moist and wet forest. Specimens have been unearthed 0.3–0.8 m below ground by a bulldozer during the construction of a road running through both primary and secondary vegetation. From 2 to12 young are born in a closely related species (*Gymnopis multiplicata*).

Distribution.—Extremely secretive, this caecilian is seen infrequently. Its known distribution is spotty: it has been recorded from the foothills of Alta Verapaz, the Sierra de las Minas, Sierra de Santa Cruz, Sierra del Merendón, and Maya Mountains of Belize and may occur in the Sierra de Chinajá on the Petén-Alta Verapaz border and other low foothill regions of northern and eastern Guatemala. In Guatemala, it is found in rainforest and cloudforest at elevations between 440 and 1,000 m.

Remarks—This species so infrequently ventures above ground that it is not well known by local inhabitants. One small individual was found dead just after sunrise on a game trail in the middle of a jaguar (*Felis onca*) track, apparently killed when that animal stepped on it during the early morning hours.

SALAMANDERS—SALAMANDRAS

Salamanders are the tailed amphibians that occur across much of the north temperate region of the world and into the American tropics. All Guatemalan species have two pairs of about equal-sized limbs and smooth, moist skin, often marked with bright colors. The salamanders occurring in Petén range in size from a diminutive species scarcely reaching 40 mm in total length to a large, robust form exceeding 200 mm. They are secretive creatures, spending most of their lives hidden in moist recesses. Only a single family occurs in the New World tropics.

To distinguish the various species of salamanders occurring in the Petén region, see appendix B.

Lungless Salamanders—Salamandras Apulmonadas

Family Plethodontidae

This family is widespread in North America, Mexico, Central America, and South America and a few species occur in southern Europe. Salamanders are not a prominent component of the herpetofauna in the Petén region, where this group may be represented by five or six species (not all these species have been confirmed). Although some species in the highlands of Guatemala are active year-round, those species inhabiting Petén usually emerge from their hiding places only during rainy periods.

All of the salamanders of Petén—indeed all salamanders of the New World tropics occurring south of the Isthmus of Tehuantepec in southern Mexico—are placed in the family Plethodontidae and are members of the tribe Bolitoglossini. The plethodontids possess several remarkable features, not the least of which is the complete absence of lungs. Respiration in this group is accomplished entirely through the skin and the lining of the mouth.

All bolitoglossine salamanders, insofar as is known, lay eggs in damp places on land and these eggs undergo direct development. All species have internal fertilization. Males produce gelatinous sperm packets called spermatophores, which are picked up from the substrate in the cloaca of females after successful courtship. Most of the species of Middle American salamanders that have been studied are highland animals that live in temperate habitats; the females of these species have biennial reproductive cycles, laying eggs every other year. The lowland species, such as those of the Petén region, are less well known but may have annual reproductive cycles. In many species the female remains wrapped around her eggs until they hatch. During the breeding season, the male develops on his chin an enlarged courtship gland, which has sometimes been referred to as a "hedonic" gland, but of course it is impossible to know if it is really pleasure-giving. Plethodontid salamanders may be sexually dimorphic in the number and size of their premaxillary teeth, which may be elongate and less numerous in the males of some species.

Another characteristic of plethodontid salamanders is a nasolabial groove under each nostril that functions as a chemoreceptor. The margin of the lip below the nostrils is swollen at the ventral terminus of each nasolabial groove in adult male bolitoglossines.

Most of the species of salamanders inhabiting the Petén region will climb on vegetation and are often encountered sitting on broad, smooth leaves at night. The digits on their hands and feet are short and connected with a full web, and the pads on the ventral surfaces of the hand and foot are smooth. These salamanders are able to climb vertical surfaces using suction created by placement of the feet on leaves or limbs; the outside margins of the feet adhere to the substrate, while the central part of the foot is lifted, causing suction. This process requires moisture, which comes from the abundant mucous glands in the skin.

Only three salamander species are known with certainty from the Department of Petén. However, *Bolitoglossa mulleri, B. odonnelli,* and *Oedipina elongata* occur in adjacent departments or Belize and possibly are even more widespread in the region. *Bolitoglossa yucatana* inhabits the relatively dry northern part of the Yucatán Peninsula and there is a slight chance that it may eventually be discovered in northern Petén.

Doflein's Salamander—Salamandra de Doflein
Bolitoglossa dofleini (Werner, 1903)
Fig. 16

Description.—Reaching a maximum size of about 125 mm in SVL and 225 mm in TL, this is the largest salamander in Guatemala. It has a robust body with 13 costal grooves between the limbs and 2 to 3 costal grooves separating adpressed legs. The snout is truncate in dorsal view, the toes are fully webbed, and the tail is robust but constricted at the base.

In adults, the ground color is uniformly grayish brown or may be mottled, spotted, or streaked with dark brown or gray. The belly and undersurface of the tail are pigmented but paler than the dorsum, often with a few dark gray spots. Juveniles have a contrasting dorsal pattern with relatively large dark brown to almost black spots and blotches on a reddish brown to tan background; large adults are more or less uniformly colored. The venter of juveniles is darker than the dorsum and has small pale flecks, and the dis-

tal portions of the limbs, hands, and feet are black.

Natural History.—Doflein's salamander is found in tropical wet forest and subtropical moist and wet forest, usually on the ground beneath piles of dead vegetation. I have never found it in bromeliads or even climbing on vegetation at night. When disturbed, these salamanders usually remain perfectly still and adpress their limbs against the body. Their cryptic coloration renders them difficult to see in leaf litter.

Distribution.—The species occurs on Atlantic slopes and lowlands from west-central Guatemala through eastern Guatemala to northwestern Honduras. In Petén, it has been recorded along the Río de La Pasión and several of its tributaries in the southwestern part of the department. Its elevational distribution is from near sea level to about 1,400 m.

Black-and-Gold Salamander—Salamandra Negridorada
Bolitoglossa mexicana Duméril, Bibron, and Duméril, 1854
Fig. 17

Description.—This moderately large, slender species reaches about 65–70 mm in SVL and 150–155 mm in TL. There are 12–13 costal grooves between the limbs, with 3–4 intercostal spaces separating the addressed legs. The snout is broadly rounded to truncate in dorsal view and the toes are fully webbed. The

tail is moderately slender and has a basal constriction.

The dorsum of the head, body, and tail is dark with a variable pattern of yellow to yellowish rust spots and blotches. These markings often fuse to form irregular dorsolateral stripes on the body but also may form irregular mottling, barring, or spotting. In a few specimens, the pale dorsal pattern is reduced to small yellow spots on a dark background. On the tail, dark markings often fuse to form an irregular dorsal stripe or an irregular series of dorsolateral blotches. The lower sides of the body and tail are dark brown to black, grading to a medium brown ventrally. The chin, throat, and undersurfaces of limbs and feet are medium brown.

Natural History.—Black-and-gold salamanders occur in tropical and subtropical wet and moist forest. They remain inactive during dry periods, hiding in the wet axils of bromeliads or in rotten logs. In Petén, individuals have been found around the edges of aguadas surrounded by forest and at night on low vegetation along streams.

Distribution.—The species is found from southern Veracruz, Mexico, through northern Guatemala and Belize to northern Honduras, exclusive of most of the northern portion of the Yucatán Peninsula; there is a single record from near Chichén-Itzá. This is the most widespread species of salamander in Petén, occurring through the southern portion of the region north to about Tikal; it appears to be absent from about the northern third of the department. In Guatemala, this salamander occurs from near sea level to about 1,000 m. In Petén, it is usually found in relatively mesic forest and near streams, although on one occasion it was collected near an aguada in savanna habitat.

Remarks.—This species may include O'donnell's salamander (see account for that species).

Müller's Salamander—Salamandra de Müller
Bolitoglossa mulleri (Brocchi, 1883)
Fig. 18

Description.—This relatively large, slender salamander reaches 60–80 mm in SVL and a TL of 135–162 mm. There are 13 costal grooves between the legs, with 4–5 between adpressed limbs. The snout is broadly truncate in dorsal view and the toes are fully webbed. The tail is slender and has a basal constriction.

Müller's salamander is nearly uniformly dark brown to black dorsally, with a narrow, pale yellow or orange dorsal stripe extending from near the back of the head onto the proximal one-half to three-fourths of the tail. This dorsal stripe may be broken and always has irregular rather than straight edges. The chin, throat, venter, and underside of the tail are also dark brown but not as heavily pigmented as the dorsum and sides.

Natural History.—This salamander inhabits tropical wet forest and subtropical wet forest. It has been found on the ground but also is somewhat arboreal and is often found in bromeliads, especially during the dry season. It has been encountered in vegetation up to 5 m above the forest floor.

Distribution.—This species has a small

distribution on the Caribbean lowlands and slopes in Alta Verapaz, Quiché, Huehuetenango, and southwestern Petén of Guatemala and eastern Chiapas, Mexico. Its elevational distribution is from about 100 m to 1,500 m.

O'donnell's Salamander—Salamandra de O'donnell
Bolitoglossa odonnelli (Stuart, 1943)
Fig. 19

Description.—This moderately large, slender salamander reaches an adult SVL of about 80 mm and a TL of about 165 mm. It has 12–13 costal grooves, and adpressed legs are separated by 3–5 costal grooves. The snout is broadly truncate in dorsal view and the toes are fully webbed. The tail has a basal constriction.

The dorsal ground color is black, and the chin, throat, venter, and undersurfaces of the hands and feet are dark gray. Two irregular dorsolateral pale yellow to cream stripes or series of spots extend from the back of the head onto the tail, where the spotting may not be confined to the dorsolateral area. Pale body stripes are almost always broken and sometimes reduced to a series of irregular spots.

Natural History.—O'donnell's salamander occurs in tropical and subtropical wet forest. I have found individuals most frequently at night on smooth, green leaves near small streams. This species has been found beneath the leaf sheaths of banana plants.

Distribution.—Known from the foothills and mountains of Alta Verapaz and Izabal, Guatemala, this species occurs in humid forests from about 100–1200 m. It may occur in the southern part of Petén.

Remarks.—This species may not be valid but instead may represent a distinct color morph of the black-and-gold salamander; both forms have been taken microsympatrically in the Montañas del Mico of Guatemala.

Common Dwarf Salamander—Salamandra Enana Común
Bolitoglossa rufescens (Cope, 1869)
Fig. 20

Description.—This small species of salamander reaches only about 35–36 mm in SVL and 65–70 in TL. Despite its small size, this salamander has a relatively robust body with 11 costal grooves between the legs and 3 costal grooves between addressed limbs. The snout is truncate and slightly scalloped anteriorly in dorsal view. Toes and fingers are fully webbed, and the third digit projects somewhat.

The dorsum is pale brown or tan to dark brown. Paler specimens often have a dorsal pattern of dark longitudinal streaks or peppering. A dark brown streak often begins behind the eyes and extends posteriorly for half the length of the body or more. In most specimens, the lower sides of the body and venter are dark gray; however, in a few specimens the venter is paler than the dorsum, or body coloration is uniform.

Natural History.—This salamander inhabits tropical and subtropical wet and moist forest. It is often found in bromeliads or under the sheaths of banana plants. On rainy nights it is frequently encountered on large smooth green leaves 1–3 m off the ground.

Distribution.—Common dwarf salamanders occur from San Luis Potosí, Veracruz, and northern Oaxaca, Mexico, through northern Chiapas and the northern foothills of Guatemala to about central Honduras. They are absent from most of Petén, which is probably too dry for this species, but have been taken in the western part of the department at Piedras Negras and are recorded to the south along the Río Usumacinta and the Río de La Pasión at Sayaxché. The species is known from east-central Petén and about the southern half of Belize. Its elevational distribution is from near sea level to about 1,500 m.

Remarks.—Probably several species are included in what is currently considered *Bolitoglossa rufescens.*

White-crowned Worm Salamander—Salmandra-lombriz de Frente Blanca
Oedipina elongata (Schmidt, 1936)
Fig. 21

Description.—This attenuate, vermiform species has short limbs and small hands and feet; it reaches about 65 mm in SVL and 150 in TL. There are 17 costal grooves between the legs and 8 costal folds between adpressed limbs. The profile of the head is rounded in dorsal view and the fingers and toes are completely webbed.

Overall color is a dark bluish gray, stippled with lichenose ash gray dots, which are more numerous on the sides. The posterior dorsal area of the head has a distinct white spot, most prominent in large individuals. The venter is not as darkly pigmented as the sides.

Natural History.—This wormlike salamander occurs in tropical and subtropical wet forest. It apparently is adapted for living in the channels of fallen logs that have been burrowed out by insect larvae and also in old termite nests on the ground. In collecting the white-crowned worm salamander, I have found that it usually avoids logs and termite nests that are so soft and rotten as to be easily pulled apart; rather it seeks out refuges in logs that retain more structural integrity and that can be broken apart only with difficulty using a machete. Three or four individuals may sometimes be found in a single log.

Distribution.—Occurring from northern Chiapas, Mexico, to Belize and eastern Guatemala, the species is not known from the Department of Petén, although it is found just to the south in the foothills of Alta Verapaz and the Sierra de Santa Cruz and to the east in the Maya Mountains. Its elevational distribution is from near sea level to about 770 m.

TOADS AND FROGS—SAPOS Y RANAS

The anurans, jumping or hopping amphibians, have four limbs. The hind limbs are elongate and particularly well developed, with several of the proximal tarsal elements having become lengthened, effectively adding an extra segment to the leg. Anurans occur practically worldwide except in the coldest environments and some oceanic islands. Adults are tailless. Most species are nocturnal and active during rainy periods. Many species have large, well-developed eyes, although the eyes are reduced in burrowing forms. Vocal slits and nuptial excrescences are characteristic of adult males of many species of anurans. These structures are never present in females. Unlike other amphibians, many anurans have loud voices. The males, especially, are often capable of producing sounds, including mating calls that attract females. Most anurans worldwide, and all Guatemalan species, have external fertilization. The classic amphibian life history is that of a frog placing its eggs in a pond, where they hatch into tadpoles that subsequently grow and eventually metamorphose into little froglets. Although many species of anurans in the Petén region adhere to this mode of reproduction, some do not. Variations on the theme include species that lay their eggs on leaves above ponds and streams, so that hatching tadpoles drop into the water; species that form foam nests; and species that lay eggs in damp places on the ground, where young undergo direct development. There are seven families of anurans in the Petén region. To distinguish the various species of anurans occurring in the Petén region, see appendix C.

Whether an anuran is called a frog or a toad is often more a matter of local usage, its habits or appearance, or human fancy than an indication of evolutionary relationships. To make matters more confusing, these terms are sometimes used interchangeably for certain species. In Europe and North America, the Ranidae and Bufonidae are the common, widespread families and have become known as true frogs and toads, respectively. However, worldwide there are about 25 anuran families and these exhibit considerable variation. In general, those species that are rotund with relatively short legs and that have rugose, warty skin are referred to as toads, especially if they happen to live in a dry environment. Those species having long legs with considerable webbing on the toes and having smooth skin are most often called frogs. But there are many exceptions, such as the Suriname toad (*Pipa pipa*), which is totally aquatic with fully webbed feet.

Some members of one group of frogs in the American tropics, commonly known as poison-dart frogs (family Dendrobatidae), are famous for their bright colors and extremely toxic skin secretions. The range of this family does not extend northward as far as Guatemala. Although no Guatemalan species of anuran has skin secretions comparable to those of the poison-dart frogs, a few species do secrete skin toxins, especially when injured or frightened, and these toxins are capable of causing serious discomfort in humans. Examples include all species of toads, which are able to exude a viscous, milky toxin from their parotoid glands, and the milky treefrog, which has a highly glandular skin covering its back.

Cats and dogs have been known to die after eating one of these anurans, and people who touch their eyes after handling these species may experience immediate and severe burning, which can last for hours.

Tadpoles are often divided into four or five different kinds, sometimes referred to as Types I-IV. Three of these types occur in the Petén region. Type I includes the family Rhinophrynidae, which has tadpoles that have no horny beaks or tooth rows; that have two separate branchial chambers, each with a separate external ventrolateral spiracle; and in which the forelimbs develop posterior to the branchial chambers. The family Microhylidae has Type II tadpoles, which lack horny beaks and tooth rows; which have two separate branchial chambers but these chambers have a common tube joining them posteriorly and opening to the exterior in a single midventral spiracle located on the posterior of the body near the base of the tail; and in which forelimbs develop posterior to the branchial chambers. All of the other anuran families in Petén (Bufonidae, Hylidae, Leptodactylidae, Ranidae) have Type IV tadpoles, which have beaks and usually tooth rows; the branchial chambers communicate with each other internally and there is a single sinistral spiracle; and the forelimbs usually develop within the branchial chambers.

Other features useful in distinguishing tadpoles of different species are the location of the mouth, which is usually anteroventral or ventral; the number of tooth rows, the generalized number being 2/3 (e.g., 2 anterior rows on upper part of oral disc and 3 posterior rows on lower part of disc); whether the marginal papillae that fringe the oral disc are continuous or have either dorsal or ventral gaps; the shape of the body and snout; the position of the eyes; the relative depth of the caudal fins; and the coloration.

MIDDLE AMERICAN BURROWING TOAD—SAPO MOI

FAMILY RHINOPHRYNIDAE

The Middle American Burrowing Toad is monotypic and the description and distribution given for the single species is therefore the same as for the family. In this species the pupil is vertical, amplexus is inguinal, and it has an aquatic Type I larva.

Middle American Burrowing Toad—Sapo Moi
Rhinophrynus dorsalis Duméril and Bibron, 1841
Fig. 22

Description.—This globular anuran has an especially fat body, a small, tapered head, and tiny eyes, and the tip of the snout is flattened and appears calloused. Adult males reach about 65–75 mm in SVL and females 70–80 mm. The skin on the back is mostly smooth but with a few minute, scattered tubercles. The limbs are exceedingly short and robust. The digits lack discs and the toes are about three-fourths webbed. The hind foot has only four digits and there is no tarsal fold; instead, along the inner tarsal surface are two large, whitish, spadelike tubercles that are used for digging. Breeding males have vocal slits and are able to inflate their internal lateral vocal sacs dramatically. Breeding males also have large, whitish nuptial excrescences that cover most of the inner surface of the pollex.

The dorsum is blackish or dark gray, usually with reddish orange markings. These markings sometimes may be yellowish in a few individuals, especially females. A pattern consisting of a middorsal stripe and mottling on the dorsolateral surface and upper lateral surface of the flanks is usually present. The venter is uniformly gray or blue-gray. The posterior surface of the thighs is blackish or gray, usually uniformly colored but sometimes with a little pale spotting.

Tadpoles lack tooth rows and beaks. Young tadpoles of this species (20 mm) possess two fleshy protuberances on the upper jaw in front of the eyes. As tadpoles mature, they lose these protuberances and develop elongate barbels at the border of the mouth. The body is wider than it is deep, the snout is truncate, and the eyes are lateral in position. There are paired ventrolateral spiracles. The dorsal and ventral caudal fins are subequal in height and the dorsal fin extends onto the posterior part of the body. Tadpoles are heavily pigmented with numerous melanophores on the dorsal surface and the venter is whitish or silver.

Natural History.—Relatively dry habitats are characteristic for the Middle American burrowing toad, including tropical dry and moist forest, where it is usually associated with the aguadas and akalchés that become seasonally flooded. This rotund anuran can be described as a "fat introvert," rarely seen above ground except after the heaviest rains of the year and for a short time thereafter when it is breeding (see "Chasing the Rain," page 47). The rest of the year it remains buried in the ground, where apparently it continues to feed, although there usually is no burrow connecting its underground retreat with the surface. It has been excavated from just 30–50 mm from the surface but may also dig much deeper into the sides of banks to aestivate during the dry season. When this toad is removed from its underground chamber, there is no evidence of the parchmentlike "cocoon" characteristic of some species that spend much time underground during the dry times of the year. Under laboratory conditions, recently metamorphosed juveniles were observed to dig to the bottom of their terrarium, which contained about 500 mm of soil.

This toad specializes on a diet consisting of ants and termites. It is reasonably certain that most feeding is done underground. The peculiar tongue mechanism, calloused snout, and flattened chin are probably adaptations for this mode of foraging.

The breeding call of this species is a low-pitched *whooooaa.* Males greatly inflate their bodies when calling. This species has inguinal amplexus; that is, the male grasps the female around the waist when mating. Amplectant pairs are sometimes found with their ventral surfaces in contact. Breeding occurs from June to September in Petén. Clutch size ranges from about 2,000 to 8,000 eggs. The eggs are laid separately and sink to the bottom where they hatch in several days, but they are sticky and sometimes small aggregations of eggs form. Tadpoles (Type I) inhabit muddy ponds that usually have a high algae content; they are filter feeders, straining algae and detritus from the water. It has been reported that burrowing toad tadpoles are carnivorous at times and feed on other tadpoles, including those of its own kind, especially under crowded conditions or when food availability is low. Tadpoles often aggregate in large numbers at midwater depths, moving through the water in schools that may be seen by day or at night. Such schooling behavior may facilitate feeding by stirring up the organic detritus on the bottom of pools. Unlike the schools of tadpoles observed in many other species of anurans, the schools of *Rhino-*

phrynus may consist of tadpoles of different sizes. Many thousands of tadpoles may metamorphose and leave the water at the same time. I have observed this remarkable phenomenon on several occasions at about mid-morning, when hordes of cricket-sized toadlets exited the water and made for muddy banks or other cover where they burrowed in. My attention was directed to these aggregations of little frogs by the activity of birds feeding on them. On one occasion, several bronze-backed parrot snakes (*Leptophis mexicanus*) were also eating the metamorphosing frogs.

Distribution.—Found from extreme southern Texas and Guerrero, Mexico, southward through Guatemala and Belize to northwestern Costa Rica, this frog occurs throughout most of central and northern Petén, Belize, and the northern Yucatán Peninsula. It inhabits just about any location where there are aguadas or other semipermanent or temporary water for several months a year, although it tends to avoid heavily forested areas. In Guatemala, the species occurs from near sea level to about 300 m.

Remarks.—Other vernacular names for the burrowing toad include *wo, sapo borracho, cameleón,* and *sapo cavador. Sapo borracho* means inebriated toad, a name alluding to the call of males during the breeding season, which sounds like a drawn-out *whooooaa*—the sound from which its Mayan name, *wo,* is derived. Choruses of these toads have been described as sounding like a shipload of sick sailors.

I know people in Petén who greatly esteem this frog as food, preferring it over many other kinds of more traditional game animals. It is impaled on the center section of a palm frond and roasted over an open fire.

Chasing the Rain.—For a herpetologist, there is practically no experience more exciting than being in the field during the first sudden downpours of the season. During this time, frogs of many species gather in great numbers at lowland breeding sites. Most tropical lowland species of frogs and toads deposit eggs that take no more than a few days to hatch, and metamorphosis ensues within several weeks to several months.

The Middle American burrowing toad or *sapo moi,* as it is known through most of Petén, is capable of reproduction over an extended period, but like almost all tropical species, it is dependent on rainfall. An opportunistic breeder, it breeds only during or after heavy rains. It is also an explosive breeder, appearing in large numbers immediately after rain to breed when conditions are suitable in temporary muddy pools, roadside ditches, and aguadas as well as more permanent bodies of water. The raucous call of the sapo moi may be heard over distances of a kilometer or more.

During the summer of 1995, Butch Brodie and I made repeated attempts to secure a series of sapos moi for laboratory experiments on their behavior. We knew that the species was abundant at the main aguada at La Libertad, where we had found them previously. We arrived in Petén on 12 July, traveling overland from Belize. From our small hotel on the northeastern shore of Lago Petén Itzá, we were about 50 airline kilometers northeast of La Libertad, but we thought we might be able to judge what the weather was like in the region of La Libertad by evaluating the large cumulus clouds that formed in the late afternoon. On the evening of July 13 conditions looked favorable. Large dark clouds had gathered on the horizon by about four o'clock in the afternoon and we could see flashes of lightning and isolated showers falling to the south.

We took off in hot pursuit of our quarry. The road was good as far as Santa Elena but quickly degenerated from that town all the way to La Libertad, a distance of about 30 bone-crunching kilometers. Butch, who was doing most of the driving, had a theory that negotiating extremely deeply rutted, washboarded roads at high rates of speed has a smoothing effect on the ride. His theory goes something like this: Because of the speed, only the high points will be touched by the tires, and because the high points are all of about the same elevation, occupants will not be as badly jolted as they would be if going more slowly. His first assumption—that he thought he was going fast enough to hit only the high points of the road—was probably accurate. The second premise—that this provided a more comfortable ride—is seriously in doubt. Several things are for certain: when we arrived at La Libertad that evening, in record time, there was no rain in sight, nor had it rained in the immediate vicinity, and the poor old Jeep Cherokee had acquired a few more unexplained rattles and clinks deep within. We dejectedly returned home.

We had to wait only until the following afternoon when an even larger storm than that of the day before formed to the south and violent squalls created whitecaps on Lago Petén Itzá. But the scenario turned out to be a repeat of the evening before. Over the next week we made half a dozen trips to La Libertad, only once getting into as much as a light sprinkle, but even that failed to quell the thick layer of dust on the road. We all but gave up hope of securing the elusive sapo moi.

On July 23, the day before we planned to leave Petén, we decided to make one last try. The weather conditions appeared to be about the same as on previous days, but as we passed through San Antonio, a small village about halfway to La Libertad from Santa Elena on Lago Petén Itza, we drove into a heavy downpour. As we continued toward La Libertad, the rain got even harder, and we were certain that we would see breeding choruses of several species of frogs when we reached the aguada at La Libertad. Unfortunately, fate intervened once again. A bright red light began to glow from the dashboard, indicating that our vehicle was overheating seriously. We received a blast of hot air from a quick look under the hood, and a pungent burning smell suggested that the light was not malfunctioning. More troubling still, there was a strong and definite smell of gasoline, though we were unable to trace the exact source.

We had no choice but to begin retracing our steps to Santa Elena, if we could make it that far, where there were mechanics and auto parts. We turned around only some seven or eight miles from La Libertad and, with Butch behind the wheel, headed for home at a rate of speed only slightly reduced. As anyone who has driven in the tropics knows, extremely humid conditions prevail during heavy showers and windshields often fog up so badly that it is necessary to drive with one hand while wiping off the glass with the other. We tried using the defogger blower, but this only made things worse. We tried turning on the air conditioner—no luck. Finally, we turned the heater on full blast and that did work, but it made conditions inside the vehicle almost unbearable. We rolled all the windows down to let in as much of the warm tropical night air as possible, which, in comparison to the hot air from the vehicle, was delightful.

As we cruised though the village of San Antonio, whence we had come about 45 minutes previously, over the din of the hot air blower, the noise of tires on the gravel road, and other vehicle noises of unknown origin, we heard in the distance the unmistakable *whooooaa* of sapo moi. We parked the Jeep in the middle of the village, grabbed our gear, and headed for the source of the calls. Before long we found a huge chorus of many hundreds of males calling. We quickly gathered up a nice sample of sapos moi and several other species of frogs as well as a cat-eyed snake that had obviously arrived with the intention of eating some of the smaller frogs. On the rest of the trip home that evening, the warning light continued to glow brightly, but we could not have cared less. The evening had been a success. Who cared if the car blew up? We had frogs!

Back at our small lakeside hotel, we decided to keep our specimens in several large plastic washtubs. The cacophony of some 80 frogs was deafening. Fortunately, the hotel was practically deserted. Even the owner had left several days before for Guatemala City. We did not realize it at the time, but two Israeli tourists were the only other occupants in the hotel. They remained huddled in their room for several hours after we arrived, terrified at what kind of beast could possibly be making the horrible racket that rocked the entire premises. When they finally ventured out, we had some explaining to do.

The next morning we placed the embattled Cherokee in the *taller*. After replacing some belts and removing the thermostat which he assured us had no known function—the mechanic patched a rather large hole in the gas tank, caused no doubt by one of the hundreds of rocks that we had kicked up on the road, and we left for Izabal. I suspect the hole had been in the gas tank for some time; Butch and I had remarked on the lousy mileage the Cherokee had been getting in Petén. A subsequent review of the gas receipts revealed that we had been getting four or five miles to the gallon. But frog collectors are very focused on their work and not easily perturbed by such details.

CHIRPING, CLIMBING, FOAM, LEAF-LITTER, AND STREAM FROGS—RANAS CHIRRIADORAS, TREPADORAS, ESPUMERAS, DE HOJARASCA, Y DE RIACHUELO

FAMILY LEPTODACTYLIDAE

This group of frogs is widespread in the Americas from the southern United States through Mexico and Central America to South America and also in the West Indies. Members of the family vary from large, smooth-skinned species to small, warty, toad-like frogs. The genus *Eleutherodactylus* contains over 500 species and is the largest genus of tetrapods in the world. Among the Guatemalan species, the skin is raised into longitudinal ridges on the back in the genus *Leptodactylus*; in *Eleutherodactylus* there may be suprascapular ridges and small tubercles on the back, but the skin is relatively smooth in most species, with the notable exception of the warty forestfrog (*E. psephosypharus*). The skin on the dorsum of the mottled chirping frog (*Syrrhophus leprus*) is slightly rugose, and in the túngara frog (*Physalaemus pustulosus*) large tubercles are scattered across the back and sides of the body. Amplexus is axillary in all species in this family. Diverse reproductive modes are exhibited by frogs of this family inhabiting the Petén. The two species of foamfrogs (*Leptodactylus*) and the túngara frog deposit their eggs on the water in a floating foam nest, where Type IV larvae hatch and complete their metamorphosis in the water. Members of the genera *Eleutherodactylus* and *Syrrhophus* lay their eggs in damp crevices or leaf litter and these eggs undergo direct development.

Alfred's Climbing Frog—Rana Trepadora de Alfred
Eleutherodactylus alfredi (Boulenger, 1898)
Fig. 23

Description.—The discs on the digits of this species are well developed and broadly expanded and the skin of the dorsum is weakly tuberculate. The first finger is shorter than the second. Adult males are 24–26 mm in SVL and females attain 40–45 mm in SVL. The toes bear only vestigial (basal) webbing. The inner tarsal fold is poorly developed or absent. Adult males lack vocal slits but have whitish nuptial excrescences.

The dorsum is tan, brown, or olive-green. A blackish interorbital bar and at least a trace of a canthal stripe usually are present. The iris is bronze. A dark subocular spot and dark markings usually are present along the lips. The dorsum has irregular black or dark brown mottling and sometimes pale flecks. Limbs usually lack distinct dark barring; often there is some black flecking, but when present, this dark pigment forms rather diffuse limb bars. Flanks are usually pale brown or purple with darker brown mottling. The venter is whitish or pale yellow with many scattered, dark melanophores. The posterior surface of the thighs lacks any contrasting pattern.

Natural History.—Alfred's climbing frog occurs in tropical moist and wet forest. It is usually encountered after dark, especially after rains, sitting on low vegetation or in the vicinity of rocky outcroppings. Its eggs are laid during the rainy season and undergo direct development.

Distribution.—The species is found from the Atlantic foothills of east-central Veracruz, Mexico, through Tabasco and northern Chiapas to northwestern Petén. It occurs at elevations ranging from near sea level to a little over 600 m. The extent of this frog's distribution in Petén is unknown. Although moderately abundant in some places in Mexico, it has been taken in Petén only once, near Piedras Negras on the Mexican border.

Remarks.—A close relative, *Eleuthero-dactylus yucatanensis*, occurs in the northeastern part of the Yucatán Peninsula in the states of Yucatán and Quintana Roo.

Chac's Leaf-litter Frog—Rana Hojarasquera de Chac
Eleutherodactylus chac Savage, 1987
Fig. 24

Description.—This frog is closely related to the larger *Eleutherodactylus laticeps*, with which it is sympatric in some areas. However, *E. chac* is almost always more abundant than *E. laticeps*. Several glandular ridges form an X or hourglass-shaped marking on the back of *E. chac*. Adult males reach 20–27 mm in SVL and females 31–39 mm. The skin of the dorsum is finely tuberculate and a few large tubercles (often black) may be present. The first finger is longer than the second and the discs on the digits are only slightly expanded. The toes bear vestigial (basal) webbing. The inner tarsal fold extends from about halfway to two-thirds from the inner metatarsal tubercle to the heel. Vocal slits and nuptial excrescences in males are absent.

Variable in color, this frog may have a tan, yellow-tan, brown, reddish brown, or gray-brown dorsum. A thin, pale middorsal line is often present. Specimens may have a uniformly colored dorsum, but usually with some dark mottling. The linear glandular ridges on the back usually are black. Below the canthus the side of the face usually is black or dark brown and this dark coloration continues posterior to the eye below a line extending from the eye across the top of the tympanum to a point about halfway down the flanks. The iris is reddish bronze above and brown below. Forearms almost always have a dark spot or bar at about mid-length. The exposed surfaces of the thighs and shanks have three to four dark brown transverse bars. The posterior surface of the thigh may be uniformly colored or mottled with brown but forming no conspicuous pattern. A black patch surrounds the vent. The venter is cream and the throat region may be dark in adult males and females.

Natural History.—This frog occurs in tropical and subtropical wet and moist forest, occupying leaf litter in the rainforest; it does not tolerate drying conditions and is restricted to forests that have not been greatly modified by human activities. Eggs of this species undergo direct development.

Distribution.—Chac's leaf-litter frog occurs in the Atlantic foothills of Guatemala from the Sierra de Chinajá to the Maya Mountains, the Montañas del Mico, the Sierra de Santa Cruz, the Sierra del Merendón, and northern Honduras, at elevations of 30–775 m.

Broad-headed Leaf-litter Frog—Rana Hojarasquera de Cabeza Ancha
Eleutherodactylus laticeps (A. Duméril, 1853)
Fig. 25

Description.—Dorsolateral glandular ridges are present but may be indistinct in some specimens; there is also a thin middorsal glandular ridge. Adult males of this species are 31–47 mm in SVL and females attain 55–80 mm. The skin of the dorsum is finely tuberculate. The first finger is longer than the second and the discs are barely wider than the digits. The toes bear only vestigial (basal) webbing. The inner metatarsal fold is strongly developed and extends from halfway to two-thirds from the inner metatarsal tubercle to the heel. Vocal slits and nuptial excrescences in males are absent.

Dorsum color is extremely variable and may be yellowish, tan, various shades of brown, or reddish brown. A dark face mask is often present, with the sides of the face below the canthus, eye, and tympanum dark. Specimens lacking a face mask have a distinct dark postocular spot and other dark spots along the lips. Usually there is at least some black pigment in the interocular region, but this may be reduced to a few small spots. The iris is copper-colored above and brown below. The dorsum may be uniformly colored but often has a series of dark brown blotches, arranged symmetrically to either side of the dorsal midline. Some individuals have a pale middorsal stripe varying from a thin line to a relatively wide stripe. The thighs and shanks are marked with about four dark brown transverse bars. The venter is cream with some brown mottling on the throat. Posterior surface of the thighs is uniformly colored or mottled with brown but without any conspicuous markings. There is no black seat patch.

Natural History.—The broad-headed leaf-litter frog inhabits tropical and subtropical wet forest. It does not appear to be common, or at least is localized, and is found in the leaf litter of mesic ravines within forest or near forested aguadas. Eggs are laid in the rainy season and undergo direct development.

Distribution.—The species is from the Sierra de Los Tuxtlas in southern Veracruz, Mexico, through the base of the Yucatán Peninsula to the Maya Mountains of Belize and southward to northeastern Honduras. In Petén, this species is recorded from several localities to the east and southeast of Laguna Yaxjá. In Guatemala, it occurs from near sea level to about 1,600 m.

Remarks.—I have not seen this species in Petén, although I have commonly encountered it farther south in Guatemala. It is closely related to the smaller *Eleutherodactylus chac*, with which it is sympatric in some places.

Warty Forestfrog—Rana del Bosque Verrugosa
Eleutherodactylus psephosypharus Campbell, Savage, and Meyer, 1994
Fig. 26

Description.—As the common name implies, the skin of the dorsum is strongly tuberculate in this species. Adult males are 29–36 mm in SVL and females attain 53–65 mm. The first finger is longer than the second and the discs on the digits are well developed and broadly expanded. Toes bear only vestigial (basal) webbing. The strongly developed inner tarsal fold extends about halfway from the inner metatarsal tubercle to the heel. Vocal slits and nuptial excrescences are absent in males.

The dorsum is brown, yellowish brown, to olive-brown with black mottling. Larger dorsal tubercles are often reddish brown in males. The posterior border of the interorbital bar is black, there are dark markings along the lips, and dark limb bars are present on females and some males. The posterior surface of the thighs is dark brown or gray-brown, more or less uniformly pigmented or with inconspicuous markings. The venter is dark brownish or purplish. The iris is metallic brown.

Natural History.—This frog occurs in tropical and subtropical wet forest. I usually have found individuals sitting in wet leaf litter in virgin forest. The warty forestfrog often occurs in karstic regions and, unlike many other large members of the genus *Eleutherodactylus* in Guatemala, this species is not associated with riparian habitats and is usually found far from streams.

A large female was found in May in a deep depression beneath a large, rotten stump, attending a clutch of 81 eggs. However, other females containing large, yolked eggs have been found in December and small juveniles have been seen in January, suggesting that the species breeds throughout most of the year. Eggs undergo direct development.

Distribution.—Occurring in the Atlantic foothills of Guatemala from the Sierra de Chinajá to the Montañas del Mico and the Sierra del Merendón, this species probably also ranges into adjacent Mexico and Honduras. It has been found at elevations from near sea level to 1,170 m. In Petén this frog occurs in the south, in the Río San Román and Río Sarstún drainages.

Remarks.—Other frogs occurring in the region that share some similarities with the warty forestfrog and may be closely related are Sanderson's streamfrog (*Eleutherodactylus sandersoni*) and the long-legged streamfrog (*Eleutherodactylus* sp.), both creatures of riparian habitats.

Common Leaf-litter Frog—Rana Hojarasquera Común*
Eleutherodactylus rhodopis (Cope, 1866)
Fig. 27

Description.—This species has dorso-lateral glandular ridges, usually a mid-dorsal glandular ridge, and a pair of suprascapular glandular ridges extending from the posterior edge of the eye to the midback region. Adult males are 19–21 mm in SVL, females 27–32 mm. The relatively smooth skin of the dorsum has a few scattered small tubercles; the flanks are covered with numerous large, rounded tubercles. The first finger is longer than the second and the tips of the digits are only slightly swollen; toes bear vestigial (basal) webbing. The inner tarsal fold is absent, but there is an inner tarsal tubercle located between one-third and one-half the distance from the inner metatarsal tubercle to the heel. Adult males have vocal slits and small whitish nuptial excrescences.

The dorsum is tan, yellowish tan, or pale brown, usually with some dark brown markings, which may take the form of irregular mottling, blotches, or longitudinal striping. A blackish interorbital bar may be present. The side of the head below the canthus and eye is dark, and a black marking extends from behind the eye across the top of the tympanum, curving downward to a point above the insertion of the forearm. The posterior surface of the thighs is mostly brown and may be marked with small pale spots. The venter is cream or yellowish. A dark brown or black seat patch is present.

Natural History.—This frog is apparently restricted to forested areas where there is ample leaf litter. It inhabits tropical and subtropical wet and moist forest and also occurs in mesic patches within the tropical dry forest. It has been taken at night along the edges of aguadas. Eggs undergo direct development.

Distribution.—The common leaf-litter frog occurs on the Caribbean watershed from southern Mexico to about northern Honduras, and on the Pacific side from Chiapas to at least south-central Guatemala, including much of the northeastern and central portions of Petén. It is found from near sea level to about 1,700 m.

Remarks.—The taxonomic status of many populations assigned to this species is confused; undoubtedly several species are involved. Although this frog has been reported from several localities in Petén, I have never collected a specimen from the Atlantic versant of Guatemala, although I have examined several preserved specimens. I have seen many thousands of individuals purportedly of this species from the Pacific versant of Guatemala, but they differ from the Petén specimens in several respects.

Sanderson's Streamfrog—Rana de Riachuelo de Sanderson
Eleutherodactylus sandersoni Schmidt, 1941
Fig. 28

Description.—The skin of the dorsum is moderately rugose with many small tubercles and there are usually large tubercles on the flanks and eyelids of this species. Adult males are 35–50 mm in SVL and females attain 70–85 mm. The first finger is about equal to, or a bit longer than, the second and the discs on the digits are well developed and expanded. Toes bear considerable webbing (compared with other members of the genus; i.e, between one-fourth and one-third webbed). The strongly developed inner tarsal fold extends from about halfway to two-thirds the distance from the inner metatarsal tubercle to the heel. Vocal slits are absent, but a whitish nuptial excrescence is present on the pollex of adult males.

The dorsum is brown or gray-brown with irregular black mottling, often with distinct orange or rust-colored spots in the interorbital region or on the back. This frog has dark markings along the lips, usually a black interorbital bar, and dark brownish gray or gray transverse bars on the limbs. The posterior surface of the thigh is dark brown or gray-brown with small pale spots. The belly is whitish or pale purplish with a suffusion of brown pigment; the throat is heavily mottled with brown or gray-brown in males and females. The iris is bronze above and below.

Natural History.—This frog occurs in tropical wet forest and subtropical wet and moist forest, usually not far from streams running through pristine forested habitats. By day, it hides under large boulders or in dirt crevices in banks, venturing out after dark to sit on banks and rocks along streams. Little is known of its biology. This frog lays eggs that undergo direct development.

Distribution.—From the Maya Mountains of Belize and the Caribbean foothills of Guatemala, including the Sierra de Santa Cruz and Montañas del Mico, this species ranges from near sea level to at least 700 m.

Remarks.—A decade or more ago, the species was abundant along certain streams in eastern Guatemala and it was possible to observe literally hundreds of individuals within several hours. Sanderson's streamfrog and its relative the long-legged streamfrog appear to be the victims of the declining-amphibian-population phenomenon that is evident worldwide. At several localities where, until recently, it was quite common, Sanderson's streamfrog now appears to be extinct. At other localities, only a dozen or so specimens may be seen after a long evening of searching (see "Harbingers of Environmental Degradation," page 58).

This species appears to be closely related to the warty streamfrog (*Eleutherodactylus psephosypharus*) and the long-legged streamfrog (*Eleutherodactylus* sp., see following account); it is found along many of the same streams as the latter species.

Long-legged Streamfrog—Rana de Riachuelo de Piernas Largas
Eleutherodactylus sp. (*rugulosus* group)
Fig. 29

Description.—The skin of the dorsum in this species is finely granular with large tubercles on the flanks. Adult males are 30–41 mm in SVL, females 60–75 mm. The first finger is a bit longer than the second, with discs on the digits well developed and moderately expanded. Toes have a moderate amount of webbing (i.e., less than one-fourth webbed). The inner tarsal fold is strongly developed and extends about halfway from the inner metatarsal tubercle to the heel. Adult males have vocal slits but no nuptial excrescences.

The dorsum is pale to dark brown or gray-brown with dark brown or black mottling and often a thin middorsal line or broad stripe. An interorbital bar is present, its posterior border usually black, and there are dark markings along the lips and three to four dark, transverse limb bars. The posterior surface of the thighs is dark brown with large pale spots. The whitish venter is suffused with brown pigment and the throat is mottled in males and females. The iris is gold above and dark brown below.

Natural History.—This frog is almost always encountered near streams running through pristine tropical wet and subtropical wet and moist forest habitats. Its activity patterns are similar to those of Sanderson's streamfrog, with which it is usually found sympatrically. I encountered an amplectant pair sitting about three-fourths buried in the soft, damp soil along the edge of a trailcut at about 4:00 P.M. on 9 July 1980. I marked the spot for future reference and when I returned the same day at about 7:00 p.m., the adults had moved and I could not find them. The nest was covered with dirt and would have been difficult to locate had I not flagged it. I excavated the clutch, which contained a total of 64 eggs at a depth of about 25–40 mm below the surface, deposited in a disc-shaped clutch only 2–3 eggs deep. Eggs undergo direct development, and 43 days later (on 21 August) the tiny young emerged.

Distribution.—Long-legged streamfrogs occur in the Atlantic foothills of northern Central America, including the Sierra de Santa Cruz and the Montañas del Mico of Guatemala and the Maya Mountains of Belize, from near sea level to at least 600 m.

Remarks.—The taxonomic placement of this species is currently under investigation. Previously, it and Sanderson's streamfrog (*Eleutherodactylus sandersoni*) have been placed by various authorities into the species *E. rugulosus*, a species in which adult males lack both vocal slits and nuptial excrescences. Like Sanderson's streamfrog, the long-legged streamfrog appears to have suffered serious population declines over the last 10–15 years.

The long-legged streamfrog is related to the warty forestfrog (*E. psephosypharus*) and Sanderson's streamfrog and is microsympatric at many localities with the latter species.

Harbingers of Environmental Degradation.—In 1980 and 1981 I spent many nights walking alongside the clear, cool streams flowing through limestone beds of the Montañas del Mico. In particular, I enjoyed visiting the Río Las Escobas, which serves as the water source for Puerto Barrios. Most of this stream flows through virgin forest that is home to a diversity of wildlife. The most abundant amphibians that I encountered on these forays were several species of streamfrogs of the genus *Eleutherodactylus* (see figs. 28–29). On any given night I would see dozens or even several hundred of these frogs sitting on rocks or banks of these streams. During several trips to Las Escobas in 1986 and 1987, I was a little surprised when I observed only about half a dozen streamfrogs each night. At the time, I attributed this lack of success to the vagaries of collecting, which afflict all field biologists. Various things are often blamed—not enough rain, too much rain, too hot, too cold, or too bright a moon. The fact is that we still do not understand very well the activity patterns of most species of animals and what causes them to be everywhere one night but to disappear the next night, when environmental conditions to the unknowing human seem to be the same. I have visited Las Escobas almost every year between 1986 and 1996 and these frogs have never returned to their former numbers. If anything, they have declined further. On some nights I have seen only one or two, or none. It seems clear to me that populations of streamfrogs in eastern Guatemala have dramatically declined, even though they occur in watershed forests that are protected and remain relatively pristine.

In 1989, I attended the First World Congress of Herpetology held in Canterbury, England. During the course of this meeting a number of scientific presentations were given that noted the disappearance or decline of amphibian species around the world. It soon became apparent to those attending the meeting that a decline in amphibian populations was possibly a global phenomenon affecting many species of anurans, both temperate and tropical, from low to high elevations, and from regions as far apart as North America and Australia. Since 1989, the disappearance of many additional species has been documented.

There is little doubt that many populations of anurans have declined and even become extinct over the last decade, and several frustrating problems face scientists investigating this phenomenon. First, no common factor has been identified that might be responsible for the majority of these declines. Possibilities suggested include chemical pollutants; habitat destruction; thinning of the ozone layer, which has led to increased ultraviolet radiation; increased atmospheric CO_2 leading to global warming; introduction of competitors, predators, or diseases; climatic stress, which has allowed certain microparasites to reach epidemic proportions; and overexploitation for food, scientific use, or the pet trade.

Chemical contaminants are perhaps the most likely cause for many amphibian declines. Chemical agents may work in a number of detrimental ways: they directly pollute the water in which amphibians live, they may pollute the air and combine with clouds to produce acid rain, or they may interact with hormones that control amphibian development. Habitat destruction is the most obvious cause for many local extinctions but fails to explain why so many species in unaltered (or so we think) habitats have disappeared in recent years. Increased ultraviolet radiation is another plausible explanation; many of the amphibians that have declined are from high elevations or parts of the world where there has been a marked increase in this radiation. Some of these species tend to be nocturnal, but perhaps their eggs or recent metamorphs are adversely affected. However, some deep forest species in which neither eggs nor adults are exposed to increased ultraviolet radiation have also declined. Various examples have been put forth of species that have declined because of such things as competitors, predators, diseases, and overexploitation, but such cases seem to pertain only to particular species and do not seem to be widespread.

A second problem confronting researchers is that little is known about natural fluctuations in amphibian populations. A good example is the golden toad (*Bufo periglenes*), which became known to science only in 1967 and is restricted to the Cordillera de Tilarán in western Costa Rica. Beginning in the 1970s, this toad was observed every year when it emerged to breed after heavy rains. In 1987 over 1,500 adults were seen, but reproductive success that year apparently was low owing to dry conditions. During surveys conducted in 1988 a total of 10 individuals (eight males, two females) were found, and in 1989 only a lonely male was encountered. From 1990 to the present, this toad has not been seen. During the first years after its disappearance, researchers hoped that its absence resulted from a natural fluctuation in its population, but its absence has been so prolonged that it is now presumed to be extinct.

The Monteverde area of Costa Rica where the golden toad occurred has been the focus of various field studies, which have revealed that 19 of the 49 anuran species present in the area a decade ago have now mysteriously disappeared. How many other species of anurans, less fetching to the human eye and not the subjects of regular surveys, have quietly left the planet? How many species, unknown to science, may be going extinct before they can even be recorded?

Finally, there are few studies of any kind that provide data on population densities of frogs. Therefore it is not possible in most instances to make quantitative comparisons of present populations with those of the past. Although scores of anecdotal accounts, such as my experiences with streamfrogs in the Montañas del Mico, have been reported over the last decade, these are subjective and by necessity invoke imprecise descriptions like "rare" and "common." Although most biologists are convinced that amphibians are in trouble, they desire hard facts and figures.

Amphibians have sometimes been likened to a canary in a coal mine; they serve warning about dangerous environmental changes that will eventually impact humans. This seems to me a fair and accurate analogy. Certain features of amphibians make them particularly sensitive to environmental changes. Amphibians tend to have delicate, permeable skin (serving as an important respiratory organ) that may be especially sensitive to increased levels of certain chemicals or ultraviolet radiation. They are the only tetrapods to have a biphasic life cycle and thus may be susceptible to any environmental changes affecting either the water or the air. It is possible that the biphasic life cycle of most amphibians makes them particularly good candidates to suffer the consequences of biomagnification of chemical contaminants, first by tadpoles ingesting plant materials that contain such toxicants as chlorinated chemicals and then by adults feeding on a variety of invertebrates known to be reservoirs for various biocides.

White-lipped Foamfrog—Ranita Espumera Labioblanco
Leptodactylus labialis (Cope, 1877)
Fig. 30

Description.—Adults are about 34–40 mm in SVL with little sexual dimorphism in size. However, the shape of the snout is strongly sexually dimorphic, with males developing an acuminate snout with a prominent shelf around the margin of the upper jaw. The snout is pointed in dorsal profile in both sexes. The skin on the dorsum is thick and glandular, usually with dorsolateral glandular ridges; the flanks have large tubercles and usually lateral glandular ridges. Digits are long and slender without discs. The toes have lateral dermal keels, but these are not flaplike. A tarsal fold extends from the inner metatarsal tubercle about halfway to the heel, where it becomes a linear series of tubercles that often reach the heel. Adult males have vocal slits and a single, moderately distensible, subgular vocal sac, but they lack nuptial excrescences.

Dorsum color is highly variable, from shades of brown to grayish brown and even greenish brown. There are often dark brown irregular dorsal markings and the longitudinal glandular ridges may be reddish. A dark canthal stripe is usually present and there is a triangular blotch on top of the head between the eyes with the apex pointing posteriorly. The white stripe along the upper jaw in juveniles and subadults may be lost in large adults. The posterior surface of the thighs is mottled with brown; usually an irregular pale stripe runs the length of the thigh along its lower posterior surface. The iris is bronze.

In tadpoles, the mouth is located anteroventrally, the beaks are finely serrated, and there are 2/3 tooth rows; all of the lower tooth rows have a narrow median gap and the lower row of the upper lip has a distinct gap. A dorsal gap is present in the marginal papillae of the oral disc. The body is broader than it is deep and the snout is rounded in dorsal view. Eyes are dorsolateral in position and there is a single sinistral spiracle. The caudal fins are subequal in height and the dorsal fin extends onto the posterior part of the body. Tadpoles are uniformly dark brown or brownish gray dorsally with a slightly paler venter and darker mottling sometimes present on the tail.

Natural History.—The white-lipped foamfrog occurs in tropical moist and dry forest and occasionally in subtropical moist forest. This species can be common in disturbed areas. It occurs in permanent ponds in open areas with abundant shoreline vegetation but also breeds in temporary flooded fields, roadside ditches, and aguadas; it breeds throughout the rainy season. These frogs call by day as well as after dark, especially on rainy or overcast days. Their call is a short, high-pitched, upwardly inflected peep or whistle, sounding like *boing* and given at irregular intervals; the sound species is deeper and

more mellow than the shrill call of the finge-toed foamfrog (*Leptodactylus melanonotus*). Eggs covered with a frothy material resembling beaten egg whites are located near water beneath rocks, tufts of grass, or overhanging vegetation. Males use their hind feet to whip eggs and the jelly capsules surrounding them, as well as seminal fluid, into a foam. Males may use their elongate snouts in excavating nest cavities. The foam nests are usually constructed 1–3 m from the shoreline during periods of increasing rains; the rising water eventually overtakes and covers these nests. Foam nests are constructed in the mud as small pockets about 65 mm in diameter. Freshly laid eggs are bright yellow and scattered throughout the froth. The number of eggs per clutch reported for this species ranges from 25 to 250. During the dry season, this species has been found under dry, cracked clods of mud in dry aguadas.

Distribution.—This frog is distributed from southwestern Texas and Guerrero, Mexico, to Costa Rica, including throughout most of Petén. In Guatemala, it occurs from near sea level to about 1,300 m.

Remarks.—The species has gone under the name *Leptodactylus fragilis* in much recent literature. *Leptodactylus labialis* and *L. fragilis* are names that have been used to refer to the same species of frog. However, it was realized recently that the name *L. labialis* was published a few months before the name *L. fragilis* in 1877 and thus has priority.

Fringe-toed Foamfrog—Ranita Espumera de Dedos Marginados
Leptodactylus melanonotus (Hallowell, 1860)
Fig. 31

Description.—Adult males are about 35–40 mm in SVL and females attain 40–45 mm. The snout is pointed in dorsal profile and males do not develop the shelflike process characteristic of the white-lipped foamfrog. The skin on the dorsum is thick and glandular with a series of longitudinal glandular ridges and small tubercles, the latter often capped with tiny pointed keratinous spines. The digits are long, slender, and without discs. A distinct tarsal fold extends most of the distance from the inner metatarsal tubercle to the heel. Flaplike lateral dermal fringes
fold downward around the toes. Breeding males have vocal slits; a single, moderately distensible, subgular vocal sac; and two black spines on the pollex. Adult males have prominent glands behind the jaw, in the pectoral and ventrolateral regions, and in the posterior abdominal area.

Dorsal color is brown, brownish gray, or gray, and sometimes so dark that the pattern may not be discernible. However, usually a pattern including a dark canthal stripe, a triangular interocular spot, and dark mottling on the dorsum is apparent. A short white streak is sometimes present beneath the eye of subadults; adults usually have a series of dark markings along the margin of the upper lip. The limbs bear dark brown or blackish transverse limb bars. Some individuals have an orange suffusion on the groin and hidden surfaces of the thigh. The posterior surface of the thighs is dark brown with irregular pale spots. The venter is darkly reticulated, especially in breeding individuals. The iris is metallic brown.

Tadpoles are similar to those of the white-lipped foamfrog (see that species account for description). The fringe-toed foamfrog tadpole's dorsal tail fin is thicker and less translucent than that of the white-lipped foamfrog and may have some pale mottling or spots. *Natural History.*—This frog occurs in tropical moist and dry forest, and sometimes enters subtropical moist forest. The species may be common in disturbed areas. It is most frequently found near permanent ponds with abundant vegetation around the edges; it often occurs sympatrically with the white-lipped foamfrog. Infrequently, it

has been taken from stream environments from within the forest. Breeding records for this frog in Petén are from April, October, and November. Foamy egg masses are deposited on the surface of the water, and a male is often found hiding beneath an egg mass. The presumed territorial call of this species has been described as a single, soft *took*. The breeding call is a rapid succession of higher pitched notes. Although mostly nocturnal, this frog calls by day when conditions are cloudy or rainy. Males are territorial; they call, display, and exhibit aggressive behavior toward other males when defending specific sites that are presumably used for calling, breeding, and feeding. Like the white-lipped frog, this species may be found in the dry season by lifting the cracked blocks of mud that cover the aguadas.

Distribution.—The fringe-toed foamfrog is distributed from Tamaulipas and Sonora, Mexico, southward through Central America to Costa Rica, occurring throughout most of Petén. It is found from near sea level to about 1,300 m.

Túngara Frog—Sapillo Túngara
Physalaemus pustulosus (Cope, 1864)
Fig. 32

Description.—The skin on the dorsum of this species is extremely tuberculate, with many small scattered glands on top of the head and on the eyelids as well as on the back. A large parotoid gland is present on the side of the neck, adding to the species' toadlike appear-

ance. Males reach about 25–30 mm in SVL and females are a little larger, attaining 28–32 mm in SVL; individuals from certain populations in lower Central America and South America may be larger. The snout is somewhat pointed in dorsal view. This species lacks an external tympanum. Fore-limbs are moderately elongate and slender. The digits are long and slender, without discs, and the fingers lack webbing, whereas the toes have vestigial webbing. One to several tubercles are present about halfway between the inner metatarsal tubercle and the heel; a tarsal fold may extend from the inner metatarsal tubercle to these tubercles or may be absent. Breeding males have a brown nuptial excrescence on the pollex, vocal slits are present, and the vocal sac is subgular and bilobed, being expanded laterally.

The dorsum may be various shades of gray or brown, often with darker mottling and reddish tubercles. Males tend to have dorsal mottling more frequently than females, which often are rather uniformly colored. Males usually have a pale middorsal stripe over the sacral region. In males the belly has large gray spots; in females the belly is usually mostly pale with a fine suffusion of small dark pigment cells. A pale midventral stripe is usually present, which is most obvious anteriorly in males. The posterior surfaces of the thighs are variable and may be dark with irregular pale spotting, or the dark bars from the dorsal surface of the thighs may extend downward onto the posterior surface. The iris is tan or pale brown. In breeding males, the vocal sac is dark gray.

In tadpoles the mouth is located anteroventrally, the beaks have small serrations, and there are 2/3 rows of teeth on a small oral disc. A dorsal gap is present in the marginal papillae of the oral disc. The body is wider than it is deep and the snout is broadly rounded in dorsal view. Eyes are directed dorsolaterally and there is a single sinistral spiracle. The caudal musculature is slender and tapering but does not extend to the tip of the pointed tail. Height of the caudal fins is subequal and the dorsal fin extends onto the posterior part of the body. The dorsum of the body is dark brown and the venter is paler. Caudal musculature is brown and the caudal fins are transparent with small brown blotches.

Natural History.—This frog is distributed mostly in tropical dry forest. It usually inhabits open, relatively dry areas, such as clearings in the dry forest and savannas, and may breed in flooded marshes, roadside ditches, or even water-filled tire ruts. The distinctive breeding call of the males consists of a whine, sometimes followed by one or several *chucks,* and has been described as resembling the sounds produced by some "star wars" video games. The reproductive period extends over much of the rainy season. Several clutches of eggs may be produced by a single female over the course of a season. Amplectant males construct a foam nest by vigorously kicking their hind legs into the egg jelly deposited by the female. Eggs deposited in this foam nest receive protection against desiccation in the dry environments inhabited by this frog. Recent evidence also suggests that the foam nest protects eggs from predation. Hierarchical social behavior based on call order has been noted in this frog species, a dominant male usually initiating a sequence of calls, followed in order by subservient males. In Panama, the fringe-lipped bat (*Trachops cirrhosus*) hunts the túngara frog by homing in on the call of male frogs. This bat occurs as far north as northern Belize, but it is not known if it preys on these frogs in the northern part of its range.

Distribution.—On the Atlantic versant, this frog occurs from southern Veracruz, Mexico, southward through Central America into northern South America; on the Pacific versant, it ranges from southern Oaxaca, Mexico, through Central America to eastern Panama. In Guatemala, it ranges from near sea level to about 1,350 m. Its distribution is disjunct in the northern part of its range. It is known from parts of Tabasco and Campeche, Mexico, and from southern Quintana Roo and northern Belize, but is absent from most of Petén; the only verified record for the species from this department is from the north shore of Laguna Yaxjá.

Remarks.—The name túngara frog is the common epithet for the species in Panama, where it has been extensively studied by Michael Ryan. In Guatemala, it is referred to simply as *sapillo*, a collective term for a number of small, fat frogs.

Mottled Chirping Frog—Ranita Chirriadora Manchada
Syrrhophus leprus Cope, 1879
Fig. 33

Description.—Long, slender digits bear discs that are slightly widened in this species, the first is longer than the second, and the toes have vestigial (basal) webbing. Adult males are 21–26 mm in SVL and adult females 25–29 mm. The snout is somewhat pointed in dorsal profile. Skin on the dorsum is slightly rugose and has many small tubercles; the flanks are covered by many large tubercles. The forelimbs are relatively slender, whereas the hind limbs are short and moderately stout. There is no tarsal fold. Breeding males have vocal slits but lack nuptial excrescences.

The dorsum is tan, yellowish green, or green with dark brown markings that may be either discrete roundish spots or may coalesce into a mottled pattern. The sides of the body have silvery white flecks. The lower jaw is faintly darkened along the edge and the rest of the venter is whitish, usually suffused with brown or gray pigment. The side of the head is dark brown to black. The posterior surface of the thighs is usually uniformly brown but may have some white spotting.

Natural History.—This frog occurs in tropical moist and dry forest. It usually is found in areas with rocky outcroppings or along roadcuts. Its call is a single shrill note. Eggs are laid during the rainy season in deep, damp crevices in banks or under large rocks and undergo direct development.

Distribution.—The mottled chirping frog occurs from central Veracruz, Mexico, through northern Guatemala to Belize, from near sea level to about 500 m. This frog has a spotty distribution in Petén, being known from the southern part of the region and several localities north of Lago Petén Itzá, including Tikal and Uaxactún.

Remarks.—The chances of seeing this small nocturnal species are diminished by their cryptic coloration and the difficulty in ascertaining the direction of their peep or chirplike call. However, in many areas they are reasonably abundant and many dozens may be heard calling from rocky hillsides or outcroppings on rainy nights. Some authorities do not recognize the genus *Syrrhopus* and place this species in the conglomerate *Eleutherodactylus*.

Toads—Sapos

Family Bufonidae

The true toads occur in most tropical and subtropical areas. Although this family possesses a diversity of body shapes and sizes, toads are usually squat-bodied with legs that are modified for hopping rather than jumping. In all Guatemalan species, the skin is warty, glandular, and dry to the touch. A pair of large parotoid glands occur on the sides of the neck behind the eyes. The skin on top of the head is co-ossified with the skull. Amplexus is axillary and the tadpoles are Type IV. Toads have a unique structure, the Bidder's organ, which is a rudimentary ovary that is retained at the anterior end of the testis.

Campbell's Forest Toad—Sapo de Bosque de Campbell
Bufo campbelli Mendelson, 1994
Fig. 34

Description.—Distinct cranial crests are present in this toad; dorsal crests include the canthal, preocular, supraorbital, postocular, supratympanic, and parietal. The latter is thin and narrow and not as high as the supraorbital crest. The parotoid gland is moderate in size, occupying an area of less than half the side of the head, and triangular, tapering to a point posteriorly and extending no farther than the level of the insertion of the forearm. Males reach about 70 mm in SVL and females grow to about 90 mm. A lateral series of enlarged tubercles extends from the posterior edge of the parotoid gland to the inguinal region. Limbs are moderately short and stout. Some of the features that distinguish this toad from the Gulf Coast toad (*Bufo valliceps*) include a relatively small tympanum, less than half the diameter of the eye;

preorbital and pretympanic crests absent or weakly developed, even in large individuals; relatively long tibia and feet, both more than 43 percent of the SVL; relatively smooth skin, that of the dorsum with a few scattered conical tubercles dorsolaterally; and a snout that is acutely rounded in lateral view and pointed in dorsal view. Pale, conical tubercles extend along the inner tarsus. Breeding males have vocal slits and brown cornified nuptial excrescences on the pollex.

In large females, the dorsum is mostly brown with a bluish brown, dark brown, or cream vertebral stripe and often with small, irregular, blackish dorsal blotches. Adult males are paler in dorsal coloration, usually being pale greenish yellow with reddish tubercles. The sides are grayish brown with dorsolateral tubercles and some intervening orange skin. The lateral row of tubercles and those at the corner of mouth are mostly whitish. Limbs are brown with black-bordered grayish bars. The highest portions of the cranial crests are black. The tympanic area and sides of the body ventral to the lateral row of tubercles are dark brown to charcoal black. Tips of digits are orange and the iris is bronze with black reticulations.

Natural History.—This toad inhabits tropical and subtropical wet forest. Occurring near streams in humid rainforest. I have heard individuals softly calling just after dark in December and January from palms less than a meter in height along streams flowing through limestone in virgin rainforest. I have also seen pairs in amplexus sitting in shallow water at the edge of fast-flowing streams. The tadpoles and eggs have not been described, but this toad almost certainly breeds in streams or small rivulets running through rainforest habitats.

Campbell's forest toad is not as widely distributed as the superficially similar Gulf Coast toad, but these species may be broadly sympatric in some areas. There seems to be a clear ecological separation of the two species, however, with Campbell's forest toad restricted to virgin mesic forest habitats and the Gulf Coast toad abundant in more open, usually disturbed, habitats such as pastures and secondary growth. Whereas Campbell's forest toad is suspected to breed in flowing streams, the Gulf Coast toad is known to breed in the still water of small ponds and roadside ditches.

Distribution.—Campbell's forest toad occurs on the slopes and foothills of Alta Verapaz, Izabal, and southern Petén, Guatemala; in the Maya Mountains of Belize; and in western Honduras in the Departments of Atlántida, Colón, Copán, and Yoro, at elevations from near sea level to over 1,000 m. In Petén this species is known only from an area 8–15 km northwest or northnorthwest of Chinanjá.

Giant Toad—Sapo Lechero
Bufo marinus (Linnaeus, 1758)
Fig. 35

Description.—Cranial crests are prominent, including the canthal, supraorbital, postocular, and supratympanic crests; there is no parietal crest. The parotoid glands are huge, occupying an area larger than the side of the head and extending posteriorly to a level well beyond the insertion of the forearm. Large adults from Petén reach 130–170 mm in SVL; in South America this species may exceed 200 mm in SVL. Females reach a larger size than males. The size attained by this species is truly impressive—no other toad in Central America approaches it in size. Larger females can mostly cover a dinner plate. The snout is somewhat pointed in dorsal view. The skin on the dorsum is rugose with numerous large tubercles. Limbs are moderately short and stout. Breeding males have vocal slits and brown cornified nuptial excrescences.

Breeding adults are sexually dimorphic. Males often are reddish brown and have spiny tubercles covering the dorsum. Females are medium brown to pale gray-brown with darker brown mottling, similar to juveniles, and have large rounded tubercles. The parotoid glands usually are colored similarly to the dorsum or sometimes are reddish brown. Males have a keratinized patch on the thumb.

Tadpoles have an anteroventral mouth, the beaks are finely serrated, and 2/3 tooth rows are present on the oral disc. Both dorsal and ventral gaps are present in the marginal papillae of the oral disc. The body is wider than it is deep and the snout is broadly rounded. Eyes are dorsolateral in position and the single spiracle is sinistral. Dorsal and ventral fins are subequal in height and the dorsal fin extends onto the posterior part of the body. The body and caudal musculature are uniformly dark brown to black; the fins are transparent or translucent, often heavily pigmented with brown or gray.

Natural History.—Tropical dry, moist, and wet forest and subtropical moist and dry forest are home to this large, nocturnal toad. It eats almost anything that moves and can be swallowed, feeding on all kinds of arthropods and also small vertebrates, including other frogs and toads. It is usually extremely abundant wherever it occurs. This toad is well protected by the toxic secretions from its huge parotoid glands. The jelly coating that surrounds its eggs and the skin of tadpoles are also toxic, lowering predation on these life stages.

Eggs are laid in strings in both temporary and permanent bodies of water. Sites that are open and unshaded are usually selected. Most frequently, this toad breeds in still bodies of water, but it may also breed in the quiet backwaters of slow-moving streams. Single clutches usually contain 5,000–25,000 eggs. Breeding has been observed in January, February, March, June, and

July. It has been suggested that this species breeds throughout most of the year, especially around permanent water, but the breeding season peak coincides with the beginning of the rainy season. Eggs and tadpoles have been observed from March to July. The tadpoles of this species are usually found in groups that school together. Toads reach adulthood in one year. Their call is a loud, rolling trill.

↙*Distribution.*—The giant toad occurs from extreme southern Texas, southward through Mexico and Central America to South America and has been widely introduced in various tropical regions, including Hawaii and northern Australia. In Guatemala, the species occurs from near sea level to about 1,650 m and is widespread in the Petén region, although it may have arrived fairly recently in some places. In one thorough study conducted in 1956, not a single giant toad was found at Tikal, although it now appears to be well established in the Tikal reservoir.

Remarks.—This species thrives in disturbed areas and is often found around human habitations. I have always found it curious that many individuals may be infested with ticks, some of which are even embedded deeply in the parotoid glands. There are reports from South America of humans dying from eating soup containing the eggs of this toad. Other names for it include *sapo corozo* (in the Nentón region), *sapo grande, sapo gigante,* and *sapo marino.*

Gulf Coast Toad—Sapo Costero
Bufo valliceps Wiegmann, 1833
Fig. 36

Description.—Distinct cranial crests include the canthal, preocular, supraorbital, postocular, supratympanic, and parietal crests, the last being especially well developed and as high as or higher than the supraorbital crest. The parotoid gland is moderate in size, occupying an area less than half the side of the head, and is triangular in shape, tapering to a point posteriorly and not extending beyond the level of the insertion of the forearm. This toad is moderately sized, only about half as big as the giant toad. The SVL of adult males is usually between 60 and 70 mm; that of females is between 80 and 90 mm. The snout is somewhat pointed in dorsal view. A lateral series of enlarged tubercles extends from the posterior edge of the parotoid gland to the inguinal region. Some of the characteristics that distinguish the Gulf Coast toad from Campbell's forest toad (*Bufo campbelli*) include a relatively large tympanum that is more than half the diameter of the eye; preorbital and pretympanic crests that are relatively well developed; relatively short tibia and feet, both less than 43 percent of the SVL; skin that is rough and warty; and a snout that is shorter and blunter in both lateral and dorsal view. A series of pale conical tubercles extends along the inner tarsus. Breeding males have vocal slits and brown cornified nuptial excrescences.

Dorsal coloration of this toad is highly variable and may be orangish, tan, yellowish tan, reddish brown, brown, or pale gray; females are usually darker than males. In some individuals, a pale dorsolateral band contrasts sharply with the darker flanks. The flanks below the lateral series of tubercles are darker than the dorsum. The venter may be uniformly whitish or cream, but most specimens have a few to many black spots, and some individuals have a black blotch on the chest. The iris is coppery red.

Tadpoles are similar to those of the giant toad (see that species account for description). In tadpoles of the Gulf Coast toad the dorsal fin is a little deeper than or subequal to the ventral fin. The dorsum of the body is uniformly brown or black and the venter is slightly paler. Darker mottling is often present on the caudal muscula-ture. The caudal fins are translucent and pigmented with brown or gray and have darker mottling.

Natural History.—This toad occurs in tropical wet, moist, and dry forest and in subtropical moist forest. It has been observed breeding in February–July in sluggish streams and temporary ponds. Near permanent water, this species may be reproductively active throughout most of the year, but it is most active after heavy rains. Eggs are deposited in strings and hatch in a few days. Its call is a short trill.

↙*Distribution.*—As its name implies, this toad occurs from the southern United States southward along the Gulf Coast to the Isthmus of Tehuantepec, where it crosses over to the Pacific watershed and continues on both coasts to Guatemala on the Pacific and to Costa Rica on the Atlantic side. Toads currently assigned to this species, but perhaps representing several different taxa, range in Guatemala from near sea level to 1,200 m. This toad is almost ubiquitous in the Petén.

GLASSFROGS—RANAS DE VIDRIO

FAMILY CENTROLENIDAE

The glassfrogs reach their greatest diversity in the South American Andes and lower Central America; only one species occurs in Guatemala and Mexico. The family derives its name from the thin translucent skin covering the belly of most species. Members of this family have finger discs and intercalary cartilages and superficially resemble treefrogs of the family Hylidae. The pupil is horizontal, amplexus is axillary, and tadpoles are aquatic Type IV.

Northern Glassfrog—Ranita de Vidrio Norteña
Hyalinobatrachium fleischmanni (Boettger, 1893)
Fig. 37

Description.—The pulsating heart, covering of the lungs, and other organs can be seen through the skin of the venter of this species, prompting one researcher to remark that "these frogs don't have many secrets." Adults reach 22–25 mm in SVL, males being slightly smaller than the females. The snout is exceptionally short and truncate in dorsal profile. The skin of the dorsum is smooth. Limbs are relatively long and slender and there is no axillary membrane. The digits have well-developed discs that are moderately expanded; the fingers are about one-half webbed and the toes are three-fourths webbed. The tarsal fold is absent. Males do not develop nuptial excrescences but vocal slits are present and the vocal sac is median, subgular, and moderately distensible.

The dorsum is pale lime green with many tiny, scattered, dark melanophores and small yellow spots. The tops of the digits and discs are yellow. These frogs derive their common name from the transparent skin covering their bellies, which allows some of their internal organs to be seen. The heart and the ventral abdominal vein are clearly evident and most of the internal organs are covered with silvery white tissue. The vocal sac is white and the iris is gold.

Tadpoles have a ventral mouth, the beaks have tiny uniform serrations, and there are 2/3 tooth rows. A dorsal gap is present in the marginal papillae of the oral disc. Tadpoles have elongate and slender bodies that are wider than they are deep. The snout is rounded in dorsal profile. Small, poorly developed eyes are dorsolateral in position. The single spiracle is sinistral. Caudal musculature is long and robust. The dorsal and ventral caudal fins are shallow and subequal, with the dorsal fin reaching the posterior part of the body. Tadpoles are mostly transparent, but have some scattered pigment on the dorsum of the body and on the dorsal tail musculature. The caudal musculature and part of the body may be bright red owing to blood showing through the skin.

Natural History.—Northern glassfrogs inhabit tropical and subtropical wet forest, preferring clear, moving streams, where they usually are found on vegetation above the water. They are active mostly at night, but occasionally on overcast or rainy days I have heard males calling just before dark.

Over most of its range, the species breeds mainly during the rainy season, which extends from May to October, but in areas in which there is no well-defined rainy period, such as eastern Guatemala, glass frogs may breed during every month of the year. Males are territorial and if one intrudes on the territory of another, a series of mew-like peeps occur, sometimes followed by four-legged push-ups and physical encounters. The advertisement call of the male is a single short, high-pitched peep. Typically, the duration of each call is about 0.1 second and calls may be repeated every 6–16 seconds. Most calling males are 0.5 to 3 m above the surface of a stream, but I have heard them up to 10 m or more above the water surface. Males usually call while hanging upside down from the lower surfaces of leaves that hang over water. Clutches of eggs are laid on the undersurfaces of leaves, on which they adhere, and are guarded by the male. Many types of leaves may be used, usually larger, smooth-surfaced leaves, such as those of philodendrons, *Dieffenbachia*, or broad-leafed ferns. The yolks of recently laid eggs are pale green and the developing embryos are yellow. The jelly enveloping the eggs is essentially clear but with a definite pale green hue. A male attempts to attract multiple females to his calling site and sometimes several clutches of eggs can be found on a single leaf. Often the males remain with the eggs during the night but move off to nearby vegetation to pass the daylight hours. The mean number of eggs varies from 18 to 30, depending on locality and time of year. There is heavy predation on the eggs by various vertebrates and invertebrates and it has been estimated that almost 80 percent of the clutches perish before hatching; the small-spotted cat-eyed snake (*Leptodeira polysticta*) is a particularly effective predator. Drosophilid flies of the genus *Zygothrica* deposit their eggs on glass-frog egg masses, the fly eggs hatching out into maggots that consume many of the frog embryos. These flies pupate within the egg mass and young flies hatch 10–13 days after the fly eggs have been laid. By the time these young flies emerge, the surviving frog embryos (if any) have already hatched and dropped into the stream below. It is tempting to speculate that the adult frogs attending the egg clutches eat some of the flies that attempt to parasitize frog eggs, but there is no evidence to support this notion. The eggs of these frogs hatch 10–15 days after deposition and the tadpoles drop into the water, where they hide in submerged detritus or in loose bottom gravel. Growth and development of tadpoles is slow, possibly taking at least one year, and up to two, for metamorphosis to occur.

Distribution.—This species occurs in wet forests from southern Mexico through most of Central America to northern South America, ranging from near sea level to over 1,600 m along clear, flowing, usually rocky streams. In southern Petén it has been found along the tributaries of the Río de La Pasión.

Remarks.—The uninitiated sometimes have trouble locating this frog, even when hearing dozens of calls over the course of a night. Individuals sit upside down on the undersurfaces of leaves of streamside vegetation, making detection difficult unless one knows where to look.

TREEFROGS—RANAS ARBORÍCOLAS

FAMILY HYLIDAE

Treefrogs occur across much of Europe and Asia to Japan and Australia (some authorities place frogs from the latter region into a separate family). They reach their greatest diversity, however, in the Americas, especially the tropics. As their common name denotes, most members of this family possess adaptations for arboreality, which include large finger discs and intercalary cartilages between the two distalmost phalanges. The leaf-frogs (*Agalychnis*) have a vertical pupil and other Guatemalan treefrogs have horizontal pupils. Amplexus is axillary and all Guatemalan species have aquatic type IV larvae. Several different reproductive modes are present among the treefrogs of Petén, including laying eggs in bromeliads where the larvae develop, laying eggs in clumps on leaves where larvae hatch and fall into the water below, and laying eggs directly in water.

Red-eyed Leaf-frog—Rana-hoja de Ojos Rojos
Agalychnis callidryas (Cope, 1862)
Fig. 38

Description.—As its name indicates, in the red-eyed leaf-frog the iris is bright red, and the palpebral membrane is reticulated with gold. Illustrations of this photogenic frog have appeared in biology texts, nature magazines, travel brochures, and the like, probably making it the most frequently photographed amphibian in the world. This frog is widespread and abundant. Choruses of several hundred males sometimes congregate in the vegetation surrounding aguadas or slow-moving streams. Adult males reach 50–55 mm in SVL and females attain SVL of 65–70 mm. The snout is somewhat pointed in dorsal view, and the skin on the dorsum is smooth. These frogs have long, slender limbs and tend often to walk rather than leap. The fingers and toes bear moderately large discs, fingers being about one-half webbed and toes about two-thirds webbed. A poorly defined tarsal fold extends the length of the tarsus. This species and Morelet's leaf-frog (*Agalychnis moreletiii*) are the only frogs in the Petén region that have vertical pupils. In breeding males, the pollex has a keratinized nuptial excrescence composed of tiny spinules; vocal slits are present and the vocal sac is median, subgular, and not greatly distensible.

The dorsal surfaces of the head, body, forearm, hind limbs, fourth fingers, and fifth toes are green, often with small, round white spots on the dorsum. The flanks are bluish with three to eight vertical cream bars, and the venter is cream. The anterior and posterior surfaces of the thighs and the dorsal and ventral surfaces of the hands and feet are mostly orange. A white line extends along the outer edge of the forearm and tarsus.

In tadpoles, the mouth is located anteroventrally (but directed anteriorly), both beaks have short, blunt serrations, and there are 2/3 tooth rows. A dorsal gap is present in the marginal papillae of the oral disc. The body of tadpoles is only slightly deeper than it is broad and the snout is truncate in dorsal profile. Eyes are dorsolaterally located and the spiracle is sinistral. Caudal musculature is slender, tapering posteriorly. Caudal fins are relatively high with the ventral fin deeper than the dorsal fin. In life, tadpoles are whitish, pale tan, dark gray, or pinkish with dark flecks on their caudal fins.

Natural History.—This frog inhabits tropical wet, moist, and dry forest. It has an extended breeding season during the rainy period and males have been found calling from late May to December. Metamorphosing individuals have been found in early February and September. Males call from vegetation along the shores of forest ponds, flooded pastures, and roadside ditches, usually at heights of 1–3 m, but may ascend to over 5 m. The call is very soft and may be a single or double note. The sound has been described as *chock* or *cluck* but it sounds more like a *click* to me. As with some other species of arboreal frogs, it is often difficult to ascertain the direction from where a call

comes. I have been in thick brush at night when this species was calling and found it difficult to locate individual specimens even though they were only a few feet above my head. During the day these frogs sit motionless, plastered against large leaves or palm fronds. I have found them up to about 10 m high in trees, but they may go considerably higher.

These frogs breed in either temporary or permanent ponds. During breeding, the female approaches a male that is calling from vegetation near water. The male amplexes the female, which is larger and which carries him down to the edge of the pond, where she sits in shallow water, taking water up in the bladder. Once her bladder is full, she moves back up into the vegetation and selects the undersurface of a leaf or slender tree branch on which she lays her eggs. These are fertilized by the male as they are deposited. The eggs are greenish at one pole and yellow at the other and are deposited in clumps of 14–90 (usually 20–50). The female then moves back down to the water and the process is repeated, with a female laying up to five clutches in a night. The water she picks up in her bladder is used to hydrate the eggs, otherwise the clutch would soon dry up. The tadpoles hatch in about five days, and fall into the water where they complete the larval stage. Metamorphosis takes place about 11–12 weeks after hatching. Sometimes egg clutches are placed above the ground rather than above water, but tadpoles are capable of flipping themselves by using their muscular tails so that some individuals that fall to the ground may be able to find water. Groups of tadpoles gather near the surface of ponds where they angle their bodies at about 45° relative to the surface of the water, with their heads up. They typically congregate where patches of sunlight fall on a pond.

✔*Distribution.*—The red-eyed leaf-frog is a creature of the Atlantic lowlands and foothills from southern Veracruz and northern Oaxaca, Mexico, southward through Mexico, Guatemala, and Belize to eastern Panama. It also occurs in the Pacific lowlands of Nicaragua, Costa Rica, and Panama. In Guatemala, this species ranges from near sea level to about 950 m, occurring throughout most of Petén.

Morelet's Leaf-frog—Rana-hoja de Montaña
Agalychnis morelettii (A. Duméril, 1853)
Fig. 39

Description.—In this species the iris is deep purple but appears black unless viewed in bright light. The palpebral membrane is reticulated with gold. This frog has a relatively restricted distribution, occurring in mesic forests along streams flowing through mountainous regions, and therefore it is less likely to be encountered then the red-eyed leaf-frog (*Agalychnis callidryas*). Adult Morelet's leaf-frogs reach 60–65 mm in SVL, females 75–80 mm. The snout is somewhat pointed in dorsal profile and the skin on the dorsum is smooth. As in other members of the genus, the limbs are slender and this species tends often to walk rather than leap. Discs on the digits are relatively large and the hands and feet are about three-fourths webbed. The tarsal fold is usually well developed and extends the length of the tarsus. This species and the red-eyed leaf-frog are the only treefrogs in the Petén region with vertical pupils. In breeding males, the pollex has a nonspinous horny nuptial excrescence, vocal slits are present, and the vocal sac is median, subgular, and not greatly distensible.

The dorsal surface of the head, body, forearm, and hind limbs are leaf green. Often small, round white spots occur on the dorsum. The flanks, anterior and posterior surfaces of the thighs, inner surfaces of the shanks and forearms, the upper arms, first three fingers, and first four toes are orange. Usually an ill-defined yellow stripe separates the green of the dorsum from the orange on the flanks. White stripes are present on the outer edges of the forearm and tarsus. The venter is cream or yellow.

In the tadpoles, the mouth is located anteroventrally (but directed anteriorly), both beaks have short, pointed serrations, and there are 2/3 tooth rows. A dorsal gap is present in the marginal papillae of the oral disc. The body of tadpoles is noticeably deeper than it is broad and the snout is truncate in dorsal profile. Eyes are dorsolaterally located and the spiracle is sinistral. The caudal musculature is fairly robust, becoming slender posteriorly. The ventral caudal fin is slightly deeper than the dorsal fin. Tadpoles are reddish, dark gray, or purplish brown in life.

Natural History.—This frog occurs in wet forest habitats in the foothills just to the south of Petén and to the east in the Maya Mountains of Belize. It inhabits tropical and subtropical wet forest. The breeding call is a single *wor-or-op* repeated every one to several minutes. The species has an extended breeding season from May to August. Eggs are greenish at one pole and cream at the other and are laid on vegetation above the water, usually at heights less than 2–3 m. Clutches usu-

ally consist of about 25–75 eggs. When tadpoles hatch, they drop into the water where they complete metamorphosis. Schools of tadpoles may be observed with their bodies and tails oriented diagonally in the water with the head up.

During the day, individuals may be found plastered tightly against the surfaces of large, green leaves with their limbs tucked against their sides, so as not to expose any of the orange coloration of the flanks or limbs.

Distribution.—Morelet's leaf-frog occurs from central Veracruz and northern Oaxaca, Mexico, southward on Atlantic slopes to Guatemala and Belize, and on Pacific slopes from southern Oaxaca to El Salvador. In Guatemala, the species ranges from about 500 m to 2,130 m.

Bromeliad Treefrog—Rana Arborícola de Bromelia
Hyla bromeliacia Schmidt, 1933
Fig. 40

Description.—Males of this species reach about 27 mm in SVL and females attain SVL of about 32 mm. The snout is somewhat pointed in dorsal profile and the skin on the dorsum is smooth. Forelimbs are moderately robust and a small axillary membrane is present. The fingers and toes have large discs, the fingers about one-fourth webbed and the toes two-thirds webbed. A poorly defined tarsal fold extends the length of the tarsus. In breeding males, the prepollex has a horny nuptial excrescence, vocal slits are present, and

the vocal sac is median, subgular, and not greatly distensible.

The dorsum is pale brown or yellowish tan, and the flanks and anterior and posterior surfaces of the thighs are pinkish tan. The ventral surfaces of the hind limbs are yellowish, usually with a fine peppering of black, and the belly is creamy white. Distal portions of the digits and toe discs are smoky gray. The iris is bronze with small black flecks.

In tadpoles, the mouth is ventrally located, the beaks have pointed serrations, and the oral disc has 2/4 or 2/5 tooth rows. A dorsal gap is present in the marginal papillae of the oral disc. The body and tail of this distinctive tadpole are extremely elongate. The body is nearly twice as wide as it is deep and the snout is bluntly rounded in dorsal profile. Eyes are directed laterally and the spiracle is sinistral. Caudal musculature is well developed and elongate, extending to the rounded tip of the tail. Caudal fins are shallow. Tadpoles are pale brown or tan dorsally with a transparent venter and fins.

Natural History.—This frog occurs primarily in subtropical wet forest. Males call after dark, especially on foggy nights, perched on the leaves of bromeliads or on nearby branches. The mating call consists of five or six soft notes repeated at intervals of 45–70 seconds. Eggs are deposited in clusters of 10–15 in the wells of bromeliads, which are usually 2–6 m above the ground, where the tadpoles hatch and develop. Tadpoles feed on the organic detritus that collects in the leaf axils of these plants. Metamorphs are 11–12 mm in SVL.

Breeding occurs throughout most of the year.

Distribution.—The bromeliad treefrog occurs on the foothills of the Caribbean slopes from the Sierra de Los Cuchumatanes through eastern Guatemala (Sierra de Santa Cruz) to the Maya Mountains of Belize and the western highlands of Honduras. In Guatemala, the species ranges from about 500 m to 1,650 m.

Remarks.—This is the only Guatemalan frog species that breeds in bromeliads. It was one of the most abundant frogs around the nature park Biotopo Mario Dary in the Department of Baja Verapaz up until the early 1980s. By the late 1980s, this frog had inexplicably become quite rare in the region, and I have not been able to find a single specimen there during recent trips. Even careful searches of large "tank" bromeliads, most of which previously contained tadpoles, have failed to reveal its presence. Curiously, the species seems not to have suffered any population decline at lower elevations at certain other locations in Guatemala.

Hourglass Treefrog—Rana Arborícola Amarillenta
Hyla ebraccata Cope, 1874
Fig. 41

Description.—Males of this species reach 24–27 mm in SVL and females attain SVL of 30–34 mm. The snout is truncate in dorsal profile, and the skin on the dorsum is smooth. Forearms are moderately robust and there is an extensive axillary membrane extending almost to the elbow. The discs on the digits are relatively large, the fingers about one-half webbed, and the toes about three-fourths webbed. A thin tarsal fold extends the length of the tarsus. Breeding males lack nuptial excrescences, but vocal slits are present and the vocal sac is median, subgular, and greatly distensible.

The dorsum is yellow or yellowish tan and may be uniformly colored, but almost all specimens from Petén have brown dorsal markings. Although highly variable, these markings often take on an hourglass shape. The side of the head is mostly dark brown with a distinct cream upper labial stripe, which usually is expanded into a pale spot beneath the eye. The thighs are uniformly yellow or pale orange. The upper arm, flanks, hands, and feet are pale yellow, the venter is cream, and the iris is reddish bronze.

In tadpoles, the mouth is terminally located, the beak bears fine serrations above and below, and rows of teeth are absent from the small, poorly developed oral disc. The body is as wide as it is deep and the snout is bluntly rounded in dorsal profile. Eyes are directed laterally and the spiracle is sinistral. The caudal musculature is deep anteriorly, becoming shallow distally. Tadpoles have very well developed, deep tail fins and a greatly elongate, sword-shaped (xiphicercal) tail. The fins are deepest at about midlength of the tail.

The larva of this species is the most beautifully colored tadpole of the Petén region. The dorsum of the body and anterior part of the tail are yellowish to brown with pale mottling; there is a black stripe on either side of and on top of the body and two black bands encircle the tail. The tail is rose red between the two tail bands, the tip of the tail often being distinctly paler than the rest of the body.

Natural History.—The hourglass tree-frog occurs in primary forest but also can survive in areas of secondary growth. It is most broadly distributed in tropical moist forest. This species has been observed breeding in forest ponds from June through September. Males call from low emergent vegetation at the edge of a pond, from dusk throughout most of the night. The call is a low insectlike *creeek* that may be followed by a short secondary note. Egg clumps containing 24–76 eggs are deposited in a single layer on the upper surfaces of leaves above water. At the time of hatching, the tadpoles wriggle to the edge of the leaf and drop into the water, where they complete metamorphosis.

Distribution.—This species occurs from the Atlantic lowlands of southern Veracruz and northern Oaxaca, Mexico, through northern Guatemala to Belize, and in lower Central America from Nicaragua through Panama into northwestern Colombia. In Guatemala, it ranges from near sea level to about 600 m. It occurs in much of central Petén and is known from the Río de La Pasión and Piedras Negras areas as well as near Tikal. However, it is absent from the northern and southern portions of Petén and from the Yucatán Peninsula in Mexico.

Remarks.—Adults have a distinctive herbal odor.

Loquacious Treefrog—Rana Arborícola Loquaz
Hyla loquax Gaige and Stuart, 1934
Fig. 42

Description.—Adults of this medium-sized frog reach 36–43 mm in SVL, with males usually larger than females. The snout is broadly rounded in dorsal profile and the skin on the dorsum is minutely corrugated. Forelimbs are moderately long and robust, with an extensive axillary membrane reaching to the elbow. The digits have well-developed discs, the fingers are two-thirds webbed and the toes nearly fully webbed. A weak tarsal fold extends from the inner metatarsal tubercle for about a third of the distance of the tarsus. Nuptial excescences are absent in breeding males, but vocal slits are present and the vocal sac is median, subgular, and moderately distensible.

The dorsum is yellowish, reddish brown, brownish, or grayish. There are often dark flecks on the dorsum, and the limbs lack transverse bars characteristic of many frogs. The venter is cream or yellowish. The hidden surfaces including the axilla, groin, anterior and posterior surfaces of the thighs, and inner surfaces of the tarsi are bright orange-red, as is the webbing of the fingers and toes. The iris is reddish tan.

In tadpoles, the mouth is anteroventrally located, the beaks bear pointed serrations, and there are 2/3 tooth rows. A dorsal gap is present in the marginal papillae of the oral disc. The body is as deep as it is wide and the snout is rounded in dorsal profile. Eyes are directed laterally and the spiracle is sinistral. Caudal musculature is slender, extending to the tip of the tail. The caudal fins are relatively deep and the dorsal fin extends onto the posterior part of the body. The dorsum is pale brown, the tail musculature is darkly mottled or reticulated, and the fins are transparent.

Natural History.—This frog occurs in tropical dry, moist, or wet forest and may be found in areas of secondary growth or in primary forest. During the dry season individuals have been found in epiphytes growing high in trees. This is one of the last frogs to appear after the beginning of the rainy season. Usually a single heavy rain is not enough to induce breeding in this species, and it appears only after about half a dozen soaking rains. Breeding takes place from May through August in temporary ponds or aguadas. Males call from low vegetation, often far out in the deeper parts of a pond. If tall trees happen to be near an aguada, these frogs may ascend high into the vegetation. The call is a series of notes that have been likened to the honking of a goose. Eggs are deposited in large clumps—up to about 250 eggs—attached to submerged vegetation. Tadpoles tend to stay at the bottom in deeper water, usually where there is an abundance of aquatic vegetation.

Distribution.—Loquacious treefrogs occur from southern Veracruz and eastern Oaxaca, Mexico, southward in the Caribbean lowlands through the southern portion of the Yucatán Peninsula, Belize, northern Guatemala, and the rest of Central America to Costa Rica. They range from near sea level to about 300 m in Guatemala but are found at higher elevations to the south. This frog occurs throughout most of Petén but is absent from the northern portion of the Yucatán Peninsula.

Remarks.—The Latin name of the species means loquatious or garrulous, an allusion to the call of breeding males.

Yellow Cricket Treefrog—Rana Arborícola Grillo Amarilla
Hyla microcephala Cope, 1886
Fig. 43

Description.—Adult males of this small species are about 25 mm in SVL, females reaching about 30 mm. The snout is somewhat pointed in dorsal profile and the skin on the dorsum is smooth. Forelimbs are short and moderately robust and an abbreviated axillary membrane is present. The fingers are about one-third webbed, the toes are about three-fourths webbed, and a poorly defined tarsal fold extends the length of the tarsus. Breeding males lack nuptial excrescences but have vocal slits, and the vocal sac is median, subgular, and greatly distensible.

The dorsum is yellowish or tan with brown markings or speckling. In specimens from Petén, dorsal markings are usually present and often form an X or H shape on the back. In other specimens, the dorsal markings may form irregular blotches, flecks, or a reticulate pattern. A dark interorbital marking is usual and there are narrow, lateral dark lines (pale bordered above) extending from behind the eyes to the sacral region. The thighs are uniformly yellow and the shanks have dark transverse markings. The venter is mostly whitish, but the vocal sac is yellow in breeding males. The iris is bronze.

In tadpoles, the mouth is terminally located, the beaks are finely serrate, and no tooth rows are present on the small oral disc. The body is slightly wider than it is deep, the snout is pointed, the eyes are situated dorsolaterally, and the spiracle is sinistral. The caudal musculature is moderately robust, becoming slender posteriorly (xiphicercal). The fins are deeper than the caudal musculature and the dorsal fin extends onto the body. The dorsum of the head and body is yellowish tan, a dark brown stripe extends from the snout through the eye, the belly is white, and the posterior half of the tail is orange.

Natural History.—This species inhabits tropical dry, moist, and wet forest, occurring in open areas such as savannas, and is common in cleared regions. The breeding season coincides with much of the rainy period; the yellow cricket frog has been found breeding in Petén from late May to December, but it also may take advantage of heavy rains during other times of the year. Recently metamorphosed frogs have been found as early as March. Males call from low emergent bushes and grass in ponds. The call resembles that of an insect and has been described as *creeek-eek-eek-eek*. The common name of this frog is derived from its cricket-like call. This species often breeds in large choruses with thousands of individuals calling at the same time. During drier periods, a single male or several may call from a drying marsh. Eggs are deposited in small clumps on vegetation just beneath the water surface.

Distribution.—This frog is distributed in southern Mexico from southern Veracruz and northern Oaxaca southward on Atlantic lowlands to Nicaragua, where it occurs on both Caribbean and Pacific lowlands, then southeastward on Pacific lowlands through Panama into South America, where it occupies various Atlantic drainages, including parts of the Amazon Basin. In Guatemala, it ranges from near sea level to about 750 m. This frog occurs throughout most of Petén. It is absent from most of the northwestern portion of the Yucatán Peninsula but occurs in the vicinity of Chichén-Itzá.

Painted Treefrog—Rana Arborícola Pintada
Hyla picta (Günther, 1901)
Fig. 44

Description.—This is a small species of frog in which males reach about 18–21 mm in SVL and females 20–23 mm. The snout is rounded in dorsal profile and the skin on the dorsum is smooth. The forearm is relatively short and slender and a distinct axillary membrane is present. The discs on the digits are relatively small, fingers are about one-third webbed, and toes are about three-fourths webbed. A poorly defined tarsal fold is present distally on the tarsus. Breeding males have vocal slits, poorly developed nuptial excrescences, and a single, median vocal sac that is greatly distensible.

This frog is yellowish, yellow-tan, or tan with small dark flecks on the dorsum. A brown dorsolateral stripe extends from the snout through the eye to about the middle of the flank, sometimes bordered above by a white or cream line. The posterior surfaces of the thighs are uniformly yellow or yellowish tan with a fine peppering of brown. The venter is mostly whitish, except for a yellow vocal sac in breeding males. The iris is pale yellow.

In tadpoles, the mouth is anteroventrally located, the beaks are finely serrated, and there are 2/3 rows of teeth on the small oral disc. A dorsal gap is present in the marginal papillae of the oral disc. The body is deeper than it is wide, the snout is bluntly rounded in dorsal profile, eyes are directed laterally, and the spiracle is sinistral. The caudal musculature is slender, extending to the pointed tip of the tail. The fins are deep with the dorsal fin extending onto the body. The body and tail are pale tan with small dark flecking on the dorsum and a dark brown stripe extending from the snout through the eye onto the body.

Natural History.—This frog occurs in tropical dry, moist, and wet forest. In the dry season it has been found in bromeliads and banana plants. It breeds during the beginning of the rainy season from late May through July in temporary bodies of water, usually in open areas. Males call from blades of tall grass or shrubs that are emergent in the water. The call of this species has been described as an insectlike buzz.

Distribution.—The painted treefrog is distributed in northeastern Mexico from southern San Luis Potosí southward through northern Guatemala and Belize to northern Honduras; it is absent from the dry northern portion of the Yucatán Peninsula. In Guatemala, this species ranges from near sea level to about 600 m. It occurs throughout much of Petén south of Lago Petén Itzá, appears to be absent from most of the northern third of the region, but is present at Tikal and to the east of Laguna Yaxjá.

Lichenose Fringe-limbed Treefrog—Rana Arborícola Liquenosa de Patas Marginadas
Hyla valancifer Firschein and Smith, 1956
Fig. 45

Description.—Adults of this species reach 70–85 mm in SVL. The snout is truncate in dorsal profile and the skin on the head is tuberculate and co-ossified with the skull. Skin on the dorsum is somewhat rugose with many tubercles. The forearm is relatively stout (hypertrophied in breeding males). Discs on the digits are well developed and moderately expanded, the fingers are over two-thirds webbed, and the toes are almost fully webbed. A low tarsal fold extends most or all of the length of the tarsus, punctuated at intervals by tubercles. Scalloped dermal fringes are present on the outside of the forearm and tarsus. Breeding males have paired vocal slits and an enlarged prepollex bearing nuptial excrescences of black keratinous spines.

The dorsum is mostly dark or reddish brown, usually possessing a lichenose pattern with various shades of brown, green, yellow, and black. Some individuals have considerable mottling of green, whereas others lack this color altogether. An irregular black marking is sometimes present on the middorsum and the hind limbs may have narrow black bars. The posterior surface of the thigh is brown mottled with dark brown. The venter is whitish mottled with brown. The iris is bronze with dark reticulations.

The tadpoles of this species are unknown.

Natural History.—This frog inhabits subtropical wet forest. Little is known about its biology. I have found it most frequently sitting on small branches 2–4 m above the ground. It seems to be most active on wet, drizzly, overcast nights. I found one specimen by day while it was asleep on a thick moss mat on the side of a giant tree. Where this species deposits its eggs remains a mystery. I assume that its tadpoles develop either in large bromeliads or in tree cavities that contain water.

Distribution.—The lichenose fringe-limbed treefrog occurs from the Los Tuxtlas Range of southern Veracruz, Mexico, through the foothills of Baja Verapaz and Izabal, Guatemala, to the Maya Mountains of Belize, at elevations from about 500 m to 1,830 m.

Remarks.—Guatemalan specimens have been recognized by some authors as a separate species, *Hyla minera*. These specimens differ from those from the Los Tuxtlas region in having more prominent dorsal tubercles.

Milky Treefrog—Rana Arborícola Lechosa
Phrynohyas venulosa (Laurenti, 1768)
Fig. 46

Description.—Skin on the dorsum of this species is thick and glandular with many large, rounded tubercles. Males reach 80–100 mm in SVL and females attain SVL of 90–110 mm. The snout is broadly rounded in dorsal profile and the forelimbs are relatively short and robust. The digital discs are fairly large, the fingers about one-half webbed and the toes about three-fourths webbed. A well developed tarsal fold is present. Breeding males have smooth, horny nuptial excrescences, vocal slits, and greatly distensible, paired, lateral vocal sacs behind the jaws.

General coloration is pale brown, pale gray, or reddish brown with large dark blotches covering most of the dorsum. Often there is but a single large dorsal splotch, but this is usually partially divided medially on the anterior of the dorsum and may also contain smaller roundish pale spots. Some individuals may have a dorsum that is uniformly colored. The limbs are marked with broad dark transverse bars. The chin, throat, and belly are white or cream. The iris is bronze with black markings.

In tadpoles, the mouth is anteroventral in position, the beaks have fine serrations and there are 4/6 tooth rows, at least in later stages of development. A dorsal gap is present in the marginal papillae of the oral disc. The body is slightly deeper than it is wide, the snout is bluntly rounded in dorsal profile, eyes are directed laterally, and the spiracle is sinistral. Caudal musculature is relatively slender, tapering to the tip of a pointed tail. The caudal fins are moderately deep with the ventral fin a little deeper than the dorsal fin, and the dorsal fin extending onto the posterior part of the body. The dorsum of the body is dark olive-brown, the musculature of the tail is pale yellow with a lateral stripe, and the fins are transparent with small dark flecks. *Natural History.*—The milky treefrog occurs in tropical and subtropical dry and moist forest. It seems to be particularly abundant in low, marshy or swampy environments. During the dry season, this frog has been found in bromeliads and the axils of banana plants. Prey of this species includes orthopterans, coleopterans, dipterans, homopterans, and spiders. There is a record of an individual ingesting a sheep toad (*Hypopachus variolosus*).

This species becomes reproductively active after the first heavy rains in late May or early June, but males may also call after heavy rains in July and August. Observations made in southern Veracruz suggest that these frogs breed on the night of the first heavy rain after a long dry period and do not breed again for several months, even though other heavy rains may be experienced and there are available breeding sites. Males often call while floating on the top of the water or while sitting near the shore in shallow water. The call is a single loud growl, sometimes described as *grrraaack.* The eggs float as a film on the surface of the water, apparently an adaptation to water with low oxygen content. Tadpoles and recent metamorphs have been observed in June and July.

These frogs have numerous granular glands on their bodies, especially in the occipital region. The glands secrete a white adhesive substance; it has been suggested that this secretion aids in reducing desiccation during the dry season. The secretion is also toxic and functions as an antipredator mechanism. As anyone who has collected these frogs knows, the secretion sticks to one's hands and is difficult to remove. Care should be taken not to touch one's eyes or nose after grabbing one of these frogs because the substance will cause a sharp burning sensation that can persist for hours.

Distribution.—Milky treefrogs occur from the lowlands of Mexico from central Tamaulipas on the Atlantic and from southern Sinaloa on the Pacific southward to central Nicaragua and then southward only on the Pacific versant through Panama into South America. In Guatemala, it ranges from near sea level to about 1,000 m. This species has a spotty distribution in Petén; it has been taken only at a few widely separated localities. I am not aware of it having been seen at Tikal, but it may occur there.

Stauffer's Longnosed Treefrog—Rana Arborícola Trompuda de Stauffer
Scinax staufferi (Cope, 1865)
Fig. 47

Description.—Adult males of this frog reach about 21–25 mm in SVL and females attain 23–27 mm. The snout is pointed and protruding in dorsal profile, the skin on the dorsum is smooth, forelimbs are moderately long and slender, and there is an abbreviated axillary membrane. The webbing is vestigial on the hands, the toes are about two-thirds webbed, and a tarsal fold is absent. There are no nuptial excrescences in breeding males, but vocal slits are present, and the vocal sac is single, median, and greatly distensible.

General coloration is tan or olive-tan with dark brown markings. There is a dark line from the nostril to the eye and a dark interorbital spot that may be triangular in some individuals. The dark longitudinal dorsolateral stripes tend to be broken in most specimens, but dark lateral stripes are often continuous, extending from behind the eye across the top of the tympanum to the inguinal region. There are usually two or three dark transverse bars on the shanks and often there is some green around the eye. Posterior surfaces of the thighs are brown. The belly is whitish and the vocal sac of breeding males is bright yellow. The iris is bronze with brown flecks.

In tadpoles, the mouth is located anteroventrally, the beaks have small serrations, and there are 2/3 rows of teeth on the small oral disc. A dorsal gap is present in the marginal papillae of the oral disc. The body is deeper than it is wide, the snout is bluntly rounded in dorsal profile, eyes are directed laterally, and the spiracle is sinistral. Caudal musculature is slender, tapering to the tip of the pointed tail. The caudal fins are deep and the dorsal fin extends onto the posterior part of the body. The body and caudal musculature are pale brown with dark brown reticulations on the tail. The caudal fins are transparent and may have a pinkish hue.

Natural History.—This frog inhabits tropical dry, moist, and wet forests and subtropical dry and moist forest. It breeds following the first heavy rains from late May to July in open areas. Recently metamorphosed individuals have been seen in July and August. Females have been found with eggs as late as September, suggesting an extended breeding season. Males call from low vegetation. The breeding call of males consists of about half a dozen high-pitched cheeps followed by a trill of about the same tone. There may be two to 30 or more consecutive notes. During the dry season this species is often found in bromeliads near permanent or intermittent bodies of water and may also be encountered under rocks or logs on the ground.

Distribution.—Stauffer's longnosed treefrog is distributed from southern Tamaulipas, Mexico, southward on the Caribbean versant to Nicaragua, and from Guerrero, Mexico, to central

Panama on the Pacific versant. In Guatemala, the species ranges from near sea level to about 1,300 m. It occurs throughout most of Petén, tending to favor the more open or drier areas.

Remarks.—The subspecies occurring in Petén is *Scinax staufferi staufferi.*

Baudin's Treefrog—Rana Arborícola de Baudin
Smilisca baudinii (Duméril and Bibron, 1841)
Figs. 48–49

Description.—This widespread species is the most common treefrog in Petén and one of the first to begin calling after heavy rains. Its loud, raucous call is one of the most frequently heard sounds in the evenings after or during rain showers. L. C. Stuart (1934:7) reported seeing a chorus that was "so numerous on the trees as to bend down the branches."

Males of this species reach 55–65 mm in SVL and females 70–85 mm. The snout is rounded in dorsal profile and the skin on the dorsum is smooth. Limbs are relatively long and robust, the digital discs are large, the fingers are less than one-fourth webbed, the toes are about three-fourths webbed, and a well-developed tarsal fold extends the length of the tarsus. Breeding males have a whitish nuptial excrescence on the prepollex; vocal slits are present, and there are paired, subgular, greatly distensible vocal sacs.

The dorsum is tan, brownish, or pale green and may be uniformly colored, but usually there are large irregular dorsal splotches that may be dark brown or olive-green. This species is capable of considerable metachrosis; a pale green specimen collected at night in the rain may become almost completely brown by the following morning. A dark canthal stripe is present, and a whitish, ash gray, or lime green spot usually occurs between the lower posterior edge of the eye and the margin of the upper lip. This spot may remain lime green even in specimens that are mostly brown. Specimens from Petén have yellowish or yellowish white flanks with brown mottling, which sometimes forms a reticulated pattern. Dark transverse limb bars are present, usually colored similarly to the dorsal blotches. The posterior surfaces of the thighs are brown with small yellowish spots (sometimes poorly defined). The venter is mostly white, but posteriorly may be yellow in some specimens. The iris is gold above and brown below.

In tadpoles, the mouth is located anteroventrally, the beaks have small blunt serrations, and there are 2/3 rows of teeth on the small oral disc. A dorsal gap is present in the marginal papillae of the oral disc. The body is slightly wider than it is deep, the snout is round in dorsal profile, eyes are directed dorsolaterally, and the spiracle is sinistral. Caudal musculature is slender and tapering but does not extend to the tip of the pointed tail. The caudal fins are not deep and the dorsal fin does not extend onto the body. The dorsum of the body is dark brown with a pale crescent-shaped marking on the posterior edge of the body, the venter is transparent with scattered brown flecks, caudal musculature is pale tan, and caudal fins are transparent with small brown flecks or blotches.

Natural History.—This frog inhabits a wide array of habitats, from xeric rain-shadow valleys to humid rainforest and cloudforest, occurring in tropical and subtropical dry, moist, and wet forest. During dry periods, it takes refuge in elephant ear and banana plants, in bromeliads, under loose bark, or in just about any other retreat where moisture may be found. The duration of the breeding season is highly variable according to geographic location but usually extends for most of the rainy season at any given locality. The mating call has been described as a series of short, explosive notes sounding like *wonk-wonk-wonk.* A call sequence consists of 2–15 notes. Amplexus is axillary and eggs form a film on top of the water. Eggs may be deposited in almost any available quiet body of water, including artificial water tanks and troughs, but the most common sites are temporary pools that form after heavy rains. Although females may contain several thousand eggs, only several hundred are deposited at a time. Newly metamorphosed young are 12–15 mm in SVL.

In Petén, the peak of the breeding season is during the early part of the rainy season from late May to July, but this species may be heard calling after heavy rains during practically any month. Tadpoles have been seen at the aguada at Tikal in mid-February and recently metamorphosed frogs have been observed in early March. During the day this species may take refuge in the axils of bromeliads or beneath logs and vegetation on the ground.

🖊*Distribution.*—Baudin's treefrog occurs on the Atlantic versant from extreme southern Texas, and on the Pacific versant from southern Sonora, Mexico, southward along both coasts and foothills to Costa Rica. This species has a continuous distribution across the Isthmus of Tehuantepec and is widespread in the Yucatán Peninsula. In Guatemala, it occurs from near sea level to about 1,500 m and is nearly ubiquitous throughout Petén.

Blue-spotted Treefrog—Rana Arborícola Flancos Azules
Smilisca cyanosticta (Smith, 1953)
Fig. 50

Description.—Males of this species reach 50–56 mm in SVL, females 60–70 mm. The snout is broadly rounded in dorsal profile, the skin on the dorsum is smooth, and the fore-limbs are relatively long and robust. Digital discs are relatively small, the fingers are about one-third webbed, the toes about three-fourths webbed, and a well-developed, thin tarsal fold extends the length of the tarsus. Breeding males have a horny nuptial excrescence on the prepollex; vocal slits are present, as are paired, subgular, greatly distensible vocal sacs.

The dorsum may be leaf green, pale green, tan, or gold depending on time of day and temperature. Dark brown or green dorsal markings are present, including markings on the occipital and interorbital regions. The thigh and shank have three or four dark brown or green transverse bands. The margin of the upper lip is creamy white, a dark brown canthal stripe extending from the nostril to the eye and a dark brown postocular mark from the eye to the axillary region, including the tympanum. A gold or bronze-colored stripe runs from the snout above the dark canthal stripe across the lateral edge of the eyelid and above the dark postocular marking onto the flank. The flanks and the anterior and posterior surfaces of the thighs are dark brown to reddish brown with many small pale blue spots. Outer edges of the forearm and tarsus are marked with a distinct white stripe, the webbing is brown, the venter is creamy white, and the iris is copper-colored. In breeding males, the throat is brown or grayish brown.

In tadpoles, the mouth is located anteroventrally, the beaks have small serrations, and there are 2/3 rows of teeth on the small oral disc. A dorsal gap is present in the marginal papillae of the oral disc. The body is slightly wider than it is deep, the snout is broadly rounded in dorsal profile, eyes are directed laterally, and the spiracle is sinistral. Caudal musculature is slender and tapering but does not extend to the tip of the pointed tail. The caudal fins are not deep; at midbody the dorsal fin is slightly deeper than the ventral fin, and the dorsal fin does not extend onto the body. The dorsum of the body is pale brown, the venter is transparent with greenish gold flecks, caudal musculature is gray, and the caudal fins are transparent and may have small brown blotches.

Natural History.—This frog occurs in tropical and subtropical wet forest. It breeds in Guatemala from March to September, but reproduction is dependent on rains, and this species may be active over much of the year during wet periods. It apparently deposits its eggs in a variety of places including pools, forks in trees, and depressions in logs. I also have found individuals calling from a small puddle of water in a culvert. The call consists of one or two short notes that have been described as a rasping squawk or *wonk-wonk*. The egg mass is deposited as a surface film. Tadpoles raised under captive conditions required 40 days to metamorphose. Newly metamorphosed young are a 14 mm in SVL.

Distribution.—Blue-spotted treefrogs occur on the Atlantic slopes of Oaxaca and southern Veracruz, Mexico, through northern Chiapas and Guatemala to the Maya Mountains of Belize. In Guatemala, this species has been found from about 200 to 750 m. In Petén, it is known from several localities along the tributaries of the Río de La Pasión, and it also has been taken at several localities in the Department of Izabal.

Yucatán Casqueheaded Treefrog—Rana Arborícola Yucateca Cabeza de Pala
Triprion petasatus (Cope, 1865)
Fig. 51

Description.—The unusual shape of the head is one of the most remarkable features of this frog. The skull is modified into a bony casque and the anterior and lateral edges are produced into a shelflike projection. The snout is upturned slightly and the eyes are directed anterolaterally. The skin is co-ossified with the skull. Males reach about 55–61 mm in SVL and females grow to about 70–74 mm. The skin on the dorsum is smooth. Limbs are relatively short and robust and the digits are moderately long and bear large discs. The fingers have only vestigial webbing, but the toes are about two-thirds webbed. A well-developed tarsal fold extends the length of the tarsus. Breeding males have paired vocal slits and a bilobed vocal sac that is situated posteriorly on the throat. A brown, keratinous nuptial excrescence is present on the pollex.

Males usually have a drab dark olive green dorsum with distinct dark brown or black flecking, spotting, or mottling. Females are not as dark and most often are pale tan to grayish green with darker brown or olive green spots or black blotches. The flanks are yellowish green or pale olive green, the limbs usually have dark transverse bars on the shanks and forearms, posterior surfaces of the thighs are dark brown or reddish brown, and the belly is white. The vocal sac of breeding males is yellow with brown flecks. The iris is gold.

In tadpoles, the mouth is anteroventral, the beaks bear small pointed serrations, and there are 2/3 rows of teeth on the small oral disc. A dorsal gap is present in the marginal papillae of the oral disc. The body is slightly wider than it is deep, the snout is bluntly rounded in dorsal profile, eyes are directed dorsolaterally, and the spiracle is sinistral. Caudal musculature is moderately robust and is attenuated distally. The caudal fins are about equal in depth to the caudal musculature at midlength of the tail and the dorsal fin extends onto the posterior part of the body. The tip of the tail is usually rounded. The body is gray-brown and the caudal musculature is tan. Fins are transparent with brown reticulations.

Natural History.—The Yucatán casqueheaded treefrog inhabits tropical dry and moist forest. This anuran, like many others in the region, is conspicuously absent during most of the year, although it may be found by digging into the dry, cracked mud of temporary aguadas where it aestivates throughout the dry season. It breeds after heavy rains from late May through August, with males often calling from perches 1–2 m up in vegetation near or in water. One report of this species calling in March may represent an unusually early rain for the season. The call has been described as a series of resonant, upwardly inflected hornlike bleats or ducklike *quacks*. Sexually aroused males produce from 33 to 54 notes in a call sequence.

Eggs are deposited in clumps; a single female may contain approximately 1,750 eggs, but it is not known if she lays all of them at a single deposition. Metamorphosed young are 15–16 mm in SVL.

This species also finds refuge in holes in trees, where it plugs the opening with its bony casquelike head. The behavior whereby tree holes are plugged in this fashion is called phragmosis. Because the skin on the top of the head is co-ossified with the skull, this frog experiences relatively little moisture loss when sequestered in its hiding places, even when environmental conditions are dry. Its diet consists mostly of insects, predominantly beetles. One of the confirmed snake predators on this species is the Yucatán cat-eyed snake (*Leptodeira frenata*).

▸*Distribution.*—This frog occurs from the northern portion of the Yucatán Peninsula southward through northern Guatemala and Belize to northern Honduras. In Guatemala, it is known only from about the northern half of Petén, and there only from a few temporary aguadas, including those at Uaxactún, Tikal, and to the southwest of Lago Petén Itzá. In Petén, the species is known from near sea level to about 300 m, but in Belize this frog has been reported to occur up to about 700 m.

NARROWMOUTHED AND SHEEP TOADS—SAPOS TERMITEROS

FAMILY MICROHYLIDAE

Members of the family Microhylidae are widely distributed in both the New World and the Old World, occurring in North, Central, and South America, Africa south of the Sahara, Asia from eastern India to the Korean Peninsula, and the Indonesian region including Malaysia and northern Australia. This is a particularly diverse family with an abundance of body shapes, sizes, colors, and natural history traits. Guatemalan species, however, are all small, rotund frogs that have short limbs, small, pointed heads, and small eyes with round pupils. The digits do not bear discs and webbing is absent or vestigial. A transverse fold of skin is present across the back of the head just behind the level of the eyes. These secretive frogs are likely to be seen or heard only after dark, and then most often only when it is raining. They feed mainly on very small insects such as ants and termites. During amplexus, which is axillary, the male adheres to the posterior part of the female's back owing to sticky secretions. All Guatemalan species have aquatic Type II larvae.

Elegant Narrowmouthed Toad—Termitero Elegante
Gastrophryne elegans (Boulenger, 1882)
Fig. 52

Description.—Adults of this fat, little toad reach 22–25 mm in SVL, with females being larger than males. The head is small and triangular. There is a transverse fold of skin across the top of the head immediately behind the eyes; however, this trait may not be obvious when the frog is at rest. The skin on the dorsum is smooth but thick, limbs are short and robust, the tips of the toes are very slightly dilated, and the toes scarcely have a trace of webbing. Breeding males have paired vocal slits, median, subgular vocal sacs that are greatly distensible, and a nuptial adhesive gland on the thorax and inner surfaces of the forelimbs, which is thought to help keep amplectant pairs united and to prevent displacement of males by rival males.

The dorsum is brown or brownish gray, the sides of the head and flanks being a darker gray or gray-brown. There is usually an inguinal spot, the ventral color pattern consists of irregular white blotches separated by a narrow dark reticulum, and the iris is medium brown. The vocal sac in breeding males is dark.

In tadpoles the mouth is terminal and unusual in lacking the horny beak and tooth rows characteristic of many species. The upper lip of this tadpole has a pair of pendent, semicircular, smooth-edged flaps which are strongly emarginate in the center and fold deeply over the mouth on either side. The body is wider than it is deep, the snout is truncate in lateral profile, eyes are lateral, and the spiracle is median and adjacent to the vent. Caudal musculature is not particularly robust and tapers to near the rounded end of the tail. The dorsal and ventral tail fins are subequal in depth and the dorsal fin slightly extends onto the posterior part of the body. The body and caudal musculature are uniformly black or dark gray with a pale lateral stripe at the base of the tail; caudal fins are pale smoky gray.

Natural History.—This species occurs over most of its range in tropical moist and dry forests and in subtropical dry forest. It has been found in small, wet depressions within the forest and in open areas surrounding aguadas. The mating call of this frog is a prolonged *baaaaaaaaaa*. Calling males are often difficult to locate because they call from within bunches of grass or beneath thick vegetation. The diet consists of small insects, especially ants and perhaps termites. The speckled racer (*Drymobius margaritiferus*) is a confirmed predator on this frog. Breeding has been observed from June to August.

Sheep Toad—Termitero Balador
Hypopachus variolosus (Cope, 1866)
Fig. 53

Description.—In this small, fat toad, adult males are 35–42 mm in SVL and females attain 40–50 mm. The head is small and triangular with relatively small eyes. There is a transverse fold or groove in the skin across the top of the head immediately behind the eyes, although this trait may not be obvious when the frog is at rest. The skin on the dorsum is moderately smooth but thick; males have small dorsal tubercles. Limbs are short and stout. The tips of the toes are not dilated, the feet have vestigial (basal) webbing, and there is no tarsal fold. Breeding males have paired vocal slits, median, subgular vocal sacs that are greatly distensible, and a nuptial adhesive gland on the thorax and inner surfaces of the forelimbs. This gland is thought to help keep amplectant pairs united and to prevent displacement of males by rival males.

The dorsum is orange or reddish brown, becoming bright orange or reddish orange in the inguinal region. A distinctive pale stripe extends from behind the eye to the anteroventral base

✔*Distribution.*—Occurring from southern Veracruz, Mexico, to northern Guatemala, Belize, and northern Honduras, this frog is found in lowland habitats from near sea level to about 900 m. It is known from a number of scattered localities throughout Petén.

of the forelimb, a thin yellow or orange middorsal line runs the length of the body, and a thin pale line often extends from above the vent across the upper posterior surface of the thighs onto the shanks. The flanks are whitish with bold dark brown or black mottling that extends to the upper inguinal region. Posterior surfaces of the thighs are orangish with distinct dark brown mottling. The venter is whitish or pale ash gray with dark brown to black mottling, which often forms a reticulated pattern, and the throat is dark gray or gray-brown. Females, especially, tend to have distinct ventral reticulations. A thin pale midventral line usually extends from the anterior margin of the lower jaw onto the belly, and often a pair of pale lines extend from the lower sternal region to the base of the upper arm. The iris is bronze

In tadpoles, the mouth is terminal and unusual in lacking the horny beak and tooth rows characteristic of many species. The upper lip of this tadpole is serrate-edged and flaplike, strongly emarginate in the center, and folded deeply over the mouth on either side. The body is wider than it is deep, the snout is bluntly rounded in dorsal profile, eyes are laterally placed, and the single spiracle is median. Caudal musculature is robust proximally and tapers almost to the tip of the acutely rounded tail. The dorsal fin is slightly deeper than the ventral fin and extends onto the posterior part of the body. The dorsum is brown, with or without small pale spots or mottling, the venter is pale brown and may have pale mottling posteriorly. Caudal musculature is brown with pale spots or mottling, and the caudal fins are translucent, mottled with brown.

Natural History.—This frog occurs in tropical and subtropical moist and dry forest. It breeds in temporary ponds and aguadas during the early rainy season in late May and early June, and in some years it has been heard calling during heavy rains through August. The breeding call is a distinctive, drawn-out *baaaaaaaaaa* that can be heard for long distances. Males sometimes call from shallow depressions beneath small plants beside water. At other times, males may call while floating on top of the water. This species usually is found in savannas or open areas. Like Middle American burrowing toads (*Rhinophrynus dorsalis*), sheep toads are rarely seen during the drier times of the year because they dig into the mud of drying ponds to aestivate in shallow cavities until the next rains. The diet consists of small insects, especially ants and termites.

Distribution.—Sheep toads occur on the Atlantic versant from southern Texas and on the Pacific versant from Sonora, Mexico, southward at low and moderate elevations through the Yucatán Peninsula, including northern Guatemala and Belize, to Costa Rica. In Guatemala, this species occurs from near sea level to about 1,500 m. It is known from many localities throughout Petén.

Remarks.—This is a species associated with temporary aguadas. After the first heavy rains individuals may appear in great numbers around aguadas that only a week before were completely dry and lined with deeply cracked earth. The common name derives from the call, which some people think resembles the prolonged, plaintive cry of a sheep. However, locating the frog when it is calling at night can be challenging. Like its relative the elegant narrow-mouthed toad (*Gastrophryne elegans*), the sheep toad usually calls from within or beneath clumps of grass or tangles of vegetation growing along the edges of aguadas or other temporary bodies of water. If the vegetation is even slightly disturbed, the frog immediately stops calling.

TRUE FROGS—RANAS VERDADERAS

FAMILY RANIDAE

True frogs occur practically worldwide in tropical and temperate habitats, exclusive of southern South America and most of Australia. As a group, ranids are extremely variable in size and shape. The largest frog in the world, the goliath frog (*Conraua goliath*) from West Africa, reaches a body length of 300 mm (it is well over twice this length with hind limbs extended) and a weight of over 3 kg. Most ranids are relatively smooth skinned and live along the shores or banks of bodies of water. The members of this family that occur in Guatemala characteristically have streamlined bodies and large, powerful hind limbs. The hind feet have extensive webbing and the toes have no enlarged discs. The pupil is horizontal, amplexus is axillary, and they have aquatic Type IV larvae.

Rio Grande Leopard Frog—Rana Leopardo de Berlandier
Rana berlandieri Baird, 1854
Fig. 54

Description.—Adult males reach 75–85 mm in SVL and females are significantly larger, up to 115–120 mm in SVL. The skin of the dorsum is smooth without denticulations, but there are well-formed dorsolateral folds. The tympanum is large, being subequal to the eye diameter and extending from the dorsolateral fold to the supralabial stripe. The webbing between the toes is extensive and the toe tips are not expanded. Adult males have brown nuptial excrescenses and a pair of vocal slits and lateral vocal sacs.

The dorsum usually is brown or olive-brown with irregular dark brown blotches, and the dorsolateral ridges are tan or yellow with a dark lower border. There is a dark canthal stripe and a white labial stripe may extend from beneath the eye to the angle of the jaw. The tympanum is pale to medium brown and the lower flanks are pale brown to whitish and marked with small dark spots. Often there are dark markings on the lower jaw, a dark stripe runs along the anteroventral surface of the upper forearm, and distinctive dark bars are present on the thigh and shank. The throat and chest of large individuals are usually dark and the belly is whitish or cream. The lower surface of the legs also tends to be dark in older specimens. I have seen a few large and presumably old individuals that were straw colored and lacked almost any trace of pattern.

In tadpoles, the mouth is anteroventral, the beaks are finely serrated, there are 2/3 or 3/3 rows of teeth, and a dorsal gap is present in the marginal papillae of the oral disc. The body is about as wide as it is deep, the snout is rounded in dorsal profile, eyes are dorsolaterally located, and the single spiracle is sinistral. Caudal musculature is moderately robust and the caudal fin is deeper than the ventral fin and extends onto the posterior part of the body. The body is brown or gray-brown, the venter is pale brown, and the caudal musculature and fins are mottled with dark brown or black.

Natural History.—This species inhabits tropical wet, moist, and dry forest and subtropical moist forest. It usually is found in the vicinity of permanent water and is common at the Tikal reservoir. I have found individuals around water at the height of the dry season, but they are much more commonly observed during the rainy season. After the first rains, this species apparently disperses widely and has been collected several miles from water. Its call species is a series of chuckles or sometimes sounds like the noise produced by rubbing two balloons together.

Tadpoles have been found from February to September, and metamorphs or juveniles have been found in March and April.

Distribution.—The Rio Grande leopard frog occurs from Texas southward on the Atlantic versant through the Yucatán Peninsula, Belize, and northern Guatemala. The southern distributional limit of this taxon is not known but may extend as far south as Nicaragua. In Guatemala frogs currently allocated to this species, but possibly representing several species, occur from near sea level to about 1,500 m. This frog is nearly ubiquitous in Petén wherever permanent bodies of water occur.

Remarks.—The systematic status of the leopard frogs of southern Mexico and Guatemala is still unresolved. A separate subspecies, *Rana berlandieri brownorum*, has been described from Campeche, Mexico, and this taxon is sometimes afforded species status.

Julian's Frog—Rana de Julian
Rana juliani Hillis and de Sá, 1988
Fig. 55

Description.—Males of this species reach about 70 mm in SVL; females presumably are somewhat larger. The skin of the dorsal surfaces is denticulate, the skin on the sides of the body is covered with raised striations, and there are distinct thin dorsolateral folds. The tympanum is large, being subequal to the diameter of the eye and

extending from the dorsolateral fold to the supralabial stripe. Webbing between the toes is extensive and the toe tips are slightly widened. As is typical in many stream-breeding species, vocal sacs and slits are absent, but large brown nuptial excrescenses are present on the pollex of breeding males.

The dorsum between the dorsolateral folds is medium brown, often with scattered dark blotches, although these may be diffuse. The sides of the body immediately below the dorsolateral folds are uniformly dark brown and the venter is cream with dusky blotches. This frog has a cream supralabial stripe, a distinct black face mask, and a pale brown tympanum. The lower border of the dorsolateral folds is black and the belly is yellow.

Tadpoles have an anteroventral mouth with finely serrate beaks. The oral disc is laterally emarginate with usually 6 (5–7) tooth rows on the upper lip and 5 (5–6) tooth rows on the lower lip; marginal teeth are present. The papillary border has a wide dorsal gap. The body is about as wide as it is deep, the snout is bluntly rounded in dorsal profile, eyes are dorsolateral, and the single spiracle is sinistral. Caudal musculature is robust and the dorsal fin, slightly deeper than the ventral fin, does not extend onto the body. Tadpoles reach about 70 mm in TL just before metamorphosis. The dorsum of the head and body is dark gray and the sides of the venter are bluish gray. Caudal musculature is tan, fins are translu-

cent, and there are distinct large dark brown or black spots on the tail.

Natural History.—Julian's frog occurs in subtropical wet and moist forest, breeding in clear, flowing streams of the Maya Mountains. Based on development of tadpoles, it has been suggested that this frog breeds during the rainy season; tadpoles collected in August have metamorphosed in September and October.

Distribution.—The species is known from Little Quartz Ridge and Mountain Pine Ridge of the Maya Mountains of Belize at elevations of 450 to 915 m. It has not been found in Guatemala, but may occur in the elevated terrain east of Dolores, Petén.

Remarks.—This species is similar to the masked mountain frog (*Rana maculata*) in overall appearance, but the two species do not occur sympatrically and are easily distinguished by several features of *R. juliani*: its larger tympanum; the absence of vocal slits and sacs; uniformly dark brown coloration of the flanks; and the presence of at least five (sometimes six) lower tooth rows in *R. juliani* tadpoles. See also Remarks under Masked Mountain Frog.

Masked Mountain Frog—Rana Montañera Enmascarada
Rana maculata Brocchi, 1877
Fig. 56

Description.—Males of this species reach about 50–75 mm in SVL, females attaining 60–113 mm. The skin of the dorsal surfaces is denticulate and there are distinct thin dorsolateral folds. The tympanum is small, being about half

the diameter of the eye. Webbing between the toes is extensive and the toe tips are slightly widened. Brown nuptial excrescences on the pollex, bilateral vocal sacs, and vocal slits are present in adult males.

The dorsum between the dorsolateral folds is medium brown to bright green with scattered dark brown blotches. These frogs have a cream supralabial stripe, a black face mask, and a dark brown tympanum. The lower border of the dorsolateral folds is black, the sides of the body below the dorsolateral folds are pale brown, usually with dark brown blotches, and the venter is cream with dusky blotches. Dark brown crossbars on the legs are about as wide as the intervening spaces.

In tadpoles the mouth is anteroventral and the beaks are finely serrate. The oral disc is not emarginate, there are 6 (5–7) tooth rows on the upper lip and 4 tooth rows on the lower lip, marginal teeth are present, and there is a dorsal gap in the marginal papillae of the oral disc. The body is about as wide as it is deep, the snout is bluntly rounded in dorsal profile, the eyes are dorsolaterally located, and the single spiracle is sinistral. Tadpoles have thick muscular tails and streamlined bodies; the dorsal fin is slightly deeper than the ventral fin and does not extend onto the body. The integument over the tail musculature and fins is heavily blotched with dark pigment, but this is more diffuse than in Julian's frog (*Rana juliani*) and the spots are smaller and more numerous, usually producing a marbled effect.

Natural History.—This species occurs mostly in subtropical wet and moist forest. It breeds in both flowing streams and still ponds. Egg masses are attached to the substrate. Because tadpoles and calling males can be found throughout the year at some localities, it has been inferred that this species breeds throughout the year. However, in the foothills to the south of Petén this species appears to breed only during the rainy season.

Distribution.—The masked mountain frog occurs from southeastern Oaxaca, Mexico, to central Nicaragua, in foothills from about 300 m to high mountain habitats of about 2,700 m. Its range borders Petén in the foothills of the departments of Alta Verapaz and Izabal.

Remarks.—This species is similar to Julian's frog in overall appearance; however, the two species do not occur sympatrically and are easily distinguished. The masked mountain frog has a smaller tympanum; vocal slits and sacs; a blotched pattern on the flanks; and no more than four lower tooth rows in its tadpoles. See also Remarks under Julian's Frog.

Vaillant's Frog—Rana de Vaillant
Rana vaillanti Brocchi, 1877
Fig. 57

Description.—Males of this species reach about 67–94 mm in SVL; females reach 76–125 mm in SVL. The skin of the dorsal surfaces is denticulate. The tympanum is large, equal to or larger than the eye diameter. Webbing between the toes is extensive and the toe tips are slightly widened. Adult males have brown nuptial excrescences on the pollex and vocal sacs and slits are usually present.

The dorsum between the dorsolateral folds usually is green anteriorly and brown posteriorly with scattered dark brown blotches, especially posteriorly. The tympanum is tan, often with irregular black markings. The supralabial stripe is absent or poorly defined and present only posterior to the eye. There is no black face mask. The lower border of the dorsolateral folds may be black but is usually poorly defined. Below the dorsolateral folds the sides of the body are brown, with darker spots or blotches, and the venter is cream colored or yellow. Usually there are dark crossbars on the lower leg, but the distinctness and width of these are variable.

In tadpoles, the mouth is anteroventral and the beaks bear fine serrations. The oral disc is laterally emarginate, there are 4/4 tooth rows, marginal teeth are absent, and a dorsal gap is present in the marginal papillae of the oral disc. The body is about as wide as it is deep, the snout is rounded in dorsal profile, the eyes are dorsolaterally placed, and the single spiracle is sinistral. A thick muscular tail is present and the dorsal fin, slightly deeper than the ventral fin, extends onto the body. The body is brown dorsally and slightly paler ventrally, the caudal musculature and fins being heavily pigmented with many small black blotches.

Natural History.—This species occurs in tropical wet, moist, and dry forest, where it inhabits sluggish lowland streams, lakes, and temporary ponds, in open areas or low bush. It is most frequently found around bodies of permanent water where it is active all year, but reproductive activity is mainly during the rainy season. Males may call from the shore, but usually they call from floating vegetation far out in the water. The call is a series of five or six grunts, each lasting for about 0.13–0.20 seconds and separated by an interval of 2–11 seconds. This call is thought to be more for territorial defense rather than for attracting females.

Distribution.—Vaillant's frog occurs from Veracruz, Mexico, southward along the Atlantic coastal plain to Nicaragua, where it crosses over to the Pacific lowlands and continues southward along both coasts through Panama into South America, where it occurs in the Pacific lowlands of Colombia and Ecuador. It is also known from the Pacific lowlands of southeastern Oaxaca and Chiapas in Mexico. The species ranges from near sea level to about 750 m. This frog is found throughout most of Petén but has not been seen at Tikal.

Part 2

REPTILES—REPTILES

Guatemala possesses many species of this class, which includes turtles, crocodiles, lizards, and snakes. Although some of these animals have become secondarily adapted to aquatic habitats, as a group the reptiles have divorced themselves from water to a much greater extent than have the amphibians. Some of
the adaptations for a terrestrial existence in reptiles are most dramatically illustrated in their integumentary and reproductive systems. The body of a reptile is
covered with a thick, keratinized layer of skin that forms protective epidermal
scales, plates, or scutes. Most reptiles lay shelled eggs and their embryos develop
in association with various extraembryonic membranes including the amnion,
chorion, allantois, and yolk sac. The presence of a shelled (cleidoic) egg permits
reptiles to live in relatively dry places, although some humidity is necessary for
the proper development of their eggs. Some groups of lizards and snakes have
secondarily become viviparous and no longer produce shelled eggs; however, all
of the embryonic membranes are still present and surround the embryos as they
develop in the oviducts.

TURTLES—TORTUGAS

Turtles are among the most interesting of vertebrates. The shell of the turtle is a remarkable structure, especially considering that the ribs which partially form the carapace are on the *outside* of the pectoral girdle. A turtle shell consists of an upper part, the carapace, and a lower portion, the plastron. Characteristic scutes or epidermal lamellae usually cover the entire shell (fig. 11). All turtles are oviparous; that is, they lay eggs. Turtle eggs may be round or oval and they may be soft and leathery or calcareous and brittle. The sex of turtles is determined in different ways. Some species, such as the giant musk turtles (*Staurotypus*) and the narrow-bridged musk turtle (*Claudius*), have genetic sex determination, whereby the sex of an individual is determined at conception by the chromosomes inherited from its parents. However, the sex of most of the species of turtles inhabiting Petén, including mud turtles (*Ki-nosternon*), the Central American river turtle (*Dermatemys*), the snapping turtle (*Chelydra*), the mesoamerican slider (*Trachemys*), and the furrowed wood turtle (*Rhinoclemmys*) is determined postconception and is dependent on the temperatures in which the eggs develop. At the relatively cool incubation temperature of 25°C, usually all of the hatchlings of *Dermatemys*, *Chelydra*, *Trachemys*, and *Rhinoclemmys* are be males, whereas at 29°C or slightly above, hatchlings will be females; intermediate temperatures produce a clutch containing both sexes. The results for mud turtles (*Kinosternon*) are not quite as dramatic, but nevertheless in one study about 70 percent of hatchlings incubated at 25°C were found to be males and 82 percent of hatchlings incubated at 29°C were found to be females.

To distinguish the various species of turtles occurring in the Petén region, see appendix D.

SNAPPING TURTLES—ZAMBUNDANGOS

FAMILY CHELYDRIDAE

This family is made up of only two genera, each containing a single species. These turtles are characterized by a carapace that is keeled dorsally, a reduced plastron, and a long tail. Highly aquatic, these turtles reach a considerable size and have large heads with powerful jaws. Although they are somewhat pugnacious and quick to defend themselves, their ferocity generally has been exaggerated. Snapping turtles range from eastern North America southward along the Gulf Coast of Mexico and Central America into South America, where they cross over to the Pacific drainages and extend into Ecuador. This family also contains the famous alligator snapping turtle of the United States, the largest species of freshwater turtle. Only a single species occurs in Mexico and Guatemala.

Central American Snapping Turtle—Zambundango
Chelydra serpentina (Linnaeus, 1758)
Fig. 58

Description.—The head of this species is large, with powerful jaws, a pointed snout, and hooked upper jaw. The top of the carapace has three low keels and the posterior margin is serrated; both the keeling and serration are most apparent in young individuals. Much reduced in size relative to that of most other turtles, the plastron is cruciform in shape. The usual complement is nine scutes on the plastron, including a single medial scute anteriorly, followed by four pairs of scutes. The bridge joining the carapace and plastron is narrow. Feet are webbed and bear long claws. The chin bears two large barbels and the neck is covered with prominent tubercles. The tail is more than half as long as the carapace in adults and may be as long as the carapace in young specimens. A series of large middorsal tubercles gives the tail a serrate appearance, and there is a smaller series of tubercles laterally. Males have a longer preanal tail length than females, with the vent situated past the posterior edge of the carapace. This turtle reaches about 50 cm in carapace length and may weigh up to about 15 kg in natural situations. Males grow larger than females.

The carapace is brown to olive-brown and the plastron is yellowish. The skin on the dorsum of the head, neck, limbs, and tail is gray or brownish gray; ventrally these parts may be paler.

Natural History.—This turtle has been well studied in the temperate parts of its range (the United States and Canada), but little is known about tropical populations. In Guatemala, it prefers quiet oxbows and backwater sloughs. It is frequently encountered in the small, slow-moving tributaries that run into large, more open bodies of water, but may also be found in large, deep rivers. I have rarely seen this species in clear water; instead it hides in the debris or vegetation of rather murky waters.

The jaws of this turtle appear to be adapted more for cutting than for crushing, lacking the crushing surface characteristic of the jaws of the northern giant musk turtle (*Staurotypus triporcatus*). Snapping turtles are omnivorous, feeding on a wide variety of foods including freshwater prawns and shrimp, crabs, clams, frogs, insects, fish and other small vertebrates that venture too near, algae and other water plants, and tree fruits that fall into the water. Most active at night, this turtle may sometimes be seen bottom-walking near the shore. I also have seen them moving at night in the shallow floodwaters of rivers. I saw one large individual capture and devour a domestic duckling near Mariscos, Izabal, during the early morning. In Guatemala, I have never seen this species bask, but they are reported to do this elsewhere in their range. When disturbed on land, this turtle rises on its hind limbs, elevating the posterior end of the carapace, and withdraws its head, ready to strike. The strike is amazingly quick, in or out of water.

The female usually digs her nest in a secluded spot covered by low vegetation rather than on open sandy beaches. Eggs are laid in April or June. The total number of eggs deposited at one time varies greatly, but 20–30 is a normal complement. Eggs are about 28–33 mm in diameter and weigh about 11–14 g. Hatching takes 80–90 days and hatchlings are 26–33 mm in carapace length and weigh about 8–9 g. Sex is determined by incubation temperature. At about 27°C approximately half of the hatchlings are male, below that temperature a greater percentage are male, and above that temperature more are female.

Distribution.—The snapping turtle occurs from southern Canada (Nova Scotia to Alberta) southward through the United States east of the Rocky Mountains to Texas. It is absent from extreme southern Texas and northeastern Mexico (the entire state of Tamaulipas), but occurs from the state of Veracruz, Mexico, southward in Atlantic drainages to Panama, where it crosses over into Pacific drainages and occurs along the Pacific coastal plain in South America to Ecuador. In Petén, this turtle occurs only in the river systems of the southern portion of the region, which include the tributaries of the Río de La Pasión.

Remarks.—Other common names for this species include *tortuga lagarto* and *tortuga cocodrilo*. Several subspecies have been recognized: *C. s. rossignonii* occurs in Petén.

MUD AND MUSK TURTLES—CHIQUIGUAO, GUAO, Y POCHITOQUES

FAMILY KINOSTERNIDAE

The family containing the mud and musk turtles is widespread in North America, Mexico, Central America, and about the northern half of South America. This family is well represented in Petén by three genera and five species. Two of these species, the northern giant musk turtle (*Staurotypus triporcatus*) and the narrow-bridged musk turtle (*Claudius angustatus*), have a reduced plastron and cannot hide completely within their shells. What they may lack in external armor, however, is fully compensated for by a large head, powerful jaws, and a pugnacious temperament. These two species are sometimes placed in the subfamily Staurotypinae.

Three species of mud turtles (*Kinosternon*) occur in Petén. These turtles have a well-developed plastron that has two hinges. All but the very fattest of turtles are able to withdraw head, neck, and limbs into the shell, which can be tightly closed. Mud turtles are noted for glands located in the inguinal region that produce a foul-smelling secretion when the turtles are frightened or injured. These turtles are placed in the subfamily Kinosterninae.

The northern giant musk turtle inhabits large bodies of permanent water and may be active any time of the year. Mud turtles and the Narrow-bridged musk turtle, however, tend to be active only seasonally. Creatures of the muddy backwaters of streams or lakes, swamps, or aguadas, they often burrow into the mud and become inactive during most of the dry season. They emerge after the first heavy rains and sometimes may be found wandering considerable distances from water. Members of this family are bottom-walkers and never emerge from the water to bask. In general, these turtles are poor swimmers and forage on the bottom of ponds or lakes. They all are most active at night.

Several species of Petén kinosternids, including the narrow-bridged and northern giant musk turtles and the red-cheeked mud turtle (*Kinosternon scorpioides*), are known to have embryonic diapause and embryonic aestivation, and probably the other two species of *Kinosternon* inhabiting the area do also. Embryonic diapause involves embryos developing very slowly in eggs already laid, despite being exposed to temperatures conducive for their development. In embryonic aestivation, embryos go into dormancy or delayed development late in their incubation, even when warm conditions prevail. This leads to a wide range of incubation times within and between clutches of eggs, even when temperatures are essentially the same. Mud and musk turtles lay elongated eggs with brittle shells.

Narrow-bridged Musk Turtle—Chiquiguao
Claudius angustatus Cope, 1865
Fig. 59

Description.—Viewed from above, the shell is oval in this species. There are three low longitudinal keels on the dorsum of the carapace; these are sometimes reduced to a trace in older specimens. The bridge connecting the carapace with the plastron is especially narrow. The plastron is greatly reduced in size, lacks gular and humeral scutes, and does not completely protect the soft underside of the turtle. There are no axillary or inguinal scutes. This is a small turtle, with males averaging about 12 cm in carapace length and females about a cm shorter. The maximum length known is about 16.5 cm for males and 150 mm for females.

The head is relatively large and the jaws, expecially the lower, are formidably hooked. A sharp maxillary cusp on each side of the upper jaw just below the front corner of the eye is a distinctive characteristic; these cusps are found in no other species of turtle. There is a pair of barbels on the chin. The toes are fully webbed, and the tail of males, considerably longer than that of females, is tipped with a hard, horny spine.

The carapace is yellowish to dark brown, often with each scute having a pattern of radiating dark streaks or spots, although these may become obfuscated with age. The plastron is paler than the carapace, usually yellowish or cream. The sides of the jaws are yellowish with vertical dark markings. In adults and juveniles the sides of the head are mottled; in very old adults the head may be uniformly plumbeous. Skin on the neck, limbs, and tail is dark gray dorsally, becoming pale gray or cream on the undersurfaces.

Natural History.—This is a turtle mostly of small, ephemeral, and usually muddy bodies of shallow water. It forages in flooded fields and shallow backwaters, marshes, small streams, and the aguadas that are abundant in the Petén region. This turtle does not bask. In some places where it occurs, the water bodies it inhabits dry up seasonally, whereupon it burrows into the mud and remains inactive during dry periods. I have seen one excavated from beneath about a foot of dried mud at the edge of an aguada. The largest specimen I have seen from Petén was from a small aguada near El Caoba, a few kilometers north of El Remate, and measured 14.8 cm in carapace length. This individual was missing a large portion of the right posterior section of its carapace—presumably the result of an encounter with a predator, perhaps a crocodile. At the time I captured this turtle, its extensive injuries had completely healed, and I have maintained it alive for many years. Although sometimes pugnacious when aroused, in captivity this species is rather timid; mine can be induced to eat earthworms and chopped fish or chicken that are placed in its tank after dark or in low light levels.

The presence of barbels is typical of bottom-walking turtles. The sharp margins of the jaws and the upper lateral cusps in narrow-bridged musk turtles suggest that they are adapted for holding and slicing prey such as frogs, which breed in great densities in some of the temporary ponds inhabited by these turtles.

Sexual maturity is reached at about 100 mm in carapace length. The breeding season approximately coincides with the beginning of the dry season and eggs usually are laid in November or December, but some females may lay a second clutch and extend the nesting season through March. Females apparently do not dig a nest but rather lay their eggs within thick mats or tangles of vegetation. From one to eight hard-shelled, oblong eggs are laid, about 30–32 × 18 mm in size. Incubation takes from 115 to 150 days in nature, but under artificial conditions incubation times range from 95 to 229 days. The hatchlings are about 35–36 mm in carapace length.

Distribution.—This turtle occurs in the Caribbean lowlands of southern Mexico from southern Veracruz to northern Guatemala and Belize, but is absent from the northern part of the Yucatán Peninsula. It is known from several widely scattered localities in Petén, including the tributaries of the Río de La Pasión and some of the small lagunas and aguadas just to the south of Lago Petén Itzá and a few kilometers to the north of El Remate. It is also relatively common in several of the aguadas of Tikal.

Remarks.—The genus *Claudius* is monotypic. A combination of a large head with powerful, hooked jaws, a long neck, and pugnacious behavior sometimes makes this turtle difficult to handle. This small turtle is sometimes eaten by humans in Petén and is reported to be tasty; I have not tried it. Other vernacular names for it include *chopontil, taimán,* and *chamarro.*

Northern Giant Musk Turtle—Guao
Staurotypus triporcatus (Wiegmann, 1828)
Fig. 60

Description.—The carapace bears three distinct keels that extend most of the length of the shell. These keels, unlike in any other species of turtle, become more prominent with age. The plastron is reduced in size. The head is large with a pointed snout, the jaws have powerful crushing surfaces, there is a pair of barbels on the chin, and the toes are fully webbed. This impressive turtle often exceeds 30 cm in carapace length, and it may occasionally approach 40 cm.

The carapace is pale to medium brown or yellowish brown with yellowish seams between the scutes. Individual scutes may be marked with dark stripes. The plastron is yellowish.

The head is usually dark gray or brown with paler reticulations or spots. Skin on the neck and limbs is gray dorsally and yellow or cream ventrally.

Natural History.—This turtle occurs in large, relatively permanent bodies of water, but often forages in flooded areas. It has been reported from clear rivers and lakes, but in flooded pastures freely enters muddy water. It is abundant around Lago Petén Itzá and fisherman often catch it in the weed-choked, marshy areas near Santa Elena. This species does not bask.

It has been suggested that the distinctive dorsal keels, and with the substantial amount of bone making up the carapace may protect this turtle from being cracked and eaten by Morelet's crocodile, with which it coexists. On the other hand, the massive, expanded alveolar surfaces of the upper jaws of this turtle are modified for crushing and allow it to feed on other species of smaller turtles, especially individuals of the genus *Kinosternon,* and on molluscs and crustaceans. This turtle also feeds on amphibians and fishes as well as on some plant material, especially tree seeds and fruits that fall into the water; it is a bottom-walker, feeding mostly on the bottom.

Nesting probably occurs in September. In captivity, the number of eggs laid by wild-caught females varies from 4 to 18, and incubation time has been reported to vary from 97 to 298 days with a mean of about 151 days. The eggs are about 35–45 × 21–26 mm. Females may lay multiple clutches per year (from 2 to 9). Hatchlings are reported to have carapaces 30–48 mm in length. Females mature in about 8–9 years.

Distribution.—Northern giant musk turtles occur in the Caribbean lowlands of southern Mexico from southern Veracruz southward through northern Guatemala, Belize, and northwestern Honduras; they are absent from the northern portion of the Yucatán Peninsula. This turtle is known from most of Petén wherever there are permanent bodies of water.

Remarks.—The vernacular name is sometimes spelled *guau.* Other Guatemalan vernacular names are *caguamo, tres lomos,* and *tres quillas;* in Belize it is referred to as *morokoi.* This turtle is capable of delivering a severe bite and readily defends itself. It should never be handled just for the hell of it.

This species is commonly eaten in Petén, but it has a musky flavor that I find unpleasant.

Tabasco Mud Turtle—Pochitoque de Monte
Kinosternon acutum Gray, 1831
Fig. 61

Description.—The carapace has a single median keel and the highest point of the carapace is located posteriorly; sometimes subadults may also have a poorly developed pair of lateral keels. The plastron is well developed and contains two hinges; the anterior and posterior lobes of the plastron can completely close up the shell openings. The anterior lobe is relatively short, equal to or shorter than the fixed midsection and is 27–33 percent of carapace length. The gular scale on the plastron is more than half the length of the anterior lobe. There is no anal notch on the posterior of the plastron. A single pair of chin barbels is present and the tip of the tail in both sexes has a hard, horny spur. This is a small species, males usually not having a carapace more than about 10.5 cm in length and females reaching 12 cm.

The carapace is yellowish to brown with black seams between the scutes or almost completely black, and the plastron is yellow or pale brown with dark seams. Upper surfaces of the head and limbs are gray-brown, yellowish brown, or reddish brown; the head has dark mottling on the top and sides. There are yellow or red markings on the side of the head and neck and the eyes are sometimes bright red.

Natural History.—The biology of this turtle is poorly known. It is reported to nest in March or April. It inhabits many bodies of water including permanent streams and lakes, small sluggish streams that periodically dry up, and temporary aguadas. Occasionally it may be found on the forest floor a considerable distance from water. Eggs hatch in 122–191 days depending on temperature, are 30–33 × 18–19 mm in size, and weigh 7–8 g.

✔*Distribution.*—The Tabasco mud turtle occupies the Caribbean lowlands of southern Mexico from southern Veracruz southward through the southern part of the Yucatán Peninsula to northern Guatemala and Belize. It occurs throughout most of Petén, inhabiting the aguadas near Tikal and the tributaries of the Río de La Pasión.

Remarks.—Other vernacular names include *casco de burro, casco de mula, casquito,* and *culuco* (Izabal).

White-lipped Mud Turtle—Pochitoque Labioblanco
Kinosternon leucostomum Duméril and Bibron, 1851
Fig. 62

Description.—The carapace of this species is oval in dorsal view and is flat on top in adults, but juveniles have a single vertebral keel. The plastron having two hinges, this turtle is able to close its shell tightly. The anterior and posterior plastral lobes are both distinctly longer than the midsection of the plastron. Although large, the gular scute is less than half of the length of the anterior plastral lobe. If present at all, the anal notch is slight. The snout is relatively protruding and the upper jaw is hooked. Anteriorly on the chin there are two large barbels followed by two smaller ones, and males have a horny spine on the tip of the tail. This species normally reaches from about

15 cm to 18 cm. Males tend to be larger than females, reaching a maximum carapace length of about 20.5 cm; females reach a maximum of about 18.5 cm. The head is larger and broader in males.

The plastron and the lower parts of the marginal scutes are yellowish with darker seams or sometimes may be almost uniformly dark brown. The head is brownish with whitish or cream jaws. Usually there is a broad cream, tan, pinkish, or yellowish band extending from behind the eye onto the neck. Development of this pale band is highly variable; it may be totally lacking in some specimens, whereas in other individuals most of the head may be pale. Limbs are pale gray or brown.

Natural History.—This widespread and abundant species occurs in the relatively still waters of lakes, ponds, marshy pastures, and backwater lagoons of rivers. It often inhabits the same waters as the Tabasco mud turtle (*Kinosternon acutum*). I have occasionally found the white-lipped mud turtle in primary forest far from water.

It is mostly nocturnal. I have seen several dozen at a time foraging at night in small, shallow lagoons where, by day, there was no evidence of turtles. The species is omnivorous, eating aquatic invertebrates such as insects, shrimps, molluscs, and crabs as well as vegetable matter (seeds, fruits, and leaves), tadpoles, and carrion.

Nesting is reported to occur throughout most of the year. Nests are simple, generally not much more than a shallow depression scraped out and then slightly covered with soil or leaf litter. This species lays its eggs in a variety of situations, including in the cooler habitat of the floor of closed-canopy forest. On several occasions, I have found eggs presumed to be of this species lying on the surface of the ground, although these may have been from nests disturbed by predators. Multiple clutches containing from one to five eggs, but usually only one or two, are laid over the course of a year. The brittle, elongate eggs are about 37×20 mm. Incubation periods are reported to vary from 126 to 148 days, and under artificially cool temperatures eggs may take up to 175 days to hatch. Hatchlings are about 33–34 mm in carapace length and weigh 4–5 g.

Distribution.—This turtle occurs from the Caribbean lowlands of southern Mexico from central Veracruz southward in Caribbean drainages through the southern and central portion of the Yucatán Peninsula to northern Guatemala and Belize to Nicaragua, then southward along both the Atlantic and Pacific coasts to northeastern Colombia, western Ecuador, and possibly northwestern Peru. Practically ubiquitous in Petén, this turtle is common in the aguadas at Tikal.

Remarks.—During my visits in the late 1950s and early 1960s, this turtle was regularly eaten by some residents in Petén. Live turtles were turned upside down and cooked in their shells directly on a bed of embers. Secretions from the musk glands of these poor distressed beasts had an overpowering effect on me and could be detected for long distances. Needless to say, I never became very fond of their flesh. Nowadays, most persons in the Petén region are relatively recent immigrants and find the flesh of this turtle repugnant. Other vernacular names for this turtle include *casco de burro, casco de mula, casquito,* and *culuco* (Izabal).

Red-cheeked Mud Turtle—Pochitoque de Carrilla Roja
Kinosternon scorpioides (Linnaeus, 1766)
Fig. 63

Description.—Three low keels are present on top of the carapace, but these become obscure in old turtles. The plastron has two hinges and is completely closeable. Its anterior lobe is about as long as its midsection and there is no interanal notch on the plastron or only a small one. The gular scute is variable in size but usually less than half the length of the anterior lobe of the plastron. There are two anterior thin barbels followed by two or three smaller ones. Males have a long, thick tail with a hard spine on the tip. The carapace of this species in Guatemala reaches about 12–15 cm.

The carapace is usually dark brown or black but sometimes may be pale brown or tan. The plastron and the ventral parts of the marginals are yellowish orange or orange with dark seams. One of the most distinctive features of this turtle are the bright red or orange blotches or spots on the side of the head. Head, neck, and limbs are gray or gray brown.

Natural History.—This omnivorous turtle lives in streams, rivers, and lakes. It reportedly nests from March to May and lays from 6 to 10 eggs that are about 35–40 × 18–19 mm and weigh 6–7 g. In nature, incubation takes about three months and hatchlings have a carapace length of about 29–30 mm and weigh 3–4 g. In captivity, 1–8 eggs are laid and incubation time is 84–258 days, with a mean of about 166 days. Hatchlings are 29–37 mm in carapace length. The smallest mature female reported was 122 mm in carapace length.

Distribution.—Red-cheeked mud turtles are widespread in tropical America, ranging from northeastern Mexico southward through Central America to the Amazonian drainage and northern Argentina in South America. The subspecies occurring in the Petén area (*Kinostemon scorpioides cruentatum*) ranges on the Caribbean coast from Tamaulipas (Mexico) southward through all of the Yucatán Peninsula to northern Guatemala and Belize, and on the Pacific coast from Oaxaca and Chiapas to El Salvador. Although I have never found this turtle to be abundant in Petén, it probably occurs throughout most of the department.

Remarks.—The subspecies in Guatemala, *K. s. cruentatum,* is sometimes considered to be a distinct species from other populations of *K. scorpioides*. Other vernacular names for this turtle include *casco de burro, casco de mula, casquito, chachaqua,* and *culuco.*

RIVER TURTLE—TORTUGA DE RÍO

FAMILY DERMATEMYDIDAE

This is a monotypic family, containing only a single living species of turtle. See description of the Central American River Turtle for a description of the family. This family, now restricted to a small area in Middle America, was once widespread and is known from fossils in North America, Europe, and eastern Asia.

Central American River Turtle—Tortuga Blanca
Dermatemys mawii Gray, 1847
Figs. 64–65

Description.—This is a large, distinctive turtle with adults reaching 45–50 cm and weighing 12 kg or more. Exceptionally large specimens, which have now become rare, may reach 65 cm. The carapace is flattened and smooth, with a flared posterior margin. In juveniles the carapace has a median ridge and the posterior margin is serrated. Although the bone of the shell is relatively thick, the scutes that cover the shell are thin, delicate and skinlike. The scutes are easily abraded and once damaged will not grow back to the original state. Captive specimens placed on concrete floors or even pebbly river banks soon badly scrape the soft integument covering their shells. In adult turtles, the individual scutes on the carapace become obscured. The bridge is wide, usually containing four or five inframarginal scales (fig. 11).

The head is relatively small for such a big turtle and has a projecting, slightly upturned snout with large nostrils. Cutting edges of the jaws are denticulate and there are no barbels on the chin. Both the forefeet and hind feet are fully webbed. The tail is much larger in males, extending well past the margin of the carapace, whereas in females the tail just reaches the edge of the carapace.

The carapace is gray, gray-brown, or olive-gray and the plastron is cream. The top of the head in adult males is bright yellow to yellow-orange; in adult females and juveniles it is gray.

Natural History.—This is a highly aquatic turtle, usually found in large permanent bodies of water including rivers and lakes. Probably the only time this turtle ever leaves the water is when the female lays eggs. Individuals do not move well on land and seem to have trouble even lifting the head when out of water. Although this species does not bask on banks or logs like many other turtles, it sometimes is found by day floating on top of the water, apparently asleep. It is reported to be most active at night. The river turtle can remain submerged for long periods and it can probably extract oxygen from the water through the nasopharyngeal epithelium. When in the water, this turtle continually brings water in through its mouth and blows it out of the nostrils.

I have never seen this species anywhere but in large bodies of permanent water. However, it has been reported from aguadas that become dry for at least part of the year. It is unclear to me how this turtle, which moves with difficulty on land, might reach these aguadas, or how it would survive for any appreciable length of time out of the water. I suspect that the records of this species from intermittent aguadas are of specimens that arrived at these locations by human agency. Captive animals placed in small to medium-sized aguadas would be easily recaptured, would provide a ready source of fresh meat, and would not be able to escape.

Adults and juveniles of this large turtle are mostly vegetarian, feeding on aquatic plants and fruit and leaves that fall into the water from riparian vegetation. These turtles are particularly fond of certain emergent grasses (*Paspalum*) and fruit from wild figs (*Ficus*). Other foods such as insects, fishes, and molluscs are infrequently taken and make up a small proportion of the diet.

River otters (*Lutra longicaudis*) apparently are one of the few predators, other than humans, that regularly feed on this turtle. However, otter populations in Central America have now been so reduced that they may be more endangered than the turtle.

Somewhat conflicting reports exist with regard to reproduction in this species; nesting and egg laying may occur over an extended period or may occur two or three times a year. Specimens from Chiapas have been reported to lay eggs from September to March, and turtles from Lago de Izabal from February to March. These periods coincide roughly with the end of the rainy season and the end of the dry season, respectively. I have observed specimens from the Río Sarstún on the Guatemala-Belize border that laid eggs in late August. As noted, this large, heavy, aquatic turtle moves laboriously when out of water to nest on open river banks, usually laying its eggs 1–3 m from the edge of the river. Nests made during the dry season are less likely to be subjected to flooding. From 6 to 20 eggs measuring about 57–65 × 32–35 mm are laid at a time; a total of about 40 brittle eggs may be laid in a single season. Individual eggs weigh about 39–43 g.

Distribution.—Central American river turtles occur in the Caribbean lowlands of southern Mexico from central Veracruz southward through the south ern portion of the Yucatán Peninsula, Belize, and northern and eastern Guatemala. In Guatemala they occupy the major rivers and lakes of southern and central Petén, reaching the southern limit of their range in Lago de Izabal and its associated rivers. Formerly abundant in Lago Petén Itzá, they are now much reduced in this lake. However, I did see juveniles during the early summer of 1995 in a river flowing into the southeastern part of the lake. The species is still moderately abundant in the Río de La Pasión and its tributaries as well as several of the larger lakes in Petén. With the sustained overharvesting of this turtle presently going on, it is likely that it will quickly become rarer over most of its range during the next decade.

Remarks.—This is the most esteemed turtle in the Petén because of its delicious meat. It undoubtedly was eaten by the Mayas and its remains have been unearthed from a burial mound at Uaxactún. This turtle almost certainly was carried to this site, because no suitable habitat (e.g., clear lakes or streams) now occurs in the immediate vicinity of Uaxactún. This turtle's Spanish name is derived from the color of its cooked flesh, which is white in contrast to the dark cooked flesh of the Mesoamerican slider (*Trachemys scripta*). The Central American river turtle is one of the most highly protected species of turtles, currently listed under various international treaty regulations and United States and Guatemalan laws; unfortunately, actual protection is not produced by legally protected status and the turtle continues to be overexploited as a food source wherever humans occur. More river turtles are captured during the last two months of the dry season, in April and early May, than at any other time. Lakes and rivers during this period are at their lowest levels, facilitating turtle hunting. The turtles are hunted by harpooning, netting, and free diving. Their future is bleak over most of the range.

Other vernacular names for this turtle are *tortuga aplanada, jicotea,* and *jincotea;* the latter two terms are also used for the Meso-American slider.

POND AND TROPICAL WOOD TURTLES—TORTUGAS DE LAGUNA Y DE BOSQUE TROPICAL

FAMILY EMYDIDAE

This family of turtles is distributed widely in Europe, northern Africa, Asia, North America, Central America, northern South America, some parts of the West Indies, eastern Brazil, and the Río de la Plata area of southern South America. The family Emydidae is the largest and most diverse group of turtles and contains the common pond turtles as well as some species that are highly terrestrial. Although many species are fully aquatic and associated with ponds, lakes, and rivers, there is tremendous variation in habits and structure among these turtles. In the Petén region there are only two species in this family—species exceedingly different from each another in appearance and habits. One is an aquatic species of the genus *Trachemys*, which includes six species of New World turtles commonly referred to as sliders. The other species is mostly terrestrial and a member of the genus *Rhinoclemmys*, which contains eight species of New World tropical wood turtles; the nearest relatives of this genus are in the Old World.

Mesoamerican Slider—Jicotea
Trachemys scripta (Schoepff, 1792)
Figs. 66–67

Description.—The carapace is oval and may be weakly keeled middorsally and slightly serrated along the posterior margin. This is a large species of freshwater turtle—the carapace of large females often exceeds 35 cm, with exceptional specimens reaching up to about 50 cm and weighing about 10 kg; males are smaller than females. There is no hinge on the plastron.

In adults, the carapace is olive-green to olive-brown with orange, often irregularly shaped ocelli on the costal and marginal scutes; several wavy longitudinal orange lines run down the top of the carapace on the central scutes. A number of yellowish and black lines are also present on the scutes of the carapace. The outer edge of the carapace has a yellow border. Very large or old specimens may lose a conspicuous pattern and have a carapace that is essentially uniformly colored. In young adults, the plastron is yellow with black mottling and in older individuals the plastron becomes mostly dark. The head, neck, limbs, and tail are marked with distinctive yellow and dark olive-brown to black longitudinal lines. The pattern in juveniles is more vivid with a bright green carapace, distinctive orange ocelli, and a yellow plastron with an intricate pattern of concentric dark lines.

Natural History.—In the Petén region this species occupies most of the larger freshwater habitats, including Lago Petén Itzá and the larger rivers, but also occurs in many of the smaller aguadas. It prefers areas that have an abundance of aquatic vegetation. The species is mostly diurnal and individuals can often be seen basking on logs.

Adults are omnivorous and feed at the water's surface as well as on the bottom, taking aquatic vegetation and tree fruits that fall into the water as well as fish, aquatic invertebrates, and carrion. Juveniles tend to be more carnivorous than adults. This turtle is known to fall prey to Morelet's crocodiles.

Females become reproductively mature at a carapace length of between 190 and 200 mm. Nesting coincides with the dry season from December through May. Females come out to lay their eggs on dark, usually moonless nights. From 5 to 22 eggs are deposited in nests scooped out on sandy river banks or the shores of lakes, with an average of about 12 eggs laid at a time. From one to four clutches may be laid in a season. The oval eggs are leathery and measure 28–49 mm in length and 19–30 mm in width; egg weights range from 6.4 to 22.7 g, with an average weight of 11.8 g. Incubation takes a little over two months. Eggs incubated at ambient temperatures (26–28°C) take 63–74 days to hatch. Under artificial conditions, a 1:1 sex ratio was produced at incubation temperatures of 27.5°C, and all females were produced at temperatures above 29°C. Hatchlings are 25–38 mm (average 32 mm) in carapace length and weigh from 3.5 to 10.7 g (average 7.2 g).

Distribution.—This widespread species occurs over much of the United States from Virginia, southern Michigan, Illinois, and Kansas to New Mexico and extends southward discontinuously in both the Atlantic and Pacific lowlands through Mexico and Central America to northern Colombia and Venezuela, with disjunct populations perhaps referrable to this species occurring as far south as temperate Argentina. There are introduced populations in the Lesser Antilles (Guadeloupe), the western United States, Europe (France, Germany, the Netherlands), Israel, and South Africa. The particular subspecies that occurs in the Petén region (*Trachemys scripta venusta*) is found in the Caribbean lowlands from northern Veracruz, Mexico, southward through most of the Yucatán Peninsula, northern Guatemala, Belize, then along the Caribbean coastal plain of Central America to northwestern Colombia. This turtle occurs throughout most of Petén. A population inhabited the Tikal reservoir as late as the 1950s and '60s, but specimens have now become rare owing to overexploitation for food.

Remarks.—This turtle is the same species as the turtle commonly known in the United States as the red-eared slider, which is sold in huge quantities in the pet trade. Numerous subspecies are recognized.

After the Central American river turtle (*Dermatemys mawii*), the jicotea is the most sought after turtle in the region. In contrast to that of the river turtle, the cooked flesh of the jicotea is quite dark. Other vernacular names are *canjicha* and *jincotea*; the latter term is also sometimes used for the Central American river turtle.

Furrowed Wood Turtle—Mojina
Rhinoclemmys areolata (Duméril and Bibron, 1851)
Figs. 68–69

Description.—The carapace of this species usually has a low median keel, highly sculptured scutes, and slightly flared posterior marginals, and it widens slightly posteriorly. Usually less than 15 cm in length, the carapace sometimes reaches 20 cm. The head is relatively small with a small median notch on the upper jaw. The feet are only slightly webbed.

In adults, the carapace is olive-brown or gray-brown. Often the adjacent portions of the marginals and costal scutes are yellowish, forming a pale ring around the carapace. The plastron is mostly dark except for its periphery and the bridge, which are yellow with dark seams. Several distinctive red bars or spots are usually present above the eye, one transverse bar on its upper anterior edge and another spot or longitudinal bar along its upper posterior edge. A brightly colored stripe extends from the parietal region onto the side of the neck; anteriorly this stripe is usually red for a short distance but becomes yellow for the rest of its length. The dorsum of the head and neck is dark gray or dark olive-brown; the sides and underside of the neck are yellow, with dark stripes and spots on the side of the neck. The forelimbs are yellow with scales that have black spots and stripes.

Natural History.—This is the most terrestrial species of turtle in the Petén region. I suspect that this species occurred primarily in wooded habitats prior to the widespread destruction of forests in Petén. However, I have frequently found this turtle along the edges of man-made clearings and some reports consider this species more of a savanna inhabitant. There is a report of as many as a dozen individuals occurring within a radius of only a few meters in savanna habitat. It also is reported from marshy situations and some individuals have algae growing on the carapace, indicating they have spent considerable time in shallow water.

Formerly, this species was quite abundant, but it has now become scarce in many areas owing to habitat loss to farming and use of the turtle as a food source. Until only about the mid-1980s, this species was frequently encountered along the trails in Tikal National Park. It is now much rarer, possibly because it has been carried off by tourists or has fallen prey to animals such as coatis (*Nasua narica*), which have increased dramatically in number within the park. In those regions of Petén where annual fires are common during the dry season, such as the savannas, many individuals lack portions of their limbs, which presumably have been burned off but may also have been lost to predators, especially coatis.

This turtle feeds primarily on plant material, including tender new shoots and the fruit of many species, but it may also eat insects. There is a record of this species in nature eating the egg shells of turtles. In captivity, it feeds on a variety of vegetables and it will also eat the egg shells of chickens, which may provide an important source of calcium.

Furrowed wood turtles lay brittle, elongate eggs about 60 × 31 mm in size and weighing about 33–34 g. Hatchlings are about 52–55 mm in carapace length and weigh 23–29 g. The shell of developing young expands during late incubation, causing the brittle outer egg layer to crack and the albumen to seep out. At the time of hatching, the carapace width of neonates is less than 40 mm. Within a day or two the shell of neonates expands to be 46–49 mm wide at the broadest point, a dimension considerably greater than the width of the egg. Under artificial conditions, incubation periods range from about 55 to 120 days depending on temperature. Eggs incubated at 27°C hatched in about 86–90 days. Eggs incubated at 30°C hatched in as little as 55 days.

Captive specimens that I have maintained have laid eggs from June to August; usually a single egg is laid at a time (rarely two), but eggs may be laid three or four times in a season from several days to over a month apart. Eggs laid in captivity were 55.7–58.7 × 29.7–30.5 mm and weighed 30.9–35.5 g.

✔*Distribution.*—This is a species of the Caribbean lowlands of southern Veracruz, Mexico, eastward through the Yucatán Peninsula and Belize to northern and eastern Guatemala; there is one questionable record for northwestern Honduras. This turtle occurs throughout most of Petén, although it is becoming less abundant just about everywhere. It ranges from near sea level to about 300 m.

Remarks.—Today, this species is heavily hunted for food and it certainly was eaten by the Mayas; remains have been excavated from burial mounds at Uaxactún.

LIZARDS—LAGARTIJAS

To many people, lizards are the most familiar reptiles. There are some 3,800 species of lizards alive in the world today and they inhabit a great variety of latitudes and terrains. Lizards, like snakes, belong to the reptilian order Squamata and have much in common with snakes, including the paired hemipenes of males. Most species of lizards are relatively small, usually less than 130 cm in SVL, but nevertheless these reptiles are often conspicuous, living in or near human habitations.

In contrast to snakes, most lizards have eyelids, external ear openings (fig. 12), and limbs. These traits characterize all species of lizards occurring in Petén, with the exception of some geckos and the night lizards, which lack eyelids. The bones of the skull are more firmly united than in most snakes; this is particularly noticeable where the two halves of the lower jaw come together in a tight mandibular symphysis. Many lizards have a well-developed pineal or "third" eye located medially on the back of the head posterior to the level of the regular eyes. The pineal eye contains a transparent, light-sensitive disc and it is thought that this structure functions in the hormonal control regulating the animal's biological clock. Most lizards have teeth that are relatively short and stout; that are all about the same shape and size (homodont) in one individual; and that lack roots penetrating into the bone of the jaws. As in snakes, the cloacal opening is a transverse slit.

Most lizards are diurnal, regulating body temperature behaviorally by basking in the sun. Only after the body temperature reaches a certain level does the lizard become active. However, in most species, activity periods are curtailed by high noontime temperatures; many species have activity periods limited to the mid- to late morning hours and become quiescent during the hotter time of the day, usually hiding in shady retreats. They may venture forth again in the late afternoon when the sun's rays are not so harsh. Nocturnal species of lizards do not bask and tend to be active at lower temperatures than diurnal species. Not surprisingly, most nocturnal species are restricted to tropical or subtropical regions and are usually found at relatively low elevations.

Because of their small size, most Guatemalan lizards have a diet consisting of insects and other small invertebrate prey. Only the black iguana (*Ctenosaura similis*) is large enough to take small vertebrates, but even this lizard does so infrequently, preferring instead to feed on various plants. The green iguana (*Iguana iguana*) is primarly a herbivore and a few other species may eat vegetable matter on occasion. Being large, the green iguana and black iguana are an esteemed source of food for humans and are overexploited almost everywhere that they occur. These two species are eaten on a regular basis, but other lizards are usually not used. On the Caribbean versant I am aware of only one instance of striped basilisk lizards (*Basiliscus vittatus*) being eaten, and this was by a starving young biologist, who told me that they were "not particularly tasty and full of bones." Interestingly, on the south (Pacific) coast of Guatemala, people now frequently eat striped basilisks, a practice unheard of several decades ago.

Most lizards have the ability to shed or autotomize their tails. Predators that seize a lizard are often distracted by a wriggling tail. This distraction allows the lizard to escape and, if it manages to continue evading capture, eventually to regenerate the tail (see "Snake and Lizard Tails," page 162). Families containing members that easily lose their tails include the anguids, gekkonids, and scincids.

Bright patches of color in lizards are frequently used in communication, either with members of the same species (especially among males) or with other intruders. The males of some of the spiny lizards (*Sceloporus*) have a pair of blue to reddish belly patches. These bright patches become conspicuous during the "push-up" displays of rival lizards. Displaying this conspicuous coloration only at certain times probably helps the owner minimize predation that such markings might otherwise provoke. Anoles (*Norops*) have a remarkable throat fan or dewlap, larger and more brightly colored in males than in females. Dewlaps may be various shades of purple, red, orange, or yellow, often with a central spot of a contrasting color. A male defending his territory against conspecific males often orients his body at right angles to an intruder and extends his dewlap to show these bright colors. The ventral surface of the tail of bark geckos is reddish or orange and its tip often has contrasting markings. These geckos often approach each other and wave their tails in a conspicuous manner; if one individual of the competing pair fails to move away, fighting may ensue.

Another remarkable trait of lizards is their ability to change colors. Practically all of the species occurring in Petén are able to alter their color to some extent, depending on temperature and emotional state. However, the most dramatic changes occur among some of the species of anoles. An adult giant green anole (*Norops biporcatus*) may change from a beautiful leaf green to a dull brown in just a matter of seconds, especially when injured or stressed.

In Petén, lizards are terrestrial or arboreal. Members of the Gekkonidae, Polychrotidae, Iguanidae, Corytophanidae, Phrynosomatidae, and Anguidae may be arboreal, with some species rarely descending from the canopy. Others may live in low brush or on the lower portion of tree trunks, and some, such as the striped basilisk, may be about equally at home on the ground or thick vegetation. All of the geckos of the region, with the exception of the Yucatán banded gecko (*Coleonyx elegans*), have modified feet that allow them to climb on vertical surfaces; they are most frequently seen on the walls of houses but also occur naturally on the trunks of large trees, especially those with loose bark that provides hiding places. The claws of some arboreal groups such as the casqueheaded basilisks (*Laemanctus*) are exceptionally sharp. Members of the families Scincidae and Teiidae are mostly terrestrial, with the former depending on crypsis or flight into leaf litter to escape predators, and the latter being exceptionally quick and agile escape artists. The limbs of skinks are relatively short and these lizards move in large part by means of serpentine undulation. In the Petén region, there are no truly aquatic or fossorial species of lizards. Some species, such as green iguanas and striped basilisks, will readily enter the water, often seeking this medium as an avenue for escape. Skinks usually are found in or near abundant leaf litter or other vegetational debris into which they will plunge when threatened, but they are not really fossorial.

Most lizard species are bisexual; that is, both males and females are present in a population. However a few lizard species reproduce parthenogenetically (see "Virgin Birth," following the species account for Maslin's whiptail, *Cnemidophorus maslini*). Most lizards lay eggs (oviparity), but a few give birth to live young (viviparity). Giving birth to live young is most often associated with lizards living at high elevations or temperate latitudes. In the tropical Petén region almost all lizards lay eggs, exceptions being Rozella's canopy lizard (*Diploglossus rozellae*) and the night lizards (*Lepidophyma*).

Lizards are divided into three major lineages, all of which occur in Petén. The iguanians include the families Polychrotidae, Iguanidae, Corytophanidae, and Phrynosomatidae; the gekkotans are represented by the family Gekkonidae; and the autarchoglossans include the families Anguidae, Scincidae, Teiidae, and Xantusiidae. To distinguish the various species of lizards occurring in the Petén region, see appendix E.

GECKOS—GECOS

FAMILY GEKKONIDAE

The Gekkonidae make up a large family of lizards containing about 80 genera and 700 species. This family is characterized by a diversity of form and adaptations, with members occurring in many different habitats.

In Petén there are three genera and four species of geckos. Three of these species have expanded digits with modified scales that allow the animals to climb on vertical surfaces. Two species, the turnip-tailed gecko (*Thecadactylus rapicaudus*) and the spotted bark gecko (*Sphaerodactylus glaucus*), are commonly found running on the walls of houses, where they prey on small invertebrates. The dwarf bark gecko (*Sphaerodactylus millepunctatus*) may also be found in houses but less frequently; it prefers nooks and crevices in tree bark and favors the leaf litter of the forest floor. Finally, the Yucatán banded gecko (*Coleonyx elegans*) is terrestrial with no modifications for climbing. This species lives on the ground under rocks and logs.

With the exception of the Yucatán banded gecko, the gecko species occurring in Petén all lack moveable eyelids. The eye is covered with a transparent scale called the brille or spectacle, which is shed periodically with the rest of the skin. The lizard keeps this transparent scale clean by wiping it with the tongue. The Yucatán banded gecko and the turnip-tailed gecko are mostly nocturnal, although it is not unusual to see the turnip-tailed gecko active inside houses on dark, cloudy days. The bark geckos may also be active at night but are mainly diurnal or crepuscular. The pupils of the Yucatán banded gecko and the Turnip-tailed gecko are narrow vertical ellipses, whereas those of the bark geckos are round or subcircular.

All Guatemalan geckos have a tail that is easily autotomized. Small scales cover their skin, which is soft and has an almost velvety texture. The skin is easily torn and may come off in patches when the lizard is seized by a predator. Such injuries look likely to be fatal, but the lizard can often recover because it soon regenerates missing skin, although the replaced skin usually is of a slightly different color and possesses scales of a smaller size than on the original piece that was lost.

Most geckos, including those species occurring in the Petén region, lay eggs. Scansorial gecko species have eggs that are soft, pliable, and sticky when first laid. As they dry, they harden within a matter of minutes and stick to the vertical surfaces on which they are laid—a fissure in a rock, the bark of a tree, or the wall of a house.

Several species of geckos are known to occur just outside the area covered in this book and may be found eventually in Petén. The weatherman gecko (*Aristelliger georgeensis*), the leaf-toed gecko (*Phyllodactylus tuberculosus*), and the island leaf-toed gecko (*Phyllodactylus insularis*) occur at various localities along coastal regions in southeastern Mexico, eastern Belize, and the Belize Keys. Several other geckos may have already been introduced into the Petén region, although not yet recorded. The house gecko (*Hemidactylus frenatus*) and its relative the Mediterranean gecko (*Hemidactylus turcicus*) occur at various localities to the north of Petén; both of these species are originally from the Eastern Hemisphere and have been widely introduced in other parts of the Neotropics. These introduced species are nocturnal, live on the walls of buildings, lay eggs that adhere to vertical surfaces, and often feed on the insects attracted by lights—traits that allow these lizards to live in close association with humans. For some of the folklore surrounding geckos, see "Unfounded Beliefs," page 31.

Yucatán Banded Gecko—Escorpión Yucateco
Coleonyx elegans Gray, 1845
Fig. 70

Description.—The snout-vent length for adults is usually about 80–90mm, but exceptional specimens may reach 120 mm. The body and tail are moderately robust, the head is large, and the limbs are long and slender. Skin covering the belly is rather translucent and some of the major blood vessels and organs can be seen. In gravid females, the whitish eggs can be observed clearly. The scales covering the dorsum of the head and body are small and granular, but there are enlarged, keeled tubercles scattered across the top of the head and back. Tubercular scales are also present on the thigh and shank; the forelimbs lack tubercles but are covered with moderately large scales. The unregenerated portion of the tail has whorls of enlarged tubercular scales that are separated by about four whorls of small granular scales. The ventro-proximal part of the tail is conspicuously swollen in males, and both sexes have a pair of large tubercular scales (sometimes referred to as cloacal or postanal spurs) on the tail just behind the thigh. The digits lack the adhesive friction pads that in other geckos are an obvious modification for climbing, but each claw is contained within a sheath composed of two enlarged lateral scales and a single elongate dorsal scale. The scales covering the venter of the body are flat, cycloid, and larger than the dorsal tubercles. This species has large eyes with vertically elliptical pupils. Unlike the other species of geckos inhabiting Petén, the Yucatán banded gecko has well-developed eyelids.

The ground color is reddish brown, apricot, yellowish tan, or pinkish gray. Usually about 4 pale yellow to tan crossbands are on the body; the tail may have 6–8 pale rings which become whitish at about midtail or the tail may be mottled or striped. Body crossbands and tail rings are boldly bordered by dark brown or black. A distinctive pale U- or V-shaped marking extends posteriorly from the eyes and across the neck; usually there is a pale crossbar on the snout in front of the eyes and a middorsal pale marking on top of the head. All head markings are darkly outlined. The lips and side of the neck are pale and marked with black spots, bars, or stripes. The venter is translucent and uniformly whitish or pinkish. Occasionally, specimens may be striped, with dark dorsolateral stripes running from the neck to above the hind legs and dark mottling on the sides. Juveniles are pinkish or reddish with whitish bands that are bordered with dark brown or black, and the caudal bands are solid black.

Natural History.—This lizard occurs in many types of tropical forests, including wet, moist, and dry forest. Specimens of this nocturnal, terrestrial species have been found beneath logs and rocks in the forest and crossing trails at night. When disturbed, this species has the interesting behavior of raising its body up by straightening its legs beneath the body, inflating the throat, and waving the tail. The Yucatán banded gecko does not climb and is completely terrestrial, living in the leaf litter of the forest floor, where it feeds mostly on small invertebrates such as crickets, cockroaches, beetles, spiders, and other arthropods.

In my experience, females usually lay two (but up to four have been reported) leathery, flexible eggs, sometimes over a period of several days. Females have been found containing well-developed eggs from February to August, suggesting that a long breeding season occurs and that perhaps multiple clutches are produced. Eggs usually are laid under rocks and logs.

Distribution.—This species occurs on the Atlantic versant from central Veracruz and Tabasco, Mexico, through the Yucatán Peninsula to northern Guatemala and Belize, and on the Pacific versant from about the Isthmus of Tehuantepec to western Guatemala. It ranges from near sea level up to about 800 m and is widespread throughout Petén, occurring in forested and open habitats.

Remarks.—This completely harmless gecko is thought to be venomous and is greatly feared in Petén. It is one of the gecko species that is capable of vocalization, emitting a soft mewing sound when frightened or attacked.

This lizard genus is sometimes placed in a separate family from other geckos in Guatemala, the Eublepharidae. Members of this group lack the subdigital specializations so characteristic of many other geckos and are the only geckos that retain moveable eyelids. The subspecies occurring in Petén is *Coleonyx elegans elegans.*

Other vernacular names for it include *niño, cuija manchada,* and *geco manchado.*

Spotted Bark Gecko—Gequillo Collarejo
Sphaerodactylus glaucus Cope, 1865
Fig. 71

Description.—The species belongs to a genus of diminutive geckos widespread in the Neotropics, including South America and the West Indies. The genus contains about 70 species, only two of which are known to occur in Guatemala. The spotted bark gecko reaches only about 22–31 mm in SVL and a TL of 45–64 mm, with females slightly larger than males. The limbs are well formed and robust; the snout is somewhat drawn out and pointed. Most of the features of scalation cannot be seen without the aid of a microscope. The tiny dorsal scales are flat, smooth, and very slightly imbricate. The tip of each digit is expanded owing to the distal subdigital lamella, which is enlarged into a friction pad. There is a single spinelike scale directly over the eye, there are no moveable eyelids, and the pupil is subcircular. Scales on the venter are flat, cycloid, and larger than the scales on the dorsum. The midventer of the unregenerated tail has a single series of enlarged, flat scales running most of its length.

The color pattern is extremely variable in this species. The body is gray, tan, reddish brown, or pale brown, often with a pale middorsal area, with a series of pale spots or stripes crossing the dorsum. There are usually a black middorsal spot (often triangular) and a pair of pale spots on the back above the forelimbs. The head may have a series of longitudinal dark stripes, including middorsal, dorsolateral, and lateral stripes. Usually 2–7 dark-bordered, pale rings or bands are on the unregenerated tail, often including one at the base of the tail and another at about midtail. The belly is usually unpigmented, but black flecking may be present on the gular area and throat. Ventrally, the tail is pink, salmon-colored, or orange.

Natural History.—This lizard inhabits tropical wet, moist, and dry forest. In natural situations, this gecko is found under loose bark in crevices in vertical rocky outcroppings, or among epiphytes; it is common around human habitations and can frequently be observed running up the walls on the inside of houses. This species may be active by day or at night. It feeds on tiny insects and spiders.

Females lay one or two eggs that are about 6 × 7 mm. In some instances, many eggs may be found together, suggesting that these lizards are attracted to specific places, which may be limited in number. Unlike those of most lizards, these eggs are not laid on the ground but rather in cracks or crevices under loose bark or in the walls of houses. When first laid, eggs are soft and sticky, but they soon dry, becoming hard-shelled and adhering to the vertical surface on which they were placed. Within a few minutes after they are laid, eggs cannot be removed without being cracked. In Chiapas, Mexico, the eggs are laid from December to February and take 80–85 days to hatch. There are records from Belize of eggs hatching in July and from Tabasco of eggs hatching in May. I have found hatchlings in Petén from May through August and they have been found in Belize in July and September. Hatchlings are about 13 mm in SVL.

Distribution.—Spotted bark geckos occur from central Veracruz, Mexico, southward, including the northern portion of the Yucatán Peninsula, through northern and eastern Guatemala and Belize to western Honduras, at elevations from near sea level to about 300 m. They inhabit most of the Petén region.

Remarks.—This small lizard is called *escorpión* throughout Petén. Other vernacular names include *cuijita collareja*, *cuida casita*, and *niño*. It is usually recognized by persons living in Petén as being inoffensive.

Dwarf Bark Gecko—Gequillo Pardo
Sphaerodactylus millepunctatus Hallowell, 1861
Fig. 72

Description.—This species reaches about 24–31 mm in SVL and a TL of about 50 mm, with females slightly larger than males. The limbs are well formed and robust; the snout is more drawn out and pointed than in the spotted bark gecko (*Spaerodactylus glaucus*). Most of the features of scalation cannot be seen by the naked eye. The tiny dorsal scales are keeled and very slightly imbricate; otherwise scalation is quite similar to that of the spotted bark gecko.

The color is variable in this species and the dorsum of the body may be brown, pale brown, or tan with small dark and pale spots. There is usually a single black middorsal spot or a pair of them on the back above the forelimbs. The head sometimes may have lateral stripes but most frequently lacks any longitudinal striping. The upper surface of the tail is colored similarly to the dorsum and has darker spots or mottling. The venter of the head and body is pale but there is fine black flecking on the gular area, throat, and belly. The venter of the tail is orange. Juveniles are pale brown with dark markings on the dorsum near the pectoral and pelvic regions. These dark markings often disappear in adults and are replaced with a peppering of dark and pale specks.

Natural History.—This diminutive lizard inhabits mostly tropical wet and moist forest. It is found on the trunks of corozo palms or under the loose bark of dead trees. Sometimes it can also be found by raking the accumulated leaf litter below large trees. Unlike its relative the spotted bark gecko, the dwarf bark gecko is infrequently found in houses.

Females lay one or two eggs. This species may reproduce over most of the year, but most records for oviposition are during the dry months, with hatching occuring during the early rainy season.

Distribution.—This gecko is distributed from the Isthmus of Tehuantepec in southern Mexico southward through northern Guatemala and Belize to northern Costa Rica, including the islands of Cozumel, Roatán, Guanaja, and Maíz Grande, from near sea level to about 300 m. This lizard occurs throughout most of the Petén region, but it is absent from the northern part of the department and from most of the Yucatán Peninsula in Mexico (except Cozumel).

Remarks.—Other vernacular names include *escorpión, cuijita pardo, cantilito,* and *cuida casita.* This small lizard is usually recognized in Petén as inoffensive.

Turnip-tailed Gecko—Cuija Cola de Nabo
Thecadactylus rapicaudus (Houttuyn, 1782)
Fig. 73

Description.—This is the largest species of gecko in the Petén region. Adults reach 90–105 mm in SVL and 140–160 mm in TL. The limbs are robust and the head is large and chunky. The tail is thick, especially proximally, and constricted at the base. The back is covered by tiny granular scales and the belly is covered by small, flat, imbricate scales that are about twice the size of the dorsals. The digits are greatly flattened and expanded; double series of large subdigital scales extend the length of each digit and form effective friction pads. The large eyes lack moveable eyelids and have vertically elliptical pupils. There are 4–5 tiny spinelike scales along the upper rear margin of the eye. The fingers and toes are heavily webbed, with only the distal two-thirds of the digits free. Males have 1–3 postanal spurs on each side; in females these structures are reduced in size.

The ground color of this species is brown, gray-brown, or yellowish tan on the dorsum with dark brown markings, usually in the form of 6 or 7 irregular crossbands. A pair of postocular stripes is usually present, the upper of which may merge with the dorsal markings, the lower one may extend for varying lengths on the the side of the body. The tail has longitudinal dark brown streaking. The venter is whitish or pale tan and heavily suffused or mottled with brown pigment.

Natural History.—This gecko occurs in tropical wet, moist, and dry forest. It is associated with large trees and is found under the loose bark of dead trees and under tangles of vines growing on live trees. It has been found at heights of 10 to 20 m and may regularly ascend even higher. This gecko is often found in buildings, especially those with ample hiding places, or under the dead fronds of large palms. I have found individuals at night in some of the larger temples at Tikal and Chichén Itzá. This lizard is nocturnal, but in deep forest it can sometimes be seen sitting in the open, especially on cloudy days. It feeds on small invertebrates, including cockroaches, crickets, grasshoppers, caterpillars, spiders, and scorpions. It is able to vocalize and emits a high-pitched *chick* or *chack*, repeated in rapid succession 15 or 20 times.

A clutch usually consists of two eggs, but these eggs may be laid several days apart. Eggs are laid on tree trunks or under bark during the *verano* or dry season.

Distribution.—The turnip-tailed gecko occurs from the Yucatán Peninsula of southern Mexico though northern Guatemala, Belize, and the Caribbean versant of Central America into South America, also occupying the Lesser Antilles. It ranges from near sea level to about 650 m. This lizard is found throughout most of the Petén region.

Remarks.—The English common name is derived from the shape of the tail, which is often swollen with fat reserves. Other vernacular names include *geco patudo* and *escorpión*.

Night Lizards—Escorpiones Nocturnos

Family Xantusiidae

The small to moderate-sized lizards that make up this family inhabit southwestern North America, Mexico, Central America, and eastern Cuba. Night lizards typically have tiny granular and tubercular scales on the back and sides of the body, larger rectangular scales on the belly, and large, platelike scales on the top of the head. They lack moveable eyelids, have vertically elliptical to subcircular pupils, and are nocturnally active, a habit that has earned them their common name. In night lizards the snout is pointed and the tail is relatively easily autotomized. Femoral pores are present. These lizards seek out dark hiding places by day and are often found beneath rock piles and in caves, abandoned mines, and Mayan temples. They move about by day in their dimly lit retreats, but I have seen them most frequently on walls or banks by night. All members of this family give birth to live young and are some of the few lizards to have a placental connection between parent and offspring. These cryptically colored lizards are usually brownish with a dorsal pattern of pale tan or yellow spots.

Yellow-spotted Tropical Night Lizard—Escorpión Nocturno Puntos Amarillos
Lepidophyma flavimaculatum A. Duméril, 1851
Fig. 74

Description.—Adults of this species are usually 90–110 mm in SVL and 210–290 mm in TL. However, I have seen several exceptional individuals that were 130 mm in SVL with a TL of 380–390 mm. The limbs are robust and the head is large with an elongate, pointed snout. The eyes have a subcircular pupil and lack moveable eyelids. Head scales are large and platelike. The dorsum of the body is covered with small, granular scales interspersed with large, pointed, trihedral tubercular scales, which are arranged in a pair of longitudinal rows, one to each side of the dorsal midline, and numerous vertical rows on the sides of the body; adjacent lateral rows of enlarged tubercular scales are irregularly arranged in vertical series and separated from each other by at least 2–3 granular scales. Labial scales are large and the anterior two pairs of infralabials make contact along the ventral midline. The gular area and undersurface of the neck are covered with tiny granular scales. The venter of the body is covered with large rectangular scales with 10 scales in a transverse series across the midbody. The proximal portion of the tail has large tubercular scales arranged in whorls that are incomplete ventrally and separated from each other on the top of the tail by 3–4 whorls of smaller tubercles; the venter of the tail is covered with flat scales similar to those on the belly but smaller.

The dorsum of the body is dark brown, usually with moderately large pale tan or yellow spots, although there is much individual variation in the development of these spots. The top of the head is paler than the dark brown on the back, usually medium brown. The lips are whitish to cream with distinctive dark vertical markings. The venter is uniformly dingy white to pale tan, without any distinctive pattern but sometimes with a light suffusion of brown pigment.

Natural History.—This lizard inhabits tropical and subtropical wet and moist forest. Like the geckos, it is a nocturnal species. It is found mostly under logs and rocks or in large rotten, hollow logs and trunks. Occasionally it may be seen out basking. This species occurs in humid forests and is most abundant in, but not limited to, shady limestone outcroppings. It is known to prey on crickets, termites, spiders, and scorpions; a close relative sometimes feeds on fruit that falls from trees and this species may have similar habits.

Females give birth to 5–8 live young in June–July. Young are about 30 mm in SVL with a TL of 70 mm.

Distribution.—The yellow-spotted tropical night lizard occurs from southern Veracruz, Mexico, southward through the Atlantic watershed of

Mexico (exclusive of most of the Yucatán Peninsula), northern Guatemala, and Belize to central Honduras; and from southern Nicaragua to central Panama. This species occurs from near sea level to about 1,500 m. This lizard is known from the southern, humid portion of the Petén region, including the area south of Sayaxché and near the Río Usumacinta in the west. I have seen one specimen from Tikal, the northernmost locality record for the species in Petén, but it is apparently rare within Tikal National Park.

Remarks.—A vernacular name for this lizard in Alta Verapaz is *reina de culebra.*

Mayan Tropical Night Lizard—Escorpión Nocturno Maya
Lepidophyma mayae Bezy, 1973
Fig. 75

Description.—Adults of this species are usually 65–90 mm in SVL and 170–210 mm in TL. The mayan tropical night lizard is similar to the yellow-spotted night lizard (*Lepidophyma flavimaculatum*) in body conformation and most aspects of scalation. It differs, however, in having numerous vertical rows of enlarged tubercular scales on the sides of the body, arranged in vertical series and usually separated from each other by only 1–2 granular scales. Some individuals have a middorsal longitudinal row of trihedral tubercular scales as well as a row to either side of the dorsal midline. The incomplete whorls on the proximal part of the tail are usually separated from each other on the top of the tail by no more than 3 whorls of smaller tubercles.

This lizard is similar to the yellow-spotted night lizard in general color pattern, but it is usually darker brown, has smaller yellow spots on the dorsum, and the dingy white venter is marked with a number of dark spots usually arranged in a checkberboard pattern.

Natural History.—This lizard occurs in tropical and subtropical wet forest. I have found it under large rocks, in limestone crevices, under rotting logs, and even in the cracks along dirt banks. It is most abundant along the edges of clearings or road cuts. It gives birth to live young.

Distribution.—The Mayan tropical night lizard occurs from the lower northern slopes of the Sierra de Los Cuchumatanes in Huehuetenango eastward through Alta Verapaz and Izabal, Guatemala, where it is found in the Montañas del Mico and the Sierra de Santa Cruz, and northward into the Maya Mountains of Belize. This species occurs in the southern portion of Petén and is known south of Sayaxché along the tributaries of the Río de La Pasión and just north of Modesto Méndez. It ranges from about 140 to 920 m.

Anoles—Abaniquillos

Family Polychrotidae

Most members of this group of lizards are commonly referred to as the anoles. Vernacular names for members of the group include *abaniquillos, bebe leches,* and *toloques.* Abaniquillo, meaning "little fan," refers to the dewlap; bebe leche is in allusion to the erroneous belief that they drink milk; and toloque is derived from the Mayan *toloc,* used in reference to a number of lizard species. This family ranges from the southeastern United States southward through Mexico and Central America to southern South America and has an extensive radiation in the West Indies. At one time, most members of this group were placed in a single genus, *Anolis,* but recent studies have suggested that several genera should be recognized. All of the anoles inhabiting Petén are placed in the genus *Norops.*

Characteristics include a dewlap, which is usually brightly colored and one of the most useful structures in species identification. The overall color of most Petén anoles is brown or brownish gray. Several species, however, stand out because of their especially distinctive patterns or colors: Becker's short-legged anole (*Norops beckeri*) with its dark reticulate pattern, the giant green anole (*N. biporcatus*) because of its green coloration, and the long-legged anole (*N. capito*) with its beautiful lichenose pattern. The overall size of an anole is often useful in identification; several diminutive species reach only about 40 mm in SVL, whereas some of the larger species easily exceed twice that length. Other important features include whether the ventrals are keeled and the relative size of the middorsal scales. Typically, a single middorsal row of keeled scales on the tail is slightly to moderately enlarged. Femoral pores are invariably absent.

The relative length of the lower portion of the hind leg, referred to as the shank, is another useful character in identifying anole species. Comparison of the shank length with the distance from the tip of the snout to some structure on the side of the head, such as the eye or ear, offers a way to distinguish between various species. However, once identification has been confirmed, it may be often easier to recognize species by other features, such as relative overall size, body color pattern, and especially dewlap coloration.

All anoles are diurnal, with round to subcircular pupils. All members of this group are climbers to some extent, with some species spending most of their time in the canopy or crowns of trees (e.g., *Norops beckeri, N. biporcatus*), others living on low shrubs, bushes, and the lower portion of large tree trunks (e.g., *N. bourgeaei, N. rodriguezi, N. sericeus*), and still others foraging in leaf litter and on small understory plants (e.g., *N. tropidonotus, N. uniformis*). Anoles feed almost exclusively on insects and other small invertebrates. Females usually lay a single egg at a time but lay multiple eggs during a season. Most anoles have a protracted breeding season that often coincides with rainy periods.

Becker's Short-legged Anole—Abaniquillo de Becker
Norops beckeri (Boulenger, 1881)
Fig. 76

Description.—Adults are 55–60 mm in SVL and 115–120 mm in TL with males larger than females. The dewlap is large in adult males, extending well onto the chest, and is deep pink to reddish purple. Unlike in most other anoles, the female of this species also has a large, well-developed dewlap, which is about the same color as in males. The head is moderately short and chunky with a broad, rounded snout in dorsal view. The limbs are very short with the tibia length about equal to the distance from the tip of the snout to the posterior margin of the eye. Scales on top of the head are smooth or slightly rugose. The dorsum and sides of the body are covered with tiny granular scales and the venter also has granular scales, but these are a little larger than those on the dorsum. There are no enlarged scales along the middorsum, but a single series of slightly enlarged, keeled scales is present on the proximal part of the tail.

The body is whitish or pale ash gray with a dark brown or gray network of reticulating lines. A fine reticulate pattern is also evident on the upper surfaces of the limbs; the forearms, thigh, and shank sometimes have about three crossbars. In a matter of minutes the pattern of this lizard may change from a bold reticulate pattern to faint and almost unicolored. The lips are marked with brown spots or bars that extend across the gular region. The venter has 5–7 irregular pairs of brown crossbars (sometimes vermiform lines) and the tail has 7–9 brown rings.

Natural History.—This lizard occurs in tropical moist and wet forest and subtropical wet forest. An arboreal species, it often prefers trees along forest margins that have an abundance of epiphytes, especially bromeliads. Individuals have been collected on low vegetation but probably spend most of their time high in the trees.

There are reports of females laying their eggs in bromeliads, during the late dry season or early part of the rainy season, that hatched in June–August, and of females laying eggs during the late rainy season that hatched in October and November. Eggs of this species are common in bromeliads growing on trees on the "forest islands" occurring in the savannas around La Libertad.

✔*Distribution.*—Becker's short-legged anole is distributed from northern Chiapas, Mexico, through northern Guatemala to Belize and Honduras. It is known from several widely separated localities in Petén. I have seen it in the forest in Tikal National Park and, as indicated, it is known from near La Libertad. There are several records from Belize and a single questionable record exists from the northern Yucatán Peninsula. This species occurs from near sea level to about 1,000 m.

Remarks.—The populations of this lizard from Petén, Belize, and the Yucatán Peninsula of Mexico have long gone under the name of *Norops pentaprion,* a species occurring to the south in lower Central America and northern South America.

Giant Green Anole—Abaniquillo Verde
Norops biporcatus (Wiegmann, 1834)
Fig. 77

Description.—This is the largest anole in the Petén, reaching 90–115 mm in snout-vent length and 315–360 mm in TL. The dewlap in males is large, extending well onto the chest, and is pale orange with a center that is lilac or pale blue; in females the dewlap is almost as large and is white (sometimes with a pale blue cast) with black streaks. The head is moderately long with a narrow, rounded snout in dorsal view. Limbs are moderately short, tibia length being about equal to the distance from the tip of the snout to slightly behind the posterior edge of the eye. Scales in the internasal and prefrontal regions are strongly keeled; those more posteriorly located on the head have low keels. The dorsum and sides of the body are covered with tiny, keeled scales, with those in the two middorsal scale rows scarcely enlarged over adjacent scales. The venter is covered with strongly keeled, imbricate scales considerably larger than the dorsal scales.

The dorsum is bright leaf green but capable of considerable and rapid color change. When green, most individuals have distinctive brownish or gray streaks or spots on the sides of the body and dorsum, sometimes with tiny blue spots also present. Injured, dead, or cold specimens may be dark brown or gray-brown. The gular area is whitish and conspicuously marked with dark streaks or lines. In males, the venter of the body is often tan or pale gray, sometimes with a few dark markings laterally; in females, the venter is usually whitish. The region immediately surrounding the eye is bright yellow.

Natural History.—This lizard inhabits tropical wet and moist forest. It is primarily an anole of the canopy, although individuals can be encountered on the limbs of small trees and occasionally on the ground.

Females usually lay a single egg at a time, although in some instances they will lay a second egg within a few hours or days of the first. Eggs are deposited throughout most of the year; they are about 23–28 × 9–11 mm in size and weigh 0.7–1.3 g. Newly hatched juveniles have been found in practically all months of the year and are about 55 mm in SVL.

↙*Distribution.*—The giant green anole is wide-ranging in mesic lowland forests, occurring from southern Veracruz, Mexico, through southern Campeche, northern Guatemala, and Belize to Panama and into South America. It occurs throughout most of Petén but appears to be absent from the drier portion of the northern third of the department. Range is from near sea level up to a little over 1,000 m.

Remarks.—In some parts of Petén, the term *toloque* is applied to all anoles as well as to the striped, helmeted, and smooth Casqueheaded basilisks. Another common name, *traicionero*, meaning "traitor," is derived from this lizard's habit of moving to the opposite side of a tree trunk to hide as people (and presumably other predators) approach; I have also heard this name applied to helmeted basilisks, which share this behavior. Another vernacular name for the giant green anole is *anolis verde.*

Bourgeau's Anole—Abaniquillo de Bourgeau
Norops bourgeaei (Bocourt, 1873)
Figs. 78–79

Description.—This is one of the most common anole species. Adults are 55–65 mm in SVL and 175–190 mm in TL, with females a little larger than males. In males the dewlap is large, extending well onto the chest; and reddish purple; in females it is small and about the same color as in males. The head is moderately short and chunky with a broad, rounded snout in dorsal view. Limbs are moderately long, with the tibia length about equal to the distance from the tip of the snout to the ear. Scales on top of the head are rugose. The dorsum and sides of the body are covered with small, keeled scales; 2–4 rows along the middorsum are very slightly enlarged. The venter is covered with keeled, imbricate scales that are considerably larger than the dorsal scales.

This species has the most variable color pattern of any anole in Petén. The body is usually some shade of brown or brownish gray and may have a dorsal pattern of pale brown or reddish brown stripes with either straight or scalloped lateral edges; of dark brown quadrangular or diamond-shaped dorsal blotches; or of a pair of pale yellowish, whitish, or tan stripes on each side that are separated by a dark brown band. A dark interorbital bar is usually evident in all but the darkest individuals. The venter is whitish or cream. Adult males have a large reddish purple dewlap; the dewlap in females is small and also reddish purple.

Natural History.—This lizard occurs in tropical wet, moist, and dry forest and subtropical wet forest. It is most frequently seen on the ground or the buttressed roots and trunks of large trees in the forest but will also invade secondary forest near human habitations.

Examination of preserved material collected in April–July shows that eggs are laid during these months, but the species is probably reproductively active throughout most of the rainy season and perhaps other parts of the year as well.

Distribution.—Bourgeau's anole occurs from about central Veracruz, Mexico, southward along the Atlantic watershed through most of the Yucatán Peninsula of Mexico, northern Guatemala, and Belize to northern Honduras. Found in many kinds of wooded habitats but usually not in open savanna, it occurs in both forested and relatively open habitats throughout the Petén region, from near sea level to over 1,000 m.

Remarks.—Another vernacular name for this species in Mexico is *lagartija chipojo.* This species is closely related to *Norops lemurinus,* and until recently the two taxa were considered to be synonymous.

Long-legged Anole—Abaniquillo Patudo
Norops capito (Peters, 1863)
Fig. 80

Description.—This large anole reaches 80–100 mm in SVL and a TL of 230–285 mm, with females a little larger than males. The dewlap in males is relatively small, extending to about the level of insertion of the forelimbs, and smoky yellow-green; in females it is dingy yellow and poorly developed. This species has the longest legs of any anole in Petén and has a short, chunky head, making comparison of shank length with head length particularly dramatic. Tibia length is about equal to the distance from the tip of the snout to a point on the neck well beyond the ear. The snout is broadly rounded in dorsal profile. Scales on top of the head are rugose and strongly unicarinate. The dorsum and sides of the body are covered with tiny, flat, irregularly arranged scales. Middorsal scales are not enlarged over adjacent scales. The venter is covered with strongly keeled, imbricate scales that are considerably larger than the dorsal scales.

The dorsum is mostly brownish or greenish with a lichenose pattern of brown, green, yellow, and reddish brown. There may be 2–3 broad and irregular crossbands on the dorsum and the tail may be marked with inconspicuous dark crossbands. A dark brown interorbital bar is present and usually dark brown markings are present beneath the eye. Some individuals (apparently always females) have a pattern of dark brown stripes or streaking on the sides of the body and a pale tan middorsal stripe that extends from the neck onto the tail. The venter is purplish gray, usually suffused with green or yellow and with faint dark mottling.

Segments of the limbs usually have dark barring.

Natural History.—An inhabitant of tropical wet and moist forest and subtropical wet forest, this large anole is most commonly found on the trunks of small to large, often moss-covered trees at heights of 2–10 m above the ground; however, it is not unusual to find individuals (especially juveniles) in leaf litter or sitting on low vegetation. In my experience, this species is mostly a deep forest anole, usually found in shady areas with only a few patches of sunlight penetrating to the forest floor. Except for forest edge situations, it appears to be absent from secondary growth.

The common bluntheaded treesnake (*Imantodes cenchoa*) and the small-spotted cat-eyed snake (*Leptodeira polysticta*) are predators of this lizard.

Distribution.—The long-legged anole is found from Tabasco, Mexico, southward along the Atlantic watershed through northern Guatemala and Belize to Panama. It occurs throughout much of Petén but is absent from the northern and northwestern part of the region. To my knowledge, this species has not been found at Tikal, but it occurs just to the east of Laguna Yaxjá and south of Sayaxché along the tributaries of the Río de La Pasión. It ranges from low elevations near sea level to 1,170 m.

Remarks.—Another vernacular name for this species is *abaniquillo jaspeado.*

Rodriguez's Anole—Abaniquillo de Rodriguez
Norops rodriguezi (Bocourt, 1873)
Fig. 81

Description.—This slender anole reaches 30–40 mm in SVL and 100–135 mm in TL. The dewlap is large in males, extending well onto the chest, and yellow; in females it is rudimentary and whitish with fine black peppering. The head is moderately long with a narrow, rounded snout in dorsal view. This is an extremely variable species. The head may be relatively broad, short, and deep or narrow, long, and shallow. The tibia may be relatively short, reaching only the posterior edge of the eye or long, reaching to about the posterior edge of the auricular opening. Scales on top of the head are smooth or very slightly rugose. The dorsum and sides of the body are covered with tiny, granular scales that are weakly keeled dorsally and weakly conical laterally; two middorsal scale rows are slightly enlarged over adjacent rows. The venter is covered with smooth, round scales that are small but nevertheless larger than the tiny dorsals.

This is a mostly brown or tan lizard. The pattern is variable, some individuals having a series of small, dark, middorsal spots. Females and juveniles often have a broad, yellow, yellow-green, pinkish, or reddish brown dorsal band running from the occiput to base of the tail. The venter is whitish. Large specimens often have a suffusion of brown pigment on the chest and belly and the gular region may be heavily speckled with brown. The dewlap in adult males appears to be somewhat geographically or individually variable. I have seen males from the Department of Izabal that had dewlaps that were orange-apricot, bright sulphur yellow, or yellowish brown with drab yellow centers and a reddish brown periphery.

Natural History.—This species occurs in tropical wet, moist, and dry forest and subtropical wet and moist forest. It appears to be more common in the more open, drier areas and is found most frequently in brushy habitats or low forest, especially around aguadas. It also may be found in the small islands of trees in the savannas.

Females lay single eggs multiple times over most of the year, but egg production is slower during the drier months.

Distribution.—Occurring from the Isthmus of Tehuantepec, Mexico, through most of the Yucatán Peninsula, northern Guatemala, and Belize to Honduras, this lizard is found throughout most of Petén. It ranges from near sea level to about 1,330 m.

Remarks.—Another vernacular name for it in Mexico is *lagartija chipojo*.

Mayan Coastal Anole—Abaniquillo Costero Maya
Norops sagrei (Duméril and Bibron, 1837)
Fig. 82

Description.—Adult males of this species reach 65–70 mm in SVL and 140–160 mm in TL; females attain SVL of 50–56 mm and TL of 130–150 mm. The dewlap is large in males and extends just onto the chest; it is rudimentary in females. Dewlap color appears to be variable according to size. In young adult males it is bright yellow; it becomes greenish yellow with an orange cast around the distal periphery in larger males, and in the largest males the dewlap is usually a smoky yellow-green. The dewlap in females is rudimentary and smoky yellow-green. The head is moderately short with a narrow, rounded snout in lateral view. Limbs are moderately long, tibia length being about equal to the distance from the tip of the snout to the posterior edge of the auricular opening. Most of the scales on top of the head are unicarinate. The dorsum and sides of the body are covered with tiny keeled or tubercular scales, with the two middorsal scale rows slightly enlarged over adjacent scales and raised into a low nuchal and middorsal crest in adult males. The venter is covered with strongly keeled, imbricate scales that are considerably larger than the dorsal scales.

The body is mostly brownish or gray-brown with the middorsal area usually a little paler than the sides. Several vertical series of small blue-gray or whitish spots are present on the sides. Females often have a pattern consisting of dorsal blotches and spots or a pale tan or yellowish dorsal stripe that is deeply incised or scalloped laterally. The gular area and throat are dark brown or gray-brown in adult males and mostly white in adult females. The venter is whitish suffused with brown.

Natural History.—This lizard inhabits tropical wet and moist forest. It is common along coastal habitats in Belize and eastern Guatemala, but also occurs at a few inland sites. It is often found around human settlements.

This species has a protracted period of reproduction during the rainy season and probably lays eggs at a reduced rate even during parts of the dry season. Multiple clutches of a single egg each are produced. Males and females reach reproductive maturity at 40 and 39 mm SVL, respectively. In Belize, mating has been observed as late as September. Juvenile specimens are absent from samples taken during the latter part of the dry season (April).

Distribution.—The Mayan coastal anole occurs from the Atlantic coast of Central Mexico to Costa Rica and in southern Florida, the Bahamas, Cuba, and Jamaica. It is found mostly near the coast of mainland Mexico and Central America. However, it is known from one locality near the Petén-Belize border, from Mérida and Chichén Itzá, and near Polyuc, which is almost in the middle of the Yucatán Peninsula. It ranges from near sea level to about 200 m.

Remarks.—Other vernacular names for this lizard include *cock maklala* (Belize) and *lagartija chipojo* (Mexico).

Blue-spot Anole—Abaniquillo Punto Azul
Norops sericeus (Hallowell, 1856)
Figs. 83–84

Description.—Adults of this slender species reach 35–53 mm in SVL and 120–140 mm in TL, with males larger than females. The dewlap in males extends onto the chest and in females is rudimentary. In adult males the dewlap is yellow, usually with reddish brown spots or streaks, and has a large blue spot in the center. In females it is sulphur yellow and may sometimes also have a blue spot in the center. The head is moderately long and slender with a narrow, rounded snout in dorsal profile. Limbs are moderately short, but variable, with tibia length about equal to the distance from the tip of the snout to between the posterior edge of the eye and the anterior edge of the auricular opening. Scales on top of the head are rugose and most are unicarinate. About 10–12 rows of scales on the middorsum are enlarged and keeled; the scales on the sides of the body are tiny and granular. The venter is covered with strongly keeled, imbricate scales considerably larger than the dorsal scales.

This lizard is most frequently pale

brown to yellowish tan. Often there is little evidence of pattern, but some individuals have a pale dorsolateral line extending from behind the eye onto the body, and sometimes rather indistinct spotting may be present on the body. Some females may have a tan to reddish brown middorsal stripe. The shanks often have a transverse dark bar. The labial area and side of the head to the auricular opening is white. The venter is whitish or cream.

Natural History.—Occurring in tropical wet, moist, and wet forest, the blue-spot anole is abundant in a number of habitats, including open, dry areas as well as more humid zones. It is usually found on low bushes and shrubs, sitting vertically on tree trunks, or in leaf litter on the ground. In wooded areas, it is more frequently seen at the edges of clearings. Reproductive females lay multiple clutches of a single egg each over the course of the rainy season.

Distribution.—Distributed from Tamaulipas on the Atlantic versant and the Isthmus of Tehuantepec on the Pacific watershed southward in lowland habitats through Central America to Costa Rica, this species occurs throughout most of Petén, the Yucatán Peninsula, and Belize. It ranges from near sea level to about 900 m.

Remarks.—This lizard is sometimes called the silky anole.

Greater Forest Anole—Abaniquillo Grande de Selva
Norops tropidonotus (Peters, 1863)
Fig. 85

Description.—Adults are 45–55 mm in SVL and 120–150 mm in TL with males larger than females. The dewlap is large in males and extends well onto the chest; it is small in females. In the Department of Izabal, adult males have a reddish orange dewlap that is darker in the center (sometimes almost black) and has a yellow distal periphery. In the Petén region, adult males have a yellowish dewlap that is reddish brown in the center. The dewlap in females is orange with a yellow distal periphery. A deep axillary pocket is present. The head is moderately short with a broadly rounded snout in dorsal view. Limbs are moderately long, tibia length being about equal to the distance from the tip of the snout to the auricular opening. Scales on the top of the head are relatively undifferentiated, with strong unicarinate keels oriented in the same direction. The back is covered with large, keeled scales, arranged in 10–14 longitudinal rows and abruptly differentiated from the scales on the sides of the body. Scales on the sides are small, keeled, and imbricate. The venter is covered with strongly keeled, imbricate scales that are roughly the same size as the dorsal scales.

The dorsum is mostly dark or reddish brown and essentially unicolored or with a pale middorsal stripe (some females), brown dorsal blotches, diamonds, or triangles. The venter is whitish with irregular clusters of small black stippling.

Natural History.—This lizard occurs in tropical moist and dry Forest. It appears to be shade-loving and does not seem to bask as much as many other species of anoles. It usually is associated with the tall forest, but I have also taken individuals infrequently in the remnants of forest bordering savannas. I have found them most often on the forest floor or on low vegetation or tree trunks. Like the lesser forest anole, this species runs with a hopping gait.

Females lay multiple clutches of a single egg each over the course of a reproductive season. Most egg-laying activity probably occurs during the rainy season and, on several occasions in July, I have observed females laying eggs in shallow depressions on shady banks.

Distribution.—The greater forest anole occurs from Veracruz, Mexico, through the Yucatán Peninsula including parts of Campeche, Yucatán, and Quintana Roo, to northern Guatemala, Belize, and Honduras. It is found throughout most of the northern half of Petén and also to the south in the Department of Izabal. In Guatemala, it ranges from near sea level to about 1,200 m.

Remarks.—The species most likely to be confused with this lizard is the lesser forest anole (*Norops uniformis*), which is smaller (maximum SVL of about 40 mm); has ventral scales that are smaller than the dorsal scales and relatively shorter legs; and differs in dewlap color. Other vernacular names for the greater forest anole in Mexico include *lagartija chipojo* and *anolis escamudo.*

Lesser Forest Anole—Abaniquillo Pequeño de Selva
Norops uniformis (Cope, 1885)
Figs. 86–87

Description.—This is the smallest of the Petén anoles, with an adult SVL of 32–40 mm and a TL of 110–150 mm, males and females being of about equal size. The dewlap in males is large, extending well onto the chest, and bright reddish purple with a central dark purple spot; in females the dewlap is small and whitish with a few small dark flecks. The lesser forest anole is similar to the greater forest anole (*Norops tropidonotus*) in having an axillary pocket and in many aspects of body conformation and scalation. However, the limbs are moderately short in the lesser forest anole, with the tibia length about equal to the distance from the tip of the snout to a point about two-thirds to the auricular opening from the eye. Scales on the sides are tiny and trihedral. The venter is covered with strongly keeled, imbricate scales that are smaller than the dorsal scales.

This lizard is mostly brown or reddish brown. Laterally, most specimens have a narrow, diagonal yellow stripe. The upper surfaces of the limbs are banded and the venter is pale brown or cream.

Natural History.—This lizard inhabits tropical wet and moist forest and subtropical wet forest. A deep forest species, it is most frequently found in leaf litter on the forest floor in heavily shaded areas or on low vegetation less than a meter in height. I have found it only in relatively undisturbed, shady, tall forest. It appears to be absent from dry, low forest and more open situations. This species runs with an unusual, almost froglike hopping gait. It can move across leaf litter surprisingly well with a quick series of short jumps.

Reproduction appears to be associated with rainfall cycles. Although some gravid females may be found throughout the year, egg production increases dramatically during the early rainy season and declines just prior to the onset of the dry season.

✔*Distribution.*—Occurring from southern Veracruz, Mexico, through northern Guatemala and Belize to northern Honduras, this lizard is found in most of Petén but is absent from most of the department north of about Uaxactún as well as from the Yucatán Peninsula to the north. The northern-most records for the species are extreme southern Campeche (Mexico), Uaxactún (Guatemala), and about central Belize. It occurs from near sea level to about 900 m.

Remarks.—The species most likely to be confused with this lizard is the greater forest anole, which is larger (average SVL over 40 mm) and has ventral scales that are about the same size as the dorsals, relatively longer legs, and in adult males a yellowish dewlap that is reddish brown in the center. A vernacular name for this lizard in Mexico is *abaniquillo de selva.*

IGUANAS—IGUANAS

FAMILY IGUANIDAE

The iguana family ranges from the southwestern United States southward through Mexico and Central America to South America; it also occurs in the West Indies, the Galapagos Islands, and the islands of Fiji and Tonga. Two species of iguanids occur in Petén and these are characteristic of the family. Both lizards are large and possess a middorsal series of spinelike scales and a prominent fold of skin that hangs down below the throat. This fold is longitudinal in the green iguana (*Iguana iguana*), forming a dewlap, and transverse in the black iguana (*Ctenosaura similis*). Femoral pores are present. Iguanids are diurnal and have subcircular or broadly elliptical pupils. The Petén species are heavily hunted by humans as a source of of protein.

Black Iguana—Iguana Negra
Ctenosaura similis (Gray, 1831)
Fig. 88

Description.—This lizard is commonly 25–35 cm in SVL, with males larger than females. Large males may reach up to 40–45 cm in SVL and 90 cm in TL and rarely may be larger (maximum of 48.9 cm SVL). Females grow to about 30 cm in SVL (maximum of 34.7 cm). Males have broader heads than females and more massive jaw musculature (see "A Lizard's Revenge," page 143). A transverse gular fold is strongly developed. The limbs are short and muscular. The top of the head is covered with small knobby scales that may have low keels. Unlike the green iguana, this species lacks a large scale on the side of the head below and slightly behind the auricular opening. The dorsum of the body is covered with small, keeled, imbricate scales; on the sides of the body the scales become smaller and tend to lose their keels. An enlarged row of mid-dorsal scales forms a serrate crest from the occiput onto the tail; this crest of spinelike scales is especially well developed in adult males and much reduced in females. The venter is covered with flat, imbricate scales that are a bit larger than the dorsal scales. On the dorsal and lateral surfaces of the tail, enlarged and strongly tuberculate scales form distinctive whorls; these whorls are separated from each other on the dorsolateral part of the tail by two whorls containing small scales. The scales on the undersurface of the tail are keeled but not tuberculate, and adjacent scales are subequal in size.

Juveniles are bright green, usually with black bands on the body and tail, and can easily be confused with small green iguanas. The bright green coloration of juveniles persists for about 3–5 months. Adults are gray, gray-brown, or brownish with 5–7 broad dark dorsal crossbands that have black anterior borders extending on to the sides. The tail has 8–11 wide dark bands (incomplete ventrally). The limbs usually have some dark spots or bars, and pale spotting may be present in large adults. The venter is pale gray with a whitish or dingy cream area midventrally.

Natural History.—This lizard lives in tropical moist and dry forest. In contrast to the green iguana, which usually is seen high in trees, the black iguana is most often encountered closer to the ground, especially basking on large fallen trunks or hollow trees in semi-open areas, on fence posts, and in old buildings, and it seems to prefer the open savanna regions. This lizard lives in ground burrows, especially in rocky terrain, or in tree cavities and hollow logs. When approached, this iguana is quick to retreat into its hiding place. Unlike most reptiles, it may be active during the hottest time of the day and maintains its body temperature during the day at 36–37°C by moving in and out of the shade.

Although it is primarily herbivorous, feeding on leaves, flowers, tender shoots, and fruits, there are records of this lizard eating nestling birds and bird eggs, small lizards (*Cnemidophorus, Sceloporus,* and *Mabuya brachypoda*), and rodents (*Oryzomys, Scotinomys,* and *Sigmodon*). Juveniles also feed on a variety of arthropods such as grasshoppers, which make up the bulk of their diet. Adults often feed heavily on brightly colored flowers and fruits available in the dry season.

This lizard breeds during the dry season. Each female lays a single annual clutch of eggs. In Chiapas, females lay 15–30 eggs from March to May that take about 90 days to hatch. In Belize, this species has been observed in courtship during the early part of the dry season (February), and females lay 15–25 eggs in May and June. Eggs hatch in mid-June and July, with the juveniles being 48–61 mm in SVL and weighing 3.5–4.5 g. It is estimated that reaching sexual maturity takes two or three years. In other parts of its range, the species has been recorded to lay as few as 12 and as many as 80 eggs in a clutch.

Distribution.—Black iguanas are creatures of the lowlands from central Veracruz, Mexico, to Panama, usually in relatively dry habitats. In Guatemala, this species occurs from near sea level to about 1,000 m. In contrast to records from other parts of Guatemala, where this lizard is quite abundant, I have seen relatively few individuals in Petén, where it is known only from a few relatively dry localities, including the southern shore of Lago Petén Itzá and the savanna region around La Libertad.

Remarks.—The meat of this species is eaten and, in some parts of Guatemala, is preferred over that of the green iguana. However, black iguanas are not used for food in most of Belize. This lizard is quick to bite when forcefully restrained. The subspecies occurring in Petén is *Ctenosaura similis similis.* Other vernacular names include *garrobo, iguana rayada,* and wish-willy (Belize).

A Lizard's Revenge.—I was party to a memorable black iguana encounter one hot summer day to the northwest of Petén along a coastal stretch of highway in central Veracruz. In this area, known locally as Punta del Moro, the coastal plain is nearly interrupted by an eastern intrusion of the Sierra Madre Oriental. Great volcanic boulders from ancient lava flows are scattered across the landscape all the way to the beach. The dark boulders provide ideal habitat and hiding places for several species of lizards, including black iguanas, which remain active after high noontime temperatures send many less heat-loving species scurrying for cooler retreats.

In August 1969 I was traveling along this road with a friend, who perhaps prefers to remain anonymous. Temperatures that day had already exceeded 33°C when we spied a number of black iguanas on the boulders along the road. This was my friend's first trip south of the Río Bravo, and he became greatly excited at the sight of these lizards. Black iguanas tend to be wary and we were not able to approach them very closely before they disappeared down burrows at the bases of the boulders or into crevices and cracks in the rocks of the lava flow. Finally, my friend cornered a fine male in a deep fissure. He reached into the crack up to his shoulder in an attempt to grab the animal.

Black Iguanas are not reluctant to defend themselves. This individual promptly seized his pursuer by the hand, just beside the little finger. This put my friend in somewhat of a predicament as he was now spread-eagled, face down, and shirtless on a large, dark, very hot rock and unable to extract his hand from the jaws of the lizard, which refused to release him but occasionally gave a strong triumphant squeeze that caused the owner of the hand to scream in pain. I worked for the better part of an hour trying to free him, with little success. There was no way to reach the lizard because my friend's arm blocked access, and I must admit that after every few minutes of working on the hot boulder, I had to move off, leaving him to sizzle.

Finally, on his own, the lizard released his grip. The bite was a nasty one but luckily had not involved any fingers. Far worse than the bite were the bad scrape and burn caused by squirming for so long on the abrasive lava boulder. Had the iguana that held him captive been one of the really large males, my friend might have lost a piece of his hand—although over the years in the retelling, his tormentor has grown to truly legendary proportions.

Green Iguana—Iguana Verde
Iguana iguana (Linnaeus, 1758)
Fig. 89

Description.—The largest lizard species in Petén, the green iguana may exceed 50 cm in SVL and 180 cm in TL, but males usually are about 40 cm in SVL and females about 30 cm. Males have larger, broader heads than females. In both sexes, a large pendant dewlap extends from behind the mental (the large triangular scale on the anterior edge of the lower jaw) to a point just in front of the level of insertion of the forelimbs; the anterior border of the dewlap is lined with large spinelike scales forming a serrate margin. The limbs are short and muscular. Scales on top of the head are mostly large and smooth. Two to three scales are raised into hornlike spines on the dorsal midline of the snout behind the rostral scale. A large roundish scale is present on the side of the head below and slightly behind the auricular opening. A number of enlarged, conical scales are present on the top and sides of the neck. The dorsum is covered with small, imbricate, weakly keeled scales that become even less keeled on the sides of the body. The scales on the venter are larger than those on the dorsum, imbricate, and either smooth or obtusely keeled. A distinctive series of enlarged, raised, spinelike scales extends along the middorsum from the occiput onto the tail. These scales are most enlarged on the back of the neck and above the shoulders in both males and females, but middorsal spines are larger in males. The tail is covered with small, imbricate, strongly to obtusely keeled scales.

Juveniles and adult females are green with black bands on the body and tail, but these become less well defined on the body of large adult females. Large adult males and some females become gray or tan, males often becoming quite orange on the anterior part of the body, including the middorsal crest of spines, and the black-banded body pattern becoming obfuscated. By day, most individuals have vivid colors, whereas at night sleeping individuals are darker.

Natural History.—The green iguana inhabits tropical wet and moist forest. It is arboreal, spending almost its entire life in trees, and is rarely found any distance from major streams, rivers, or lakes. If a predator ascends a tree in pursuit of a green iguana that happens to be on a limb above the water, this lizard has no hesitancy in launching itself from a considerable height into the water to escape (see "The Iguana Hunters," page 146). It can swim well underwater as well as at the surface and sometimes remains underwater when hiding from enemies. These lizards swim by undulating motion of the body and tail, their limbs folded along the sides of the body. Adults are most often seen high in trees, whereas juveniles may often descend to the ground or frequent low vegetation. By night, these lizards sleep on slender branches and clumps of vegetation, usually facing toward the outside of the bush or tree.

This is a docile lizard, but large individuals sometimes try to bite when mistreated; large adults also lash out with their tails at aggressors. The species is mostly vegetarian, feeding on tree leaves and certain fruits, although small juveniles reportedly eat insects.

The mating season is October–December and females lay 15–60 eggs in February–May (usually March or April). Nests are excavated in sandy areas near water and eggs hatch in about 90 days.

Eggs were found to incubate at 31–32°C in natural nests in Panama. The relatively high temperatures necessary for successful incubation of eggs of this species may help explain why it is mostly restricted to open areas such as along rivers, where sunlight penetrates to the banks.

Distribution.—Green iguanas occur from Sinaloa and Veracruz, Mexico, southward through Central America into South America. Because of its propensity to be restricted to habitats near permanent water, this species is absent from most parts of Petén, and apparently does not occur around the major lakes of the northern half of the department, including Lago Petén Itzá. However, it is known from riparian forests along the Río Mopán and Río de La Pasión and their tributaries. In Guatemala, this species occurs from near sea level to about 875 m.

Remarks.—A vernacular name for this lizard is *iguana de ribera*, meaning "shoreline" or "riparian" iguana and referring to its most common haunts. In southern Petén, female iguanas are sometime simply called *iguana*, whereas adult males are called *garrobo*, a name also used for the black iguana. The subspecies occurring in Petén is *Iguana iguana rhinolopha*. Green iguana populations have been reduced drastically in most areas in Guatemala owing to consumption by humans.

The Iguana Hunters.—Most green iguana populations have declined precipitously in recent years because of overexploitation for human consumption. In years past, persons known as *iguaneros* made their living by hunting iguanas. The iguana hunters, usually with several mangy mongrels in tow, used to be quite common along the Canal de Chiquimulilla and associated rivers of the Pacific coast of Guatemala. They could be seen poling their dugout canoes along the edges of the waterways or camped out on the banks. It was wise to keep a careful eye on one's possessions when iguaneros were nearby; they were invariably dressed in tatters and looked impressively disreputable.

On finding a tree with a large iguana, they would make a small clearing underneath and then climb the tree to dislodge the iguana. When the iguana jumped to the ground it was met by the dogs, which grabbed the lizard and held it until the iguanero descended the tree. Sometimes, if the tree was close enough to the river, the iguana made good its escape by plunging into the water, where it remained submerged until danger had passed. Nevertheless, iguaneros were remarkably efficient, severely depleting areas in which they worked. The limbs of the hapless iguana were tied behind its back by breaking and pulling off the terminal portion of several fingers and toes, thus exposing the tendons, which were used for ligatures. Iguanas were accumulated and eventually taken to various towns in Guatemala for sale. In the early 1960s it was commonplace to see iguanas stacked like cordwood in the La Terminal marketplace of Guatemala City, and this sight was repeated in most of the lowland markets in tropical areas where the lizards lived. Iguanas could be purchased and taken home alive or butchered and cooked on the spot in a nearby charcoal pit.

The unlaid, yellow eggs of iguanas were considered a special treat and females were sometimes doomed to a particularly horrible death. An incision was made on the bellies of females that were obviously gravid and the eggs were removed; the abdominal cavity of the female was then filled with leaves and she was released under the mistaken assumption that she would recover and go on to produce more eggs that could be harvested at a later date.

BASILISKS—CUTETES Y TRAICIONEROS

FAMILY CORYTOPHANIDAE

The basilisk lizards range from about central Mexico through Central America to northern South America. Members of this family are usually immediately recognizable by their crests, casques, or helmets. Adult male striped basilisks (*Basilisus vittatus*) have a large flaplike crest on the back of the head; this crest is also present in adult females but much reduced in size. Helmeted basilisks (*Corytophanes*) also have a nuchal crest, but in these lizards the crest is strongly reinforced along its dorsal edge with a projection of the parietal bone. Finally, casqueheaded basilisks (*Laemanctus*) have a flat-topped cephalic crest that is also bony. The helmeted and casqueheaded basilisks have laterally compressed bodies; the body is less compressed in striped basilisks. All members of this group have extremely long legs and tail. The dorsal and ventral scales are keeled and imbricate and the middorsal scale row is usually enlarged. Femoral pores are absent. The claws are exceptionally sharp, especially in helmeted and casqueheaded basilisks. These diurnal lizards sit quietly waiting for prey for most of the day, but the striped basilisk is one of the most frequently seen reptiles as it dashes across roads on its hind legs.

Striped Basilisk—Cutete Rayada
Basiliscus vittatus Wiegmann, 1828
Figs. 90–91

Description.—Adult males have a large flaplike crest that is supported by flexible cartilage and projects from the back of the head in the parietal region and extends onto the neck; this crest is present, but small, in adult females and subadults. Recently hatched individuals have no crests but within a few months acquire a small flap on the neck similar to that of grown females. Adult males also have a high middorsal crest extending from above the shoulders to about the level of the hind limbs and continuing down the tail as a low dorsal keel; in females and juveniles this crest is low or reduced to a strongly keeled row of middorsal scales. Males are larger than females, reaching about 17 cm in SVL and over 60 cm in TL; females usually are no more than 14–15 cm in SVL and 55–60 cm in TL. The head is large and males have a more elongate snout than females. The limbs and tail are long and slender, the toes have a distinctive series of scales that form a ventrolateral fringe on each side, and the tail is laterally compressed. Scales on top of the head are rugose in adults. The dorsum and sides of the body are covered with small, keeled, imbricate scales, with the scales on the sides smaller than on the dorsum. Scales that cover the gular area are smooth and there is no series of enlarged midventral scales; a distinctive transverse gular fold is present. The venter of the body is covered with keeled, imbricate scales which are larger than those of the dorsum.

Adult males are brown or olive-brown with a pair of distinct yellow dorsolateral stripes extending from behind the upper temporal region to above the hind limbs. Another yellow stripe is usually present from just above the insertion of the forelimb to the inguinal region; below this stripe the ventrolateral region may be whitish, beige, or brown. The venter is pale to medium brown and often suffused with pink or red. Below the eye and auricular opening the side of the head is white and this color extends as a stripe posteriorly to above the forelimb. The limbs and proximal section of the tail often are indistinctly banded with alternating shades of brown or olive-brown. In adult females, the dorsolateral stripes are usually gray-brown or reddish brown, the ground color is yellow brown, and there are 6–7 dark brown squarish blotches on the back that extend ventrally to the dorsolateral stripes. The top of the head is olive-brown and the tail has alternating yellow-brown and darker brown bands. The throat, belly, and undersurfaces of the hind limbs are dingy white, with black flecks on the lateral portions of the belly and ventral parts of the hind limbs. Juveniles have a more vivid pattern than adults. The iris is yellow or greenish yellow darkly suffused with black, with a yellow ring around the pupil.

Natural History.—This common species can be found in tropical and subtropical wet, moist, and dry forest. It occurs in dense vegetation along the margin of practically any body of water. This lizard is quite arboreal, often to be seen in bushes and the lower branches of trees or thickets, but also spends much time on the ground. It feeds mostly on insects but is reported sometimes to feed on fallen berries. At night it often can be found sleeping in vine-covered thickets or in the open on low bushes, usually in the vicinity of water. I have noted that individuals return night after night to the same perch, usually 1–4 m above the ground. When this perch is a small shrub or tree, these lizards invariably sleep on the drooping distal portion of branches and turn to face inward toward the trunk, so that the head is higher than the body. If disturbed at their perch site, these lizards often do not return to their perches, at least for several nights. I have watched on several occasions as these lizards leave their perches. Just after first light, but before sunup, they jump abruptly from their perches to the ground, usually hitting the ground running, and dash off to the nearest cover.

When alarmed, this lizard runs on its hind legs. It escapes into dense vegetation, especially thick brush along banks and stream courses, or by running across the surface of the water to the other side of the stream. It is able to move across the water surface because of the well-developed fringes on the sides of the hind toes. Normally folded, these fringes open up as the lizard dashes across the water, giving the animal more area to support its weight with the surface tension of the water. These lizards also sometime escape by diving into the water.

Sexual maturity is reached at about 9–10 cm SVL at less than a year of age, and during the wet season it has been estimated that hatchlings may reach sexual maturity in as little as three months. Females lay 3–8 eggs from May to about August and the young hatch during the early part of the rainy season from June through September. The breeding season may sometimes be more protracted, with another peak of hatchlings in evidence in October and November. Females may lay up to three clutches of eggs during a single season. Eggs are 17 × 11 mm and weigh about 1.2 g. The average number of eggs is about four and the gestation period is 50–55 days. Hatchlings are about 4 cm in SVL.

This species falls prey to a variety of animals, including snakes (the tropical indigo snake, *Drymarchon corais*; black mussurana, *Clelia clelia*; common bluntheaded treesnake, *Imantodes cenchoa*) and birds (the great black hawk, *Buteogallus urubitinga*). It has been estimated that only about 2 percent of hatchlings survive two years. Longevity for this species in captivity is 5 years and 11 months.

Distribution.—Striped basilisks occupy the lowlands of both coasts of Mexico from southern Tamaulipas and Jalisco southward through Central America to northwestern Colombia. In Guatemala, this species is widespread, found throughout Petén practically wherever there is a water source. It occurs in mesic to dry forests from about sea level to about 1,400 m.

Remarks.—Because of this lizard's ability to run short distances over the surface of water, in certain circles it has been christened the *lagartija de Jesú Cristo*, Jesus Christ lizard. Vernacular names for it in Guatemala include *tel, taparulejo, pokmol* (lower Polochic Valley, term used for juveniles), *toloc* (lower Polochic Valley, term used for adults), *toloque rayada; pasarríos*, and *orejón*; in Belize it is known as the *cock lizard* or *cock malakka*.

Elegant Helmeted Basilisk—Traicionero Elegante
Corytophanes cristatus (Merrem, 1820)
Fig. 92

Description.—The casque in this species is triangular and supported dorsally by a projection of the parietal bone. The canthus is raised into a sharp ridge that extends as a broad arch over the eyes and then posteriorly to form the distinct raised casque; the ridges forming the posterior edges of the casque unite and continue posteriorly for a considerable distance as a vertical crest extending onto the shoulders. A low crest is present on the back topped with a single series of triangular scales that are continuous with those on the posterior margin of the crest. This lizard attains 10.5–12.5 cm in SVL and a TL of 35–39 cm; males and females show little sexual dimorphism in size, but the crest may be a bit larger in males. The limbs and tail are long and slender. The area above and in front of the auricular opening is slightly raised into an inconspicuous ridge. The dorsum and sides of the body and the sides of the crest are covered by heterogeneous, imbricate scales, most of which are flat. On the venter the keeled, imbricate scales are roughly equal in size. The upper head scales are smooth to slightly rugose and irregularly arranged. The gular region is covered with strongly keeled scales and a serrate, midventral row of enlarged scales; a distinct gular fold is present. Scales on the tail are keeled but the tail lacks any middorsal keel or crest (except sometime proximally). The ventral scales are larger than the dorsals, subequal in size, strongly keeled, and arranged in transverse series. On the limbs the large, imbricate scales are mostly keeled except on top of the thigh and on the front of the forearm.

This lizard is pale ash gray, tan, reddish brown, or green dorsally with 5–6 dark brown or black crossmarkings, which are coarsely marbled to finely mottled. Usually somewhat lichenose, the dorsal pattern may have a heavy suffusion of brown, black, green, rust, or yellow. The upper surface of each segment of the limbs is marked with 3–4 dark crossbars. There are 10–12 dark tail rings. The venter is cream or beige, usually with a few dark spots or a little mottling. Several dark bars or lines radiate away from the lower half of the orbit. The iris is copper in color.

Natural History.—This species inhabits tropical wet, moist, and dry forest and subtropical wet forest. It is usually found sitting vertically in a head-up position on small to medium-sized tree trunks at heights of 2–5 m above the ground. This lizard usually does not move when approached, depending instead on its cryptic color pattern to avoid detection; sometimes it simply moves to the far side of a trunk to hide. It is not a particularly agile species but may move quickly for short distances using a bipedal gait or sometimes in a series of awkward-appearing leaps.

When threatened by predators such as snakes, or even humans, this lizard orients its body so that one side faces the intruder, then elevates its laterally compressed body on stiffened legs, depresses the head to raise the nuchal crest, and expands the throat fan, greatly increasing the animal's apparent size. If further provoked, this lizard may bob its head or lunge forward with open mouth and even bite whatever threatens it.

Helmeted basilisks are sit-and-wait predators that feed mostly on large insects, especially orthopterans (grasshoppers, crickets, and cockroaches) and, to a lesser extent, on lepidopterans and coleopteran larvae (the presence in stomach content analyses of the latter, which live in rotten logs or beneath the surface of the ground, is not readily explainable). Studies in Costa Rica and Panama have revealed that the elegant helmeted basilisk spends most of its time immobile, occasionally making a bipedal dash on the forest floor to capture a prey item. Because of the large size of its prey, it has been estimated that a single prey item more than satisfies the daily requirements of this lizard. It therefore need not forage actively for long periods, thus exposing itself to the many lizard predators of the rainforest. The sedentary nature of this lizard in wet forest habitat is demonstrated by the fact that it is one of the few lizards on which liverworts and filamentous algae are occasionally known to grow. These plants have been found growing on the top of the head of this species and may serve as a camouflage for an already cryptically colored lizard. Adult lizards shed infrequently, but would lose the plants growing on them at the time of shedding.

A clutch consists of 5–8 eggs. When freshly laid, the leathery, oblong eggs are 20–25 mm in length, 12–14 mm in width, and 2.0–2.8 g in weight. The dimensions of eggs increase considerably before hatching, with more than a trebling of weight. In the northern part of the species' range, nesting occurs from June through November, coinciding with the rainy season. However a captive specimen from Panama, captured in August, did not lay eggs until February. Nests are usually placed in relatively open ground devoid of leaf litter and are usually about 50 mm in diameter and excavated to a depth of about 50–100 mm. It has been suggested that the casque may be employed as a scoop in nest excavation, but, if true, exactly how this is accomplished is not certain. Under captive conditions, incubation takes about five months. Juveniles are about 3–3.7 cm in SVL and 7–8 cm in TL and have been found in April. Longevity in captivity is 2 years and 5 months.

Distribution.—This lizard ranges from central Veracruz and the southern part of the Yucatán Peninsula in Mexico southward on the Atlantic versant and lowlands of Central America through northern Guatemala and Belize to Costa Rica, where it occurs on both the Atlantic and Pacific slopes into northwestern Colombia. It occurs throughout most of the forested areas in Petén, ranging in Guatemala from near sea level to about 1300 m.

Remarks.—It has been reported that this species is referred to as *piende jente* in some parts of Petén, but I have never heard this term. Other vernacular names are *turipache de selva, guardia de hacienda,* and old man (Belize). See Remarks under Giant Green Anole for discussion of the name *traicionero.*

Hernandez's Helmeted Basilisk—Traicionero de Hernandez
Corytophanes hernandezii (Wiegmann, 1831)
Fig. 93

Description.—The casque in this species is triangular and supported dorsally by a projection of the parietal bone. The canthus is raised into a sharp ridge that extends as a raised peak over the eye and then posteriorly to form the distinct raised casque; the ridges forming the posterior edges of the casque unite and curve downward almost immediately onto the neck. Large triangular scales border the upper posterior margin of the crest, but these become small on the lower posterior margin and are not continuous with the dorsal crest. This lizard attains 10–10.5 cm in SVL and a TL of 35–36.5 cm with no distinct sexual dimorphism in size. The limbs and tail are long and slender. A distinct large spine formed from the squamosal bone is present in the lower temporal region just above the tympanum. The low crest on the back is topped with a single serrate series of enlarged triangular scales extending from above the shoulders to the level of the hind limbs. The dorsum and sides of the body and the sides of the crest are covered by heterogeneous, imbricate scales; most of these are flat but scales in a few vertical series of lateral scales bear tubercular keels. On the venter the keeled, imbricate scales that are roughly equal in size. The upper head scales are slightly to moderately rugose and irregularly arranged. The gular region is covered with strongly keeled scales but there is no serrate, midventral row of enlarged scales; a distinct gular fold is present. Scales on the tail are keeled but the tail lacks any middorsal keel or crest (except sometimes proximally). The ventral scales are larger than the dorsals, subequal in size, strongly keeled, and arranged in transverse series. The limbs are covered with large, imbricate scales, that are mostly keeled except for some scales on the posterior surface of the thigh, which are smooth.

This lizard is mostly reddish brown or olive-brown. The side of the head from the eye through the tympanum is dark brown; below the side of the head the labials are white to pale orange-rust. The sides of the crest are tan to pale orange-brown. On the sides of the shoulder region there is usually a large dark blotch outlined dorsally by a thin white or yellow line in the form of an arch. A dark brown middorsal blotch is above the shoulders. The limbs and tail are brown with indistinct darker bars or markings. The throat and venter of the body are dingy white, usually suffused with orange, tan, or brown pigment. The iris is dark red-copper.

Natural History.—Associated with forested habitats, this lizard occurs in tropical wet, moist, and dry forest and in subtropical moist forest. Like other species of helmeted basilisks, this cryptically colored lizard usually sits motionless to escape detection. It often sits in leaf litter on the ground. It runs bipedally.

Females lay 3–7 eggs in May–September and have a gestation period of 67 days; eggs are usually laid in sunny places within the forest, such as an area of treefall. Eggs are about 30 × 20 mm. Juveniles have been collected from March to May in Petén. A female was observed in Veracruz, Mexico, to lay seven eggs on the ground without excavating a nest. She covered her nest with leaves using the sides of her body and head. Removed and artificially incubated at ambient temperatures, the eggs hatched in 67–70 days. The hatchlings were 3.5 cm in SVL and 9 cm in TL. Available evidence suggests that this species may lay several clutches of eggs over an extended breeding season. It has been suggested that the casque may be employed as a scoop in nest excavation.

Distribution.—Hernandez's helmeted basilisk occurs on the Atlantic slopes and lowlands from central Veracruz in Mexico southward through northern Guatemala to Belize. It is known from scattered localities in Petén, including Tikal and Uaxactún. It occurs from near sea level to about 1,300 m.

Remarks.—Other vernacular names for this lizard are *turipache de Hernandez, guardia de Hernandez,* and old man (Belize). See Remarks under Giant Green Anole for discussion of the name *traicionero.*

Smooth Casqueheaded Basilisk—Cutete Policía
Laemanctus longipes Wiegmann, 1834
Fig. 94

Description.—A flat-topped cephalic casque projects over the neck in this species. The posterior edge of this casque is smooth without projecting spines. On top of the casque, scales are rugose and unequal in size, those covering the anterior and posterior portions relatively small compared with those in the central location. This lizard is about 12–15 cm in SVL and 65–70 cm in TL. The head, limbs, and tail are slender and elongate and the body is laterally compressed. Scales in the gular area are smooth and imbricate. The transverse gular fold is complete, with 2–3 rows of granules. Dorsal scales are smooth and imbricate, except for the middorsal scale row, in which scales are keeled but not enlarged over adjacent ones; there are 34–47 scales around the midbody. Scales on the sides of the body are smaller than those on the dorsum and become weakly keeled on the lower flanks. The ventral scales are keeled and larger than the dorsals. Scales on the limbs are large, most on the forelimb are bicarinate, and most on the hind limb have either one or two keels. Scales on the tail are large, imbricate, and keeled.

The dorsum is bright green with 4–6 dark green crossbars that may be narrowly black-margined and may contain black-outlined scales on the dorsum. The green tail is distinctly marked by dark or pale bars. The top of the head is yellow-green to golden brown (darker brown in juveniles), with the posterior edge of the casque outlined in black. The sides of the head are bright yellow-green and large males often develop a striking yellow-orange head. A whitish or cream colored stripe extends from the anterior supralabials to the anterior surface of the upper forelimb, and from the axilla to the groin. The venter is pale green and the iris is yellowish brown.

In juveniles the head casque is low, and consisting of little more than a hump that does not project posteriorly. There are usually a single dark brown or black quadrangular nape blotch, four dorsal blotches on the body, and on the proximal portion of the tail a few longitudinally elongate dark blotches that become rings before the distal portion of the tail becomes mostly black. The dorsum and tail are usually yellow or yellow-green. The area from behind the upper posterior edge of the orbits along the lower black margin of the casque and across the neck is bright yellow or pale lime green. A brown marking extends from the lower posterior edge of the orbit through the auricular opening onto the neck. The venter is yellow.

Natural History.—This species occurs in tropical wet, moist, and dry forest. It spends most of its time in the canopy or trees, although specimens may sometimes be found in bushes or on the ground. This lizard seems to avoid the harsh, seasonally deciduous forest of the northern Yucatán Peninsula and inhabits areas receiving 2,000–4,000 mm of rain per year, with a relatively short dry season. When frightened, this species runs bipedally like its relative, the striped basilisk. It is insectivorous.

This species lays 3–6 eggs measuring about 23–25 × 14–16 mm in June-September, with weights of 2–3 g; these eggs hatch from July to September after incubation of about 45 days. Four eggs that I dug up at the base of a great buttressed tree on 19 June hatched in my hands upon being disturbed. Eggs also have been found buried in rotting logs and in a shallow burrows beneath tree roots. The young are 4–4.5 cm in SVL and 17.5–18.5 cm in TL.

Distribution.—The smooth casque-headed basilisk occurs in Eastern Mexico from central Veracruz southward through the southern and eastern portion of the Yucatán Peninsula into Petén and the Atlantic lowlands of Guatemala, Belize, and northwestern Honduras. It is restricted to Atlantic lowlands and foothills throughout its range, except in the Isthmus of Tehuantepec region in Mexico and in southeastern Guatemala, where it crosses over onto the Pacific versant. It occurs throughout most of the Petén and from about sea level to about 750 m.

Remarks.—The subspecies occurring in the Petén is *Laemanctus longipes deborrei*. Its vernacular name, *cutete policía,* is in allusion to the flat casque, said by some to resemble the service cap worn by Guatemalan police.

Serrate Casqueheaded Basilisk—Cutete Espinudo
Laemanctus serratus Cope, 1864
Fig. 95

Description.—In this species a flat-topped cephalic casque projects over the neck, the posterior edge of the casque distinctly serrated with large projecting triangular spines. Scales on top of the casque are strongly rugose and those covering the anterior portion from the rostral to the level of the orbits are enlarged and more or less bilaterally symmetrical. This lizard is about 12–13 cm in SVL and 44–45 cm in TL, with a maximum reported SVL of 19 cm. The limbs and tail are extremely slender and long and the body is laterally compressed. Scales in the gular area are smooth or obtusely keeled. The transverse gular fold is complete, with 4–5 rows of granules. Dorsal and lateral body scales are keeled, the lateral scales smaller than dorsals, and there are 49–62 scales around midbody. A distinctive serrate crest of large triangular scales extends from the posterior of the neck to a level a little in front of the hind limb insertion. Ventral scales are keeled and slightly larger than the dorsals. The scales covering the limbs and tail are large, imbricate, and unicarinate.

The ground color is bright lime

green, beige, or pale yellow green, and these lizards are capable of undergoing considerable overall color change from some shade of green to brown, or the reverse, in just a matter of minutes. Individuals may have one of several distinct color patterns. Some specimens have a broad brown dorsal stripe extending from the neck onto the tail and 4–5 small dark brown dorsal blotches, the interspaces between these about twice the width of the blotches themselves. The tail is green or pale brown and marked with diffuse dark-bordered dark brown rings. The top of the casque is bright green to golden brown. A white stripe extends from the supralabials to behind the angle of the jaw and below the ear to the insertion of the forelimb, where it is interrupted, but it continues from behind the axilla to the inguinal region. A pale brown or golden brown narrow lateral stripe extends from above the forearm to near the hind limb; narrow stripes of the same color extend the length of the limbs on their posterolateral surfaces, contrasting with their otherwise green coloration, and these limb stripes often merge with the lateral brown body stripe. The dorsal pattern in some specimens consists of broad dark dorsal crossbars, which are often black and sharply defined middorsally but may become diffuse laterally, and which extend laterally onto the side of the body but always fade out completely somewhere above the ventrolateral stripe; in these specimens the brown dorsal, lateral, and limb stripes

are absent. The venter is pale green and the iris is orange with a yellow ring around the pupil.

Natural History.—This species occurs in seasonally dry habitats and seems to be most abundant in the tropical dry forest of the northwestern portion of the Yucatán Peninsula. It spends most of its time in trees or shrubs and inhabits areas receiving less than 2,000 mm of rain per year and where there is a long dry season. When frightened, this lizard runs bipedally like its relative, the striped basilisk. It is known to eat insects, snails, small lizards (anoles), and frogs (*Eleutherodactylus*).

Females lay 3–7 eggs measuring about 22–23 × 12 mm in June–July; nests are usually shallow excavations near the bases of large trees. Hatchlings have been found in August and the young are 4.1–4.6 cm in SVL and 17.5–18.5 cm in TL.

Distribution.—The serrate casque-headed basilisk occurs from southern Tamaulipas, Mexico, southward through Veracruz, across the Isthmus of Tehuantepec eastward through the Río Grijalva Depression to the Guatemalan border; and from southern Campeche northward through most of the Yucatán Peninsula. It has not been recorded from Petén but is known from about 50 km to the north of this department in the Mexican state of Campeche and probably occurs in the poorly explored northern portion of Petén. In the Yucatán, it is known from elevations ranging from near sea level to about 200 m.

Remarks.—This species is easily distinguished from the smooth casqueheaded basilisk by the formation of the head casque, which in the serrate casqueheaded basilisk is rimmed by a series of thick spinelike scales, and by the distinctive serrate dorsal crest. The subspecies occurring in the Petén region is *Laemanctus serratus alticoronatus*.

SPINY LIZARDS—LAGARTIJAS ESPINUDAS

FAMILY PHRYNOSOMATIDAE

This family occurs throughout most of the United States, Mexico, and Central America to western Panama. Only a single genus within this family occurs in Petén, the spiny Lizards (*Sceloporus*). Members of this genus are typically medium-sized; they have well-developed limbs, and their backs are covered with sharply projecting imbricate scales. Femoral pores are present and the animals are diurnal, with round pupils. These lizards often display at intruders by vigorously bobbing their heads up and down. They are adept climbers and can be seen sitting on rock piles, logs, trees, and Mayan ruins. They prefer locations that receive plenty of sun. Adults, especially males, usually have a pair of brightly colored belly and throat patches, although these are absent in one species in Petén, the Yucatán spiny lizard (*Sceloporus chrysostictus*).

Yucatán Spiny Lizard—Lagartija Espinosa Yucateca
Sceloporus chrysostictus Cope, 1866
Fig. 96

Description.—In Petén, this lizard appears to be restricted to small patches of bush scattered across the savannas and to the edges of rather dry forest. It is absent from forested habitats. Adult males usually reach 50–55 mm in SVL and 120–130 mm in TL, with a maximum of about 62 mm in SVL and 170 mm in TL; females reach 48–54 mm in SVL and 115–130 mm in TL. A distinctive lateral nuchal pocket is present behind the auricular opening; there is no postfemoral dermal pocket. The dorsum and the sides of the body are covered with mucronate, keeled scales—scales ending in a sharp spine—with those on the sides being smaller than dorsal scales. Scales on the venter are slightly smaller than dorsal scales and smooth, imbricate, and rounded posteriorly; each scale usually has a pair of notches posteriorly. The posterior surface of the thigh is covered with keeled, imbricate scales. There are 42–57 dorsal scales between the interparietal and the level of the posterior margins of the hind limbs and 12–17 femoral pores on each side.

Males have bright yellow dorsolateral lines, about two scales wide, extending from the eye over the shoulder and down the side of the body onto the base of the tail. Bordering the lower edge of this yellow line is a black band that fades into brown and then buff posteriorly and ventrally. Between the dorsolateral lines is a broad brown or gray-brown median band about seven scales wide at midbody. Within this median brown band may be a series of 6–10 paired dark brown diagonal markings, forming or almost forming posteriorly directed chevrons. There is a distinctive black spot in and above the axillary region. The sides of the body are brown above and pinkish to tan below and often have yellow or orange spotting. Females often lack pale dorsolateral lines, although a vague indication of these may be present in some individuals, and have a pale to medium brown or grayish dorsum, with dark brown dorsolateral markings similar in shape to those of males but usually more distinct. In females the sides of the body are reddish and the jaws bright red, with the lower jaw more so than the upper. In males the head and lower jaw are reddish brown speckled with black. A narrow vertical black bar extends from the lower edge of the eye to the margin of the upper lip and the limbs are barred on both sexes, although usually these markings are better defined in males. The tail has 11–12 indistinct, dorsal, saddlelike blotches. The venter is uniformly white in both males and females.

Natural History.—This lizard occurs in tropical moist and dry forest. It is mostly a terrestrial species, seeking refuge in rock crevices or holes at the bases of trees, and occurs in open areas such as savannas and secondary growth. This lizard feeds mainly on insects and arachnids but is also occasionally known to eat small individuals of its own species.

Females usually lay 2–3 eggs, and occasionally 1 or 4. Gravid females have been collected almost year-round; however, they are rare during July. Egg-laying activity rises in August and September, with another peak in January and February. The small clutch size and long reproductive period of this species suggests that females may typically lay multiple clutches of eggs per season. In central Petén, hatchlings have been reported in late May, at about the time of the first heavy rains of the rainy season. Hatchlings are about 23 mm in SVL.

Distribution.—The Yucatán spiny lizard occurs from about west-central Petén, Guatemala, and west-central Belize northward through the Yucatán Peninsula. It is common in the northern portion of the peninsula, but in the southern part of its distribution it is known only from several localities in central and northern Petén and west-central Belize. This species has been found at elevations between sea level and 300 m.

Lundell's Spiny Lizard—Largartija Espinosa de Lundell
Sceloporus lundelli Smith, 1939
Fig. 97

Description.—Mainly arboreal, this lizard is found in forested areas, often on tree trunks, and has been observed more than 20 m above the ground. Individuals reach about 85–95 mm in SVL and about 200–235 mm in TL, with females attaining slightly greater lengths than males. A distinctive lateral nuchal pocket is present behind the auricular opening; there is no postfemoral dermal pocket. The dorsum and the sides of the body are covered with mucronate, keeled scales, those on the sides being smaller than dorsal scales. Scales on the venter are considerably smaller than dorsal scales and are smooth, imbricate, and pointed posteriorly, with a single apical notch. The posterior surface of the thigh is covered with keeled, imbricate scales. There are 28–34 dorsal scales between the interparietal and the level of the posterior margins of the hind limbs and 8–12 femoral pores on each side.

In adult males, the ground color is grayish or gray-brown. The dorsum may be essentially uniformly colored or there may be a pair of black shoulder spots, which are sometimes connected dorsally, and irregular dark markings across the back extending onto the sides of the body. The anterior part of the gular region is pale orange, becoming greenish blue or dark blue on the throat. The belly patches are blue and usually continuous across the chest; the midventer of the chest is dark blue or sometimes black and the chest scales may be edged with black; the sides of the belly are lavender. A dark stripe is present on the posterior surface of the thigh. Adult females are gray or gray-brown, but usually paler than males, and have 3–4 narrow, jagged black or gray markings across the back. The venter of females is whitish or pale gray and the throat is dingy white, with faint barring sometimes evident.

Natural History.—This lizard inhabits tropical moist and dry forest. It tends to be wary and when acosted on or near the ground, usually ascending high into a tree to escape. This species may be viviparous.

✔*Distribution.*—Lundell's spiny lizard occurs from near the Laguna de Términos northward through western Campeche, Mexico, and across the northern portion of the state of Yucatán to the Quintana Roo border; a disjunct population occurs in east-central Petén and west-central Belize. This lizard is common in the northern portion of the Yucatán Peninsula, but not in Petén, where it is known only from several northern localities, including Uaxactún and Tikal. It is known from elevations between sea level and 300 m.

Remarks.—The subspecies in Petén is *Sceloporus lundelli lundelli;* another subspecies, *S. l. gaigeae,* occurs in the northern part of the Yucatán Peninsula.

Blue-Spotted Spiny Lizard—Largartija Espinosa de Puntos Azules
Sceloporus serrifer Cope, 1866
Fig. 98

Description.—This lizard is common in the northern portion of the Yucatán Peninsula but in Petén is known only from several central localities, including Uaxactún and Zotz. Adults usually reach 80–95 mm in SVL and 210–250 mm in TL. A distinctive lateral nuchal pocket is present behind the auricular opening; there is no postfemoral dermal pocket. The dorsal and lateral body scales are mucronate and keeled with lateral and dorsal scales about the same size. The ventral scales are smaller than the dorsals and they are smooth, imbricate, and pointed posteriorly, with one or several posterior notches. The posterior surface of the thigh is covered with imbricate, keeled scales. There are 28–34 dorsal scales between the interparietal and the level of the posterior margins of the hind limbs and 8–14 femoral pores on each side.

Ground color is gray or gray-brown, with females often darker than males. Both sexes have a conspicuous black nuchal collar, which is bordered anteriorly and posteriorly by white bands that may be interrupted medially. In females, this collar extends ventrally only to the shoulder, but in males it extends uninterrupted across the throat. The dorsum of males often is essentially uniformly colored, but in females there are about four broad transverse bands, each bordered posteriorly by narrow pale gray or blue edging. In both sexes, the keels of many of the dorsal scales are more heavily pigmented than the rest of the scale, giving a streaked effect. The top of the head in both sexes is dark brown or black, usually boldly marked with yellow or blue spots. A distinctive crescent-shaped pale marking extends from the posterior corner of the eye to over the temporal region. Many of the posterior dorsal scales on the body and tail are marked with blue. The throat of males is pale lavender-blue medially and pink laterally. Males also have pale blue belly patches that are broadly bordered with black medially and separated from one another by a narrow white band. The tail is distinctly banded with white and black in juveniles and females; in adult males this banding pattern is less conspicuous. Juveniles have brilliant yellow and black spots and bars on the crown of the head.

Natural History.—Although it tends to be more terrestrial than Lundell's spiny lizard, the blue-spotted spiny lizard has been found on abandoned thatch-roofed huts in clearings and on the trunks of large trees. Extremely wary, it readily climbs to escape. It is thought to be viviparous. Neonates have been found about mid-May, just before the beginning of the rainy season in late May.

Distribution.—This lizard occurs from Tamaulipas, Mexico, southward to the Yucatán Peninsula, central Guatemala, and central Belize. Populations in Petén and Belize are disjunct from other populations to the north. This species, as presently recognized, occurs at elevations from near sea level to 2,300 m.

Remarks.—Populations in Petén and Belize have been assigned to several different subspecies; the systematics of this group are in need of study.

Rosebellied Spiny Lizard—Lagartija Espinosa Panza Rosada
Sceloporus teapensis Günther, 1890
Fig. 99

Description.—This is one of the most common and widespread lizards wherever it occurs. Despite its common name, the belly patches of adult males usually tend to be lavender rather than pink. Adults usually reach 50–60 mm in SVL and 130–150 mm in TL, with males attaining a greater size than females. A lateral nuchal pocket is present behind and a little below the auricular opening. A postfemoral dermal pocket is characteristic of this species. The dorsal and lateral body scales are mucronate and keeled with lateral scales smaller than dorsal scales. The scales covering the venter are smaller than the dorsal scales and they are smooth, imbricate, and pointed posteriorly with one to several notches. The posterior surface of the thigh is covered with small, granular scales. There are 36–49 dorsal scales between the interparietal and the level of the posterior margins of the hind limbs and 9–15 femoral pores on each side.

Males have a pair of dorsolateral stripes that extend from above the ear to above the hind limb and onto the proximal part of the tail. The dorsum between the dorsolateral stripes is brown, often with pale or dark spots. The sides of the body are brown and punctated with yellow spots. The belly patches are lavender with dark blue or black medial borders. In females, dorsolateral stripes are vague or absent, there are 9–10 pairs of dark brown spots on the dorsum, the sides of the head are bright reddish orange, and the belly is uniformly whitish. Both sexes have a black patch above the axillary region that contains a vertical yellow streak above the fore limbs. The limbs are brown, usually marked with small dark brown markings.

Natural History.—This species is usually found on or near the gound, basking on rocks or at the bases of trees. I have frequently seen it on Mayan ruins, including near the top of the some of the higher temples.

Most species of spiny lizards are heavily parasitized by mites, which in some instances may cause physical damage to the lizard. In the rosebellied spiny lizard, the lateral nuchal and postfemoral dermal pockets are usually packed with mites. It has been suggested that in this species, which is mostly terrestrial and perhaps more susceptible to heavy mite infestation, the postfemoral pocket has developed to keep mites away from more vulnerable areas such as the ears, vent, and head. The diet of these lizards is mainly insects, especially orthopterans, lepidopterans and their larvae, homopterans, and coleopterans.

Females lay 3–5 eggs over a prolonged breeding season. I have seen hatchlings from July to September and also in December. Adult females probably produce multiple clutches during a breeding season.

✔*Distribution.*—Rosebellied spiny lizards occur from southern Veracruz, Mexico, through about the southern half of the Yucatán Peninsula, including northern Guatemala and Belize. They are encountered in open sunny areas and are relatively common on the Mayan edifices of Tikal, Uaxactún, and elsewhere. They are also common in the savanna, southern, and central portions of Petén, ranging from near sea level to about 1,300 m.

Remarks.—This species sometimes has been considered to be the same as *Sceloporus variabilis*.

Snake and Lizard Tails.—Lizards and snakes are preyed upon by many different species of birds, mammals, other reptiles, and even some invertebrates. Therefore, it is not surprising that a variety of antipredator mechanisms have evolved in reptiles. One mechanism frequently employed among lizards is tail autotomy—shedding the tail. The efficacy of this evolutionary strategy was made evident to me recently when several colleagues and I were searching for reptiles in the poorly explored Sierra de Los Cuchumatanes of northwestern Guatemala. After a brutal day of collecting at an elevation of almost 3,000 m, one member of our party returned with nothing but a sheepish grin on his face and a lizard tail in his collecting bag.

An examination of the tail, which was over 100 mm in length and elegantly marked with green and black, revealed that it belonged to a member of a group on which Darrel Frost and I had recently written a monograph (arboreal alligator lizards, genus *Abronia*). It was obvious that the tail belonged to a species never before described by a biologist—that it represented a species new to science. How frustrating! The owner of the tail still lurked in the forest and the exact identity of this wonderful beast remained unknown to us. It had outmaneuvered us with an old lizard trick. The tail, however, was sufficient to motivate further efforts, and after two days of intense searching we were able to secure five more specimens, complete with body and tail. In several of these lizards the tail had been regenerated (this lizard did indeed represent an unknown species, a geographical relic occupying a single mountainside, so far as we know).

In many lizards and some salamanders that are easily able to shed their tails when attacked by predators, the tail continues to writhe after it is broken off, often for several minutes. Not only does this adaptation allow a lizard to break loose from a predator; the wriggling, detached tail often distracts a predator, which may proceed to eat it while the lizard makes its escape. Tail loss can hardly be considered completely beneficial to the lizard, but it is decidedly better than the alternative.

A cost in losing the tail is that this is one of the places lizards often store fat. Members of the gecko and skink families are especially noteworthy in this regard. These reserves are important in maintaining the animal through harsh, nonfeeding periods, such as most of the dry season. The loss of its tail may affect not only survival of the individual but also its future reproductive success. The lizard will eventually grow a new tail, but the replacement is not quite the same as the original, being a little shorter, usually of a slightly different color, having a different scale arrangement, and lacking caudal vertebrae. The new tail is also capable of autotomy and some lizards may lose their tails multiple times over the course of their lives. Many species of lizards frequently have broken tails; sometimes the majority of individuals in certain populations have regenerated tails, which is often accepted as an indicator of the effectiveness of this mechanism.

The place where the tail breaks varies among species. In many lizards the tail breaks intravertebrally, and a specialized fracture plane runs through most of the individual caudal vertebrae. The intravertebral fracture plane coincides with the primary segmentation of the body and thus separates adjacent muscle segments of the tail. Many lizards also have particularly fragile skin between caudal whorls of scales that further facilitates breakage. In lizards having intravertebral breakage, the ability to autotomize the tail is often highly developed, as is the ability to regenerate the tail. The term tail autotomy is probably best restricted to those species having intravertebral breakage and neural control over the event: in other words, they are able to break their own tails when they are restrained. In other species of lizards, breakage occurs intervertebrally; that is, between adjacent caudal vertebrae. Where this kind of breakage occurs, the ability to regenerate the tail is not as well developed and the amount of postbreakage tail thrashing is considerably diminished.

Many groups of lizards occurring in Petén have the capability to autotomize their tails freely, including the geckos, night lizards, anoles, spiny lizards, skinks, ameivas and whiptails, and alligator lizards. Some terrestrial species of lizards use their tails in locomotion and experiments have shown that their speed may be reduced after losing their tails (e.g., skinks). In arboreal species, the tail seems to act as a balancer and loss of this organ significantly diminishes their agility across leaves and branches. Some lizards, such as iguanas, are able to shed their tails but not easily. Observations on basilisk lizards have shown that they are unable to run bipedally, their usual method of escape, after losing only the distal third of the tail. Not surprisingly, these lizards and their close relatives also do not have tails that break easily, especially in adults.

Snakes have many of the same problems as lizards and form an important part of the diet of many predators. Few snakes employ tail breakage as an antipredator mechanism and no snake is able to regenerate its tail once this is broken off, but it is now recognized that several long-tailed species have fragile tails that they readily give up when restrained by predators. Among the species of snakes that are frequently encountered with blunt tails are the white-lipped spotbelly snake *(Coniophanes fissidens)*, two racers *(Dendrophidion vinitor and Drymobius margaritiferus)*, the long-tailed false coral *(Pliocercus elapoides)*, the striped forest snake *(Rhadinaea decorata)*, and the half coral snake *(Scaphiodontophis annulatus)*.

The most thorough study of this phenomenon in snakes was undertaken on the white-lipped spotbelly snake as a thesis project by Joe Mendelson while he was a graduate student at the University of Texas at Arlington. He confirmed that the tails of these snakes are not as specialized as lizard tails and their caudal vertebrae do not have fracture planes, but at least some species of snakes have tails that wriggle on becoming detached. Frequency of tail breakage in *Coniophanes fissidens* varied among populations and age classes and between sexes, but there were no consistent trends. It has been suggested that snakes may have specific zones of weakness in their tails and that long-tailed species may benefit because of potential multiple breaks (and, thus, multiple escapes) over a lifetime. Joe found that in *C. fissidens* the tail was not broken consistently at any particular site and he found no evidence for a significant number of multiple breaks for individual snakes.

The half coral snake proportionally has the longest tail of any terrestrial snake in Petén; it represents almost half of the snake's total length. Most adults have lost at least a portion of their tail. In contrast to the indications for the white-lipped spotbelly snake, several authors have suggested that the half coral snake is an example of a species that commonly may undergo multiple tail breaks during its lifetime.

Skinks—Salamanquezas

Family Scincidae

This family occurs worldwide in tropical and temperate habitats. Most skinks have smooth, shiny, cycloid scales that are mostly subequal in size and underlain by bony osteoderms. Limbs are present in all of the Guatemalan species but are small and relatively short. Femoral pores are absent. All Guatemalan species of skinks are oviparous except for *Mabuya*, which gives birth to live young. Skink species inhabiting Petén are brown, tan, yellow, or black, and usually have some striping on the sides. They are small to moderate-sized, diurnal lizards with round pupils.

Schwartze's Skink—Salamanqueza de Schwartze
Eumeces schwartzei Fischer, 1885
Figs. 100–101

Description.—This large skink attains 110–125 mm in SVL and a TL of 250–300 mm; the tails of adults are usually regenerated. The head is scarcely wider than the neck, the body is robust and somewhat cylindrical, and the limbs are short and fail to meet when adpressed. The scales on top of the head are large, smooth, and platelike. There is a paired series of broad scales on the neck, becoming a single series of broad scales on the dorsum; scales on the middorsum are 2–3 times wider than adjacent dorsal scales. Other scales on the dorsum, sides, and venter of the body are smooth, imbricate, cycloid, and (except for the enlarged dorsals) subequal in size; a single row of enlarged scales is on the midventer of the tail. There are 21 scales around midbody.

The head and neck are dark brown with a pair of yellowish to tan stripes extending from the rostral over the top of the eye and through the parietal region and dorsolateral part of the neck on the anterior part of the body where they merge; the dorsum of the body is mostly beige or tan with many small squarish or quadrangular dark brown spots that sometimes form an irregular checkerboard pattern. A white stripe extends along the upper lip; the lower lip is white, barred with dark brown. The sides of the body are dark brown punctated with small white spots. The tail has many narrow, alternating tan and dark brown crossbars; the dark brown crossbars are often broken up into transverse series of quadrangular spots. The venter of the head, body, and tail is beige or cream.

Natural History.—This lizard inhabits tropical moist and dry forest. It is often found in sun spots in the forest as it basks in the leaf litter or on large logs.

Snake predators on this species include the tropical indigo snake (*Drymarchon corais*), the half coral snake (*Scaphiodontophis annulatus*), and the variable coral snake (*Micrurus diastema*). Schwartze's skink probably lays eggs.

Distribution.—It occurs from the northern shore of Lago de Izabal northward through northern Guatemala and Belize and the northern portion of the Yucatán Peninsula. This lizard is found throughout most of Petén and the Yucatán Peninsula, from near sea level to about 300 m.

Sumichrast's Skink—Salamanqueza de Sumichrast
Eumeces sumichrasti (Cope, 1866)
Figs. 102–103

Description.—This large skink attains 90–100 mm in SVL and a TL of 240–270 mm. The head is about as wide as the neck, the body is robust and somewhat cylindrical, and the adpressed limbs just barely touch, if at all. The scales on top of the head are large, flat, and platelike. The scales covering the dorsum, sides, and venter are smooth, imbricate, subequal in size, and cycloid; a series of enlarged midventral scales is present on the tail. There are 26–30 scales around midbody.

The dorsum from the head onto the tail is a medium to reddish brown. A blackish lateral band extends from the posterior edge of the eye above the insertion of the forearm along the side of body and onto the tail; anteriorly this band is usually diffuse, amounting to little more than black-edged scales.

Below the black lateral stripe, the body is beige fading to a yellowish beige or cream color more ventrolaterally, many of the scales in this region having black spots. The venter of the head and neck are yellowish or cream, the body is grayish yellow or pale blue-gray, and the tail is pinkish, brownish gray, or orange.

Juveniles are mostly black or very dark brown with pale lateral, dorsolateral, and middorsal stripes that extend the length of the body onto the proximal portion of the tail. These stripes are whitish or cream on the head and neck but become blue or blue-gray on the body and bright blue on the tail. The lateral stripe begins on the rostral and extends posteriorly below the auricular opening; the dorsolateral stripe extends from the rostral to a point in front of and above the eye, where it bifurcates, with one fork continuing above the eye as the dorsolateral stripe and the other directed posteromedially, where it unites on the posterior part of the frontal area with its sister stripe from the other side of the head and continues as the middorsal stripe. Most of the tail is bright blue. The undersurface of the head and neck is whitish or cream; the venter is blue-gray.

Natural History.—Sumichrast's skink inhabits tropical wet, moist, and dry forest and subtropical wet forest. I have found adults most frequently at about midmorning by searching in the patches of sunlight that penetrate primary forest to the forest floor and also on the horizontal trunks of large fallen trees; juveniles are sometimes common along the edges of clearings. This species feeds mostly on insects and occasionally on small lizards. It lays eggs in March, April, and May, with 10 to 13 eggs in an individual clutch. In Belize an adult female, along with what were presumed to be her eggs, was encountered in a tree cavity about 20 m above the ground. The average measurement of the eggs was 15 × 11 mm, and each weighed less than a gram. Four hatchlings from the eggs averaged 26 mm in SVL, 70 mm in TL, and 0.67 g.

Distribution.—This lizard occurs from central Veracruz, Mexico, through northern Guatemala and Belize to Honduras, with an isolated population in the northeastern Yucatán Peninsula. It is found in the southern and central portions of Petén and ranges from near sea level to about 900 m.

Remarks.—Another vernacular name for this species is *eumeces listado*.

Viviparous Skink—Salamanqueza Vivípara
Mabuya brachypoda Taylor, 1956
Fig. 104

Description.—This skink reaches about 68–90 mm in SVL and 160–220 mm in TL, with females attaining a greater body size than males. The body is robust and somewhat cylindrical, with short forelimbs and hind limbs that do not touch when adpressed. The head is covered with large, flat, plate-like scales. The central portion of the lower eyelid is covered with a large translucent scale. It has been suggested that this "window" allows this lizard to see even with its eyes closed. The dorsal, lateral, and ventral body scales are smooth and shiny, subequal in size, imbricate, and cycloid. Scales in the midventral series on the tail are not enlarged over adjacent scales. There are 28–32 scale at midbody.

The body is medium brown with dark brown lateral stripes, about 1–1.5 scales wide at midbody, extending from the snout through the eyes onto the shoulders and onto the sides to above the hind limbs. This dark stripe is bordered below by a white stripe, less than a scale wide at midbody, that extends from the supralabials below the auricular opening and just over the insertion of the forelimb and then onto the body to the level of the hind limb. Both the dark and white lateral stripes may be bordered by small dark dashes. The dorsal area between dark lateral stripes is usually unicolored, but some specimens have scattered small dark spots. The venter is whitish to pale ash gray. The pattern of juveniles is similar to that of adults, but juveniles show more color contrast and a pale tan stripe is sometime present *above* the dark lateral stripe.

Natural History.—This lizard inhabits tropical moist and dry forest and subtropical moist forest. It lives mostly on the ground but readily climbs and is often seen sunning on tree trunks, fence posts, or the lower limbs of trees. Almost invariably, the lizard is near dense piles of rubbish, logs, or thick vegetation into which it can escape if disturbed, but it seems to prefer relatively dry microhabitats. This lizard is often around human habitations, some-time even in the thatch of roofs. It is primarily insectivorous.

Females reach sexual maturity at about 60 mm SVL. They give birth to 4–9 live young in May–August. Although I have never observed the phenomenon, it is reported that the female stays with her young for at least a few days after giving birth and that she and her young may bask together.

Distribution.—The viviparous skink is distributed from central Mexico through most of the Yucatán Peninsula and Central America into South America. It occurs throughout most of Petén and Belize. In Guatemala, this species occurs from near sea level to about 910 m.

Remarks.—The species of *Mabuya* inhabiting Petén has sometimes been considered to be *Mabuya unimarginata*. This harmless little lizard is thought by some persons in Petén to be venomous. Other vernacular names include *lagartija lisa* and snake waiting boy (Belize).

Brown Forest Skink—Salamanqueza Parda
Sphenomorphus cherriei (Cope, 1893)
Fig. 105

Description.—Adults reach a length of about 50–60 mm in SVL and 140–165 mm in TL in those individuals that have not had their tail broken off. The scales on top of the head are large, flat and platelike. The central portion of the lower eyelid is covered with a large translucent scale. The head is scarcely distinct from the neck, the body is robust and some-what cylindrical, and the relative length of the limbs is variable. The adpressed limbs of juveniles and many females usually meet or overlap slightly, whereas in adult males and large females, adpressed limbs may narrowly approach each other but do not overlap. The scales on the dorsum, sides, and venter of the body are smooth, imbricate, subequal in size, and cycloid. There are usually 26–34 scales at midbody.

This little lizard has a mostly pale to dark brown dorsum, with a dull bluish gray or dark brown tail in adults. There is a dark brown stripe that usually begins on the side of the head, extending through the posterior edge of the eye, above the auricular opening, and onto the side of the body, becoming diffuse about halfway between the levels of the axilla and groin in paler specimens; in dark individuals this dark lateral stripe merges with the dark coloration on the sides. Small whitish or yellowish dots occur on the side of the neck, above the insertion of the forelimb, and on the flanks below this dark lateral stripe as well as on the upper surfaces of the limbs. The dorsal field between the dark lateral stripes is usually spotted or streaked with dark brown in pale specimens and lightly spotted with tan scales in darker individuals. The venter is cream, often with a suffusion of pink or salmon.

Natural History.—This lizard occurs in tropical wet, moist, and dry forest and subtropical wet and moist forest. It is most active about midmorning and becomes scarce during the midday heat. A lizard of the forest floor, usually seen as it rustles through and quickly disappears in leaflitter, this species is seen infrequently during the dry season but is one of the more commonly observed of forest floor lizards once the rainy season begins. Its tail readily autotomizes. The diet mainly comprises small arthropods.

Females become reproductively mature at about 44 mm SVL. They are known to lay 1–4 eggs (usually 2) about 14–15 mm in length in shallow depressions under the leaflitter or in rotten logs. The peak of the reproductive season appears to be during June–July, but reproduction at a reduced level may extend over most of the year. Hatchlings are about 21–23 mm in SVL and reach maturity in 7–8 months.

Snake predators of this common leaflitter inhabitant include the white-lipped spotbelly snake (*Coniophanes fissidens*), the half coral snake (*Scaphiodontophis annulatus*), and the variable coral snake (*Micrurus diastema*).

Distribution.—The brown forest skink occurs on the Atlantic versant from Tabasco and northern Chiapas, Mexico, through Central America to Panama, and on the Pacific watershed of Nicaragua, Costa Rica, and Panama. It is found throughout most of Petén and there is an isolated population in the northern part of the Yucatán Peninsula. In Guatemala, this species ranges from near sea level to about 1,300 m.

Remarks.—Other vernacular names include *escincela parda* and *galliwasp* (Belize). Two subpecies are recognized in Petén: *Sphenomorphus cherriei cherriei* in about the southern half of the department, and *S. c. ixbaac* in the north.

Ameivas and Whiptails—Ameivas y Murishcas

Family Teiidae

This family is widespread in tropical and temperate New World habitats and is distributed from the United States southward through Mexico and Central America into temperate south South America; the family is also present in the West Indies. Ameivas and whiptails are moderate-sized lizards that have an elongate and pointed snout; a head distinct from the neck; large, flat platelike scales on the head; tiny, granular scales on the dorsum; and large, quadrangular scales on the venter. The limbs are well developed, and these lizards are diurnal, terrestrial, and quick. The long, slender tail is covered by whorls of scales that are keeled except for those on the venter, which are smooth. Femoral pores are present. All Guatemalan species of teiids are oviparous and at least one species occurring in Petén is parthenogenetic (see "Virgin Birth," page 177).

Species of teiids inhabiting Petén have pointed snouts and long, slender tails, subcircular pupils, and femoral pores. They are usually striped with various shades of brown, tan, yellow, or black, and may have some bright blue barring or mottling on the sides. The venters of males in breeding condition may be bright reddish, pinkish, or blue.

It is possible that the diminutive *Gymnophthalmus speciosus* occurs in Petén, but I am not aware of confirmed records for this department, although it is known from adjacent northern Belize and Chiapas, Mexico. The body of this lizard is covered with large, shiny scales, and only four digits are present on each hand. *Gymnophthalmus speciosus* is a member of a group of lizards often placed in their own family, the Gymnophthalmidae, apart from the Teiidae.

Chaitzam's Ameiva—Ameiva de Chaitzam
Ameiva chaitzami Stuart, 1942

Description.—Adults are 75–85 mm in SVL and have a TL of about 220 mm, with males larger than females. The interparietal is sometimes divided longitudinally and there are two parietal and two frontoparietal scales, producing a total of six scales in the parietal region. The dorsum and sides of the body are covered with tiny granular scales that are raised and tubercular;

the venter is covered with large rectangular scales. The median enlarged gulars grade into the surrounding subequal granules, one row of enlarged upper antebrachials is present, and there usually are eight longitudinal rows of ventral scales. There are two complete transverse gular folds with 2–3 rows of enlarged, irregularly arranged mesoptychial scales that are distinctly set off from the surrounding granular scales.

The top of the head and dorsum is olive-brown or gray-brown and a yellow-green dorsolateral stripe extends from the posterior of the eye down the body and onto about the proximal one-third of the tail. This lateral stripe is usually bordered above and below by irregular black bands. A pale yellow or white ventrolateral stripe extends posteriorly from the auricular opening and continues onto the groin; this stripe may be broken into a series of spots in the axillary region and is interrupted by the insertions of the fore and hind limbs. Below this pale stripe, in the ventrolateral region, the body is black with a few irregular, vertical greenish bars. The limbs are olive-brown above with black and greenish mottling. Anterior surfaces of the thighs are black with greenish spots. The sides of the head are bluish with black mottling. Brown above, the tail has a dorsal black stripe that is often discontinuous; laterally the proximal part of the tail is marked with the continuation of pale body stripes, and below the tail is brownish white. The venter is bluish, becoming especially dark on the abdomen.

Natural History.—Chaitzam's ameiva is known from the pine savannas of southeastern Petén. A female 66 mm in SVL contained well formed eggs in April.

Distribution.—This lizard is known from several widely separated areas, including the upper Río Grijalva valley in eastern Chiapas (Mexico) and western Guatemala, east-central Alta Verapaz, and near Poptun in southeastern Petén. It occurs from about 400 to 1,350 m.

Festive Ameiva—Ameiva de Fiesta
Ameiva festiva (Lichtenstein, 1856)
Fig. 106

Description.—Adults are about 85–130 mm in SVL and have a TL of about 270–430 mm, with males larger than females. The interparietal is usually single and there are two parietal and two frontoparietal scales, producing a total of five scales in the parietal region. The dorsum and sides of the body are covered with tiny granular scales that are mostly keeled or pointed except on the lower flanks, where they are rounded. The venter is covered with large, flat rectangular scales. The median gulars are large and abruptly differentiated from the surrounding tiny granules. There is a single row of enlarged upper antebrachials and longitudinal rows of ventral scales usually number eight. There are two complete gular folds with a single large series of mesoptychial scales distinctly set off from the surrounding granular scales.

The color pattern is highly variable and subject to sexual and ontogenetic variation. Adult males may have a bluish, reddish orange, coppery, or yellowish gular area and chest; a pale blue medial portion of the belly; and laterally the belly may be pale blue with black blotches. The middorsum is brown or gray-brown and often has a pale, wavy, yellow or tan vertebral stripe, which may be vague in older specimens; dorsolaterally there is a broad dark brown to black band bordered above and below by narrow, broken, yellow stripes; and ventrolaterally the body is brown or olive-brown with narrow yellow bars. In adult females, the venter is a pale bronze or pinkish and the pale vertebral stripe is more evident. The palmar and plantar surfaces of the feet are pinkish in adults. Juveniles have brightly colored yellow or blue-green vertebral stripes, bright yellow dorsolateral and ventrolateral stripes, and bright blue tails.

Natural History.—This species inhabits tropical or subtropical wet and moist forest. It is widespread and may be found in virgin forest or in secondary forest near human habitations. Although it occurs from very humid forests to the semiarid interior valleys of Central Guatemala, it appears to be absent from the savanna region around La Libertad. In dry areas, it is mostly restricted to habitats along watercourses. This diurnal species becomes active as soon as the sun sufficiently warms patches of the forest floor. Individuals are often seen basking in these sunny spots from mid- to late morning; once the sun becomes too hot, usually by about noon, they disappear into shady retreats to wait for the more subdued sun of the later afternoon, at which time they again become active.

I have found this lizard most often in primary forest, where it forages in the leaf litter, but it also enters secondary growth, especially along the edges of clearings.

This lizard feeds mostly on insects and other arthropods that it hunts in the leaf litter; the diet is composed mostly of crickets, spiders, roaches, and katydids. Rarely, it eats small vertebrates such as other lizards and frogs.

Females are reported to lay 2–10 eggs from May to July, but the reproductive season may extend over most of the year. Juveniles have been observed in February and March and are about 40 mm in SVL.

Distribution.—The festive ameiva occurs in southern Mexico from Tabasco and Chiapas, excluding most of the Yucatán Peninsula, through much of northern Guatemala and southern Belize southward on the Caribbean versant of Central America to Colombia, and on the Pacific versant from Costa Rica to Colombia. In Guatemala, it occurs from near sea level to about 1,020 m. This lizard is common in the southern and central portions of Petén. Although it occurs around and a little to the north of Lago Petén Itzá, I have not seen this species at Tikal.

Remarks.—The subspecies occurring in Petén is *Ameiva festiva edwardsi.*

COLOR PLATES

2

Fig. 14. Plumbeous Central American Caecilian—Tapalcua Grande de Costa *(Dermophis mexicanus)*, adult male, 318 mm TL (UTA A-25396); Finca Bandegua, near Quiriguá, Izabal, Guatemala, 100 m elevation. WWL

Fig. 15. Mountain Caecilian—Tapalcua Pequeña de Montaña *(Gymnopis syntrema)*, female, 257 mm TL (UTA A-33612); near Casco of Finca Semuc (Sierra de Santa Cruz), Izabal, Guatemala, *ca.* 500 m elevation. JAC

Fig. 16. Doflein's Salamander—Salamandra de Doflein *(Bolitoglossa dofleini)*, juvenile, 45 mm SVL, 71 mm TL (UTA A-34082); 11.6 km west-southwest of Puerto Santo Tomás (Montañas del Mico), Izabal, Guatemala, 744 m elevation. JAC

Fig. 17. Black-and-Gold Salamander—Salamandra Negridorada *(Bolitoglossa mexicana)*, adult, 70 mm SVL, 147 mm TL (UTA A-33628); Las Escobas, 5.1 km west-southwest of Puerto Santo Tomás (Montañas del Mico) Izabal, Guatemala, *ca.* 200 m elevation. JAC

Fig. 18. Müller's Salamander—Salamandra de Müller *(Bolitoglossa mulleri)*, adult, 65 mm SVL, 140 mm TL (UTA A-50475); Parque Nacional Laguna Lachuá, Alta Verapaz, Guatemala, 150 m elevation. ENS

Fig. 19. O'donnell's Salamander—Salamandra de O'donnell *(Bolitoglossa odonnelli)*, adult, 80 mm SVL, 165 mm TL (UTA A-25412); Finca Semuc (Sierra de Santa Cruz), Izabal, Guatemala, 460 m elevation. WWL

Fig. 20. Common Dwarf Salamander—Salamandra Enana Común *(Bolitoglossa rufescens)*, adult, 37 mm SVL, 66 mm TL (UTA A-45328); east of San Miguelito, along tributary of Río Bobos (Sierra de Caral), Izabal, Guatemala, *ca.* 510 m elevation. JAC

Fig. 21. White-crowned Worm Salamander—Salamandra-lombriz de Frente Blanca *(Oedipina elongata)*, adult, 62 mm SVL, 150 mm TL (UTA A-21568); *ca.* 2.5 km south of Lago de Izabal, along Río Mariscos, Izabal, Guatemala, 50 m elevation. EDB

Fig. 22. Middle American Burrowing Toad—Sapo Moi *(Rhinophrynus dorsalis)*, adult male, 59 mm SVL (UTA A-47352); La Libertad, Petén, Guatemala, 180 m elevation. JAC

Fig. 23. Alfred's Climbing Frog—Rana Trepadora de Alfred *(Eleutherodactylus alfredi)*, adult male, 27 mm SVL (UTA A-12974); 20.1 km north of Vista Hermosa, Oaxaca, Mexico, 610 m elevation. WWL

Fig. 24. Chac's Leaf-litter Frog—Rana Hojarasquera de Chac *(Eleutherodactylus chac)*, adult female, 32 mm SVL (UTA A-26198); Las Escobas, 5.1 km west-south-west of Puerto Santo Tomás (Montañas del Mico), Izabal, Guatemala, *ca.* 200 m elevation. WWL

Fig. 25. Broad-headed Leaf-litter Frog—Rana Hojarasquera de Cabeza Ancha *(Eleutherodactylus laticeps)*, adult female, 70 mm SVL (UTA A-49614); east side of Cerro 1019 (Sierra de Santa Cruz), Izabal, Guatemala, 970 m elevations. ENS

Fig. 26. Warty Forestfrog—Rana del Bosque Verrugosa *(Eleutherodactylus psephosypharus)*, holotype, adult female, 55 mm SVL (UTA A-18194); 7.8 km west-southwest of Puerto Santo Tomás (Montañas del Mico), Izabal, Guatemala, 375 m elevation. JAC

Fig. 27. Common Leaf-litter Frog—Rana Hojarasquera Común *(Eleutherodactylus rhodopis)*, adult female, *ca.* 30 mm; Estación de Biología Tropical Los Tuxtlas, Veracruz, Mexico. RCV

Fig. 28. Sanderson's Streamfrog—Rana de Riachuelo de Sanderson *(Eleutherodactylus sandersoni)*, adult female, 70 mm SVL (UTA A-33444); Finca Semuc, 1–3 km south of main ranch house (Sierra de Santa Cruz), Izabal, Guatemala, *ca.* 420 m elevation. WWL

Fig. 29. Long-legged Streamfrog—Rana de Riachuelo de Piernas Largas *(Eleutherodactylus* sp.), adult female, 62 mm SVL (UTA A-24425); Las Escobas, 5.1 km west-southwest of Puerto Santo Tomás (Montañas del Mico), Izabal, Guatemala, *ca.* 200 m elevation. JAC

Fig. 30. White-lipped Foamfrog—Ranita Espumera Labioblanco *(Leptodactylus labialis)*, adult male, 32 mm SVL (UTA A-26019); Tikal, Petén, Guatemala, 200 m elevation. WWL

Fig. 31. Fringe-toed Foamfrog—Ranita Espumera de Dedos Marginados *(Leptodactylus melanonotus)*, adult male, 36 mm SVL (UTA A-24510); Finca El Faro, 4 km north of El Palmar (south slope of Volcán Santa María), Guatemala, 875 m elevation. WWL

Fig. 32. Túngara Frog—Sapillo Túngara *(Physalaemus pustulosus)*, adult male, 24 mm SVL (UTA A-26034); 3.2 km north of Champerico, Retalhuleu, Guatemala, 20 m elevation. WWL

Fig. 33. Mottled Chirping Frog—Ranita Chirriadora Manchada *(Syrrhophus leprus)*, adult male, 23 mm SVL (UTA A-29629); west slope Río Tinajas/Río Chiquito Divide, 5.5 km (airline) south-southeast of Pueblo Viejo (Sierra de las Minas), Alta Verapaz, Guatemala, 396 m elevation. MN

Fig. 34. Campbell's Forest Toad—Sapo de Bosque de Campbell *(Bufo campbelli)*, subadult, 54 mm SVL (UTA A-18196); 11.8 km west-southwest of Puerto Santo Tomás (Montañas del Mico), Izabal, Guatemala, 744 m elevation. JAC

Fig. 35. Giant Toad—Sapo Lechero *(Bufo marinus)*, adult female, 102 mm SVL (UTA A-32999); Las Escobas, 5.1 km west-southwest of Puerto Santo Tomás (Montañas del Mico), Guatemala, 150 m elevation. JAC

Fig. 36. Gulf Coast Toad—Sapo Costero *(Bufo valliceps)*, adult male, 62 mm SVL (UTA A-47677); 16.8 km north of El Remate, Petén, Guatemala, 335 m elevation. JAC

Fig. 37. Northern Glassfrog—Ranita de Vidrio Norteña *(Hyalinobatrachium fleischmanni)*, adult male, 23 mm SVL (UTA A-44067); San Miguelito (Sierra de Caral), Izabal, Guatemala, 450 m elevation. JAC

Fig. 38. Red-eyed Leaf-frog—Rana-hoja de Ojos Rojos *(Agalychnis callidryas)*, subadult female, 43 mm SVL (UTA A-45485); San Miguelito (Sierra de Caral), Izabal, Guatemala, 450 m elevation. JAC

Fig. 39. Morelet's Leaf-frog—Rana-hoja de Montaña *(Agalychnis moreletii)*, adult male, *ca.* 50 mm SVL (UTA A-30510); Finca Chiblac, 21.7 km north-north-east of Barillas (Sierra de Los Cuchumatanes), Huehuetenango, Guatemala, 900 m elevation. EDB

Fig. 40. Bromeliad Treefrog—Rana Arborícola de Bromelia *(Hyla bromeliacia)*, adult female, 36 mm SVL (UTA A-44027); Aldea Negro Norte (Sierra de Caral), Izabal, Guatemala, 1,100 m elevation. JAC

Fig. 41. Hourglass Treefrog—Rana Arborícola Amarillenta *(Hyla ebraccata)*, adult male, 25 mm SVL (UTA A-51438); Puente Zapotón, Parque Nacional Laguna Lachuá, Alta Verapaz, Guatemala, 180 m elevation. ENS

Fig. 42. Loquacious Treefrog—Rana Arborícola Loquaz *(Hyla loquax)*, adult male, 37 mm SVL (UTA A-47786); La Libertad, Petén, Guatemala, 180 m elevation. JAC

Fig. 43. Yellow Cricket Treefrog—Rana Arborícola Grillo Amarilla *(Hyla microcephala)*, adult male, 25 mm SVL (UTA A-24635); 4.2 km west-southwest of Puerto Santo Tomás (Montañas del Mico), Izabal, Guatemala, 90 m elevation. WWL

Fig. 44. Painted Treefrog—Rana Arborícola Pintada *(Hyla picta)*, adult male, 19 mm SVL (UTA A-33501); 3.2 km west of Puerto Santo Tomás (Montañas del Mico), Izabal, Guatemala, 50 m elevation. WWL

Fig. 45. Lichenose Fringe-limbed Treefrog—Rana Arborícola Liquenosa de Patas Marginadas *(Hyla valancifer)*, adult male, 77 mm SVL (UTA A-20000); Vuelta del Quetzal, across highway from Biotopo Mario Dary Rivera (Sierra de las Minas), Baja Verapaz, Guatemala, *ca.* 1,500 m elevation. WWL

Fig. 46. Milky Treefrog—Rana Arborícola Lechosa *(Phrynohyas venulosa)*, adult male, 75 mm SVL (UTA A-38279); along highway CA-10, 7.4 km north-northwest of intersection of highways CA-10 and 21, Chiquimula, Guatemala, 370 m elevation. JAC

Fig. 47. Stauffer's Longnosed Treefrog—Rana Arborícola Trompuda de Stauffer *(Scinax staufferi)*, adult male, 27 mm SVL (UTA A-47458); Gringo Perdido, *ca.* 3.0 km W El Remate-Tikal road, on road to San José, Petén, Guatemala, 120 m elevation. JAC

Fig. 48. Baudin's Treefrog—Rana Arborícola de Baudin *(Smilisca baudinii)*, adult male, 57 mm SVL (UTA A-48127); *ca.* 1.0 km southwest of main aguada at Tikal, Petén, Guatemala, 260 m elevation. JAC

Fig. 49. Baudin's Treefrog—Rana Arborícola de Baudin *(Smilisca baudinii)*, adult male, 69 mm SVL (UTA A-49613); Chixoy, San Cristóbal Verapaz, Alta Verapaz, Guatemala, 630 m elevation. ENS

Fig. 50. Blue-spotted Treefrog—Rana Arborícola Flancos Azules *(Smilisca cyanosticta)*, adult male, 51 mm SVL (UTA A-33564); Río San Agustín, 8.8 km west-southwest of Puerto Santo Tomás (Montañas del Mico), Izabal, Guatemala, 457 m elevation. JAC

Fig. 51. Yucatán Casqueheaded Treefrog—Rana Arborícola Yucateca Cabeza de Pala *(Triprion petasatus)*, adult male, 51 mm SVL (UTA A-26016); San Francisco, Petén, Guatemala, *ca.* 200 m elevation. WWL

Fig. 52. Elegant Narrowmouthed Toad—Termitero Elegante *(Gastrophryne elegans)*, adult male, *ca.* 23 mm SVL; Laguna de Zacatal, Sierra de Los Tuxtlas, Veracruz, Mexico. RCV

Fig. 53. Sheep Toad—Termitero Balador *(Hypopachus variolosus)*, adult female, 41 mm SVL (UTA A-48424); main aguada at Tikal, Petén, Guatemala, 220 m elevation. JAC

Fig. 54. Rio Grande Leopard Frog—Rana Leopardo de Berlandier *(Rana berlandieri)*, adult male, 85 mm SVL (UTA A-47787); San Antonio, *ca.* 15 km southwest of San Benito, Petén, Guatemala, *ca.* 200 m elevation. JAC

Fig. 55. Julian's Frog—Rana de Julian *(Rana juliani)*, Doyle's Delight (16° 29' 65" N, 89° 02' 72" W), Bladen Nature Reserve, Cayo/Toledo, Belize, 1,124 m elevation. CC

Fig. 56. Masked Mountain Frog—Rana Montañera Enmascarada *(Rana maculata)*, adult female, 73 mm SVL (KU 186676); 2.0 km east-southeast of Purulhá, Baja Verapaz, Guatemala, 1,524 m elevation. JAC

Fig. 57. Vaillant's Frog—Rana de Vaillant *(Rana vaillanti)*, adult female, 90 mm SVL (UTA A-24818); Semococh, Finca Semuc (Sierra de Santa Cruz), Izabal, Guatemala, 675 m elevation. WWL

Fig. 58. Central American Common Snapping Turtle—Zambundango *(Chelydra serpentina)*, adult male, carapace length 21.5 cm (UTA R-36472); near Mariscos, in small stream flowing into Lago de Izabal, Izabal, Guatemala, 10 m elevation. JAC

Fig. 59. Narrow-bridged Musk Turtle—Chiquiguao *(Claudius angustatus)*, adult male, carapace length 14.8 cm (UTA Live Collection); near El Caoba, Petén, Guatemala, 300 m elevation. ENS

Fig. 60. Northern Giant Musk Turtle—Guao *(Staurotypus triporcatus)*, adult male, carapace length 22.5 cm (UTA R-23553); Lago Petén Itzá, Santa Elena, near Hotel Maya Internacional, Petén, Guatemala, 110 m elevation. DGB

Fig. 61. Tabasco Mud Turtle—Pochitoque de Monte *(Kinosternon acutum)*, adult female; Lerdo de Tejada, Veracruz, Mexico, 10 m elevation. RCV

Fig. 62. White-lipped Mud Turtle—Pochitoque Labio-blanco *(Kinosternon leucostomum)*, adult male, carapace length 12.2 cm (UTA R-30842); Finca Yolanda, Izabal, Guatemala, 50 m elevation. JAC

Fig. 63. Red-cheeked Mud Turtle—Pochitoque de Carrilla Roja *(Kinosternon scorpioides)*, adult male, carapace length 13.8 cm (UTA R-11410); Tapanate-pec, Oaxaca, Mexico, 122 m elevation. WWL

Fig. 64. Central American River Turtle—Tortuga Blanca *(Dermatemys mawii)*, subadult female, cara-pace length 25 cm; Lago de Izabal, near confluence of Río Polochic, Izabal, Guatemala, 10 m elevation. WWL

Fig. 65. Central American River Turtle—Tortuga Blanca *(Dermatemys mawii)*, data as for fig. 64. The skin covering the plastron has been scraped by main-taining this turtle on a cement floor of the market-place where it was purchased. WWL

Fig. 66. Mesoamerican Slider—Jicotea *(Trachemys scripta)*, adult male, carapace length 18 cm (UTA R-41202); northeast edge of Lago Petén Itzá, 1.0 km west of El Remate, Petén, Guatemala, 115 m eleva-tion. JAC

Fig. 67. Mesoamerican Slider—Jicotea *(Trachemys scripta)*, data as for fig. 66. The plastron of small specimens is yellow with an intricate pattern of lines, but it becomes dark in large adults such as the individual figured here. JAC

Fig. 68. Furrowed Wood Turtle—Mojina *(Rhinoclemmys areolata)*, adult female, carapace length 12 cm (UTA Live Collection); near San Miguel, southwestern edge of Lago Petén Itzá, Petén, Guatemala, 140 m elevation. JAC

Fig. 69. Furrowed Wood Turtle—Mojina *(Rhinoclemmys areolata)*, hatchling male, carapace length 5.5 cm (UTA Live Collection); female parent from near El Caoba, Petén, Guatemala, 400 m elevation. JAC

Fig. 70. Yucatán Banded Gecko—Escorpión Yucateco *(Coleonyx elegans)*, adult male, 68 mm SVL, 132 mm TL (UTA R-33237); Tikal, Petén, Guatemala, 250 m elevation. JAC

Fig. 71. Spotted Bark Gecko—Gequillo Collarejo *(Sphaerodactylus glaucus)*, adult male, 25 mm SVL, 44 mm TL, tail regenerated (UTA R-39915); 2.5 km west of El Remate, northeast edge of Lago Petén Itzá, Petén, Guatemala, 120 m elevation. JAC

Fig. 72. Dwarf Bark Gecko—Gequillo Pardo *(Sphaerodactylus millepunctatus)*, adult male, 30 mm SVL, 59 mm TL (UTA R-39961); Finca El Pantano, near Puerto Barrios, Izabal, Guatemala, 1 m elevation. ENS

Fig. 73. Turnip-tailed Gecko—Cuija Cola de Nabo *(Thecadactylus rapicaudus)*, adult male, 99 mm SVL (UTA R-23446); vicinity of Chiquimula, Chiquimula, Guatemala. JAC

Fig. 74. Yellow-spotted Tropical Night Lizard—Escorpión Nocturno Puntos Amarillos *(Lepidophyma flavimaculatum)*, adult female, 91 mm SVL, 171 mm TL, tail regenerated (UTA R-39663); Aldea La Libertad, Km Post 285 on road to Petén, Izabal, Guatemala, 70 m elevation. ENS

Fig. 75. Mayan Tropical Night Lizard—Escorpión Nocturno Maya *(Lepidophyma mayae)*, adult female, 54 mm SVL, 125 mm TL (UTA R-27454); Finca Chiblac (Sierra de los Cuchumatanes), Huehuetenango, Guatemala, 1,150 m elevation. EDB

Fig. 76. Becker's Short-legged Anole—Abaniquillo de Becker *(Norops beckeri)*, adult female, *ca.* 55 mm SVL; El Corral Workers' Camp, Tikal, Petén, Guatemala, 250 m elevation. JAC

Fig. 77. Giant Green Anole—Abaniquillo Verde *(Norops biporcatus)*, adult female, 84 mm SVL, 269 TL (UTA R-29747); San Miguelito (Sierra de Caral), Izabal, Guatemala, 450 m elevation. JAC

Fig. 78. Bourgeau's Anole—Abaniquillo de Bourgeau *(Norops bourgeaei)*, adult male, 60 mm SVL, 191 mm TL (UTA R-23056); Mundo Perdido Complex, Tikal, Petén, Guatemala, 250 m elevation. JAC

Fig. 79. Bourgeau's Anole—Abaniquillo de Bourgeau *(Norops bourgeaei)*, adult male, 58 mm SVL, 182 mm TL (UTA R-40119); Tikal, Petén, Guatemala, *ca.* 250 m elevation. JAC

Fig. 80. Long-legged Anole—Abaniquillo Patuda *(Norops capito)*, subadult female, 51 mm SVL, 134 mm TL (UTA R-19876); Las Escobas, 5.1 km west-southwest of Puerto Santo Tomás (Montañas del Mico), Izabal, Guatemala, *ca.* 200 m elevation. WWL

Fig. 81. Rodriguez's Anole—Abaniquillo de Rodriguez *(Norops rodriguezi)*, adult male, 40 mm SVL, 93 mm TL (UTA R-39830); Uaxactún, Petén, Guatemala, 200 m elevation. JAC

Fig. 82. Mayan Coastal Anole—Abaniquillo Costero Maya *(Norops sagrei)*, adult male, 67 mm SVL (UTA R-29794); Puerto Barrios, Izabal, Guatemala, 5 m elevation. JAC

Fig. 83. Blue-spot Anole—Abaniquillo Punto Azul *(Norops sericeus)*, adult female, 43 mm SVL (UTA R-39929); Aldea La Libertad, near Km Post 285 on road to Petén, Izabal, Guatemala, 80 m elevation. ENS

Fig. 84. Blue-spot Anole—Abaniquillo Punto Azul *(Norops sericeus)*, adult male, 50 mm SVL (UTA R-39951); Caserio Mojubal, Cuilco, Huehuetenango, Guatemala, 1,125 m elevation. ENS

Fig. 85. Greater Forest Anole—Abaniquillo Grande de Selva *(Norops tropidonotus)*, adult female, 50 mm SVL, 135 mm TL (UTA R-40606); El Remate, Petén, Guatemala, 140 m elevation. JAC

Fig. 86. Lesser Forest Anole—Abaniquillo Pequeño de Selva *(Norops uniformis)*, adult male, 40 mm SVL (UTA R-29536); 12.0 km west-southwest of Puerto Santo Tomás (Montañas del Mico), Izabal, Guatemala, 786 m elevation. JAC

Fig. 87. Lesser Forest Anole—Abaniquillo Pequeño de Selva *(Norops uniformis)*, adult male, 39 mm SVL, 93 mm TL (UTA R-15986); Las Escobas, 5.1 km west-southwest of Puerto Santo Tomás (Montañas del Mico), Izabal, Guatemala, 104 m elevation. WWL

Fig. 88. Black Iguana—Iguana Negra *(Ctenosaura similis)*, subadult female, 15 cm SVL, 48 cm TL (UTA R-29038); San Buenaventura, Chuarrancho, Guatemala, Guatemala, 480 m elevation. ENS

Fig. 89. Green Iguana—Iguana Verde *(Iguana iguana)*, juvenile, 7.3 cm SVL, 25.3 cm TL (UTA R-37870); Quebradas (Sierra de Caral), Izabal, Guatemala, 95 m elevation. JAC

Fig. 90. Striped Basilisk—Cutete Rayada *(Basiliscus vittatus)*, adult male, 12.2 cm SVL (UTA R-39686); San Antonio, *ca.* 15 km southwest of San Benito, Petén, Guatemala, 200 m elevation. JAC

Fig. 91. Striped Basilisk—Cutete Rayada *(Basiliscus vittatus)*, adult female, 12 cm SVL (UTA R-39685); El Remate, Petén, Guatemala, 120 m elevation. JAC

Fig. 92. Elegant Helmeted Basilisk—Traicionero Elegante *(Corytophanes cristatus)*, adult female, 9.6 cm SVL, 28.5 cm TL (UTA R-29016); Las Escobas, 5.1 km west-southwest of Puerto Santo Tomás (Montañas del Mico), Izabal, Guatemala, *ca.* 200 m elevation. JAC

Fig. 93. Hernandez's Helmeted Basilisk—Traicionero de Hernandez *(Corytophanes hernandezii)*, adult male, 8.9 cm SVL, 31.8 cm TL (UTA R-39633); Uaxactún, Petén, Guatemala, 180 m elevation. JAC

Fig. 94. Smooth Casqueheaded Basilisk—Cutete Policía *(Laemanctus longipes)*, adult male, 10.5 cm SVL, 52.8 cm TL (UTA R-22021); Finca Semuc (Sierra de Santa Cruz), Izabal, Guatemala, 460 m elevation. DGB

Fig. 95. Serrate Casqueheaded Basilisk—Cutete Espinudo *(Laemanctus serratus)*, adult male, 11 cm SVL, 52 cm TL (UTA R-33236); Cholul, Yucatán, Mexico, 150 m elevation. JAC

Fig. 96. Yucatán Spiny Lizard—Lagartija Espinosa Yucateca *(Sceloporus chrysostictus)*, adult male, 59 mm SVL (KU 70433); Pisté, Yucatán, Mexico, *ca.* 10 m elevation. WED

Fig. 97. Lundell's Spiny Lizard—Lagartija Espinosa de Lundell *(Sceloporus lundelli)*, adult female, 97 mm SVL (KU 70537); Pisté, Yucatán, Mexico, *ca.* 10 m elevation. WED

Fig. 98. Blue-spotted Spiny Lizard—Lagartija Espinosa de Puntos Azules *(Sceloporus serrifer)*, adult; Ruinas Oxkintok, Yucatán, Mexico. JCL

Fig. 99. Rosebellied Spiny Lizard—Lagartija Espinosa Panza Rosada *(Sceloporus teapensis)*, adult male, 60 mm SVL, 150 mm TL (UTA R-40053); San Antonio, *ca.* 15 km southwest of San Benito, Petén, Guatemala, 200 m elevation. JAC

Fig. 100. Schwartze's Skink—Salamanqueza de Schwartze *(Eumeces schwartzei)*, adult male, 102 mm SVL, 238 mm TL, tail regenerated (UTA R-41136); 2.5 km west of El Remate, northeast edge of Lago Petén Itzá, Petén, Guatemala, 140 m elevation. JAC

Fig. 101. Schwartze's Skink—Salamanqueza de Schwartze *(Eumeces schwartzei)*, data as for fig. 100. JAC

Fig. 102. Sumichrast's Skink—Salamanqueza de Sumichrast *(Eumeces sumichrasti)*, adult female, 100 mm SVL (UTA R-37455); San Miguelito (Sierra de Caral), Izabal, Guatemala, 480 m elevation. JAC

Fig. 103. Sumichrast's Skink—Salamanqueza de Sumichrast *(Eumeces sumichrasti)*, data as for fig. 102. JAC

Fig. 104. Viviparous Skink—Salamanqueza Vivípara *(Mabuya brachypoda)*, adult male, 75 mm SVL, 212 mm TL (UTA R-39636); El Remate, Petén, Guatemala, 140 m elevation. JAC

Fig. 105. Brown Forest Skink—Salamanqueza Parda *(Sphenomorphus cherriei)*, adult male, 58 mm SVL (UTA R-29842); 11.6 km west-southwest of Puerto Santo Tomás (Montañas del Mico), Izabal, Guatemala, 744 m elevation. JAC

Fig. 106. Festive Ameiva—Ameiva de Fiesta *(Ameiva festiva)*, subadult male, 50 mm SVL, 157 mm TL (UTA R-19742); Las Escobas, 5.1 km west-southwest of Puerto Santo Tomás, Izabal, Guatemala, *ca.* 200 m elevation. WWL

Fig. 107. Metallic Ameiva—Ameiva Metálica *(Ameiva undulata)*, adult male, 130 mm SVL (UTA R-39854); northeast edge of Lago Petén Itzá, Petén, Guatemala, 120 m elevation. JAC

Fig. 108. Metallic Ameiva—Ameiva Metálica *(Ameiva undulata)*, subadult female, 75 mm SVL, 242 mm TL (UTA R-39851); El Remate, Petén, Guatemala, 120 m elevation. JAC

Fig. 109. Yucatán Whiptail—Murishca Yucateca *(Cnemidophorus angusticeps)*, adult; Cobá, Quintana Roo, Mexico. JCL

Fig. 110. Maslin's Whiptail—Murishca de Maslin *(Cnemidophorus maslini)*, juvenile, 33 mm SVL, 96 mm TL (UTA R-41196); near El Remate, Petén, Guatemala, 140 m elevation. JAC

Fig. 111. Rozella's Canopy Lizard—Salamanqueza de Rozella *(Diploglossus rozellae)*, adult male, 83 mm SVL, 212 mm TL (UTA R-41138); Gringo Perdido, *ca.* 3.0 km west of El Remate–Tikal road, on road to San José, Petén, Guatemala, 120 m elevation. JAC

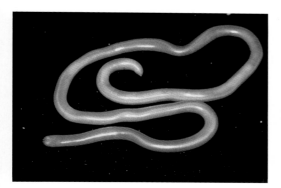

Fig. 112. Yucatán Blind Snake—Culebrilla Ciega Yucateca *(Typhlops microstomus)*, adult female, 327 mm TL (KU 70816); Pisté, Yucatán, Mexico, 10 m elevation. WED

Fig. 113. Goudot's Thread Snake—Culebrilla Hilo de Goudot *(Leptotyphlops goudotii)*, adult female, 118 mm TL (UTA R-30282); Huité, Zacapa, Guatemala. JAC

Fig. 114. Boa Constrictor—Mazacuata *(Boa constrictor)*, adult female, *ca.* 150 cm TL (KU 190885); 13.3 km west-southwest of Puerto Santo Tomás (Montañas del Mico), Izabal, Guatemala, 945 m elevation. JAC

Fig. 115. Annulated Boa—Boa Anillada *(Corallus annulatus)*, adult female, 172.5 cm TL (UTA R-38864); Quebrada El Branchi, Izabal, Guatemala, 45 m elevation. ENS

Fig. 116. Four-lined Middle American Earth Snake—Busca-lombriz Rayada *(Adelphicos quadrivirgatus),* subadult female, 22.6 cm SVL, 23.9 cm TL, tail incomplete (UTA R-37408); Aldea Negro Norte (Sierra de Caral), Izabal, Guatemala, 1,100 m elevation. JAC

Fig. 117. Rufous-headed Snake—Culebra Cabeza Colorada *(Amastridium veliferum),* subadult female, 28.6 cm TL (UTA R-20683); 5.5 km west-southwest of Puerto Santo Tomás (Montañas del Mico), Izabal, Guatemala, 350 m elevation. JAC

Fig. 118. Black Mussurana—Mata Culebra *(Clelia clelia),* adult female, 234 cm TL (UTA R-22253); Finca Semuc (Sierra de Santa Cruz), Izabal, Guatemala, 460 m elevation. WWL

Fig. 119. Southern Racer—Zumbadora Olivácea *(Coluber constrictor),* adult female, near Brownsville, Cameron, Texas, *ca.* 20 m elevation. JEW

Fig. 120. Mottled-jaw Spotbelly Snake—Culebra Vientre-punteado Labiomoteado *(Coniophanes bipunctatus),* adult female, 77.9 cm TL (UTA R-29848); El Chupón (Lago de Izabal), near El Estor, Izabal, Guatemala, 2 m elevation. JAC

Fig. 121. White-lipped Spotbelly Snake—Culebra Vientre-punteado Labioblanco *(Coniophanes fissidens),* subadult female, 23.5 cm SVL, 30.3 cm TL (UTA R-39152); on trail between La Firmeza and Cerro Pozo de Agua (Sierra de Caral), Izabal, Guatemala, 970 m elevation. JAC

Fig. 122. Black-striped Snake—Culebra Rayas Negras *(Coniophanes imperialis)*, adult female, 25.2 cm SVL, 34.4 cm TL, tail incomplete (UTA R-38213); Aldea La Libertad, near Km Post 285 on road to Petén, Izabal, Guatemala, 77 m elevation. ENS

Fig. 123. Striped Spotbelly Snake—Culebra Vientre-punteado Listada *(Coniophanes quinquevittatus)*, adult male; near Tlacotalpán, Veracruz, Mexico. RCV

Fig. 124. Schmidt's Striped Snake—Culebra Rayada de Schmidt *(Coniophanes schmidti)*, adult female, 65.5 cm TL (KU 70829); Pisté, Yucatán, Mexico, *ca.* 10 m elevation. WED

Fig. 125. Lizard Killer—Lagartijera *(Conophis lineatus)*, adult female, 62.1 cm TL (UTA R-28300); Aldea El Rosario, Zacapa, Guatemala. JAC

Fig. 126. Three-colored Keeled Racer—Zumbadora Aquillada de Tres Colores *(Dendrophidion nuchale)*, adult male, 164 cm TL; Cuxta Bani, Raspaculo River Valley, Cayo, Belize. PJS

Fig. 127. Barred Keeled Racer—Zumbadora Aquillada de Barras *(Dendrophidion vinitor)*, adult; Sierra de Los Tuxtlas, Veracruz, Mexico. RCV

Fig. 128. Short-faced Snail-eater—Caracolera de Cara Corta *(Dipsas brevifacies)*, adult; *ca.* 2 km SE Cobá, Quintana Roo, Mexico. JCL

Fig. 129. Middle American Smooth-scaled Racer—Lagartijera Lisa Olivácea *(Dryadophis melanolomus)*, subadult male, 78 cm TL (UTA R-22153); Finca Semuc (Sierra de Santa Cruz), Izabal, Guatemala, *ca.* 500 m elevation. WWL

Fig. 130. Tropical Indigo Snake—Arroyera de Cola Negra *(Drymarchon corais)*, subadult male, 132.5 cm TL (UTA R-28323); Aldea El Rosario, Zacapa, Guatemala. JAC

Fig. 131. Speckled Racer—Ranera Salpicada *(Drymobius margaritiferus)*, subadult female, 73.6 cm TL (UTA R-21791); Las Escobas, 5.1 km west-southwest of Puerto Santo Tomás (Montañas del Mico), Izabal, Guatemala, 150 m elevation. WWL

Fig. 132. Red-blotched Ratsnake—Ratonera Manchada *(Elaphe flavirufa)*, subadult male, 44 cm SVL, 55.4 cm TL (UTA R-41189); Tikal, Petén, Guatemala, ca. 200 m. ENS

Fig. 133. Blotched Hooknosed Snake—Naricilla Manchada *(Ficimia publia)*, adult female, 31.7 cm TL (UTA R-39214); El Caoba, Petén, Guatemala, 400 m elevation. JAC

Fig. 134. Common Bluntheaded Treesnake—Cordelilla Común *(Imantodes cenchoa)*, adult male, 101 cm TL (UTA R-39232); near El Caoba, Petén, Guatemala, 400 m elevation. JAC

Fig. 135. Spotted Bluntheaded Treesnake—Cordelilla Manchada *(Imantodes gemmistratus)*, adult male, 71.8 cm TL (UTA R-22807); Finca Medio Monte, Escuintla, Guatemala, *ca.* 500 m elevation. WWL

Fig. 136. Tropical Milksnake—Coral Falsa *(Lampropeltis triangulum)*, adult male, 73.7 cm SVL, 85 cm TL (UTA R-40092); 30.6 km north El Remate, on road to Tikal, Petén, Guatemala, 317 m elevation. JAC

Fig. 137. Yucatán Cat-eyed Snake—Escombrera Yucateca *(Leptodeira frenata)*, subadult female, 26.4 cm TL (UTA R-26105); La Esperanza, Petén, Guatemala, *ca.* 200 m elevation. EDB

Fig. 138. Small-spotted Cat-eyed Snake—Escombrera de Manchitas *(Leptodeira polysticta)*, subadult female, 68.3 cm TL (UTA R-39345); *ca.* 8.5 km southwest of main aguada at Tikal, Petén, Guatemala, 220 m elevation. JAC

Fig. 139. Green Parrot Snake—Ranera Verde *(Leptophis ahaetulla)*, adult male, 153 cm SVL, 247.5 cm TL (UTA R-41190); near Río Bobos, Finca Quebradas, Izabal, Guatemala, 100 m elevation. ENS

Fig. 140. Bronze-backed Parrot Snake—Ranera Dorso-bronceada *(Leptophis mexicanus)*, adult female, 74 cm SVL, tail incomplete (UTA R-39228); Gringo Perdido, *ca.* 3.0 km west of El Remate–Tikal road, on road to San José, Petén, Guatemala, 120 m elevation. JAC

Fig. 141. Neotropical Coachwhip—Chirrionera Café *(Masticophis mentovarius)*, subadult female, 50.6 cm TL (UTA R-39210); 35.2 km east of Belmopan, Belize, Belize, 91 m elevation. JAC

Fig. 142. Black Coffee Snake—Basurera Negra *(Ninia diademata)*, adult female, 36.9 cm TL (UTA R-38212); Km 137.5 on road to Cobán, Baja Verapaz, Guatemala, 1480 m elevation. ENS

Fig. 143. Red Coffee Snake—Basurera Roja *(Ninia sebae)*, adult female, 30.6 cm TL (UTA R-21682); Las Escobas, 5.1 km west-southwest of Puerto Santo Tomás (Montañas del Mico), Izabal, Guatemala, *ca.* 200 m elevation. WWL

Fig. 144. Brown Vine Snake—Bejuquillo Café *(Oxybelis aeneus)*, adult female, 108 cm TL, tip of tail missing (UTA R-22183); Semococh, Finca Semuc (Sierra de Santa Cruz), Izabal, Guatemala, *ca.* 750 m elevation. DGB

Fig. 145. Green Vine Snake—Bejuquillo Verde *(Oxybelis fulgidus)*, adult female, 184.5 cm TL (UTA R-19911); Las Escobas, 5.1 km west-southwest of Puerto Santo Tomás (Montañas del Mico), Izabal, Guatemala, 150 m elevation. WWL

Fig. 146. White-bellied False Coral—Falso Coral Panza Blanca *(Oxyrhopus petola),* adult male, 66.5 cm TL (UTA R-39224); *ca.* 8.5 km southwest of main aguada at Tikal, Petén, Guatemala, 220 m elevation. JAC

Fig. 147. Long-tailed False Coral—Coralillo Cola Larga *(Pliocercus elapoides),* adult male, 28.2 cm SVL, 49.8 cm TL (UTA R-41191); Finca Chiblac Buena Vista (now Aldea Buenos Aires), Sierra de los Cuchumatanes, Huehuetenango, Guatemala, *ca.* 900 m elevation. ENS

Fig. 148. Bird-eating Treesnake—Pajarera *(Pseustes poecilonotus),* subadult male, 111.8 cm TL (UTA R-39271); Finca El Pantano, near Puerto Barrios, Izabal, Guatemala, 1 m elevation. ENS

Fig. 149. Striped Forest Snake—Hojarasquera Rayada *(Rhadinaea decorata),* adult male, 36.7 cm TL (UTA R-22188); Finca Semuc (Sierra de Santa Cruz), Izabal, Guatemala. DGB

Fig. 150. Half Coral Snake—Media Coralilla *(Scaphiodontophis annulatus),* adult male, 30.2 cm SVL, 52.1 cm TL, tail incomplete (UTA R-39179); near El Caoba, Petén, Guatemala, 400 m elevation. JAC

Fig. 151. Common Tropical Ratsnake—Ratonera Tropical Común *(Senticolis triaspis),* adult male, 106 cm TL (UTA R-28489); Quebrada Los Chorros, Santa Elena, San Diego, Zacapa, Guatemala, 650 m elevation. JAC

Fig. 152. Coral-backed Snail-eater—Tragababosa Espalda Coral *(Sibon dimidiata)*, subadult male, 28.4 cm SVL, 42.5 cm TL (UTA R-29909); Las Escobas, 5.1 km west-southwest of Puerto Santo Tomás (Montañas del Mico), Izabal, Guatemala, *ca.* 150 m elevation. JAC

Fig. 153. Cloudy Snail-eater—Tragababosa Jaspeada *(Sibon nebulata)*, adult male, 62.4 cm TL (UTA R-26321); Finca Chiblac, 3.7 south of Casa Grande (Sierra de los Cuchumatanes), Huehuetenango, Guatemala, 1,100 m elevation. EDB

Fig. 154. Yucatán Snail-eater—Tragababosa Yucateca *(Sibon sanniola)*, near Big Eddy on Macal River, Cayo, Belize. RAL

Fig. 155. Ringed Snail-eater—Tragababosa Anillada *(Sibon sartorii)*, adult female, 62 cm TL (UTA R-39154); Zocotzal, just south of south entrance to Tikal National Park, Petén, Guatemala, 320 m elevation. JAC

Fig. 156. Tiger Treesnake—Chichicua *(Spilotes pullatus)*, adult male, *ca.* 200 cm TL (UTA Live Collection); road between San Miguelito and Finca Quebradas (Sierra de Caral), Izabal, Guatemala, 350 m elevation. JAC

Fig. 157. Tiger Treesnake—Chichicua *(Spilotes pullatus)*, adult female in defensive pose, 141.5 cm SVL, 192 cm TL (UTA R-40787); Finca El Jabalí, Puerto Barrios, Izabal, Guatemala, 3 m elevation. ENS

Fig. 158. Degenhardt's Scorpion-hunter—Alacranera de Degenhardt *(Stenorrhina degenhardtii)*, adult female, 60 cm TL (UTA R-22206); Finca Semuc (Sierra de Santa Cruz), Guatemala. WWL

Fig. 159. Freminville's Scorpion-hunter—Alacranera de Freminville *(Stenorrhina freminvillii)*, subadult male, 33.3 cm TL (UTA R-22847); Champerico, Retalhuleu, Guatemala, 20 m elevation. WWL

Fig. 160. Tropical Brown Snake—Traga-lombriz Café *(Storeria dekayi)*, juvenile female, 11.3 cm SVL, 14.1 cm TL (UTA R-26336); vicinity of La Unión Barrios, Baja Verapaz, Guatemala, 1,500 m elevation. EDB

Fig. 161. Mayan Golden-backed Snake—Culebra Maya Dorso Dorado *(Symphimus mayae)*, adult male, 70.9 cm TL (UTA R-16870); between Tulum and Cobá at Km 33, Quintana Roo, Mexico. WWL

Fig. 162. Mayan Black-headed Centipede-eater—Traga-cienpiés Maya Cabeza Negra *(Tantilla cuniculator)*, adult male, 22 cm TL (UTA R-35012); Tikal, Petén, Guatemala, *ca.* 240 m elevation. PR

Fig. 163. Black-bellied Centipede-eater—Traga-cienpiés Panza Negra *(Tantilla moesta)*; 14 km SE Cobá, Quintana Roo, Mexico. JCL

Fig. 164. Lesser Centipede-eater—Traga-cienpiés Pequeña *(Tantilla schistosa)*, adult female, 11.1 cm SVL, 13.3 cm TL (UTA R-41193); Finca Sabó, near Purulhá, Baja Verapaz, Guatemala, 1,175 m elevation. ENS

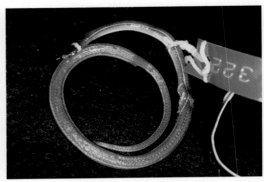

Fig. 165. White-striped Centipede-eater—Traga-cienpiés Listado de Blanco *(Tantilla tecta)* adult female, 22.2 cm TL (UVG R-1742); northeast of Laguna Yaxá, Petén, Guatemala, *ca.* 220 m elevation. JAC

Fig. 166. Yucatán Dwarf Centipede-eater—Traga-cienpiés Enana Yucateca *(Tantillita canula)*, male, 21.2 cm SVL, tail incomplete (UTA R-39161); El Caoba, Petén, Guatemala, 400 m elevation. EDB

Fig. 167. Linton's Dwarf Centipede-eater—Traga-cienpiés Enana de Linton *(Tantillita lintoni)*, adult male, 20.6 cm TL (British Museum of Natural History 1996.90); Las Cuevas, Chiquibul Forest, Cayo District, Belize. PJS.

Fig. 168. Checkered Garter Snake—Ranera Cuadriculada *(Thamnophis marcianus)*, adult female, 56.5 cm SVL, 75.6 cm TL (UTA R-22796); shore of Lago de Izabal, Finca Marruecos, Punta Caymanes, Izabal, Guatemala, 10 m elevation. WWL

Fig. 169. Middle American Ribbon Snake—Ranera Listada *(Thamnophis proximus)*, adult female, 47 cm SVL, 65 mm TL (UTA R-43561); southern shore of Lago Petén Itzá, Petén, Guatemala, 120 m elevation. ENS

Fig. 170. Middle American Swamp Snake—Buceadora *(Tretanorhinus nigroluteus)*, adult male, 44 cm TL (UTA R-29939); El Chupón, near El Estor (Lago de Izabal), Izabal, Guatemala, 2 m elevation. JAC

Fig. 171. False Barba Amarilla—Engañosa *(Xenodon rabdocephalus)*, juvenile female, 23.2 cm TL (UTA R-23057); Tikal, near Temple V, Petén, Guatemala, 250 m elevation. WWL

Fig. 172. Variable Coral Snake—Coral Variable *(Micrurus diastema)*, adult female, 57.5 cm TL (UTA R-39212); between Km Posts 5 and 6, east of Santa Elena (Santa Elena–El Remate road), Petén, Guatemala, 140 m elevation. JAC

Fig. 173. Variable Coral Snake—Coral Variable *(Micrurus diastema)*, adult male, 57.4 cm TL (UTA R-22768); Finca Santa María Chaylá, Zona Reina, Quiché, Guatemala, 300 m elevation. WWL

Fig. 174. Mayan Coral Snake—Coral Maya *(Micrurus hippocrepis)*, subadult female, 26.8 cm TL (UTA R-21805); Las Escobas, 5.1 km west-southwest of Puerto Santo Tomás (Montañas del Mico), Izabal, Guatemala, ca. 200 m elevation. JAC

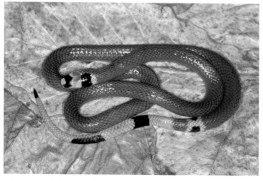

Fig. 175. Mayan Coral Snake—Coral Maya *(Micrurus hippocrepis)*, adult male, 48.2 cm SVL, 57 cm TL (UTA R-40095); 12.6 km west of Puerto Santo Tomás (Montañas del Mico), Izabal, Guatemala, 866 m elevation. JAC

Fig. 176. Central American Coral Snake—Coral Centro Americano *(Micrurus nigrocinctus)*, adult male, 63.7 cm TL (UTA R-15787); on mainland opposite Cayos Cochinos, Atlántida, Honduras. WWL

Fig. 177. Cantil—Cantil *(Agkistrodon bilineatus)*, subadult male, ca. 60 cm TL; vicinity of Mérida, Yucatán, Mexico, 50 m elevation. WWL

Fig. 178. Jumping Pitviper—Chalpate *(Atropoides nummifer)*, adult female, 90.1 cm TL (UTA R-30286); Semococh, Finca Semuc (Sierra de Santa Cruz), Izabal, Guatemala, 750 m elevation. WWL

Fig. 179. Jumping Pitviper—Chalpate *(Atropoides nummifer)*, adult female, 66.2 cm TL (UTA R-16104); 7.2 km west-southwest of Puerto Santo Tomás (Montañas del Mico), Izabal, Guatemala, 300 m elevation. WWL

Fig. 180. Eyelash Palm-pitviper—Víbora de Pestañas *(Bothriechis schlegelii)*, adult male, 33 cm SVL, 39.2 cm TL (UTA R-41195); on trail between Finca Quebradas and Cerro Poso de Agua (Sierra de Caral), Izabal, Guatemala, 830 m elevation. ENS

Fig. 181. Eyelash Palm-pitviper—Víbora de Pestañas *(Bothriechis schlegelii)*, adult female in defensive pose, 68.5 cm TL (KU 187441); 12.6 km west of Puerto Santo Tomás (Montañas del Mico), Izabal, Guatemala, 774 m elevation. JAC

Fig. 182. Barba Amarilla—Barba Amarilla *(Bothrops asper)*, adult female, 150.1 cm TL (UTA R-40353); Quebrada El Branchi, near Aldea La Libertad, Izabal, Guatemala, 35 m elevation. ENS

Fig. 183. Barba Amarilla—Barba Amarilla *(Bothrops asper)*, subadult female, 84.5 cm TL (UTA R-40331); Finca Karen, near Km Post 275 on Atlantic highway, Izabal, Guatemala, 40 m elevation. ENS

Fig. 184. Rainforest Hognosed Pitviper—Víbora Chatilla de la Selva *(Porthidium nasutum)*, adult male, 31.6 cm TL (UTA R-39162); Gringo Perdido, *ca.* 3.0 km west of El Remate–Tikal road, on road to San José, Guatemala, 120 m elevation. JAC

Fig. 185. Neotropical Rattlesnake—Víbora de Cascabel Neotropical *(Crotalus durissus)*, adult; Yucatán, Mexico. LP

Fig. 186. American Crocodile—Cocodrilo de Río (*Crocodylus acutus*), juvenile, 62.3 cm TL; Izabal, Guatemala. ENS

Fig. 187. American Crocodile—Cocodrilo de Río (*Crocodylus acutus*), female, 193.2 cm TL; mouth of the Río Polochic, Izabal, Guatemala, 5 m elevation. ENS

Fig. 188. Morelet's Crocodile—Cocodrilo de Pantano (*Crocodylus moreletii*), juvenile, *ca.* 50 cm TL; Lago Petén Itzá, Petén, Guatemala, 110 m elevation. JAC

Fig. 189. Morelet's Crocodile—Cocodrilo de Pantano (*Crocodylus moreletii*), subadult, *ca.* 100 cm TL; Lago Petén Itzá, Petén, Guatemala, 110 m elevation. JAC

Metallic Ameiva—Ameiva Metálica
Ameiva undulata (Wiegmann, 1834)
Figs. 107–108

Description.—Adults are about 80–130 mm in SVL and have a TL of about 260–430 mm, with males larger than females. The interparietal is usually single and there are two lateral parietal and two frontoparietal scales, producing a total of five scales in the parietal region. The dorsum and sides of the body are covered with tiny granular scales that are mostly keeled or pointed. The venter is covered with large, flat rectangular scales. The median gulars are moderate in size and grade into the surrounding gular scales. There is a single row of enlarged upper antebrachials and longitudinal rows of ventral scales usually number eight. Two complete transverse gular folds have 2–3 rows of enlarged, irregularly arranged mesoptychial scales that are distinctly set off from the surrounding granular scales.

The color pattern is highly variable and, as in other species in this genus, subject to sexual, ontogenetic, and geographical variation. In adult males, the top of the head and dorsum of the body are medium to dark brown or gray-brown with scattered dark spots or bars. The flanks are marked with alternating, irregular, vertical chestnut brown and turquoise bars; usually a pale turquoise or blue-green lateral stripe bisects the vertical barring. In breeding males, the venter is bright blue and the gular area and throat are bright red-orange. Large adult females may be patterned on their flanks similarly to males but are not as brightly colored. Females usually have a pale to medium brown dorsum with some dark barring posteriorly, a broad, dark brown lateral band that may have darker vertical barring, and a thin cream or yellow lateral stripe bordering the dark lateral band. The lateral stripe is usually broken, at least anteriorly, and interrupted by the hind limb, but continues onto the tail as a ventrolateral stripe. The venter is whitish and may be lightly suffused with pink, yellow, or blue pigment.

Natural History.—This species occurs in many types of habitats, including tropical and subtropical wet, moist, and dry forest, but appears to be most common in the forest bordering the edges of clearings or in places where a fair amount of sunlight penetrates to the forest floor. It is abundant in the acahuales. The diet of this species consists mostly of insects. A number of snakes are known to prey on this lizard, including the aptly named lizard killer (*Conophis lineatus*), Middle American smooth-scaled racer (*Dryadophis melanolomus*), tropical indigo snake (*Drymarchon corais*), and Neotropical coachwhip (*Masticophis mentovarius*).

Reproductive information for this species suggests an extended reproductive period. Females lay 2–7 eggs from July to about September. In a large series collected at Tikal between February and May, there were 56 juveniles and only four adults. Sexual maturity reportedly is attained in as little as four months.

Distribution.—The metallic ameiva occurs on the Atlantic versant from northern Tamaulipas, Mexico, southward through the Yucatán Peninsula and Central America to Nicaragua, and on the Pacific versant from Nayarit, Mexico, through Central America to Costa Rica. It is found throughout most of Petén, occurring in forest, secondary growth, and savannas. It ranges from near sea level to about 1,830 m.

Remarks.—Another vernacular name for this species is *lagartija metálica*. The subspecies occurring in Petén are *Ameiva undulata hartwegi* in the southern and central portion of the department and *A. u. gaigeae* in the northern part.

Yucatán Whiptail—Murishca Yucateca
Cnemidophorus angusticeps Cope, 1877
Fig. 109

Description.—This lizard reaches a maximum adult SVL of about 100–115 mm and a maximum TL of 250–270 mm, with males being larger than females. There are four supraocular scales (the posterior scale is smaller than the preceding three or about the size of the anterior scale in the series). The interparietal is usually single and there are two parietals and two frontoparietal scales, producing a total of five scales in the parietal region. There are multiple rows of enlarged upper antebrachials. The dorsum and sides of the body are covered with tiny granular scales and the venter with large, flat rectangular scales, usually arranged in eight longitudinal rows. The median gulars are not distinctly enlarged over surrounding gular scales. There are two complete transverse gular folds with the mesoptychials only slightly enlarged and grading into adjacent anterior scales.

Six well-defined cream stripes are present on the back and sides in juveniles and adult females. These stripes are also present in young males, but as males mature small spots appear between the stripes. These spots continue to enlarge with age until they eventually coalesce to form a lichenose or tessellated pattern in large males. The paravertebral and dorsolateral stripes extend to a level about even with the posterior insertion of the hind limbs; the lateral stripes extend only to about the level of the anterior insertion of the hind limbs. Adult males have a broad median dorsal band extending from the parietals to the base of the tail; this vertebral band is only vaguely present in the larger females. In juveniles, females, and young males, the area between stripes is immaculate brownish black, except for the dark zone between the lower two stripes, which may be somewhat tessellated, at least posteriorly. In adult males, the chin and gular area are pink, and the belly is black or bluish black from the gular fold to the preanal scales; black pigment extends onto the ventral surfaces of the fore- and hind limbs. The venters of subadult males are less extensively blackened than in mature males, and the posterior ventrals, preanal scales, and ventral surfaces of the hind limbs may be cream. In females and juveniles the venter is pale blue laterally, becoming cream or pale gray near the ventral midline; the throat is blue, suffused with cream, and the preanal scales and ventral surfaces of the limbs and tail are also cream. Dorsally, the tail is orange or reddish brown in juveniles and subadults and becomes brownish or blue-gray in adults; the tail is white or pale gray ventrally.

Natural History.—The Yucatán whiptail inhabits tropical moist and dry forest. In a series of 122 specimens collected in the Yucatán between mid-June and mid-July, there were only two juveniles, measuring 39 and 41 mm in SVL. That there were so few juveniles in this sample is possibly because it was early in the season for hatchlings to emerge. This suggests that the reproductive pattern in this species may be similar to that of *Ameiva undulata*, with most of the hatchlings appearing during the late rainy season.

Distribution.—This lizard occurs in most of the Yucatán Peninsula, including central Petén, Guatemala, and east-central Belize. It is common in the northern part of the Yucatán Peninsula, but in Petén it is known only from the savanna region southwest of Lago Petén Itzá, where it is usually encountered along the edges of forested islands surrounded by savanna and in acahual habitat. It occurs at elevations between sea level and 300 m.

Remarks.—This lizard is a member of the *Cnemidophorus sexlineatus* group. Other vernacular names include *huico rayado* and *lagartija llanera.*

Maslin's Whiptail—Murishca de Maslin
Cnemidophorus maslini Fritts, 1969
Fig. 110

Description.—This lizard reaches a maximum adult SVL of about 70–83 mm and a maximum TL of 210–230 mm. There usually are three supraocular scales. The interparietal is usually single and there are two parietals, two frontoparietal scales, and at least one scale on either side between the frontonasal and parietal, producing a total of seven scales or more in the parietal region. There are multiple rows of enlarged upper antebrachials. The dorsum and sides of the body are covered with tiny granulars and the venter is covered with large, flat rectangular scales, usually arranged in eight longitudinal rows. Median gulars are not distinctly enlarged over surrounding gular scales. There are two complete transverse gular folds with the mesoptychials only slightly enlarged from and grading into adjacent anterior scales.

The dorsum of the head and body are medium brown to pale olive-brown, the sides of the head and throat and the ventrolateral surface of the body are whitish to pinkish gray. On each side of the body are three yellow stripes that extend from the neck posteriorly for the length of the body; the upper two stripes run above the insertion of the hind limb and onto the tail and the lowest stripe terminates in front of the hind limb. A fourth yellow stripe is present on the neck and extends from the posterior edge of the auricular opening to above the insertion of the fore limb. The dorsal field between yellow stripes is pale brownish olive to dark brown and the sides of the body below the stripes are paler than the middorsal field. The labials, throat, and lower surface of the thighs and tail are pinkish. The subcaudal and subfemoral surfaces are pale pinkish cinnamon. The venter of the body and tail is cream to pale gray. Unlike most members of the genus, the young of this species do not undergo an ontogenetic change of color pattern.

Natural History.—This species inhabits tropical dry forest along the eastern shore of Lago Petén Itzá at El Remate, where it occurs near the shore in low bushy habitats and areas of secondary growth.

This lizard is apparently unisexual, with only females being known. The species reproduces parthenogenetically, which is to say that it can reproduce without males (see "Virgin Birth"). It may have a protracted reproductive season and may lay several clutches of eggs per season. Almost 20 percent of a series of 78 of a closely related species collected during June and July in the Yucatán contained nearly mature eggs. Hatchlings have been found near El Remate in October and March.

Distribution.—Maslin's whiptail and its close relatives occur at several localities in Belize, several localities near the beach in Campeche and Quintana Roo, Mexico, and on a number of islands off of the Yucatán Peninsula, including Isla de Cozumel, Isla Mujeres, Isla Contoy, and Isla de Carmen. This species occurs at elevations between sea level and 200 m. It is known in Petén from near the eastern and northern shores of Lago Petén Itzá and one locality to the south, where it occurs in low forest habitats.

Remarks.—The range of this species appears to be largely complementary to that of the larger Yucatán whiptail (*Cnemidophorus angusticeps*), which is thought to be one of the parental species (see "Virgin Birth"). Maslin's whiptail is sometimes considered to be a subspecies of the Cozumel whiptail (*C. cozumela*). Another vernacular name for it is *huico*.

Virgin Birth.—Males and females are present in most populations of vertebrates. There is a good reason for this—biparental populations usually are able to maintain genetic variability that helps ensure their survival. On the other hand, in parthenogenesis (virgin birth), only females usually occur in a population, and they are able to give birth without the benefit of males. Parthenogenesis is relatively common in invertebrates but unusual in vertebrates. It was first demonstrated in vertebrates in 1932 when the Amazon molly *Poecilia formosa* was shown to have arisen through hybridization between two other distinct fish species. Uniparental salamanders were discovered next, with a series of reports appearing in the decades from 1930 through 1950.

It was not until 1958 that a Russian scientist reported for the first time parthenogenesis in reptiles, having found it in a lizard species from the Caucasus Mountains. Soon American scientists began to note that they could find no males among large museum samples of certain species of whiptail and racerunner lizards (*Cnemidophorus*). By the early 1960s, it had been established that in the genus *Cnemidophorus*, parthenogenesis could result from speciation by interspecific hybridization. Parthenogenesis is now known be present in five, and may occur in as many as seven, families of lizards. The offspring of these parthenogenetic species are clones of their mother and genetic variability is low in these populations. It has been suggested that these species are of recent origin and have a relatively short evolutionary life.

In the Petén region, Maslin's whiptail (*Cnemidophorus maslini*) reproduces parthenogenetically. No males of this species have ever been found and it is therefore known as an obligatory parthenogen. Occurring in the Yucatán Peninsula are a number of closely related parthenogenetic populations that sometimes are recognized as *C. cozumela, C. rodecki,* and *C. maslini.* How to treat these populations taxonomically remains controversial. Morphological, cytological, and biochemical evidence suggests that all of the parthenogenetic populations of whiptails occurring in the Yucatán Peninsula originated from hybridization between female Yucatán Whiptails (*C. angusticeps*) and male Deppe's whiptails (*C. deppei*), the two gonochoristic species (i.e., having both male and female sexes) of whiptails inhabiting the Yucatán Peninsula. *Cnemidophorus deppei* occurs at present only peripherally around the Yucatán Peninsula on Isla del Carmen, in parts of Chiapas, and in the Motagua Valley of Guatemala. *Cnemidophorus angusticeps,* however, occurs throughout most of the Yucatán Peninsula.

Even though there is general agreement that all of these parthenogenetic populations share the same parental species, the number of times that parthenogenetic populations may have arisen independently is unknown. The reason this is important is that if all populations of uniparental whiptails in the Yucatán are the result of a single event and current distributions are the result of subsequent fragmentation of ancestral distributions, then only a single species should be recognized. On the other hand, if some of the populations are the result of two or more independent hybridization events, then some biologists argue that an equal number of species should be recognized.

The various populations of whiptails inhabiting the Yucatán Peninsula provide a good example of a tangled taxonomic history. From the time that *Cnemidophorus cozumela* was described in 1906 until the early 1960s it was considered to be a subspecies of the wide-ranging *C. deppei.* But in the early 1960s, *C. cozumela* was elevated to a full species and three subspecies were recognized (*cozumela, maslini,* and *rodeki*). In 1969, *C. rodecki* was elevated to a full species, but *cozumela* and *maslini* were retained as subspecies. It was not until 1995 that *C. maslini* and *C. cozumela* were each suggested to represent full species, although at this time the evidence remains inconclusive as to whether *C. cozumela* and *C. maslini* are indeed distinct species.

There are at least five or six populations of *C. maslini,* and three of these are morphologically different and are statistically distinguishable. Allopatric populations of *C. maslini* occur southwest of Champotón in Campeche, on Isla del Carmen and the adjacent mainland to the northeast in Campeche, near El Remate on the east side of Lago Petén Itzá, about 20 km northwest of Poptún, in southern Quintana Roo, and in northern Belize. Because these populations share similarities of color pattern, they are recognized as a single parthenospecies. If, in the future, it can be demonstrated that these populations arose through independent hybridization events, then some or all might be recognized as a separate species.

ALLIGATOR LIZARDS—LAGARTIJAS DE LAGARTO

FAMILY ANGUIDAE

The alligator lizards and their relatives are widespread in Europe and Asia as well as in the Americas. The family is represented by about a dozen species in the Guatemalan highlands, but only one species occurs in Petén, Rozella's canopy lizard (*Diploglossus rozellae*).

Despite its relatively small, short limbs, this diurnal species spends most of its time high in trees. The shiny, flat, cycloid scales give it a skink-like overall appearance. Femoral pores are absent.

Rozella's Canopy Lizard—Salamanqueza de Rozella
Diploglossus rozellae (Smith, 1942)
Fig. 111

Description.—This skinklike lizard reaches a maximum SVL of about 100 mm and a TL of 230–235 mm in individuals with unregenerated tails. The head is scarcely wider than the neck, the body is robust and somewhat cylindrical, and the limbs are short and fail to meet when adpressed. Scales on top of the head are large, smooth, and platelike. The scales on the dorsum, sides, and venter of the body are smooth, imbricate, cycloid, striated, and about equal in size. There are 31–33 scales around midbody.

In adults, the body is coppery brown (a little darker on the dorsum than sides) with scattered dark spots, the sides of the body, have irregular, vertical series of yellow spots, the venter is greenish with a distinct metallic sheen, and the tail is coppery brown or brownish gray. Juveniles have a dark brown ground color, well-defined copper-colored dorsolateral stripes, black vertical bars, and a bright orange tail.

Natural History.—This lizard occurs in tropical wet and moist forest. Mostly arboreal, it has been observed at heights of 10–20 m basking on limbs in patches of sunlight. It is usually near clumps of epiphytes, into which it escapes when threatened. This lizard is not commonly seen, probably more because of its habits than its actual relative abundance. Females give birth to three to five young from May through July.

Distribution.—Rozella's canopy lizard occurs from the Atlantic slopes and lowlands of southeastern Oaxaca and northern Chiapas, Mexico, across northern Guatemala and southern Belize to the Sierra del Merendón in eastern Guatemala. There is a single record for the Pacific versant of Guatemala. This species occurs from near sea level to over 1,350 m and is known from several widely separated localities in Petén, including Tikal.

SNAKES—CULEBRAS

Snakes are a fascinating and variable group of organisms. The more that is learned about them, the more interesting they become. Superficially, some lizards may resemble snakes and there is a close evolutionary relationship between the two groups, such that they are placed in the same order, the Squamata. One of the most obvious differences between snakes and lizards is the presence or absence of limbs; most lizards have well-developed fore and hind limbs, whereas most snakes have none. Confusing the issue, however, are some lizards that have lost their limbs, but none of these occur in Petén. Also, some snakes, including the boa constrictor, retain small vestiges of the pelvic girdle and hind limbs, but these are evident externally only as a small spur on either side of the vent and are not likely to be noticed without careful scrutiny.

Most lizards have well-developed eyelids. Whereas snakes never have moveable eyelids, they do have a transparent scale, called the brille or spectacle, that covers the eye. This scale is shed periodically with the rest of the skin. However, some lizards occurring in Petén, including the night lizards and some of the geckos, also lack moveable eyelids. The scales covering most snakes are clearly differentiated into smaller, imbricate scales on the side and top of the body and the series of large straplike scales, called ventrals, that run along their bellies. In lizards, the scales of the dorsum and venter may be of different sizes and shapes, but straplike ventrals are never present. Ventral scales are reduced in size in the boa constrictor and absent altogether in blind snakes and thread snakes.

In general, snakes are capable of swallowing larger prey in relation to their head size than are lizards. In part, this is because the mandibles of snakes are connected by a highly elastic ligament, whereas in lizards both of the bony mandibles come together to form a suture. Another difference between snakes and lizards concerns tail autotomy. In most lizards, the tail is fragile and easily breaks when seized. This defense mechanism allows the lizard to scamper safely off while a predator is distracted by the wriggling broken segment of the tail. The lizard will regenerate a tail over the next few months, which subsequently may be broken by another predator. In contrast, snakes are not able to regenerate a new tail, although it is not unusual for individuals in long-tailed species to have only a stub for a tail, obviously the result of a close encounter with a predator.

Snakes may be active at any time of the day or night. During the cool early morning hours, many of the smaller leaf-litter inhabitants such as the white-lipped spotbelly snake (*Coniophanes fissidens*), striped forest snake (*Rhadinaea decorata*), or coral snakes (*Micrurus*) are out searching for their favorite prey, generally small species of amphibians or reptiles. At about midmorning, the greatest number of diurnal species may be found active, including the different tropical racers (*Dendrophidion, Dryadophis, Drymobius, Masticophis*), indigo snakes (*Drymarchon corais*), and lizard killers (*Conophis lineatus*). Snake activity diminishes dramatically during the hotter times of the day, especially when there are few clouds in the sky. I have generally found that the hours from

about noon until around 4:00 P.M. are best reserved for siestas and not snake hunting. A few of the large diurnal hunters may still be out, particularly where they can rest periodically in the shade during their foraging activities, but generally when they are found, they are coiled motionless under a bush or in some recess, waiting for the rays of the sun to wane. There is another peak period of activity for diurnal snakes in the late evening. I believe I have seen more milksnakes (*Lampropeltis*), parrot snakes (*Leptophis*), and vine snakes (*Oxybelis*) during the hour before sunset than at any other time.

After dark, an entirely different assemblage of snakes becomes active. Most but not all of these are small species. Bluntheaded treesnakes (*Imantodes*), snail-eaters (*Sibon*), and cat-eyed snakes (*Leptophis*) crawl from their hiding places on the forest floor and in hollowed-out logs to begin their search for anoles, molluscs, and frogs, respectively. These snakes usally patrol low vegetation in the vicinity of streams or ponds. Several aquatic species including the Middle American swamp snake (*Tretanorhinus nigroluteus*) and the mottled-jaw spotbelly snake (*Coniophanes bipunctatus*) enter the water from their nearby refuges and begin hunting for fish, frogs, and other aquatic prey.

Several impressively large species, including the boa constrictor (*Boa constrictor*), black mussurana (*Clelia clelia*), and barba amarilla (*Bothrops asper*), are also nocturnal. Boa constrictors are rather infrequently found over much of Petén; I have found them active most frequently on rainy nights along river banks. By day these snakes retreat to deep armadillo or tepezcuintle (*Agouti paca*) burrows or to the hollows of trees. The black mussurana often is found on steep, root-covered stream banks, where it preys on other large snakes and striped basilisk lizards. The most fearsome snake in the region, the barba amarilla, reaches lengths in excess of two meters and may have a head as large as a man's fist. The barba amarilla feeds on many different kinds of animals as a juvenile (even venomous centipedes!) but as an adult tends to prey mostly on small mammals. It has sometimes been regarded as a sit-and-wait type of predator, but judging from the frequency with which it is seen moving across paths or the forest floor, it must also actively seek prey at times. The activity periods of snakes during the night are not well known. Certainly, I have found most species from about sundown to midnight, but this may be a function of my activity rather than that of snakes. At those times that I have remained abroad all night, I have continued to see snakes, although perhaps fewer species and in smaller numbers.

Snakes may reproduce by laying eggs or by giving birth to live young. Most snakes lay eggs, but in Petén the boa constrictor, some of the colubrids, and all of the vipers have live young.

Snakes of the Petén region are placed into six families. To distinguish the various species of snakes occurring in the region, see appendix F. The blind snakes and thread snakes belong to the families Typhlopidae and Leptotyphlopidae, respectively; these diminutive, inconspicuous snakes spend most of their lives underground. They are highly adapted to a subterranean life, having reduced eyes, a very small mouth, a rigid skull, smooth and strongly overlapping scales, and short, blunt tails. Both of these families have a vestigial pelvis. However, in blind snakes the maxillary bones bear teeth and the lower jaw is edentate, whereas thread snakes lack teeth on the maxillae but have teeth on the lower jaw.

The boa constrictor is a member of the family Boidae, which contains the various species of boas and anacondas, most of which inhabit the New World. Some species in this family reach huge sizes and all bear live young. Boas have a vestigial pelvis and hind limbs, which are reduced externally to a small spur on either side of the vent. These are large, muscular snakes that suffocate their prey by constriction.

The vast majority of snakes are placed in the family Colubridae, which contains large and small species, diurnal and nocturnal species, and harmless and rear-fanged species. None has any remnant of a pelvis or hind limbs, but many modifications of maxillary dentition have evolved. The maxillary teeth of aglyphous colubrids are relatively unmodified, usually roughly subequal in size, and venom glands are absent. Snakes having this kind of dentition include the indigo snake, which simply rushes and swallows its prey, and milksnakes, which kill by constriction. Snakes with aglyphous dentition have a number of modifications. In the half coral snake (*Scaphiodontophis annulatus*), for example, the maxillary teeth are peculiarly hinged and shovel-like, an adaptation for feeding on skinks; and the black coffee snake (*Ninia diademata*) has long and needle-like maxillary teeth, an adaptation for feeding on slugs, earthworms, and other soft-bodied invertebrate prey.

In opisthoglyphous colubrids, commonly known as rear-fanged snakes, several of the posterior teeth on the maxillary are enlarged and each of these teeth often has an open groove running its length. For subduing prey, these snakes produce toxins that are transmitted into a bite via the grooves in the enlarged rear teeth. Many colubrids in Petén are opisthoglyphous with the lizard killer and the false barba amarilla *(Xenodon rabdocephalus)* having especially large rear fangs. Colubrids subdue their prey by simply seizing, overpowering, and swallowing it, by envenomation, or by constriction. A few species, such as the black

mussurana (*Clelia clelia*) may both envenomate and constrict prey.

The venomous coral snakes (*Micrurus*) are placed in the family Elapidae, which also contains the cobras, kraits, mambas, and sea snakes. These snakes have proteroglyphous dentition in which there are relatively short, relatively immobile, hollow fangs in the front of the mouth on the maxillary. Coral snakes subdue their prey through envenomation and are dangerously venomous to humans. The common belief that because of their relatively small size coral snakes are unable to bite unless they happen to grab a small part of the body, such as the web between fingers, is pure hokum.

Finally, species such as the barba amarilla, jumping pitviper, and rainforest hognosed pitviper are all in the family Viperidae and have solenoglyphous dentition. In this type of dentition the hollow fangs are relatively long and affixed to the front of a highly moveable, short maxillary. Fangs are folded backward in the mouth when at rest but swing forward into an erect position during a bite. These snakes feed on a variety of mostly vertebrate prey and are dangerous to humans.

BLIND SNAKES—CULEBRILLAS CIEGAS

FAMILY TYPHLOPIDAE

The blind snakes occur throughout the tropics of the world, including in Africa, Asia, and Australia as well as in Mexico, Central and South America,

and the Antilles. There are nine species on the mainland of the Americas and some 20 more in the Antilles. The New World species are small, most less than 35 cm in TL; some of the African species easily exceed twice this length. In members of this family the maxillae bear teeth, but the dentaries are toothless. A vestigial pelvis is present. The left lung and oviduct are absent, and most, but not all, species are oviparous.

Only a single species of this secretive family is known from Petén, but it is possible that *Typhlops tenuis*, which is known from Alta Verapaz and from southern Mexico, also occurs in the lower foothills of the region.

Yucatán Blind Snake—Culebrilla Ciega Yucateca
Typhlops microstomus Cope, 1866
Fig. 112

Description.—This wormlike snake reaches a maximum length of about 366 mm in TL and a midbody diameter of about 5 mm. The head is rounded and vestigial eyes are reduced to tiny black dots just barely discernible beneath the ocular scale. The tail terminates in a spine. A large rostral scale curves up over the top of the snout. The prefrontal, supraoculars, parietals, occipitals, interparietal, and interoccipital scales are all subequal and not greatly differentiated from each other. A subocular scale is present and the nasal suture is complete. There are four supralabials bordering the margin of the upper lip; the lip margin is not interrupted by the ocular. The dorsal scales, counted from the posterior edge of the rostral to the tail spine, are 484–566; there are 5–10 subcaudals, counted from the posterior edge of the cloaca to the tail spine; and there are 18 longitudinal rows of scales throughout the body. The ventral scales are not enlarged and are similar in size and shape to other cycloid body scales.

The coloration of this snake is usually rosy pink or pinkish tan, becoming a bit paler on the posterior part of the body, but one specimen was described as being "pure white, showing no pink coloration." The rostral scale may have a vertical dark marking.

Natural History.—This species occurs in tropical dry forest. Almost nothing is known about its habits. This secretive snake rarely ventures above ground and is most likely to be found during excavations or above ground at night after heavy rains have flooded it out of its subterranean refuge. Similar to other blind snakes, it probably feeds primarily on the larvae and eggs of termites and ants and it probably lays eggs.

Distribution.—The Yucatán blind snake occurs from the northern portion of the Yucatán Peninsula of Mexico to the northern portion of Belize and the Petén region of Guatemala. I am aware of a single record from Guatemala, from near El Paso [= Paso Caballos] along the Río San Pedro. The apparent rarity of this snake in Guatemala is probably a reflection of a dearth of collecting activity and the animal's small size and secretive nature. It occurs from near sea level to about 200 m.

THREAD SNAKES—CULEBRILLAS HILO

FAMILY LEPTOTYPHLOPIDAE

Members of this family are burrowing or subterranean species with rudimentary eyes and and a vestigial pelvis. The right lung and the right oviduct are functional, but these organs on the left side are absent or vestigial. Thread snakes are unique among snakes in having teeth confined to only the lower jaw; they feed primarily on the larvae and eggs of ants and termites. When arriving at a new ant or termite colony, some species are able to elevate the free margins of their body scales to keep attacking insects at a distance. A repellent substance is secreted, which discourages ants or termites from continuing their attack, and the body scales regain their original flat, imbricate conformation. In time, the snake acquires the odor of the colony of insects and is not molested further. Some species apparently spend most of their lives within ant or termite nests, food and shelter being readily available.

Goudot's Thread Snake—Culebrilla Hilo de Goudot
Leptotyphlops goudotii (Duméril and Bibron, 1844)
Fig. 113

Description.—This diminutive, vermiform snake reaches about 140 mm in TL. The head is tiny, not broader than the neck, and rounded in dorsal view. The vestigial eye is located near the anterior edge of the ocular scale. The tail is short and terminates in a spinelike scale. A large rostral scale curves up over the top of the snout, and there are upper and lower nasals, an anterior supralabial between the lower nasal and the ocular, a large ocular that completely covers the eye, and a posterior supralabial bordering the upper posterior corner of the jaw. Scales in the longitudinal series behind the rostral, including the prefrontal, frontal, interparietal, and interoccipital, are of about equal size and are not differentiated from more posterior body scales. The supraoculars are 3–4 times wider than the prefrontal, and the parietals are broad, extending from the frontal to the posterior supralabial. The dorsal scales are cycloid in shape. There are 14 scale rows throughout the body, about 250 scales from head to vent, and 14–17 scales from vent to tip of tail. The ventral scales are not enlarged and are similar to other dorsal scales.

The upper seven dorsal scale rows are dark brown. In some individuals scales have pale lateral edges, creating longitudinal stripes on the dorsum; in other specimens the dorsum is almost uniformly dark. The lower seven dorsal scale rows are paler than the dorsum, varying from pale pinkish gray to medium brown. The rostral and sometimes the nasals have a distinct white spot, and the tail spine is yellow or white.

Natural History.—This species inhabits tropical and subtropical wet, moist, and dry forest. These little snakes are most frequently encountered above ground after heavy rains, when they are flooded out of their subterreanean hiding places. Like other species in the family Leptotyphlopidae, this snake is specialized for feeding on the eggs, larvae, and adults of termites and ants and other soft-bodied arthropods. It is often found in the nests of ants or termites. Although the entire prey item may be ingested, the highly modified jaws and teeth allow these snakes simply to suck out the prey's body contents, leaving the chitinous body covering behind. This species lays 8–12 elongate eggs in June or July.

Distribution.—Goudot's thread snake has a disjunct distribution. It occurs in Veracruz, Mexico, and the northern portion of the Yucatán Peninsula, is widespread across much of central and southern Guatemala, and ranges southward through Central America into Colombia and Venezuela. It is known from a number of localities in the northern part of the Yucatán Peninsula, from several localities in Corozal and Stann Creek districts in Belize, and from near El Estor on the north side of Lago de Izabal. Eventually, this secretive snake will probably prove to be more widely distributed in the Petén region of Guatemala. Elsewhere in Guatemala, I have found it in habitats ranging from near desert to cloud forest and at elevations from near sea level to 1,610 m.

Remarks.—Other vernacular names for this species include *agujilla* and *culebra lumbricoide.*

Boas—Mazacuatas y Boas

Family Boidae

This family of small to huge snakes inhabits parts of Africa, southeastern Europe, western Asia, Madagascar, New Guinea and nearby islands, western North America, Mexico, Central America, South America, and the West Indies. Members of the family vary from slender to thick-bodied but all have a chunky, viperine head and vertical pupil. A vestigial pelvic girdle is present and both the left and right lungs are functional. All species of boas subdue their prey by constriction with their coils. Contrary to popular belief, constriction does not crush the prey but serves to suffocate it. Most boas tend to have relatively small dorsal scales and the scales on top of the head are also small and fragmented. Compared with those of most snakes, the ventral scales of boas are rather narrow. Unlike pythons, boas give birth to live young.

Boa constrictor—Mazacuata
Boa constrictor Linnaeus, 1758
Fig. 114

Description.—This moderately stout snake has a large, somewhat viperine head, vertical pupils, and small spine-like spurs that are vestiges of a thigh bone on either side of the vent. These spurs are larger in males than in females. This is a large species but rarely exceeds 300 cm in TL. Adult individuals of 150–220 cm are much more common. There usually are 19–20 supralabials, 22–24 infralabials, (57–59)–(55–79)–(39–43) dorsal scale rows, 225–253 ventrals, an undivided anal plate, and 47–69 undivided subcaudals. Scales on top of the head are small and not well differentiated from the more posterior dorsal scales.

The ground color is yellowish brown, pale gray-brown, tan, or medium brown. There are 22–30 medium to dark brown or black dorsal saddles; these are usually 10 or more scales long and each is interrupted dorsolaterally by a yellow streak. The dorsal blotches on the posterior of the body and tail become rust-colored to orange and are sharply separated by yellow. A series of grayish brown to dark brown roundish to vertically elliptical, lateral blotches, is arranged either alternately with or opposite the dorsal blotches and sometimes coalescing with the dorsal blotches. The head is often golden brown. A mid-dorsal head stripe extends from the tip of the snout to the occipital region, becoming broader posteriorly. There usually is a dark rectangular blotch on the side of the head in the loreal region, a dark vertical streak below the eye, and a dark postocular stripe extending from the posterior edge of the eye and curving downward to the angle of the jaw. The lower jaw usually has 3–4 irregular dark blotches. The venter is cream or pinkish to almost salmon with black speckling and mottling, with many black spots present at the level where the lateral blotches encroach onto the ventrals. The undersurface of the tail usually has distinct black bars or spots, separated by immaculate yellow. Juveniles are patterned similarly to adults but are usually more brightly colored.

Natural History.—This snake occurs in tropical and subtropical wet, moist, and dry forest. Mostly nocturnal, it is often found active on the forest floor, frequently in secondary vegetation. I have also taken this species from tepezcuintle and armadillo burrows on hillsides, from hollow trees and logs, coiled in trees at heights of 2–5 m (see "To Catch a Boa," page 190), and from the deep recesses of overhanging banks carved by streams. I have occasionally found this snake out and about by day, usually in heavily forested situations. Boa constrictors are good climbers and may ascend high into trees. It has been reported that juveniles are more arboreal than adults, but I have found the reverse to be true. There seems to be a strong geographic component to the behavior of this species. Most South American boas that I have come across tend to be rather mild mannered and easily handled. Conversely, many Central American boas are easily aroused and aggressive when first encountered. They hiss loudly, mouth partly opened, and readily strike at any intruder. However, these snakes usually calm down in captivity.

Boa constrictors look for good places to ambush prey, often lying coiled in mammal burrows or along the edges of stream courses. They feed on most kinds of small to moderately sized vertebrates, such as iguanas (*Ctenosaura, Iguana*), smaller lizards (*Ameiva, Cnemidophorus*), birds (blue-gray tanager, antbird), spiny pocket mice (*Heteromys*), agoutis (*Dasyprocta*), tree porcupines (*Coendou*), common opossums (*Didelphis*) and woolly opossums (*Caluromys*) and four-eyed opossums (*Philander*), bats (*Artibeus, Desmodus*), rabbits (*Sylvilagus*), and pizotes (also known in English as coatimundis, *Nasua*). There are even records of ocelots (*Felis pardalis*, 15 kg) and young brocket deer (*Mazama*, 20 kg) being eaten by boas. I know of two instances in Guatemala where boa constrictors entered houses and ate house cats. Smaller specimens tend to feed heavily on small lizards and small rodents, whereas larger specimens feed mostly on larger mammals and an occasional iguana. Boa constrictors, of course, sometimes fall prey themselves; one individual measuring 1683 mm in TL was found while being eaten by an even larger snake (see Tropical Indigo Snake account).

Females give birth to 12–64 live young that are about 35–45 cm in TL. Juveniles have been found in May, June, July, and August in Petén. The anal spurs of males are larger than those of females and used to stroke the female during courtship. This is a long-lived species with a record longevity of 38 years, 10 months in captivity.

✔*Distribution.*—Boa constrictors are wide-ranging, occurring from Mexico to Argentina and also on a number of islands, including the Tres Marías Islands of Pacific Mexico, and Saint Lucia, Dominica, Trinidad, and Tobago in the Caribbean. They are found throughout most of Petén in both forested and relatively open habitats and range from near sea level to about 1,200 m.

Remarks.—This is the largest species of snake occuring in the Petén region. As with all large species of snakes, it has been the subject of much exaggeration. I have heard incredible tales of huge serpents in many villages around Petén that would make even a Texan blush. Almost everywhere, it seems, there are reputed to be monsters of this species as big around as mahogany trees and capable of eating cattle. Most of the large specimens that I have seen over the years have been about 2 m or a little more in length, and I have encountered perhaps half a dozen individuals that were around 2.5 m. The largest specimen I have seen from Guatemala was one 3.2 m (10.5 feet) in TL from the Río Polochic valley, found in a local resident's hut in the process of eating the village cat and collected by Joe Mendelson. This boa constrictor (but not the cat) was preserved in its entirety and now is in the University of Texas at Arlington herpetology collection; as far as I know, it represents the largest snake ever found in Guatemala for which there is documented evidence. Some 20 years ago there were two large, mounted specimens of boa constrictors in the Museo Nacional de Historia Natural in Guatemala City, the larger of which measured almost 4 m. However, the skins of these mounted specimens had been greatly stretched and, judging from their head sizes, I do not think that in life either would have exceeded the Polochic snake in size.

Other vernacular names include *boa* in Guatemala and *wanasai* and *wowla* in Belize.

To Catch a Boa.—I was introduced to my first boa constrictor over 35 years ago on the Río Oscuro on the southwestern side of Lago de Izabal in eastern Guatemala. With a couple of friends, I was hunting and fishing from a dugout canoe along this river early one morning when our local guide, whom we knew only as Octavio, casually mentioned seeing a boa. Curiously, this is the local name for the snake in this part of Guatemala, whereas it is known as mazacuata almost everywhere else. (I suspect that the snake is called a boa here because the United Fruit Company had extensive holdings in the Motagua Valley between Gualán and Puerto Barrios from about 1920 to 1954 and employed many North Americans, who may have referred to this snake by its common English name.)

Although I was only 12 or 13 years old, I already had a blinding interest in snakes and greatly desired to add a fine boa constrictor to my collection. This was early in the rainy season and the first torrential rains had caused the lower Río Oscuro to overflow its banks into the surrounding forest. Many of the trees along the banks were heavily laden with epiphytes, particularly bromeliads that had died and dried out during the dry season. Octavio pointed up into one of these bromeliad-covered trees standing in water on the edge of the river. There, some 4 or 5 m above the water, the coils of the boa were clearly evident.

We tied our dugout to the tree and I ascended to about the level of the snake. Unfortunately for me, the snake was tightly coiled in the vegetation and I had difficulty in ascertaining exactly where its head was positoned. At the time, I was inexperienced with large snakes and more than slightly terrified when I realized I was precariously perched high in a tree with the biggest snake I had ever seen. Presently, after some prodding, the snake became irritated and began to strike and hiss. I tried in vain to gain a vantage to grab it behind the head, but the snake would not cooperate, and I could not get up my nerve to seize it at midbody.

Finally, bored with these proceedings, Octavio yelled that he was going to help me. But instead of climbing into the tree with me, he put a lighted match to the dry bromeliads on the lower branches. These quickly burst into flame and soon the entire tree was engulfed in fire. There was no choice but to abandon my precarious perch. I jumped for the river. The snake soon followed and swam to the opposite bank, where it disappeared into the brush.

Inquiry after Octavio during a visit to the region in 1994 yielded word that he was still actively fishing the waters of Lago de Izabal, although by my calculations he was by then well over 80 years old. I was on a tight schedule and regretted not being able to go and see him. I hope he has retained his sense of humor.

Annulated Boa—Boa Anillada
Corallus annulatus (Cope, 1876)
Fig. 115

Description.—This snake has vertical pupils and a large, somewhat viperine head well set off from the slender neck. On either side of the vent there are small spinelike spurs that are vestiges of a thigh bone. This is a slender species, which in Guatemala reaches at least 172.5 cm in TL. The long, slender tail is prehensile. There are 3 or 4 loreals, 14 supralabials, 18 infralabials, 50–54 dorsal scale rows at midbody, 251–255 ventrals, an undivided anal plate, and 80–87 undivided subcaudals.

In adults the ground color is pale brown with the dorsum slightly darker than the sides. On either side of the body is a series of about 44–47 large dark brown annuli that have salmon-colored centers, and the venter is pale pinkish buff. Juveniles are cinnamon colored, with the dorsum slightly darker than the sides. Juveniles apparently go through an ontogenetic change in color, becoming salmon colored with better defined dark-edged annuli before attaining the adult coloration.

Natural History.—This species inhabits tropical wet forest. In Guatemala, it has been found active at night 1.5–2 m above the ground on the buttressed root of a huge tree or stretched out on a palm leaf. A juvenile, collected in January, had a distinct umbilical scar and was estimated to be no more than two months old. This juvenile was 51.2 cm in TL when collected and fed on anoles in captivity. A captive adult fed on mice. This species gives birth to live young.

Distribution.—The annulated boa is known in Guatemala only from a small portion of northeastern Izabal, but it probably occurs in neighboring Belize and nearby Petén. It is also known from the Sierra del Merendón in Honduras. In lower Central America, this snake ranges from southern Nicaragua to Panama and Colombia east of the Andes; it also occurs in the Pacific lowlands of Colombia and Ecuador. In Guatemala, it occurs in wet rainforest at elevations of less than 100 m.

Remarks.—The populations of this snake in Nicaragua and Costa Rica are of the subspecies *Corallus annulatus annulatus;* whether snakes from Guatemala should be allocated to this subspecies remains to be ascertained.

COLUBRIDS—COLUBRIDOS

FAMILY COLUBRIDAE

The vast majority of snakes belong to this family. Colubrids occur worldwide on all continents except Antarctica. Most species have a typical complement of nine large supracephalic plates, the ventrals are well developed, and the subcaudals are usually divided. No trace of the pelvis is present. No species of colubrid has a functional left lung.

Species of colubrids living in Petén exemplify the variety present in this family. There are burrowers (*Adelphicos*), tree dwellers (*Leptophis*), aquatic inhabitants (*Tretanorhinus*), and terrestrial racers (*Dendrophidion, Dryadophis*). Some species forage by night and have a vertically elliptical pupil (*Leptodeira*); some are mostly diurnal and have a round pupil (*Drymobius*), and still others may be found abroad by day or at night (*Coniophanes*). There are colubrid species that feed on earthworms such as *Adelphicos*, on snails and slugs (*Ninia, Sibon*), frogs (*Leptodeira*), lizards (*Conophis, Imantodes, Scaphiodontophis*), birds (*Pseustes*), and on mammals (*Drymarchon, Spilotes*). The posterior teeth on the maxilla are enlarged in some species of colubrids and may bear open grooves that function in channeling a weak venom (*Conophis, Xenodon*). In other species, the maxillary teeth are not modified (*Coluber, Dryadophis*). Most species lay eggs, but a few (*Storeria, Thamnophis*) bear live young. Some species are tiny, rarely reaching much more than 18 cm in TL (*Tantillita*), whereas others commonly exceed 250 cm (*Drymarchon, Spilotes*).

Several species of colubrids not included in this book may eventually prove to be present in Petén. The brown mussurana (*Clelia scytalina*) is reported from extreme northern Belize but otherwise is absent from the entire Yucatán Peninsula. The systematics of this genus are poorly known and the two Belize records may prove to be variants of the black mussurana (*Clelia clelia*) or something other than the brown mussurana, which is otherwise known from the Pacific versant from west-central Mexico southward to Costa Rica. Werler's diamondback watersnake (*Nerodia rhombifer werleri*) is known from the Río Usumacinta and its tributaries in Tabasco and northern Chiapas, Mexico. It is possible that further exploration of the Río Usumacinta along the western border of Petén will reveal the presence of this snake there.

Four-lined Middle American Earth Snake—Busca-lombriz Rayada
Adelphicos quadrivirgatus (Jan, 1862)
Fig. 116

Description.—The head is small, somewhat conical, and barely wider than the neck. The small dark eyes have a round pupil. There are usually 7 supralabials, 6–8 infralabials, a single scale in the loreal-preocular area, 1 + 1 temporals, 15–15–15 smooth dorsal scale rows, 117–149 ventrals, a divided anal plate, and 36–49 divided subcaudals. The anterior chinshields are large, the first pair of infralabials meet at the ventral midline, and infralabials 2–3 are narrow and reduced to form a narrow border along the margin of the lip. This species reaches about 40 cm in TL.

The dorsal color is pale brown, pale gray, or medium brown. There usually are four black longitudinal lines, but these may be faint or obfuscated by dark ground color. Dark brown dorsolateral stripes are present on scale row 5, or on the lower part of scale row 4 and upper part of scale row 5. Dark lateral stripes are present on scale rows 1–2 and sometimes the lower half of scale row 3. The central portions of the scales of rows 1–2 are often pale, creating three thin lines on the sides of the body: one along the juncture of the ventrals and scale row 1, another involving the borders of rows 1–2, and another along the borders of scale rows 2–3. The top and sides of the head are dark brown. The venter may be cream, yellow, pink, or salmon. In some specimens the venter is almost immaculate, with only a few dark specks on the body posteriorly, and the subcaudals are pale except for a dark brown midventral stripe. In other individuals, the entire venter is heavily speckled with dark pigment, especially on the lateral and anterior portions of the ventrals, and the subcaudals are mostly dark brown. Most of the labials, chin, and throat may be pale, but there is almost always a little dark pigment on the anterior chinshields, and often the undersurface of the head is heavily speckled with dark pigment. A black midventral line on the tail may extend forward for 12–15 scales anterior to the vent.

Natural History.—This snake occurs in tropical and subtropical wet and moist forest. A burrowing species, it is more active below ground than on the surface. It is often associated with deep leaf litter or other piles of plant rubbish and may be found by raking litter in moist areas or by looking under logs. I have sometimes found individuals crossing roads or trails at night, especially after heavy rains that undoubtedly flooded their abodes. The species occurs in both the primary and secondary forests of Petén but does not seem to be nearly as abundant in the region as it is on the Pacific versant of Guatemala. It feeds almost exclusively on soft-bodied invertebrates, particularly earthworms. This snake is preyed upon by the white-lipped spotbelly snake (*Coniophanes fissidens*) and variable coral snake (*Micrurus diastema*).

Eggs are laid during the early rainy season in May and June. Hatchlings are about 10 cm in TL. In southern Veracruz, a clutch of three eggs was found in a termite nest some 1–1.5 m above ground. The eggs were about 10 cm from the surface of the nest, which was 70 cm in diameter. It has been suggested that the snake possibly exploits this niche, which may afford it some protection against ants and other predators as well as providing a suitable microenvironment for incubation.

Distribution.—The four-lined Middle American earth snake occurs from Tamaulipas, Mexico, southward along the Atlantic watershed through northern Guatemala, Belize, and into northwestern Honduras; and on the Pacific versant from Oaxaca, Mexico, to Guatemala. It probably occurs throughout most of Petén and Belize in moist microhabitats. It is absent from the central and northern portion of the Yucatán Peninsula. In Guatemala, it occurs from near sea level to about 1,300 m.

Remarks.—Several subspecies are recognized, mostly on the basis of the size of the chinshields and anterior infralabials, number of ventrals and subcaudals, and body striping. The subspecies that occurs in Petén is *Adelphicos quadrivirgatus visoninus.* Another vernacular name is *zacatera.*

Rufous-headed Snake—Culebra Cabeza Colorada
Amastridium veliferum Cope, 1860
Fig. 117

Description.—The head is moderately large and the eyes are large with round pupils. The head is somewhat angular with a sharp canthal ridge. There are usually 7 supralabials, 9 infralabials, a loreal, 1 preocular, 2 preoculars, 1 + 2 temporals, 17–17–17 dorsal scale rows, 144–170 ventrals, a divided anal plate, and 77–86 divided subcaudals. The dorsal scales are weakly keeled on the posterior portion of the body. This species reaches a maximum length of about 47 cm in TL.

The overall coloration is dark gray to

black, with a series of small white dots on scale rows 5 or 6; these dots are separated from each other by 1–5 scales. The venter is also dark, heavily mottled with gray or dark gray-brown, but a little paler than the dorsum. The top of the head is orange, with the internasals, prefrontals, frontal, supraoculars, and parietals with irregular black streaks. A finger of dark pigment from the neck extends forward middorsally into the rufous head coloration and reaches about to the parietals. Each labial scale usually has a white spot. A dark brown postocular stripe, distinctly bordered below by a white streak, extends from the posterior edge of the eye to the angle of the jaw and sometimes beyond.

Natural History.—This snake inhabits tropical wet forest. I have found this individual under a small log along the edge of a stream and beneath a large fallen leaf on top of a large log. I have encountered active rufous-headed snakes just after nightfall and they have been observed crawling through moist leaf litter by day. This snake appears to be restricted to primary forest.

One specimen from Veracruz contained small myriapods in its stomach, and another from the same area contained an unidentified lizard, possibly a night lizard (*Lepidophyma*). Stomach contents of these snakes from Chiapas and Tamaulipas included small frogs, one of which was identified as a species of *Eleutherodactylus*.

Distribution.—This snake occurs on the Atlantic versant from Nuevo León, Mexico, to Panama, exclusive of most of the Yucatán Peninsula. It occurs locally on the Pacific versant in southeastern Chiapas–southwestern Guatemala and in central Panama. Known from southeastern Petén and southern and central Belize, it probably occurs in the western part of Petén as well. This snake occurs in the foothills of the northern highlands of Alta Verapaz and Izabal at elevations of 150–650 m.

Black Mussurana—Mata Culebra
Clelia clelia (Daudin, 1803)
Fig. 118

Description.—This snake has small dark eyes with subcircular pupils. The head of juveniles is moderately large, but that of adults is not much wider than the body. There usually are 7–8 supralabials, 7–9 infralabials, a single loreal, 1 preocular, 2 postoculars, 2 + 3 temporals, 19–19–17 smooth dorsal scale rows, 210–240 ventrals, an undivided anal plate, and 71–87 divided subcaudals. This is a large, robust species, sometimes exceeding 200 cm.

Adults are uniformly shiny black above with the dark pigment extending over the lateral edges of the ventrals and subcaudals. The infralabials, chin, throat, and venter are cream, usually with a suffusion of dark pigment along the infralabial sutures and on portions of the infralabials adjacent to the chinshields.

Individuals undergo a remarkable ontogenetic color change. Juveniles are red dorsally, with black-tipped dorsal scales. The scales on the back have more dark pigment than do those on the sides. Usually, the vertebral row is particularly darkly tipped, forming a dotted middorsal line. The top of the head is black to about the posterior edge of the parietals. Posterior to the black head cap is a yellow collar 3–5 scales long, which is followed by a black nape patch 5–8 scales long and extending laterally to about scale row 3. The infralabials, chin, throat, and all but the upper portion of the supralabials are mostly cream, but the anterior infralabials and mental are lightly suffused with dark pigment. Dorsally, about the distal half of the tail is black. Subadults in transition between the juvenile and adult colorations have a brown dorsum and black head.

Natural History.—This snake inhabits tropical wet and moist forest. The posterior teeth on the maxillary are enlarged, grooved, and associated with venom glands. This is one of the comparatively few species of snakes that employs both venom and constriction in subduing its prey (but see "Docile Snakes," page 197). It is nocturnal and I have found it most frequently at night stretched out on the banks of streams or steep paths.

This species feeds primarily on other snakes. There is a reliable record of a 2 m (6½-foot) individual that contained a 1.8 m (6-foot) barba amarilla (*Bothrops asper*). Other species of snakes preyed on include a racer (*Dryadophis melanolomus*) and treesnake (*Spilotes pullatus*). I have seen specimens eat striped basilisks (*Basiliscus vittatus*), which were seized at night as they were sleeping on low streamside vegetation. A specimen from Panama contained a teiid lizard.

During the late rainy season (August through November) females lay 18–22 eggs, which hatch in 85–90 days. The eggs were 46–48 mm long in a clutch laid by a Guatemalan female and the hatchlings were 31–33 cm in TL.

Distribution.—The black mussurana occurs from Veracruz and Guerrero, Mexico, southward through Central America to Argentina in South America. It is found in the southern, humid portion of Petén near and south of Petén near and south of Sayaxché and in central Belize. This species occurs from near sea level to about 700 m in Guatemala.

Remarks.—The closely related brown mussurana (*Clelia scytalina*) is reported from two specimens from extreme northern Belize and may occur in northeastern Petén. However, with only a single museum specimen available, evaluation of the status of this population is not possible. The brown mussurana purportedly differs from the black mussurana in having 17 rather than 19 dorsal scale rows at midbody, although this character is likely variable. The subspecies of black mussurana occurring in Petén is *Clelia clelia clelia*. Other vernacular names include *zumbadora, zopilota,* and *culebrera.*

Docile Snakes.—Despite its large size and powerful body, the black mussurana *(Clelia clelia)* is of mellow disposition. I have encountered many of these snakes over the years and have never had one attempt to bite me. Nevertheless, they command respect by their size and the fact that they are opisthoglyphous, and rarely have I given one the chance to bite. On one occasion, I had the good fortune to witness just how mild-mannered this snake can be. While searching for frogs along a stream in the Montañas del Mico in eastern Guatemala one night, I spied a very large specimen of black mussurana stretched out along the bank near the water's edge. I collected this snake, which was about 2 m in length, and put it in a large pillowcase that I carried specifically for holding large snakes. I hung the pillow case from my belt and proceeded upstream, continuing to collect frogs.

I had reached the top of a small waterfall when the snake made a strong surge and managed to push itself out of the pillowcase from under my belt and got into my shirt, which I had not tucked into my trousers. I could feel the snake's large coils on my body and chest and quickly began trying to locate its head. In the struggle I lost my balance and toppled headlong off the edge of the waterfall into the pool at its base, severely bruising myself on some large boulders and losing my light in the process. I grabbed the snake as it finally managed to exit from a sleeve of my shirt.

In the dark, I was sorely tempted to part company with the mussurana and fling it away into the stream. But such fine specimens are not easy to find. Probably somewhat imprudently, I held on, fighting my way through the streamside vegetation to a small trail and stumbling about a kilometer back to camp with the writhing snake in my hands. If ever a snake had reason or opportunity to bite, it was this large mussurana, and it was with great reluctance the next morning that I prepared it as a scientific specimen. It is now in the University of Kansas collection.

Southern Racer—Zumbadora Olivácea
Coluber constrictor Linnaeus, 1758
Fig. 119

Description.—The head is moderately distinct from the neck and the eye is large with a round pupil. There usually are 7–8 supralabials, 8–9 infralabials, a single loreal, 1–2 preoculars, 2 postoculars, 1 + 2 or 2 + 2 temporals (rarely 3 + 2 temporals), 17(15)–15(17)–15(13) smooth dorsal scale rows, 151–172 ventrals, a divided anal plate, and 78–108 divided subcaudals. The largest individual I have seen in Guatemala was 72.2 cm in TL, but this species grows to over 1 m.

The dorsum is olive-brown or greenish gray, with the sides of the body paler. The venter is bright yellow to pale yellow-green. The top of the head is colored similarly to the dorsum of the body and the labials, chin, and throat are yellow. In juveniles the ground color is pale tan. They have a distinct pattern of dark brown, jagged-edged bands at least on the anterior two-thirds of the body and irregular dark brown spotting on the sides. This pattern fades out on the posterior part of the body and may become vaguely striped with brown; the dorsum of the tail is usually uniformly brown.

Natural History.—This diurnal forager appears to be restricted to savannas and open, sparsely wooded regions of tropical moist forest. It may be found in grassy fields and also climbs into low shrubs and bushes. Juveniles consume insects such as grasshoppers and crickets and an occasional lizard, whereas adults feed mostly on vertebrates, including rodents, lizards, and other snakes. The ecology of this snake has been well studied in the United States, but little is known about the fecundity, reproductive season, or young of tropical populations. Females lay 5–12 eggs early in the rainy season.

Distribution.—The southern racer occurs from extreme southwestern Canada eastward to New England and southward along both the Atlantic and Pacific slopes (disjunct populations) to Oaxaca, Mexico, and northern and eastern Guatemala. In Guatemala it is uncommon and is known from only a few specimens. I have seen it from the dry slopes near Doña María in the Motagua Valley. In Petén, this snake occurs in the savanna regions around La Libertad to the southwest of Lago Petén Itzá, and in Belize it inhabits open areas of Mountain Pine Ridge. This species occurs from about 50 to 800 m in Guatemala.

Remarks.—The subspecies occurring in Guatemala is *Coluber constrictor oaxaca,* which ranges from southern Texas to the Motagua Valley. Another vernacular name is *zumbadora.*

Mottled-jaw Spotbelly Snake—Culebra Vientre-punteado Labiomoteado
Coniophanes bipunctatus (Günther, 1858)
Fig. 120

Description.—The head is moderately sized, the snout is sharp, and the eyes are medium sized with round pupils. There usually are 7–9 supralabials, 8–11 infralabials, a single loreal, 1 preocular, 2 postoculars, 1 + 2 temporals, 21–21(19)–17 smooth dorsal scale rows, 128–147 ventrals, a divided anal plate, and 72–94 divided subcaudals. Adult males have keeled scales above the vent. This snake reaches a maximum adult size of about 80 cm in TL.

Usually a black-bordered pale streak or series of spots extends from the nostril to the upper anterior edge of the eye and from the upper posterior edge of the eye to the temporal area. A distinct black-bordered pale postocular stripe extends from the lower posterior edge of the eye across the angle of the jaw and onto the neck. The dorsum is pale to medium brown or reddish brown. A middorsal blackish stripe, usually poorly defined at best, extends from about the parietals for the length of the body and onto the tail. Whether or not a middorsal stripe is defined, the middorsal 3–5 longitudinal scale rows are usually darker than the more lateral scales between the lateral stripes. A blackish lateral stripe is present on scale row 4 and adjacent portions of scale rows 3 and 5 (darkest along its upper edge on scale row 5). The top and sides of the head are dark brown. The labials, chin, and gulars possess an intricate pattern of dark vermiform markings, mostly along the edges of scales, and irregular pale yellow markings in the center of most scales; the labials often have pale vertical bars. The belly is cream or pale orange and each ventral scute has a pair of large brown or black spots. The ventral black spots continue onto the subcaudals but may disappear on about the distal fourth of the tail. The ventral spots are larger on the neck and anterior part of the body and become smaller posteriorly.

Natural History.—This snake inhabits tropical wet, moist, and dry forest. It has been recorded from the forest floor, but I have encountered most specimens at night lying on aquatic vegetation in marshy areas or by day under logs or debris at the edges of bodies of water. Infrequently, it is active by day. The major part of its diet includes various species of frogs. Eggs are laid during the rainy season.

Distribution.—The mottled-jaw spotbelly snake occurs from Veracruz, Mexico, southward through the Yucatán Peninsula and northern Central America to Panama. It is found at scattered localities throughout Petén, almost always near water. It ranges from near sea level to about 400 m in Guatemala.

Remarks.—The subspecies occurring in Petén is *Coniophanes bipunctatus bipunctatus*. Another vernacular name for it is *tabaquilla*.

White-lipped Spotbelly Snake—Culebra Vientre-punteado Labioblanco
Coniophanes fissidens (Günther, 1858)
Fig. 121

Description.—The head is moderately distinct from the neck and the eyes are medium-sized with round pupils. There are usually 8 supralabials, 8–10 infralabials, a single loreal, 1–2 preoculars, 2 postoculars, 1 + 2 temporals, 21(19)–21–17 smooth dorsal scale rows, 116–132 ventrals, a divided anal plate, and 72–85 divided subcaudals. Adult males have anal ridges. The maximum TL reached by this common snake is about 70 cm.

A dark streak extends from the rostral across the nasals and lower edge of the eye to past the angle of the jaw, usually well onto the neck. This dark streak is bordered below by a distinctive white stripe extending across the supralabials onto scales on the side of the neck. The lower part of the rostral and supralabials is darkly mottled. The dorsum is medium brown, often darker middorsally. The scales of the vertebral scale row sometimes are black around their periphery, creating an ill-defined middorsal line. There is a thin black lateral stripe on scale row 5, sometimes with a thin pale border above. The dorsal scales below this line are usually a little darker than the dorsum; the dark color on the sides of the body and tail encroaches on the lateral portions of the ventrals and subcaudals. The dorsum of the tail is medium brown, often with a black-edged dorsal stripe, a dark lateral stripe, and dark brown sides below the lateral stripe. The top of the head is brown or reddish brown, usually with a few black-edged yellow spots on the temporal region. A pair of cream but black-edged dorsolateral spots is present on the neck, followed posteriorly by dark-edged cream dorsolateral stripes. These stripes may be vaguely indicated on the the anterior one-fourth of the body, but in some specimens may continue as a pale upper border of the black lateral stripe for most of the length of the body. The venter is whitish, sometimes with a pinkish tinge. The chin and throat are heavily stippled with black punctations of different sizes. The outer edges of the ventrals have distinctive small black spots, usually one per side, but sometimes there are several present. These spots become smaller on the posterior of the body, and on the tail spotting may become irregular.

Natural History.—This snake occurs in tropical and subtropical wet and moist forest. It is active by day and by night, foraging in leaf litter. Although most often encountered in forested terrain, it may also be found in cultivated areas if there is abundant shade available. Adults frequently have incomplete tails, the result of an accident (see "Snake and Lizard Tails," page 162).

A wide variety of prey items are taken, including salamanders (*Bolitoglossa* sp.), frogs (*Eleutherodactylus* sp. and their eggs), toads (*Bufo*), lizards (*Norops* and *Sphenomorphus*), other snakes (*Adelphicos, Ninia, Rhadinaea,* and *Tantilla*), reptile eggs, and invertebrates (earthworms and lepidopteran larvae). Frogs are the most common item eaten. Occasionally, this species is cannibalistic.

Females become mature at about 25 cm SVL and males presumably at a somewhat smaller size. From 1 to 5 (usually 2–4) elongate eggs are laid from March through July. Hatchlings are about 14–15 cm in TL.

Distribution.—The white-lipped spotbelly snake is distributed from southern San Luis Potosí and southern Michoacán, Mexico, southward through Central America to northwestern Ecuador. It occurs in the southern half of Petén in mesic, well-drained forests. In Guatemala, it ranges from near sea level to about 1,830 m.

Remarks.—The subspecies occurring in Petén is *Coniophanes fissidens fissidens.*

Black-striped Snake—Culebra Rayas Negras
Coniophanes imperialis (Baird and Girard, 1859)
Fig. 122

Description.—The head is moderately distinct from the neck and the eye is medium sized with a round pupil. There usually are 8 supralabials, 9–10 infralabials, a single loreal, 1 preocular, 2 postoculars, 1 + 2 temporals, 19–19(21)–15 smooth dorsal scale rows, 117–141 ventrals, a divided anal plate, and 70–94 divided subcaudals. This species reaches about 60 cm in TL.

The upper parts of the supralabials are black, forming an irregular black line that curves downward at about the angle of the jaw and continues onto the neck. The supralabials and infralabials are mostly white with black flecks. The dorsum is pale to medium brown, usually with a black middorsal stripe, but this may be vague, absent, or broken into a series of dashes. If present, the middorsal stripe is usually confined to the vertebral scale row. There is a thin black line on dorsal scale row 4 or adjacent portions of dorsal scale rows 4–5, bordered above by a pale cream line on dorsal scale rows 5–6, which in turn has an irregular and often broken upper black edging. In some snakes, this pale line may be barely distinguishable, only slightly paler than the dorsum ground color. The sides of the body and tail below the lateral black line are dark brown, with this dark coloration extending onto the outer edges of the ventrals and subcaudals. Dark pigment on the outer edges of the ventrals may form a series of spots or dashes, or it may be more or less evenly distributed and continuous with the dark pigment on the sides of the body. The top of the head is dark brown with a pair of black-edged, yellow parietal spots. A black-edged yellow streak extends from the upper posterior edge of the eye across the upper temporal region; it is usually followed by a yellow spot or streak on the back of the head that may be fused with the dark-edged dorsolateral stripes on the neck. These yellow dorsolateral stripes become tan or pale brown posteriorly. The yellow temporal stripe continues anterior to the eye across the canthus, but this may be indistinct. The chin, throat, and anterior part of the venter are white, grading to yellow or yellow-orange at about midbody and to salmon or orange posteriorly. The chin and throat are marked with black punctations. A series of irregular black mid-ventral spots is present on the anterior part of the body, and these may extend most of the length of the body in some specimens, whereas in others, the spots are restricted to the anterior half.

Natural History.—This species inhabits tropical wet, moist, and dry forest. Active by day or at night, it is often seen crawling in leaf litter or coiled under rotten logs or piles of plant debris. It may be observed in open habitats or along the edges of wet or marshy areas. It is opisthoglyphous and feeds mostly on frogs and lizards. There are records of the species eating the yellow cricket treefrog (*Hyla microcephala*), milky treefrog (*Phrynohyas venulosa*), toads (*Bufo* sp.), Yucatán blind snake (*Typhlops microstomus*), and insects.

Females lay 3–10 elongate eggs that are about 18 × 8 mm and hatch after about 40 days. Juveniles have been reported in February-March and are approximately 15 cm in TL. A female containing well-developed eggs was collected in mid-May, suggesting an extended breeding season.

Distribution.—The black-striped snake occurs from southern Texas southward on the Atlantic watershed through eastern Mexico, the Yucatán, Belize, and northern and eastern Guatemala to Honduras; it also occurs locally on Pacific slopes in Oaxaca. This snake is found throughout most of Petén. In Guatemala, it occurs from near sea level to about 600 m.

Remarks.—The subspecies in Petén is *Coniophanes imperialis clavatus.*

Striped Spotbelly Snake—Culebra Vientre-punteado Listada
Coniophanes quinquevittatus (Duméril, Bibron, and Duméril, 1854)
Fig. 123

Description.—The head is small, scarcely distinct from the neck. The eye is small with a round pupil. There usually are 8 supralabials, 10–11 infralabials, a single loreal, 1 preocular, 2 postoculars, 1 + 2 temporals, 21(23)–21(19)–17 smooth dorsal scale rows, 157–164 ventrals, a divided anal plate, and 63–70 subcaudals. Adult males have anal ridges. This species reaches at least 87 cm in TL.

The supralabials are cream with a distinct black spot on each scale. The infralabials are also cream with black spots, but the spots are usually more irregular than on the supralabials. The dorsum is pale brown with a dark brown middorsal stripe on the vertebral scale row and sometimes on adjacent portions of the paravertebral scale rows, extending from the back of the head to the tip of the tail. Usually, the two dorsal scale rows on either side of the middorsal stripe are darker than several of the dorsal scale rows immediately lateral to them. At midbody, a dark gray to gray-brown lateral stripe is present on scale rows 3–5 and adjacent lower portions of scale row 6. On the posterior part of the body, the dark lateral stripe occupies scale rows 3–4 and adjacent portions of scale rows 2 and 5. The dark lateral stripe extends anteriorly across the temporal region and through the eye to the snout. The top of the head is brown, heavily suffused with dark gray. The venter is cream anteriorly, often becoming yellowish or pinkish posteriorly. The chin is punctated with many black spots, and most ventrals have large bold black spots on the lateral edges; often there is a midventral series of smaller black spots on most of the ventrals. The venter of the tail has paired black spots at least proximally, but these spots may fuse distally in some specimens, forming a zigzag line.

Natural History.—This aquatic species of tropical moist and dry forest is usually found in marshy or swampy areas with thick vegetation along the edges of lakes, ponds, or rivers. It is nocturnal and feeds on frogs and fish.

Distribution.—The striped spotbelly snake is distributed from southern Veracruz, Mexico, to central Petén. In the Yucatán Peninsula, it is known from relatively few specimens; it has been collected around the edges of Lago Petén Itzá and along the the northern coastal area of the Yucatán Peninsula. It occurs from near sea level to about 200 m.

Remarks.—No subspecies are recognized.

Schmidt's Striped Snake—Culebra Rayada de Schmidt
Coniophanes schmidti Bailey, 1937
Fig. 124

Description.—The head is moderately distinct from the neck and the eye is medium sized with a round pupil. There are usually 8 supralabials, 9–10 infralabials, a single loreal, 2 preoculars, 2 postoculars, 1 + 2 temporals, 23 (21–25)–25(23)–19 smooth dorsal scale rows, 153–175 ventrals, a divided anal plate, and 83–115 subcaudals. There is a small subpreocular scale on each side of the head. Adult males have keeled scales above the vent. This snake reaches a maximum of about 70 cm in TL.

The supralabials are mostly cream with some brown mottling. A distinctive yellow dorsolateral stripe on dorsal scale rows 8–9 begins on the anterior fourth of the body and extends onto the tail. A narrow, dark-edged, cream or yellow stripe extends from the upper posterior edge of the eye across the upper temporal region and may be discontinuous, forming a discrete nape spot or streak, or may be continuous with the dorsolateral stripe. The dorsal coloration between the pale dorsolateral stripes is dark brown; the dorsolateral stripes are edged ventrally with dark brown and the more ventral scales (scale rows 1–6 and the lower part of 7) on the side of the body are pale brown. The top of the head is reddish brown. The chin is mostly cream with a suffusion of a little brown pigment. The ventrals and subcaudals are immaculate cream.

Natural History.—This snake occurs in tropical moist and dry forest, usually in relatively open situations. It occurs at scattered localities in Petén and is found in forested habitats as well as secondary growth. Most of the specimens with which I am familiar came from hilly areas. This species feeds on lizards and frogs and lays 4–5 eggs during the rainy season.

Distribution.—Schmidt's striped snake is distributed from the northern Yucatán Peninsula to northern Chiapas (Mexico), central Petén (Guatemala), and Cayo (Belize). It is found at elevations between sea level and 300 m in Guatemala.

Remarks.—This species has sometimes been considered a subspecies of Cope's striped snake (*Coniophanes piceivittis*), a species occurring to the south of the Yucatán Peninsula from Pacific Mexico to Costa Rica.

Lizard Killer—Lagartijera
Conophis lineatus (Duméril, Bibron, and Duméril, 1854)
Fig. 125

Description.—This snake has a sleek, somewhat conical head that is only a little wider than its body. The eyes are moderately large with round pupils. There are usually 8 supralabials, 9–10 infralabials, 1 preocular, 2 postoculars, 2 + 2 or 2 + 3 temporals, 19(17)–19–17 smooth dorsal scale rows, 158–178 ventrals, a divided anal plate, and 56–80 divided subcaudals. This species reaches a maximum TL of about 120 cm.

Individuals from the northern part of the Yucatán Peninsula, northern Belize, and possibly northern Petén are uniformly gray or grayish brown dorsally, lacking any distinct striping on the body except for the head and neck. The lower two scale rows are slightly paler than the dorsum, the venter is pinkish, there is a suffusion of dark pigment on the chinshields and edges of the infralabials, and the supralabials are also pinkish, with the anterior scales of this series edged with gray along the margin of the lip. There are short dorsal and lateral stripes on the head and nape, with a reddish brown stripe beginning on the anterior portion of the nasal scale and extending posteriorly through the lower half of the eye to the beginning of the neck; this stripe is narrowly bordered in black above and below. There may be short paravertebral or lateral series of black dots on the nape, continuing onto the body on scale rows 4 or 7.

Snakes from central and southern Petén are striped throughout their body, with a pattern consisting of narrow dark lines and wider pale to brown stripes. Usually there are four narrow black lines on either side of the body: a ventrolateral line on dorsal scale row 1, a lower lateral line on scale row 2, an upper lateral line on the upper part of scale row 4 and the lower part of row 5, and a dorsolateral line on scale row 7. Additionally, on the paravertebral scale rows, there may be thin black lines that become more distinct posteriorly. The dorsal color between the dorsolateral lines and between the two lateral lines is medium to dark brown. If paravertebral dark lines are present, the color between them is pale gray-brown, with this color grading into brown on the anterior part of the body and proximal part of the tail. The stripes between the ventrolateral and lower lateral lines and between the upper lateral and dorsolateral lines are cream to almost white. The brown dorsal stripes, the whitish dorsolateral stripes, and brown lateral stripes continue onto the head to the tip of the snout. The whitish ventrolateral stripes also continue onto the head, where they merge with the mostly white supralabials. The margin of the upper jaw is darkly pigmented. The venter is immaculate cream colored or whitish except for the lateral edges of the ventrals, which may be pigmented or spotted in some specimens.

Natural History.—This diurnal species inhabits tropical and subtropical moist and dry forest. As its name suggests, it eats mostly lizards, especially those in the family Teiidae (ameivas and whiptails). There are records of this species eating a Gaumer's spiny pocket mouse (*Heteromys gaumeri*) and the eggs of ground-nesting birds. This snake lays 4–6 eggs in June or July.

Distribution.—The lizard killer occurs on the Atlantic versant from Veracruz and Oaxaca, Mexico, southward through northern Guatemala, the northern Yucatán Peninsula, and Belize to Costa Rica; and on the Pacific versant from Chiapas, Mexico, to Costa Rica. It is found at several localities in central Petén but may be absent from much of the southern, humid portion of the region. Areas of secondary growth, pastures, and natural clearings are frequented by these snakes. In Guatemala, the species occurs from near sea level to about 1,500 m.

Remarks.—This small-headed, innocuous-looking snake is quick to bite. It has well-developed rear teeth and a fairly potent venom that are used for subduing lizards. Anyone who handles these quick, agile snakes carelessly or attempts to restrain them runs a good risk of being bitten. I have witnessed about half a dozen bites from this species, several my own, and in every instance there was pain and swelling in the the bitten area, followed by some discoloration and discomfort. In the worst case, a bite from a snake from the Pacific coast of Guatemala caused my thumb to become discolored and provoked swelling that extended to my shoulder and persisted for several days. Wounds inflicted by these bites tend to bleed freely for some time; it is possible that these snakes possess an anticoagulant in their venom. They tend to hang on when they bite, and in the bites described, the snake was always forcibly removed.

Because of the considerable variation in color pattern of this snake, several different subspecies have been recognized: *Conophis lineatus lineatus*, *C. l. dunni*, and *C. l. concolor*. Some have been suggested to be full species. Other vernacular names are *guarda camino* and *sabanera*.

Three-colored Keeled Racer—Zumbadora Aquillada de Tres Colores
Dendrophidion nuchale (Peters, 1863)
Fig. 126

Description.—The head of this slender species is well distinguished from the neck and the large eye has a round pupil. On each side of the head there usually are a single preocular, 2 postoculars, 2 + 2 temporals, 9 supralabials, and 10 infralabials. The anal scute is divided or undivided; dorsal scales are disposed in 17–17–15 rows and most are strongly keeled. There are 153–175 ventrals and 132–163 divided subcaudals. The tail is often incomplete in this species. This snake reaches a maximum TL of a little over 150 cm.

The anterior supralabials are whitish, cream, or tan. The top of the head is reddish brown and the anterior third of the dorsum is reddish brown, pale greenish gray, or greenish and may have dark-edged pale crossbands or spots less than one scale row wide, or may lack any distinctive pattern. The middle part of the body usually has dark-bordered pale spots arranged as crossbands, and posteriorly the body becomes darker brown to almost black, usually with rows of pale, dorsolateral spots. The upper surface of the tail is reddish brown to coral red and may have traces of irregular pale crossbands; the subcaudals are salmon or orange. The chin and throat are yellowish. The venter is mostly immaculate cream or pale yellow, but a suffusion of dark pigment is present on the lateral portions of the ventrals and subcaudals.

Natural History.—This large-eyed snake inhabits tropical and subtropical wet forest. It is diurnal, exceedingly quick and agile, and apparently restricted to primary forest. This species is known to feed on frogs of the genus *Eleutherodactylus*. A hatchling was found in August, suggesting a breeding cycle similar to that of most other snakes in the region. Little is known about its reproductive biology other than that it lays about six eggs.

Distribution.—This species occurs in several disjunct areas including parts of Belize, northern and eastern Guatemala, northwestern Honduras, Costa Rica and Panama, and northern South America. In the northern part of its range, it occurs in the hills associated with the Maya Mountains and on the lower slopes of the northern and eastern Guatemalan highlands, usually inhabiting hilly situations at elevations of 100–1,000 m.

Remarks.—The three-colored keeled racer is one of the quickest, most alert snakes occurring in the Petén region. I have seen individuals launch themselves into the air off the tops of steep hillsides or from the edges of cliffs into deep ravines to escape predators.

Barred Keeled Racer—Zumbadora Aquillada de Barras
Dendrophidion vinitor Smith, 1941
Fig. 127

Description.—There usually are 9 supralabials, 10 infralabials, a single loreal, 1 preocular, 2 postoculars, 2 + 2 temporals, 17–17–15 dorsal scale rows, 148–165 ventrals, an anal plate that is usually divided (rarely single), and 111–128 divided subcaudals. Most of the dorsal scales are strongly keeled.

The tail is often incomplete in this species. Smaller than the three-colored keeled racer (*Dendrophidion nuchale*), this species reaches a TL of only about 100 cm.

The ground color is brown, darker middorsally. Distinct dark-edged, pale yellow or tan crossbands over most of the body are more than one scale row wide; posteriorly the body is patterned with crossbands, pale spots, dark longitudinal stripes, or some combination thereof. The venter is immaculate cream or yellow.

Natural History.—This snake inhabits tropical wet forest and perhaps tropical moist forest. It is a large-eyed, diurnal species that is restricted to primary forest. The biology and distribution of this snake are poorly known. It feeds on frogs. It presumably lays eggs; a hatchling 23 cm in TL, probably not more than a couple of months old, was captured in mid-October.

Distribution.—The barred keeled racer occurs in disjunct populations from southern Veracruz, Mexico, southward through parts of western and southern Petén, and then from Nicaragua through Costa Rica to eastern Panama and adjacent Colombia. In the northern part of its range it is known only from the mesic forests of the Sierra de Los Tuxtlas in Mexico, along the portion of the Río Usumacinta forming the border between Guatemala and Mexico, and from several foothill localities in southern Petén, Izabal, and Alta Verapaz. It occurs at low elevations of less than 1,300 m in humid forests.

Remarks.—Another vernacular name is *culebra barrada.*

Short-faced Snail-eater—Caracolera de Cara Corta
Dipsas brevifacies (Cope, 1866)
Fig. 128

Description.—The head is distinctly wider than the neck and the relatively large, protruding eyes have vertically elliptical pupils. The body is laterally compressed. The prefrontal borders the orbit in almost half of the specimens I have examined. The number of scales on the side of the head in front of the eye is highly variable: the total number between the nasal and eye (preoculars plus loreals) may be 1–6, with 2–5 most frequently found. Usually there are 3 postoculars, 2 + 2 or 2 + 3 temporals, 9–10 supralabials, and 10–12 infralabials. There are 15–15–15 smooth dorsal scale rows, and scales in the vertebral row are not or are only slightly wider than adjacent dorsal scales. There are 162–180 ventrals, an undivided anal, and 70–101 subcaudals. Usually two pairs of infralabials meet along the ventral midline behind the mental. This species reaches a maximum TL of about 60 cm.

The body and tail have alternating black and pale rings. There are 9–15 pale rings on the body and 5–12 on the tail. In life the pale rings may be pink, orange, or white with pink saddles. The black rings are 1.3–3 times longer than the pale rings that follow, and the pale body rings are 2–8 scales long at middorsum and usually a little longer ventrolaterally. The anterior portion of the head is black above and below. The color of the nuchal collar is usually more intense than the succeeding pale body rings and may be scarlet or bright orange. The nuchal collar extends from about the posterior edge of the parietals posteriorly for 2–4 scale lengths and may be interrupted middorsally, either partially or completely, by a posterior protrusion of black pigment from the top of the head.

Natural History.—This species occurs in tropical dry forest. It is nocturnal and appears to be most active on rainy nights. Although the short-faced snail-eater has many of the adaptations associated with arboreal snakes, including a laterally compressed and elongated body, an abrupt narrowing of the neck behind head, and enlarged and protruding eyes, it is often found on the ground. Unlike most members of its genus, it lacks the widened vertebral scale row, which is often associated with arboreality. Given the dry habitat in which this species lives, it seems likely that it remains in underground retreats most of the time, foraging above ground and perhaps climbing in vegetation only when environmental conditions are favorable (i.e., after dark, especially when the humidity is high). The diet consists of snails, which are extracted from their shells before being swallowed.

This snake lays 2–5 eggs, with 2–3 being most common. The smallest hatchlings known for this species were 18.6–19.1 cm in TL. Females containing shelled eggs with embryos in the early stages of development have been collected in March and July; hatchlings have been collected in September and December.

Distribution.—This snail-eater occurs in the northern Yucatán Peninsula, including most of the state of Yucatán and the eastern half of Quintana Roo, Mexico, and east-central Belize, at elevations between sea level and 300 m. I am not aware of records from Petén, but given the paucity of collections in the northern part of this department, this species probably will eventually prove to be a component of the Guatemalan herpetofauna.

Remarks.—Another vernacular name is *chupa caracoles.*

Middle American Smooth-scaled Racer—Lagartijera Lisa Olivácea
Dryadophis melanolomus (Cope, 1868)
Fig. 129

Description.—The head is moderately distinct from the neck and the eyes are large with round pupils. There usually are 9 supralabials, 10–11 infralabials, a single loreal, 1 preocular, 2 postoculars, 2 + 2 temporals, 17–17–15 smooth dorsal scale rows, 171–188 ventrals, a divided anal plate, and 114–136 divided subcaudals. This species reaches about 150 cm in TL; males attain a larger size than females.

This racer is subject to much individual and ontogenetic variation. Other than the dark brown or black edging that is usually present on the anterior half of most dorsal scales, the dorsum of large adults is usually more or less uniformly colored, being olive-tan, olive-brown, olive-green, or reddish brown. In Alta Verapaz and Izabal two distinct color phases occur sympatrically, one olive-brown and the other a deep reddish orange, but whether variation of color pattern in Petén snakes is the result of individual variation or geographic variation has not been demonstrated. In juveniles, there is a banded pattern of up to about 65 narrow, whitish to pale gray bands on the body about a single scale wide or less, but these bands become less evident or disappear as the snake matures. In young adults, the black edging of scales in dorsal rows 1–2 and 4–5 is often reduced, thus creating a pair of pale lateral stripes on each side, but these become obfuscated with age. The head is often brownish, regardless of body color, and there is a dark postocular stripe from the posterior edge of the eye to above the angle of the jaw. Usually there is a dark streak across the loreal region from the posterior nasal to the anterior edge of the eye. The venter is cream, pale yellow, or reddish orange; often the anterior two-thirds of the venter is pale yellow or cream, grading on the posterior part of the body and tail to a brilliant pink. The supralabials are whitish to yellow, sometimes suffused with gray mottling. The chin and throat may be uniformly white but usually are spotted with gray or brown pigment.

Natural History.—This snake inhabits tropical wet, moist, and dry forest and subtropical wet and moist forest. Large-eyed, alert, and quick, this diurnal species often is found on the forest floor or as it crosses paths and roads through either secondary or primary vegetation.

It feeds mostly on reptiles, especially lizards (there are records of this species ingesting *Norops* sp., *Ameiva undulata*, *Cnemidophorus angusticeps*, *Basiliscus vittatus*, *Sceloporus teapensis*, *Sphenomorphus cherriei*, *Lepidophyma flavimaculatum*, and *Diploglossus rozellae*), as well as unidentified reptile eggs, small colubrid snakes, frogs (*Eleutherodactylus*), neonatal cricetine rodents, and shrews (*Cryptotis* sp.).

Females reach maturity at about 58 cm SVL, at minimally 18 months of age. It is thought that females reproduce biennially. Two to five eggs are laid in the late rainy season between August and November. Eggs are about 45–55 mm in length.

Distribution.—The Middle American smooth-scaled racer occurs from Tamaulipas and Sinaloa, Mexico, southward through Central America to Panama. Found throughout most of Petén, the northern Yucatán Peninsula, and Belize, it is most common in forested habitats. However, it also occurs in secondary growth and the forested islands of the savanna region. This species occurs from near sea level to about 1,250 m.

Remarks.—The subspecies occurring over most of Petén and the Yucatán Peninsula is *Dryadophis melanolomus melanolomus*. Another subspecies, *D. m. laevis*, occurs in the foothills of Alta Verapaz and Izabal and possibly intergrades with *D. m. melanolomus* in southern Petén and parts of Belize. The genus *Dryadophis* sometimes has been synonymized with *Mastigodryas* but these two genera appear to be distinct. Another vernacular name is *zumbadora*.

Tropical Indigo Snake—Arroyera de Cola Negra
Drymarchon corais (Boie, 1827)
Fig. 130

Description.—This is one of the largest species of snakes found in Petén, surpassed in length only by the boa constrictor (*Boa constrictor*) and tiger treesnake (*Spilotes pullatus*). Individuals commonly exceed 220 cm in TL, and there is a verified record for one huge old specimen from Guatemala measuring 295 cm; an individual from Belize was 279 cm in total length. In most colubrid snakes females usually grow to greater lengths than males, but the larger tropical indigo snakes all seem to be males. The head is moderately distinct from the neck and the eye is large with a round pupil. There usually are 8 supralabials, 8 infralabials, a single loreal, 1 preocular, 2 postoculars, 2 + 2 temporals, 17-17-15 smooth dorsal scale rows, 195–201 ventrals, an undivided anal plate, and 73–80 divided subcaudals.

The ground color of the anterior half of the body is pale brown to olive-tan, becoming darker posteriorly so that the tail and about the posterior fourth of the body are blackish. Juveniles often have irregular black mottling anteriorly, with black dorsal crossbands on the posterior of the body. In adults, the dorsum of the anterior part of the body is more uniform with less mottling. A distinctive black marking is present on the side of the neck beginning in the dorsolateral area less than a head length behind the head and extending diagonally downward to the ventrals; this black marking sometimes is followed a short distance behind by a second similar marking. The top of the head is uniformly pale to medium brown and the sides of the head are a little paler. Usually, there are four bold black vertical or diagonal streaks below and behind the eye; these streaks occupy the posterior portions of supralabial scales. Usually three of these black streaks continue onto the infralabials, where they are also located on the posterior portions of the scales. Apart from these black streaks, the chin and throat are immaculate cream. The ventrals on the anterior two-thirds of the body are cream colored with transverse black streaks extending about a third of the way across the venter at intervals of every 2–5 ventrals. About the posterior one-third of the venter is dark gray to black; the subcaudals are uniformly dark.

Natural History.—This snake inhabits tropical and subtropical wet, moist, and dry forest. A diurnal species, it frequents stream and river valleys and the riparian forests running through open areas and appears to be more abundant in secondary growth. This species also occurs in parts of the southern United States, where it has a reputation for being docile and mild-mannered. This is not true of tropical indigos, which are easily irritated to the point of inflating the throat and vibrating the tails, and often delivering a powerful, although nonvenomous, bite. However, after a short time in captivity tropical indigos usually settle down and can safely be handled.

The diet of this snake includes most groups of terrestrial vertebrates—frogs, lizards, snakes, birds, and mammals. Specific prey items of Guatemalan specimens include toads (*Bufo marinus, B. valliceps*), lizards (*Eumeces schwartzei, Lepidophyma flavimaculatum, Basiliscus vittatus*), and snakes (*Boa constrictor, Ninia sebae*). The tail of a long-tailed false coral (*Pliocercus elapoides*) was found in the stomach of one Guatemalan indigo snake. This snake is neither opisthoglyphous nor a constrictor—it simply rushes and seizes its prey, which it then swallows alive. Seeing a snake capturing or eating prey in the field is a rare and special occasion. I have twice come across tropical indigos eating frogs in the vegetation along fencerows. Both times, I would not have found the snake were it not for the distress calls of the frog. On another occasion, I investigated the rustling under some bushes and found a tropical indigo about 2 m long, with another individual of the same species, only slightly smaller, about half ingested. As soon as I grabbed these snakes, the smaller was regurgitated relatively unharmed except for a number of needlelike teeth marks along its back.

The abilities of this snake at subduing relatively large and powerful prey should not be underestimated. A huge specimen of tropical indigo, measuring 295 cm in TL, was found thrashing on the forest floor while eating a boa constrictor 168.3 cm long. This same tropical indigo specimen also contained a jumping pitviper *(Atropoides nummifer)* 95.3 cm in TL.

Males from Belize have been observed in ritual combat dances (these usually occur just prior to mating) in February. Eggs are laid over an extended period during the early rainy season, from about May to July, and hatchlings have been seen from July through October.

Distribution.—A disjunct population of the tropical indigo snake occurs in the southeastern United States; it also occurs from southern Texas and southern Sonora, Mexico, southward through Central America and South America to Argentina. Widespread in Petén, the northern Yucatán Peninsula, and Belize, it frequents the edges of clearings in forested areas and the riparian forests in open country. In Guatemala, this species occurs from near sea level to about 1,900 m.

Remarks.—The subspecies in Petén is *Drymarchon corais melanurus.* Another vernacular name is *zumbadora.*

Speckled Racer—Ranera Salpicada
Drymobius margaritiferus (Schlegel, 1837)
Fig. 131

Description.—The head is moderately large and the eyes are very large with round pupils. There usually are 9 supralabials, 8–11 infralabials, a single loreal, 1 preocular, 2 postoculars, 2 + 2 temporals, 17–17–15 keeled dorsal scale rows, 144–158 ventrals, a divided anal plate, and 107–130 divided subcaudals. The tail is often incomplete. This species reaches a maximum total length of about 120 cm.

The anterior portion of most dorsal scales is turquoise, the posterior portion is heavily blackened, and there is a bright orange streak on at least the proximal part of the scale, often extending most of the length of the keel. The turquoise is more intense on the anterior part of the body. The top of the head is brown and the supralabials are cream, edged posteriorly and above with black; a few of the posterior infralabials are also posteriorly edged with black. The chin, throat, and anterior part of the body are cream, becoming pale turquoise or turquoise-gray on the posterior two-thirds of the body. A dark transverse streak, which is darker laterally, is present on the posterior part of each ventral scale. The posterior edges of the subcaudals are black.

Natural History.—This snake inhabits tropical and subtropical wet, moist, and dry forest. A large-eyed, diurnal species, it is usually found near water and along the edges of clearings in the forest. It is also common in secondary vegetation. Individuals do wander widely, however, and I have occasionally found one on the forest floor far from water.

The speckled racer feeds mostly on anurans. Frog and toad prey recorded are *Eleutherodactylus* sp., *Hypopachus variolosus*, *Leptodactylus labialis*, *L. melanonotus*, *Syrrophus* sp., *Rhinophrynus dorsalis*, *Smilisca baudinii*, *Bufo marinus*, *B. valliceps*, *Rana berlandieri*, and *R. maculata*. This snake also feeds on reptiles, with records of anoles, ameivas, the brown forest skink (*Sphenomorphus cherriei*), striped basilisk (*Basiliscus vittatus*), small colubrid snakes, and unidentified reptile eggs. Rodents, shrews (*Cryptotis* sp.), and crickets are also known food items. Like some other racer-type snakes, this snake does not subdue prey with venom or by constriction but rather swallows it alive.

From April through August females lay 2–7 eggs, which have an incubation period of 64–68 days. Hatchlings have been found from June through October in Guatemala.

Distribution.—The speckled racer is distributed from southern Texas and southern Sonora, Mexico, southward through Central America to Colombia.

It is widespread in Petén, the northern Yucatán Peninsula, and Belize. In Petén it is found in many types of habitat, including virgin forest, secondary growth, and savannas. In Guatemala, this species occurs from near sea level to about 1,830 m.

Remarks.—Many people living where this common snake occurs are familiar with its habits and call it *ranera*, meaning "frog hunter." This name can be ambiguous, however, because many other snakes eat frogs and are sometimes also called raneras, including ribbon snakes, parrot snakes, and cat-eyed snakes. Other vernacular names for the speckled racer are *petatilla* and guinea hen snake (Belize).

A remarkable photograph of this species, taken near the entrance of the Biotopo Cerro Cahuí on 16 September 1986, was shown to me at Gringo Perdido by my host, Eduardo Cofiño. In the photo at least seven snakes are intertwined together. All appear to be adults, with one snake considerably larger than the others. This may represent a breeding aggregation of a single female and at least six males. I have never been fortunate enough to witness such a phenomenon.

The subspecies *Drymobius margaritifrus margaritiferus* occurs in Petén.

Red-blotched Ratsnake—Ratonera Manchada
Elaphe flavirufa (Cope, 1867)
Fig. 132

Description.—The head is moderately distinct from the neck and the eye is large with a round pupil. There usually are 9–10 supralabials, 12–14 infralabials, a single loreal, 1–2 preoculars, 2 postoculars, 25(27)–29(27–31)–21(19–23) dorsal scale rows, 249–263 ventrals, a divided anal plate, and 94–116 divided subcaudals. Only the middorsal scales are keeled, and usually scale rows 1–8 (sometimes more) are smooth; keeling is often not apparent in juveniles. This species reaches a maximum size of about 150 cm in TL.

There are 33–46 reddish brown, black-bordered blotches on body, which at midbody extend laterally to dorsal scale rows 6–8. The dorsal blotches are 6–8 scales long, with interspaces 1–3 scales long, or the blotches are often joined to form a zigzag pattern. There are 15–24 dorsal blotches on the tail. A series of small, oval reddish brown blotches is present laterally, extending from the ventrals up to dorsal scale rows 7–9; a smaller ventrolateral series of blotches is present on the lateral portions of the ventrals and scale rows 1–2. The top of the head is reddish brown with a pattern of small spots, streaks, or bars, and a narrow—often broken—postorbital stripe extends from behind the eye to the posterior supralabials. Except where the dark pigment from the lateral or ventrolateral series of blotches encroaches on the lateral portions of the ventrals, the venter is im-maculate pale yellow or whitish in all but the largest specimens, which often have gray mottling posteriorly.

Natural History.—This snake lives in a variety of habitats ranging from tropical dry to tropical wet forest and even the very dry forests of the interior valleys of central Guatemala. It is nocturnal, and I have found it to be uncommon over most of its range. There are records for this species having eaten rodents, bats, birds, and lizards. Other than that it lays eggs, little is known about its reproductive biology.

Distribution.—The red-blotched ratsnake is distributed from central Tamaulipas, Mexico, southward through the Yucatán Peninsula and on the Atlantic watershed of Central America to eastern Nicaragua and Corn Island; it occurs locally on the Pacific versant of Oaxaca and Chiapas, Mexico. It is found throughout most of the Petén region but does not seem to be common anywhere. Elevational records for this snake in Guatemala are from below 300 m.

Remarks.—The subspecies occurring in most of Petén is considered to be *Elaphe flavirufa pardalina*, but in the western and northern parts of the department *E. f. flavirufa* may intergrade with this subspecies.

Blotched Hooknosed Snake—Naricilla Manchada
Ficimia publia Cope, 1866
Fig. 133

Description.—The head is small and scarcely wider than the neck. The eye is small with a round pupil. The tip of the snout in this species in unusual in that the top of the rostral is sharply edged and upturned, intervening between the internasals and extending posteriorly to contact the frontal. The dorsal surface of the rostral behind the sharp edge is concave. There usually are 7 supralabials, 7–8 infralabials, 1 preocular, 2 postoculars, 1 + 2 temporals, 17(19)–17–17 smooth dorsal scale rows, 127–145 ventrals, a divided anal plate, and 26–44 divided subcaudals. A loreal scale is absent. Most large adults reach between 35 and 45 cm in TL; there is a record of almost 60 cm for one exceptionally large male.

The ground color is pale tan, pale brown, yellowish tan, orange-tan, or reddish brown. There are 17–35 dark brown to almost black dorsal body blotches and 6–13 tail blotches. Smaller lateral blotches are present on the body. The top of the head usually has a pattern of dark bars, spots, or mottling, but these markings sometimes may be indistinct or absent. A subocular spot is usually present. The venter is im-maculate white, sometimes with small spots on the lateral portions of the ventrals. The subcaudals are usually immaculate white, but a midventral zigzag pattern is sometimes present.

Natural History.—This snake occurs in tropical moist and dry forest. It sometimes attempts to bite when handled. Defensive behavior includes coiling into a ball and gaping with its mouth. Its diet includes mostly spiders and some insects. This species is oviparous; a female from Belize contained two large eggs.

Distribution.—The blotched hooknosed snake occurs from northern Veracruz, Mexico, to northern Honduras on the Atlantic watershed and from Guerrero, Mexico, to Guatemala on the Pacific versant. It is found throughout most of the northern half of Petén. In Guatemala, this snake occurs from near sea level to about 600 m.

Remarks.—Several subspecies have been described, but many authors no longer consider these valid. *Ficimia publia wolffsohni* is based on specimens from Belize, and *F. p. publia* is sometimes considered to be the race inhabiting most of Petén.

Common Bluntheaded Treesnake—Cordelilla Común
Imantodes cenchoa (Linnaeus, 1758)
Fig. 134

Description.—The body of this snake is exceptionally slender and somewhat laterally compressed, as is typical of many arboreal species. The head is not elongate; instead it is rather chunky and well differentiated from the slender neck. The eyes are large and have vertical pupils. There are usually 8 supralabials, 9–11 infralabials, a single loreal, 1 preocular, 2–4 (usually 3) postoculars, 2 + 3 temporals, 19(21)–17–17 smooth dorsal scale rows, 227–248 ventrals, a divided anal plate, and 144–166 subcaudals. Scales in the vertebral dorsal row are enlarged and about 3–4 times larger than scales in adjacent rows. Adults usually attain about 100 cm in TL but some occasionally reach about 130 cm.

The dorsum is creamy tan, pale gray-brown, or pale brown, with 28–37 brown blotches on the body and 19–26 on the tail. The dorsal blotches are deep reddish to chocolate brown, narrowly edged with white or cream, and longest at middorsum, usually 3–5 scales long; the blotches are triangular in lateral view with the apex reaching the outside edges of the ventrals. The top of the head usually has 1–3 brown blotches in the internasal and anterior part of frontal region and a pair of elongate blotches extending posteriorly from the supraocular region and posterior part of frontal-parietal region to merge with the first body blotch on the nape. The supralabials are mostly white or cream but usually have some dark speckling or spotting. The infralabials, chin, and throat are immaculate white or cream; posteriorly, the venter is whitish with small dark flecks. Juveniles tend to have more contrasting patterns than do adults.

Natural History.—This snake occurs in tropical wet, moist, and dry forest and subtropical wet and moist forest. When not active, this nocturnal species almost always hides in arboreal retreats, including inside of bromeliads and holes in trees, but it has also been found on the ground under rotting logs, and I have encountered it by day coiled in the centers of low palms. I have most frequently found individuals active at night stretched out in low vegetation, especially along small streams, apparently foraging for sleeping anoles. Like many other arboreal species, this snake drinks rainwater droplets that bead up on its coils or on leaves. I have handled many of these snakes, and I have never had one attempt to bite.

They feed mostly on anole lizards; specimens from Guatemala have contained *Norops uniformis, N. bourgeaei, N. rodriguezi,* and *N. capito.* Less frequently, small anurans are eaten and Guatemalan specimens have contained frogs of the genera *Hyla, Scinax,* and *Eleutherodactylus.*

Females reach reproductive maturity at about 62 cm SVL and lay 1–8 (usually 2–3) elongate eggs about 35–38 mm long. Females collected in April and June contained well-formed eggs, and hatchlings have been found in June, July, and August. Hatchlings are about 34–37 cm in TL.

Distribution.—The common bluntheaded treesnake occurs along Atlantic drainages from southern Tamaulipas, Mexico, southward through Central America and South America to Argentina and on the Pacific versant from Oaxaca, Mexico, to Guatemala. It is found throughout most of Petén, Belize, and the northeastern portion of the Yucatán Peninsula. In Guatemala, this species occurs from near sea level to about 1,800 m.

Remarks.—The population occurring in Petén is considered a distinct subspecies, *Imantodes cenchoa leucomelas,* by some authors. Another vernacular name is *bejuquilla.*

Spotted Bluntheaded Treesnake—Cordelilla Manchada
Imantodes gemmistratus (Cope, 1861)
Fig. 135

Description.—This snake is similar to the common bluntheaded treesnake (*Imantodes cenchoa*) in having an exceptionally slender and somewhat laterally compressed body. The head is rather chunky, much broader than the slender neck, and the eyes are large with vertical pupils. There are usually 8 supralabials, 9–11 infralabials, a single loreal, 1 preocular, 2 postoculars, 1 + 2 temporals, 17–17–17 smooth dorsal scale rows, 215–238 ventrals, a divided anal plate, and 120–155 divided subcaudals. Scales in the vertebral dorsal row are less enlarged than in *I. cenchoa,* being only about twice as large as the scales in adjacent rows. Individuals are usually about 50–60 cm in TL but may occasionally exceed 800 mm.

The dorsum is pale brown with 35–70 brown crossbands or spots on the body and 30–35 on the tail. On the anterior portion of the body, the dorsal markings are usually in the form of crossbands that extend at least to scale rows 1 or 2 and often to the lateral edges of the ventrals. At about midbody these crossbands become broken laterally, forming discrete dorsal and lateral spots 5–7 scales wide. The top of the head is pale brown; the internasal-prefrontal region is usually not spotted but may have dark brown mottling. The posterior part of the frontal and the parietal regions usually have small dark brown spots or, less frequently, may have a pair of dorsolateral longitudinal stripes extending from the posterior part of the supraocular and frontal regions to the first dark nape marking, but these stripes are often broken. The supralabials are cream with a few dark flecks. The infralabials, chin, and throat are white or cream and usually immaculate but sometimes have a few dark flecks. The venter is whitish or cream speckled with dark brown or black.

Natural History.—This snake occurs in tropical moist and dry forest and subtropical moist forest. I have most frequently found it active at night as it crossed a footpath. By day, it has been found in bromeliads, under loose bark, and on the ground beneath piles of dead palm leaves. This species will not bite, even when handled roughly. It feeds mostly on lizards of the genus *Norops.* In one captive study, individuals could not be induced to eat small frogs. Females lay 2–3 elongate eggs during the rainy season.

Distribution.—The spotted blunt-headed treesnake is distributed from northern Veracruz and southern Sonora, Mexico, southward through Central America to Colombia. It occurs in the northern part of the Yucatán Peninsula and in Petén is known from several localities near Sayaxché along tributaries of the Río de La Pasión. To my knowledge, it has not been found in Belize. In Guatemala, this species occurs from near sea level to about 750 m.

Remarks.—The subspecies occurring in the northern part of the Yucatán Peninsula is *Imantodes gemmistratus splendidus;* it is uncertain whether Petén snakes should also be considered this subspecies. Another vernacular name is *bejuquilla.*

Tropical Milksnake—Coral Falsa
Lampropeltis triangulum (Lacépède, 1789)
Fig. 136

Description.—The head is moderately distinct from the neck and the eyes are medium sized with round pupils. There usually are 7–8 supralabials, 8–11 infralabials, a single loreal, 1 preocular, 2(2–4) postoculars, 2 + 3 temporals, 21–23(21)–19(17) smooth dorsal scale rows, 203–244 ventrals, an undivided anal plate, and 47–61 divided subcaudals. In Petén, I have not seen individuals of this snake over 150 cm in TL; however, in the Verapaz highlands to the south I have encountered huge specimens close to 200 cm.

The pattern of this species is extremely variable. Usually, the body is boldly patterned with rings of red, black, and yellow that completely encircle the body. These rings are arranged in a sequence of red-black-yellow-black-red, such that the yellow and red rings are never adjacent but are always separated by black. This species may have a completely black snout, including the anterior five supralabials, or a white crossbar may be present on the posterior edges of the internasals and the anterior half of the prefrontals, extending down on the side of the head on portions of supralabials 1–2. The extent of the black head cap is likewise variable; it may extend posteriorly to cover all of the parietals or it may cover only about three-fourths of these scales. The first black ring may encroach on the posterior tips of the parietals or it may not extend forward farther than 1–2 scale lengths posterior to the parietals. In general, snakes from the northern part of the Petén region tend to have less pale coloration on the snout (or none) and a more extensive black head cap than snakes from central and southern Petén, but this is variable. Most individuals have the red and yellow dorsal scales tipped with black. Snakes from northern Petén tend to have fewer red body rings (14–20) than do those in southern Petén (20–32). I have seen snakes from southeastern Petén that were orange rather than red, and snakes from this region may also lack yellow or white bands as adults, whether they are red or orange. Regardless of geographic locality, most large individuals tend to become melanistic.

Natural History.—This species is widespread geographically and occurs in many kinds of habitats, including tropical and subtropical wet, moist, and dry forest. I have seen smaller specimens active by day in leaf litter, and it is not unusual to see individuals that have recently taken a large meal basking in sunny patches on the forest floor. However, most large specimens have been seen after dark or, less frequently, during the early morning or late afternoon. In Petén, the species occurs in primary forest but appears to be more common in the secondary forest along the edges of primary forest. I have seen individuals entering burrows at the bases of large, buttressed trees.

This snake is a constrictor, feeding on lizards, other snakes, and mammals. Specimens from Guatemala have contained rodents, shrews (*Cryptotis* sp.), and fragments of egg shells that presumably were reptilian.

Females lay 5–12 eggs that have an incubation period of 35–50 days and hatch from July through August.

Distribution.—The milksnake is distributed from southern Ontario and Quebec, Canada, through most of the United States east of the Rocky Mountains, most of Mexico (exclusive of the Sonoran Desert and most of the Chihuahuan Desert), and most of Central America to Colombia, Ecuador, and Venezuela. It is found throughout most of Petén, Belize, and the Yucatán Peninsula. In Guatemala, this species occurs from near sea level to about 1,650 m.

Remarks.—For those enamored of subspecies, allocating individuals of this species from Petén can be an impossible challenge. The subspecies occurring over most of Petén is considered to be either *Lampropeltis triangulum polyzona* or *L. t. abnorma*, depending on which authority is followed. On biogeographical grounds, the former perhaps makes more sense, with this subspecies ranging northward in lowland tropical habitats into Campeche and Veracruz, Mexico. On the other hand, the subspecies *abnorma* is generally considered to be the snake found in the rugged highlands of Guatemala. Two other subspecies closely approach or enter Petén; *L. t. blanchardi* of the Yucatán Peninsula occurs in northern Petén, or at least it intergrades with another subspecies in this area, and characteristics often considered diagnostic of *L. t. hondurensis* are evident in many snakes from southeastern Petén. A problem with subspecies that make broad contact with each other is that there are no distinct genetic boundaries differentiating them, and the variation inherent in certain species such as milksnakes makes recognition of subspecies an exercise of questionable utility.

Other vernacular names include *coralillo falso* and in Belize bead and coral.

Yucatán Cat-eyed Snake—Escombrera Yucateca
Leptodeira frenata (Cope, 1886)
Fig. 137

Description.—The head is relatively large and the eye is medium sized with vertical pupils. There are usually 8 supralabials, 10 infralabials, a single loreal, 2 preoculars, 2 postoculars, 1 + 2 temporals, 21(19)–21(23)–15(17) smooth dorsal scale rows, 170–188 ventrals, a divided anal plate, and 61–85 divided subcaudals. This snake reaches an adult size of about 60–74 cm in TL.

The dorsum is pinkish tan to gray-brown with 20–39 brown to olive-green blotches. The dorsal blotches are edged with dark brown or black, are 3–7 scales in length, and are separated middorsally by 1–3 scales; they extend laterally at least to scale rows 2–3 and usually to the lateral portion of the ventrals. Often the dorsal blotches coalesce, especially posteriorly, forming a zigzag pattern. A series of dark ventrolateral spots is present on the edges of the ventrals and the first several dorsal scale rows. The top of the head is pale grayish brown mottled with dark brown, and usually each parietal bears a brown spot or two. A median nape stripe usually extends from the posterior edges of the parietals for 2–5 scale lengths. The postorbital stripe extends posteriorly from the eye to the angle of the jaw or beyond, and may be continuous with the first dark body blotch. The labials are cream with broad dark edging, as are the ventral surfaces of the chin and body. The venter is rosy pink.

Natural History.—This species inhabits tropical wet, moist, and dry forest. It has been found beneath the bark of a log in primary forest, in a hole in a decayed stump on the edge of an aguada in savanna habitat, and in bromeliads.

This snake feeds mostly on anurans and is known to prey on *Triprion petasatus, Smilisca baudinii, Bufo valliceps,* and other species of frogs. It also feeds on lizards, including *Norops bourgeaei, Ctenosaura similis,* and *Sceloporus* sp.

One female from Petén contained seven well-developed eggs in April and another from Isla Cozumel contained three well-developed eggs in February, suggesting that egg deposition occurs during the early rainy season. Juveniles have been seen in July.

Distribution.—The Yucatán cat-eyed snake occurs from central Veracruz, Mexico, eastward through the Yucatán Peninsula, northern Belize, and northern Petén and on the Isla de Cozumel. It is known from scattered localities in the northern half of Petén. It occurs from near sea level to about 300 m.

Remarks.—Three subspecies are recognized: *Leptodeira frenata frenata* in Veracruz, *L. f. yucatanensis* in the northern part of the Yucatán Peninsula and the Isla de Cozumel, and *L. f. malleisi* in the southern portion of the peninsula, including Petén and northern Belize. Other vernacular names include *cantil* and *cohune tommygoff* (Belize).

Small-spotted Cat-eyed Snake—Escombrera de Manchitas
Leptodeira polysticta Günther, 1895
Fig. 138

Description.—The small-spotted cat-eyed snake occurs throughout most of Petén and is the most common nocturnal snake at many localities. It has a long, slender, slightly laterally compressed body, somewhat resembling a Bluntheaded treesnake (*Imantodes*), but is not as attenuate. The head is large and well differentiated from the neck and the large eyes have vertical pupils. There usually are 8 supralabials, 10 infralabials, a single loreal, 3 preoculars, 2 postoculars, 1 + 2 temporals, 21(19)–23(21)–15(17) smooth dorsal scale rows, 186–211 ventrals, a divided anal plate, and 73–106 divided subcaudals. The vertebral and paravertebral scale rows may be slightly enlarged. This species reaches about 90–106 cm in TL.

The dorsum is yellowish brown to grayish tan with 38–70 small brown blotches on the body; these continue onto the tail as an irregular row of dark spots. At midbody, the blotches are 1–3 scales long and extend laterally to scale rows 5–7. A series of smaller brown lateral spots is mostly arranged at intervals between the dorsal blotches. The paired nuchal blotches are 4–6 scales in length, and the posterior edges of these blotches may fuse to form a U- or Y-shaped mark. The top of the head is yellowish to grayish brown, often with irregular dark spots or streaks, especially on the frontal and parietal. A dark brown median nape stripe extends posteriorly from the posterior edge of the parietals for about 4–6 scale lengths. A thin, brown postorbital stripe extends from the posterior edge of the eye to about the angle of the jaw; the postorbital stripe may be vague or even absent in some specimens. The labials are mostly cream and may have diffuse gray or brown pigment. The ventral surfaces are cream or pale yellow with a light dusting of darker pigment.

Natural History.—This common nocturnal snake inhabits tropical wet, moist, and dry forests and subtropical wet and moist forest. It is quite arboreal, often climbing up to 10 m or more in trees along streams. During the day it hides in bromeliads or tree hollows and may also be found on the ground under logs or piles of debris, almost always near water. It frequently is found around breeding choruses of frogs, its principal prey. It is known to eat *Agalychnis callidryas* and its eggs, *A. moreletii*, *Hyla loquax*, *H. microcephala*, *Smilisca baudinii*, *Scinax staufferi*, *Eleutherodactylus* sp., *Leptodactylus melanonotus*, and *Bufo valliceps*. This snake eats reptiles, especially anoles, ameivas, and the red coffee snake, *Ninia sebae*. Salamanders (*Bolitoglossa*) are also taken. I have encounted this snake eating the eggs of the red-eyed treefrog (*A. callidryas*), which are laid on leaves above the water, on about half a dozen occasions. I watched one snake for about half an hour as it foraged on multiple clutches in the vegetation bordering a small pond. The snake would find a clutch of eggs, then quickly seize and engulf them. Some of the eggs clung to the snake's mouth and it would scrape the side of its head against a leaf to manipulate these into it mouth.

Females lay 6–12 eggs during the late dry season in February–May. The incubation time for eggs is 70–85 days. Hatchlings have been found in July-August. One remarkable aspect of reproduction in this species is the apparent capacity of females to store sperm. In one instance, a female captured in 1934 was reported to lay clutches of fertile eggs in 1936, 1938, and 1939, despite the fact that she was maintained in isolation. Whether this ability is characteristic for the species or only for certain populations is not known.

✓*Distribution.*—The small-spotted cat-eyed snake occurs from southern Veracruz and Nayarit, Mexico, southward through the Yucatán Peninsula, Guatemala, Belize, and both coasts of Cen-tral America to Costa Rica. It has a considerable vertical distribution in Guatemala; I have taken it practically at sea level in rainforest near Puerto Barrios and at about 2,300 m in cloud-forest of the Sierra de las Minas. It also occurs in pine-oak forest in parts of the Guatemalan highlands.

Remarks.—The taxonomic status of this snake is in a confused state. Most recently, it has been referred to as *Leptodeira septentrionalis polysticta*. Because I do not believe it is conspecific with *L. s. septentrionalis* of northern Mexico and Texas, I have chosen to recognize Petén snakes as *L. polysticta*. However, if future systematic studies can demonstrate that *L. polysticta* Günther, (1895) is conspecific with *Comastes ornatus* Bocourt (1884) of lower Central America and South America, then the Law of Priority would dictate that the Petén snake be known as *Leptodeira ornata*.

Other vernacular names for this snake include *cantil ojo de gato* and *cantil desteñido*.

Green Parrot Snake—Ranera Verde
Leptophis ahaetulla (Linnaeus, 1758)
Fig. 139

Description.—The body is slender and the head is moderately elongate and distinct from the neck. The large eyes have yellow irises and round pupils. There usually are 8–9 supralabials, 10–11 infralabials, 1 preocular, 2 postoculars, 1 + 2 temporals, 15–15–11 dorsal scale rows, 166–185 ventrals, a divided anal plate, and 153–185 divided sub-caudals. The loreal is usually absent in this species. The dorsal scales, exclusive of the paraventral row, are keeled. The keels of the paravertebral row are especially well developed and prominent. This species often exceeds 200 cm in TL and may occasionally reach about 230 cm.

This snake has a leaf green dorsum.

The interstitial skin and edges of some scales in the dorsolateral region are bright yellow, forming irregular diagonal markings that are most evident when the body is inflated. The keels on the dorsal scales are black. The labials, chin, throat, and venter of the body and tail are pale green or yellow-green.

Natural History.—This snake inhabits tropical wet, moist, and dry forest. Although this diurnal, arboreal species is by no means rare, I suspect that it spends much time in the canopy of tall trees, and that people pass unknowingly underneath it much more frequently than they realize. It is most commonly found in forested habitats, especially in bushes along rivers and large streams, but also ranges into mature secondary growth. This snake threatens adversaries with an open mouth, which is particularly dramatic owing to the bluish oral lining. It also inflates the anterior part of its body, revealing the bright yellow of the skin between the scales.

This snake feeds mostly on frogs (especially treefrogs); there are records of it eating Baudin's tree frog (*Smilisca baudinii*), *Eleutherodactylus* sp., and *Rana* sp. in Guatemala. It also preys on lizards and occasionally birds, bird eggs, and grasshoppers.

About 3–5 eggs are laid during the early rainy season.

Distribution.—As currently recognized, the green parrot snake ranges from central Veracruz, Mexico, southward through the Yucatán Peninsula and onto Atlantic lowlands and foothills of Central America; it occurs on the Pacific in Costa Rica and Panama. It also has an extensive distribution in South America, on the Pacific from Colombia to Ecuador and in most of the lowlands east of the Andes to the Río de la Plata drainage of southern South America. It is widespread in forested areas of Petén and Belize but apparently restricted to the eastern part of the northern Yucatán Peninsula. In Guatemala, this species occurs from near sea level to about 990 m.

Remarks.—Members of the genus *Leptophis* are commonly called parrot snakes, presumably for no other reason than that many species are of least partially bright green. The subspecies *Leptophis ahaetulla praestans* occurs in Petén.

Bronze-backed Parrot Snake—Ranera Dorso-bronceada
Leptophis mexicanus Duméril, Bibron, and Duméril, 1854
Fig. 140

Description.—The head is moderately large, elongate, and well differentiated from the neck. The eye is large with a round pupil and the iris yellow above and dark brown below. There usually are 8 supralabials, 10–11 infralabials, a single loreal, 1 preocular, 2 postoculars, 1 + 2 temporals, 15–15–11 dorsal scale rows, 148–174 ventrals, a divided anal plate, and 140–175 divided subcaudals. Most of the dorsal scales, especially those of the paravertebral scale rows, are strongly keeled in adult males. In females only some of the scales on the proximal part of the tail may be keeled and in juveniles even these keels may be weak. The lateral portions of the ventrals project upward. The ⊔-shaped ventrals are thought to be an adaptation to arboreality, giving the snake better traction when gliding over branches. This snake reaches about 120 cm in TL, and a few individuals may exceed this length.

The middorsum is golden tan or bronze and the top of the head is green. Dorsal scales on the side (usually rows 3–6) are heavily marked with green and black on the anterior two-thirds of the body. A black stripe extends from the tip of the snout through the eye to above the angle of the jaw and onto the neck. Ventrolaterally (dorsal scale rows 1–2), the body is pale gray-brown. Most parts of the labials, chin, and throat are whitish; posteriorly, the ventrals and subcaudals are pale gray-brown.

Natural History.—This snake occurs in tropical wet, moist, and dry forest and subtropical wet and moist forest. Diurnal and arboreal and an active forager, it is often observed in low bushes and trees in the forest or at the edges of clearings. When threatened, this snake usually climbs into bushes or other low vegetation, and when cornered it displays its purple mouth lining in an open-mouth challenge.

Frogs are an important component of the diet, with records of *Hyla loquax, Phrynohyas venulosa, Smilisca baudinii,* and *Bufo valliceps* having been eaten. One specimen was captured while trying to dislodge a Yucatán casqueheaded treefrog (*Triprion petasatus*) from a hole in a stump. Another specimen contained two salamanders (*Bolitoglossa rufescens, B. odonnelli*). This snake also eats lizards, especially anoles; there are records of it consuming *Norops sagrei, N. bourgeaei, N. rodriguezi,* and *Thecadactylus rapicaudus.*

Females mature at about 54–55 cm SVL, at about 18 months of age. They reproduce annually, depositing from 2 to 11 eggs from March through October. Eggs are 29–43 mm in length. Juveniles have been seen in August and are 14.5–18.5 cm in TL.

✒*Distribution.*—The bronze-backed parrot snake occurs from southern Tamaulipas, Mexico, southward through the Yucatán Peninsula, where it continues southward in the lowlands of the Atlantic to Costa Rica, and across the Isthmus of Tehuantepec onto the Pacific, where it occurs discontinuously from Oaxaca through Chiapas and Guatemala to Costa Rica. This snake is found throughout most of Petén, Belize, and the northern Yucatán Peninsula. In Guatemala, it occurs from near sea level to about 1,360 m.

Remarks.—The subspecies in Petén is *Leptophis mexicanus mexicanus; L. m. yucatanensis* occurs in the northern Yucatán Peninsula. Another vernacular name is *bejuquillo.*

Neotropical Coachwhip—Chirrionera Café
Masticophis mentovarius (Duméril, Bibron, and Duméril, 1854)
Fig. 141

Description.—The head is moderately distinct from the neck and the eyes are large with round pupils. There usually are 7–8 supralabials, 8–11 infralabials, a single loreal, 2 preoculars, 2 postoculars, 1 + 2 to 3 + 4 temporals, 19–17–13 smooth dorsal scale rows, 181–205 ventrals, a divided anal plate, and 102–123 divided subcaudals. The number of temporals is quite variable, with from 1 to 3 anterior temporals. This species often exceeds 200 cm in TL and reaches a maximum of about 250 mm in TL.

The dorsum is pale brown or gray-brown, usually more reddish posteriorly. Dorsal scales are narrowly edged with dark brown. The top of the head is pale to medium brown and the side of the head in front of and behind the eye and in the posterior temporal region is marked with irregular, vertical white bars. The supralabials are mostly white and the chin and throat are marked with gray spots. The venter is cream or white, grading to pink on the posterior part of the body and the subcaudals. The iris is yellow to pale bronze with a red ring around the pupil. Juveniles usually have two narrow pale stripes on each side of the neck.

Natural History.—This snake inhabits tropical and subtropical moist and dry forest. An agile, diurnal species, it is found mostly in open areas or on the edges of clearings. It is usually seen on the ground but often escapes by climbing into low vegetation. It feeds mostly on lizards, especially those in the family Teiidae (whiptails and ameivas), and also feeds on rodents. I have often seen individuals foraging in low trees and bushes, and I once found a specimen that contained five nestling birds. In March–April females lay 7–30 eggs that are a little over 50 mm in length. This agile snake is quick to defend itself, biting repeatedly if restrained.

Distribution.—The Neotropical coachwhip is distributed from northern Veracruz and southern Sonora, Mexico, southward through lowlands and foothills to the Yucatán Peninsula and Central America to Costa Rica. It is also known from central Panama, northern Colombia, and northern and central Venezuela. This snake is widespread in the northern Yucatán Peninsula and Belize. In Petén, it is known from the savanna region around La Libertad and from around Sayaxché. In Guatemala, this species occurs from near sea level to about 1,400 m.

Remarks.—The subspecies *Masticophis mentovarius mentovarius* occurs in Petén. Some authors place this species in the genus *Coluber*. Another vernacular name is *zumbadora*.

Black Coffee Snake—Basurera Negra
Ninia diademata Baird and Girard, 1853
Fig. 142

Description.—The head is scarcely distinct from the neck. The eyes are small with a round pupil. Adult males have tubercles on the mental, the anterior chinshields, and several anterior infralabials. There usually are 6 supralabials, 6 infralabials, a single scale in the loreal-preocular region, 2 postoculars, 1 + 2 temporals, 19–19–19 dorsal scale rows, 127–150 ventrals, an undivided anal plate, and 86–106 divided subcaudals. The dorsal scales are strongly keeled, including the paraventral row. This snake reaches about 35 cm in TL.

The dorsal ground color is dark gray, which may extend to the lateral edges of the ventrals; the keels of the dorsal scales are often whitish. I have examined a specimen from Tikal in which each scale of the first three dorsal scale rows had a distinct yellow center, forming a spotted ventrolateral stripe, and the keels of the more dorsal scales were uniformly dark without white keels. An orange or yellow collar may be continuous across the neck or interrupted middorsally. This collar often crosses the posterior half of the parietals or may be located entirely behind them. Ventrally, the pale collar merges with the pale coloration of the supralabials and that of the throat. The top of the head is dark gray, with dark pigment extending down the side of the head to the upper edges of the supralabials. Most of the supralabials are whitish. The infralabials and chin are mostly whitish with some gray mottling along scale sutures. The venter is whitish or cream with a series of black midventral markings, ranging from small round spots to larger blotches that are about half as wide as the ventrals. The tail usually has a continuous midventral dark stripe along the subcaudal sutures.

Natural History.—This snake inhabits tropical and subtropical wet and moist forest. It is a secretive species, usually found in areas of abundant leaf litter or other ground cover, where it feeds almost exclusively on slugs. Females lay 2–4 eggs during the rainy season.

Distribution.—The black coffee snake occurs from San Luis Potosí, Mexico, to central Honduras on the Atlantic watershed and from Oaxaca, Mexico, to Guatemala on the Pacific versant. Although not common in Petén, it may be widespread. It is known from Uaxactún and Tikal. A single specimen has been reported from Belize, from Toledo District. In Guatemala, this species occurs from about 100 to 1,830 m.

Remarks.—The Spanish common name *basurera* refers to this snake's habit of seeking refuge in piles of leaves or other vegetational refuse. Subspecies of the black coffee snake are not well defined; the subspecies occurring in Petén is *Ninia diademata nietoi*.

Red Coffee Snake—Basurera Roja
Ninia sebae (Duméril, Bibron, and Duméril, 1854)
Fig. 143

Description.—The head is scarcely distinct from the neck. The eyes are small with round pupils. Adult males have tubercles on the mental, the anterior chinshields, and several anterior infralabials. There usually are 7 supralabials, 7 infralabials, a single scale in the loreal-preocular region, 1 postocular, 1 + 2 temporals, 19–19–19 dorsal scale rows, 128–159 ventrals, an undivided anal plate, and 38–71 divided subcaudals. The dorsal scales are strongly keeled, including the paraventral row. This species reaches about 35 cm in TL.

This wide-ranging common species is subject to considerable geographic variation. Specimens from central and northern Petén have a reddish dorsum and show a great deal of variation with regard to dorsal pattern; often the dorsum is without pattern, but some individuals are black-spotted on the anterior two-thirds of the body. In the southern part of Petén and adjacent Alta Verapaz and Izabal, specimens usually have 16–43 distinctive black dorsal crossbands narrowly edged with yellow. These crossbands are often continuous across the dorsum or broken and staggered along the dorsal midline. The top and sides of the head to at least the upper edges of the supralabials are black; sometimes the anterior supralabials are black. A yellow, usually unbroken collar extends across the back of the neck behind the parietals and is 1–3 dorsal scales long. Laterally, the yellow collar merges with the pale coloration of the posterior supralabials and the throat. Posterior to the yellow collar is a long black nape crossband, usually 6–12 scales long. The collar and nape crossband are present in almost all individuals. The supralabials are usually mostly yellow, but often dark pigment intervenes along their vertical sutures. The infralabials and chin are yellowish, mottled with dark pigment. The ventrals and subcaudals are immaculate white or yellowish. Juveniles resemble adults except that they lack the narrow yellow edging of the black dorsal bands that is sometimes present in adults.

Natural History.—This snake occurs in tropical wet, moist, and dry forests and subtropical wet and moist forest. It appears to be much more abundant in cleared areas than in primary forest (see "The Serpent Brokers," page 228), and it is generally found under rocks and logs or beneath leaf litter or piles of decaying vegetation. I have taken relatively few specimens in virgin forest, but occasionally I have found individuals beneath the bark of dead trees or in rotten logs. Almost always these logs have been where sun penetrated to the forest floor for at least several hours sometime during the day. This secretive snake is not frequently seen on the surface; it usually moves along under debris or loose soil. I have seen this species active at night after moderate to heavy rains.

When threatened, red coffee snakes will flatten the head and body dorsoventrally. Some individuals also go through a rather dramatic display in which they raise the head and about the anterior third of the body vertically, angle the head at almost 90 degrees to the axis of the neck, and spread the posterior ends of the mandibles, clearly exposing the pale nape band. Despite this elaborate display, these snakes never make any attempt to bite. They feed mostly on eathworms, slugs, and land snails.

Over most of the Petén region, females lay 1–4 eggs, usually from about March to September. A single nesting site, such as a cavity beneath a log, is sometimes utilized by multiple females. Juveniles have been found from about May to September. In the more mesic areas, the reproductive season may extend over a longer period, because eggs have been found in January and juveniles have been seen as early as mid-March. Several clutches of eggs from northern Chiapas hatched in late August. Eggs are 16–31 mm × 7–11 mm and hatch in 75–79 days. Hatchlings are 8.5–13.5 cm in TL and weigh 0.57–0.94 g. Females reach maturity at about 25 cm TL.

✔*Distribution.*—The red coffee snake occurs from Veracruz and Oaxaca, Mexico, southward through Central America to Costa Rica. Found throughout most of Petén, Belize, and the northern Yucatán Peninsula, it is abundant at many localities. In Guatemala it ranges from near sea level to about 2,000 m.

Remarks.—One of this snake's Spanish common names is *basurera*, in allusion to its habit of seeking refuge in mounds of dead leaves or other vegetation. This snake is also referred to as *dormilona* ("sleeper") in some places owing to its habit of sometimes remaining motionless when discovered beneath a log or in some other hiding place. Other vernacular names include *madre de coral, coral,* and in Belize bead and coral.

A number of subspecies have been proposed for the red coffee snake, but there appear to be few characters that distinguish these with any certainty. The range of *Ninia sebae sebae* is generally thought to include most of central and southern Petén, and *N. s. morleyi* occurs from northern Petén northward in the Yucatán Peninsula.

The Serpent Brokers.—The red coffee snake seems to reach its greatest abundance at moderate elevations in areas that are partially cleared and receive abundant rainfall. Such areas include many of the coffee farms or *fincas* on the Pacific versant of Guatemala, where dozens of these snakes can be seen in a single day of diligent searching. During a collecting trip to Finca El Faro, about 5 km north of El Palmar in Quezaltenango, I recruited the help of the local inhabitants in securing specimens. The children on this finca proved to be especially enthusiastic and effective collectors and were rewarded with 5 centavos for every red coffee snake they brought me.

Even though I had planned this in advance and had brought 10 quetzales of 5-centavo coins with me, these were soon exhausted. I was reduced to passing out handwritten IOUs, which were eagerly accepted in lieu of payment, although I am reasonably sure that this fiduciary concept was new to the region. This system seemed to work well for a while. Every few days I went to the nearest town to beg all of the available coins from several *tiendas* (small stores) to pay off my continually accumulating debts—until I discovered that several talented young entrepreneurs had learned to forge my signature with such exactitude that even I had trouble distinguishing a copy from the real thing. The error that led to their apprehension lay in using blue rather than black ink. This brought my snake-buying days on this finca to a halt, and when I accused several of the little delinquents, they readily admitted their crime and we all had a good laugh.

Brown Vine Snake—Bejuquillo Café
Oxybelis aeneus (Wagler, 1824)
Fig. 144

Description.—This a particularly slender species that has an elongate, attenuate head with an acutely pointed snout. The eye is medium sized with a round pupil. There are usually 8–9 supralabials, 8–9 infralabials, 1 preocular, 2 postoculars, 1 + 2 temporals, 17– 17–13 dorsal scale rows, 180–197 ventrals, a divided anal plate, and 169–197 divided subcaudals. The loreal is usually absent in this species. Dorsal scales may be smooth or weekly keeled. This species rarely exceeds 150 cm in TL, and most individuals may reach only about 120 cm; males are a little smaller than females.

The body is brownish or grayish above, with the middorsum and sides of the head usually a bit darker. There are black or dark brown streaks or dashes arranged in diagonal rows for about two-thirds of the body length (this pattern is most conspicuous when the skin is stretched). The interstitial skin between the dorsal scales often has white or yellowish spots. The labials and throat are white to yellow. A dark stripe usually begins at about the posterior edge of the nasal and extends posteriorly along the upper edges of the supralabials and lower edges of adjacent scales to terminate on the neck. The venter is mostly grayish, a little paler anteriorly and becoming darker posteriorly. Often a vague indication of a pair of dark stripes is on the venter, one to either side of the midline. The lining of the mouth is a startling dark gray or black.

Natural History.—This snake occurs in tropical wet, moist, and dry forest and subtropical moist and dry forest. Arboreal and diurnal, it appears to have acute eyesight and probably has a wide binocular field of vision. It is usually found in open areas with low bushes, shrubs, or tall grasses; it frequents sunny areas and is common in secondary growth. Its body so closely resembles woody vegetation that it is often almost impossible to see when it is draped in tangles of vines or on small branches. By day, this snake is usually found stretched out in vegetation between 0.5 and 2 m above the ground. At night, it can be found in a loosely coiled, head-down sleeping position, usually located slightly higher (2 to 5 m above the ground) in vegetation than by day.

This snake sometimes exhibits a curious jerky motion of the anterior part of the body as it crawls forward with the anterior part of the body extended and unsupported by branches; at the same time, the tongue is often protruded and held rigid and motionless. The tongue remains extended out of the mouth for varying periods, usually for at least several seconds at a time. It has been suggested that this tongue be-havior functions for "prey fascination" or "lingual-lure deception," but it is doubtful that either of these notions is accurate, and the precise role of this behavior remains unknown. When threatened, this snake assumes a defensive posture of an S-shaped curve with an open mouth, revealing a dark blue-black lining that may serve to startle potential predators. When irritated, it often vibrates its tail.

The brown vine snakes feeds mostly on lizards, especially anoles, including *Norops rodriguezi, N. bourgeaei,* and *N. uniformis,* and there are records for predation on juvenile striped basilisks (*Basiliscus vittatus*), juvenile green iguanas (*Iguana iguana*), spiny lizards (*Sceloporus* sp.), and whiptails (*Cnemidophorus* sp.). It also eats frogs (hylids and leptodactylids), small or nestling birds, small rodents, and even insects. This species appears to ambush its prey rather than to forage actively.

Human envenomation by this snake produces itching, swelling, redness, and blisters near the site of the bite.

Females reach maturity at about 65 cm SVL, at about 24 months of age. They reproduce annually, usually laying 3–5 eggs from March to August. These eggs are about 45 mm in length and hatchlings are about 37–38 cm in TL. Juveniles have been seen during the late rainy season and early dry season, suggesting that this species lays eggs throughout much of the rainy season. A nest containing four eggs was discovered in a depression in leaf litter near a large tree in Panama.

✔*Distribution.*—This snake is distributed on the Atlantic from southern Tamaulipas, Mexico, and on the Pacific from extreme southern Arizona and from Sonora, Mexico, southward through Mexico and Central America and South America to southern Brazil. It is found throughout most of Petén, Belize, and the northern Yucatán Peninsula. In Guatemala, it occurs from near sea level to about 1,500 m.

Remarks.—No subspecies are presently recognized.

Green Vine Snake—Bejuquillo Verde
Oxybelis fulgidus (Daudin, 1803)
Fig. 145

Description.—The body is slender and the elongate, attenuate head has an acutely pointed snout. The eye is medium sized with a round pupil. There usually are 9–10 supralabials, 9–11 infralabials, no loreal, 1 preocular, 2 postoculars, 1 + 2 temporals, 17–17–13 dorsal scale rows, 209–217 ventrals, a divided anal plate, and 150–186 divided subcaudals. The dorsal scales are keeled except for about the first five scale rows on the side of the body. This snake reaches about 200 cm in TL.

The dorsum is green, with this color extending laterally to the outside portions of the ventrals. Distinctive ventrolateral yellow or white stripes are present along the lateral portions of the ventrals; these stripes extend from near the first ventral throughout the body and tail. A thin, black line extends from the snout to the lower temporal area, running through the eye; ventrally, this line is bordered by yellow. The labials, chin, and throat are pale green or yellow-green. The ventrals and subcaudals between the ventrolateral stripes are pale green.

Natural History.—This arboreal species occurs in tropical wet, moist, and dry forest and subtropical wet and moist forest. It is diurnal, and like other vine snakes that forage by day, it appears to have keen eyesight. It is abundant near forest edges and along sandy beaches where there are large populations of lizards. The curious habit of motionless extended-tongue behavior noted for the brown vine snake (*Oxybelis aeneus*) is also characteristic of the green vine snake, which (again like the brown vine snake) may often employ a sit-and-wait strategy for securing its prey, rather than actively foraging.

Green vine snakes feed heavily on birds, but also prey on rodents, anoles, and other lizards (*Basiliscus vittatus, Ctenosaura similis, Sceloporus* sp., and teiids). One specimen from Guatemala had a black-headed siskin (*Spinus notatus*) in its stomach.

Eggs are laid from April to June, and probably earlier, because juveniles have been seen in April and May. A captive specimen of unknown provenance laid 10 eggs in May that hatched in August after an incubation period of 105–106 days; hatchlings were 33.5–36.0 cm in TL.

‣Distribution.—This snake occurs from the Isthmus of Tehuantepec, Mexico, southward through Central America and South America to Argentina. It is found throughout most of Petén, Belize, and the northern Yucatán Peninsula, occurring in Guatemala from near sea level to about 1,100 m.

Remarks.—No subspecies are recognized.

White-bellied False Coral—Falso Coral Panza Blanca
Oxyrhopus petola (Linnaeus, 1758)
Fig. 146

Description.—The head is moderately distinct from the neck and the eyes are medium sized with vertically elliptical pupils. There are usually 8 supralabials, 10 infralabials, a single loreal, 1 preocular, 2 postoculars, 2 + 3 or 2 + 4 temporals, 19–19–17 smooth dorsal scale rows, 200–211 ventrals, an undivided anal, and 77–83 divided subcaudals. This species reaches about 90 cm in TL.

There is a pattern of alternating red and black crossbands on the body and tail, with both the red and black coloration extending ventrally to the lateral edges of the ventrals. The red scales may be immaculate or may be heavily outlined or tipped with black. There are 20–25 black bands on the body and 10–12 on the tail. Just posterior to the parietals is a yellow nuchal collar, which is 2–3 scales wide middorsally and a little wider laterally, merging with the pale coloration of the throat. The anterior supralabials are dark, while those posterior to the eye usually have some pale mottling extending forward from the collar. The mental and anterior infralabials are cream and somewhat dusky along the lip margin. The ventrals are white and the subcaudals are darkly edged; the red bands sometimes form rings on the tail.

Natural History.—This nocturnal, terrestrial species occurs in tropical wet and moist forest. Adults feed on lizards and rodents.

This species lays 5–10 eggs which hatch about 90 days later in March or April. A clutch of about 10 eggs discovered in March near Paso Caballos beneath a log had embryos about ready to hatch. The eggs are 31–34 mm long and 18–19 mm wide. Hatchlings are probably a little over 20 cm in TL.

‣Distribution.—The white-bellied false coral is distributed from Veracruz, Mexico, southward on the Atlantic watershed through Central America and South America to northern Brazil and Bolivia and on the Pacific versant from Costa Rica to Ecuador. It occurs throughout most of Petén and west-central Belize but is absent from the extreme northern portion of Petén, northern Belize, and the Yucatán Peninsula in Mexico. In Guatemala, this species occurs from near sea level to about 650 m.

Remarks.—The subspecies *Oxyrhopus petola sebae* occurs in the Petén region.

Long-tailed False Coral—Coralillo Cola Larga
Pliocercus elapoides Cope, 1860
Fig. 147

Description.—This is one of the best mimics of venomous coral snakes to be found anywhere in the New World tropics (see "Deceit among Snakes," p. 264). The head is only a little wider than the neck and the eye is medium sized with a round pupil. There usually are 8 supralabials, 9–10 infralabials, a single loreal, 2 preoculars, 2 postoculars, 1 + 1 temporals, 17–17–17 smooth dorsal scale rows, 128–136 ventrals, a divided anal plate, and 97–112 divided subcaudals. This species attains a length of about 70 cm in TL, but in large individuals the long tail is usually incomplete (see "Snake and Lizard Tails," page 162).

The body is patterned with rings usually in a sequence similar to that of the variable coral snake, that is, black-yellow-red-yellow-black, but specimens having only red and black rings are known and a few all red individuals have been found. The red scales are usually black tipped and may also have irregular black mottling, sometimes forming one or two accessory rings within a red ring. In Petén, this snake usually has 6–16 black body bands or rings that tend to cross the venter but often are broken middorsally or laterally. Black bands are usually 3–4 dorsal scales and 2–3 ventrals long. A yellow collar extends across the back of the head, usually involving the posterior tip of the frontal, one-half to three-fourths of the parietals, the anterior and posterior temporals, and the three posteriormost supralabials. Most of the top of the head anterior to the yellow collar is black and this extends laterally to the upper portion of the anterior supralabials. The margin of the upper jaw including the rostral is usually yellow. The infralabials, chin, and throat are immaculate yellow.

Natural History.—This snake inhabits tropical wet, moist, and dry forest and subtropical wet and moist forest. I have found individuals most frequently as they crawled through leaf litter by day, especially in the early morning, although they also may be active after dark. I have found them beneath or in rotten logs and in the dirt crevices of banks. In this species the tail is particularly long, being 35–40 percent of the TL. It is fragile and easily broken; as a result, most large adults have blunt tails.

Prey consists mostly of salamanders (specimens from Guatemala have contained *Bolitoglossa rufescens, B. mulleri, B. odonnelli,* and *B. dofleini*) frogs, (*Eleutherodactylus* sp.), and the terrestrial eggs of amphibians. These snakes usually are mild in disposition but do have a venom associated with the enlarged teeth on the rear of the maxillary. There is a report of a long-tailed false coral bite on a human finger causing immediate pain and swelling and subsequent discoloration of the skin; the finger remained sore for several weeks.

This snake lays 4–8 eggs, apparently over an extended period coinciding with the rainy season. A specimen from the Department of Huehuetenango laid five eggs on 8 August, which hatched 108 days later. This represents a long incubation period and may be the result of the rather cool temperatures (room temperature, 70–72°F) at which these eggs were maintained. On the other hand, the locality where these eggs were collected lies at about 1,400 m where a decidedly cool environment prevails.

Distribution.—The species occurs on the Atlantic from southern Tamaulipas, Mexico, to central Honduras and on the Pacific versant from Oaxaca, Mexico, to El Salvador. It is found throughout most of Petén, Belize, and the northern Yucatán Peninsula, occurring in Guatemala from near sea level to about 1,830 m.

Remarks.—This variable snake mimics different species of coral snakes at different geographic localities. Because of its extreme color morphs, a number of different subspecies have been recognized. The subspecies inhabiting Petén has been referred to as *Pliocercus elapoides aequalis.* The population inhabiting the northern portion of the Yucatán Peninsula has sometimes been recognized as a full species, *Pliocercus andrewsi.* Snakes of the genus *Pliocercus* are sometimes placed in the genus *Urotheca.*

Bird-eating Treesnake—Pajarera
Pseustes poecilonotus (Günther, 1858)
Fig. 148

Description.—The head is moderately large and distinct from the neck and the eye is large with a round pupil. There usually are 7–9 supralabials, 11–14 infralabials, a single loreal, 1 preocular, 2–3 postoculars, 2(1) + 2(3) temporals, 25–23(25)–15 dorsal scale rows, 205–223 ventrals, an undivided anal plate, and 127–143 divided subcaudals. The dorsal scales are keeled on the middorsum, but the lower 5–7 scale rows on the sides are smooth. Adults of this species exceed 200 cm in TL.

Large adults are colored somewhat similarly to the tiger treesnake (*Spilotes pullatus*), having a black body punctated with bright yellow spots, but in *Pseustes poecilontus* the spotting tends to be more or less uniform. A specimen from Tikal, 850 mm in TL, retained the juvenile color pattern with no hint of the adult coloration. The venter is whitish on the anterior part of the body, with some dark spotting or mottling, becoming brown or gray-brown posteriorly with heavy dark mottling. Juveniles are pale brown, tan, or brick red with 27–32 dark brown, black-edged dorsal blotches, which are roughly chevrons in shape with the apex pointed anteriorly. A series of small ventrolateral blotches is present on the first scale row and the lateral edges of the ventrals; on the neck they appear as small black spots. The top of the head is pale brown with a dark brown bar across the snout just anterior to the eyes and often with dark brown spots in the frontal and parietal regions. A dark brown postocular stripe extends to the angle of the jaw, and the labials usually have irregular spotting or barring. Much of the dorsal pattern becomes obfuscated in older juveniles or subadults, but some blotches and mottling remain and the overall color is brownish.

Natural History.—This diurnal, arboreal snake occurs in humid forested areas. I have found juveniles on the forest floor, where their color pattern made them quite cryptic in the leaf litter. There are records of adults having been found in low bushes as well as in the canopy of tall trees. One individual was taken about 1.5 m above the ground from a hole in an escoba palm. This species, like the tiger treesnake, inflates its throat when irritated. In this defensive posture, the mandibles are spread, the anterior part of the body is laterally compressed and thrown into an S-shaped coil, the neck is expanded, and the mouth is held open. Snakes often strike from this display position and the strike may fall short of the target or they may bite and immediately release. They feed mostly on birds, bird eggs, and arboreal rodents; juveniles probably eat lizards. This species lays eggs.

Distribution.—The bird-eating treesnake occurs from San Luis Potosí and Oaxaca, Mexico, southward through Central America to Brazil and Bolivia in South America. It is found throughout most of Petén, Belize, and about the eastern half of the northern portion of the Yucatán Peninsula. In Guatemala, this species is known from near sea level to 1,000 m but may occur somewhat higher.

Remarks.—In my wanderings through Guatemala, I have never seen an adult, although several have been brought to me. This may be a matter of chance, but I suspect it is truly a rare thing to see a mature black-and-yellow adult; possibly they almost never descend to the ground. A number of subspecies have been proposed for this wide-ranging snake. The subspecies occurring in Petén is *Pseustes poecilonotus poecilonotus.*

Reclusive Forest Snake—Hojarasquera Reclusa
Rhadinaea anachoreta Smith and Campbell, 1994

Description.—The head is small and only slightly distinct from the neck. The eye is relatively large and has a subcircular pupil. There usually are 8 supralabials, 8 infralabials, a single loreal, 1 preocular, 1 postocular, 1 + 1 temporals, 17–17–17 smooth dorsal scale rows, 139–151 ventrals, a divided anal plate, and 74–80 divided subcaudals. In adult males anal tubercles are present (e.g., some of the dorsal scales above the vent are keeled). Adult specimens of this diminutive species reach about 26 cm in TL.

This snake is striped throughout its body with a number of narrow dark brown stripes: ventrolateral stripes on the lateral portions of the ventrals— the first dorsal scale row and adjacent portions of scale rows 1–2; a lateral stripe on adjacent portions of scale rows 3–4; dorsolateral stripes on adjacent portions of scale rows 6–7; and a middorsal stripe on the vertebral scale row and adjacent portions of the paravertebral rows. Ground color on the dorsum of the body is pale to medium brown and a yellow or tan spot is present in the central part of most dorsal scales. The dorsal ground color becomes a bit darker on the tail. The dorsum of the head is dark brown with scattered pale spots and flecks on the internasals, prefrontals, frontal, supraoculars, parietals, and temporals. A pair of small, yellow, oval spots are present on the parietals, one on either side of the interparietal suture. A pale yellow nuchal collar is interrupted medially and extends slightly posteriorly and laterally for four or five scales to form a broken, obtuse chevron. A cream postocular stripe extends from the lower posterior corner of the orbit across the antepenultimate supralabial to the edge of the lip on the penulti-mate supralabial. A cream streak or series of spots extends from behind the ultimate supralabial to the ventrolateral nuchal region. The supralabials are narrowly bordered anteriorly with cream. The mental and anterior infralabials are mostly dark brown, and the posterior infralabials are yellow or cream, with dark markings posteriorly. The venter is yellowish, becoming cream posteriorly.

Natural History.—This secretive snake inhabits tropical wet, moist, and dry forest and subtropical wet forest. It has been found in leaf litter in forested areas and in heavy secondary growth bordering primary forest. One individual was found beneath a rotten log and several specimens were dug up by a bulldozer during the construction of a road. Nothing is known of its feeding or reproductive biology.

Distribution.—The reclusive forest snake occurs in the Sierra de Santa Cruz and the Sierra de Caral in eastern Guatemala and at Tikal in Petén. Its distribution is apparently disjunct in Guatemala. It almost certainly occurs in Belize and Honduras. This snake is known from elevations of 200 m to 1,180 m.

Striped Forest Snake—Hojarasquera Rayada
Rhadinaea decorata (Günther, 1858)
Fig. 149

Description.—The head is small and only slightly distinct from the neck. The eye is relatively large and has a subcircular pupil. There usually are 8 supralabials, 10 infralabials, a single loreal, 1–2 preoculars (sometimes also a subpreocular), 2 postoculars, 1 + 2 temporals, 17–17–17 mostly smooth dorsal scale rows, 112–134 ventrals, a divided anal plate, and 100–123 divided subcaudals. In most individuals, some of the dorsal scales above and in front of the vent are weakly (sometimes strongly) keeled. Large specimens of this snake may exceed 40 cm in TL.

Two narrow dorsolateral cream stripes extend posteriorly from the neck, grading to pale brown on the posterior half of the body. The middorsum between the stripes is brown, either uniformly or sometimes with an ill-defined darker vertebral line that disappears on the posterior part of the body. The sides of the body are darker brown than the dorsum and delimited by a lateral dark line situated on parts of scale rows 4–5 immediately below the dorsolateral pale line. A white streak on the first scale row extends posteriorly from the throat to the anterior part of the body. The dorsum of the head is brown and has a bold pattern of black-edged lines or spots. The pale head pattern is variable, but usually a distinct whitish streak or spot lies posterior to the upper postocular region and another is in the posterior temporal area just anterior to the beginning of the pale dorsolateral body stripe; sometimes the upper postocular stripe is continuous with the dorsolateral body stripe. A blackish line edges the upper portion of the supralabials, passing under the eye onto the neck. Beneath this dark line the supralabials are whitish, sometimes immaculate or lightly spotted with dark pigment. The underside of the head is pale yellow to

orange and some black dots may be on the chin. A series of black dots or dashes is present laterally on the ventrals, as is a solid black ventrolateral line on the tail. The ventrals grade from pale orange to a deeper uniform reddish to reddish orange on the anterior third of the body. The upper part of the iris is usually colored pale copper and the lower part dark brown.

Natural History.—This diurnal snake inhabits tropical wet and moist forest and subtropical wet forest. It is usually found in leaf litter in forested areas but also tolerates a limited amount of human disturbance and is found in some patches of secondary forest. It feeds primarly on salamanders (*Bolitoglossa*) and frogs (*Eleutherodactylus*) and the terrestrial eggs of these groups. Occasionally, this snake may also feed on lizards. This is an egg-laying species, but little is known of its reproductive biology. When cornered, this snake often coils and hides its head beneath its body, raising and wriggling its tail.

Distribution.—The striped forest snake occurs from northern San Luis Potosí, Mexico, south to Panama and perhaps to the Pacific lowlands of Ecuador. It is restricted to the Atlantic watershed over most of its range but also occurs on the Pacific side of Costa Rica and Panama. In northern Guatemala, this snake is known from only a few localties but probably occurs throughout most of Petén, except perhaps the extreme northern portion of the region, which may be too dry. It occurs in southern Belize but not in the northern part of that country or the Yucatán Peninsula in Mexico. In Guatemala, it is most frequently found at elevations below 600 m, but there are records as high as 1,200 m.

Remarks.—No subspecies are recog nized.

Half Coral Snake—Media Coralilla
Scaphiodontophis annulatus (Duméril, Bibron, and Duméril, 1854)
Fig. 150

Description.—The tail is exceptionally long, comprising 40–50 percent of the TL. The head is only moderately distinct from the neck and the eye is large with a round pupil. There usually are 9–10 supralabials, 9–11 infralabials, a single loreal, 1 preocular, 2 postoculars, 1 + 2 or 2 + 2 temporals, 17–17–17 smooth dorsal scale rows, 139–156 ventrals, a divided anal plate, and 121–149 divided subcaudals. This species reaches about 90 cm in TL, but large adults usually lack a portion of the tail.

This snake is variable in the extent of banding pattern, with some individuals showing the brightly colored pattern only on the anterior third or less of their bodies and others having a banded pattern throughout the body and tail. Specimens I have seen from the Petén region have banding only on the anterior part of the body. The sequence of bands is red-black-yellow-black-red. The red bands exhibit the most variation, with some snakes having bands only about two scales in width and the red bands in others being up to eight scales wide. The red scales may be dusky or black tipped. Posterior to the bands the body is brown, with the scales of the vertebral row and scale row 5 heavily black tipped, forming dotted lines that extend onto the tail. The upper parts of the rostral internasals, and most of the prefrontals are black. A pale band extends across the top of the head between the eyes the back of the head including the pari etals and sometimes up to about 4–6 scales behind the parietals is black The supralabials are mostly pale, usu ally with several dark spots beneath the eye. The infralabials, chin, and throa are cream usually with a little darke mottling. The venter is cream excep for the lateral edges of the ventrals which are mottled with black.

Natural History.—This sharp-eyed, di urnal snake occurs in tropical wet moist, and dry forest and subtropica wet and moist forest. It is most fre quently encountered in primary fores but also occurs in old coffee groves and along the edges of other cultivated areas. It is agile and usually disappears quickly beneath the leaf litter of the forest floor when disturbed. It is mos active in the early morning and late af ternoon. The long tail of this species i easily broken and adults usually have blunt tails.

This snake appears to be adapted to feed primarily on skinks, especially the brown forest skink (*Sphenomorphu cherriei*), which it can swallow with amazing speed (usually less than 10 seconds). These lizards have smooth, hard scales (with osteroderms underneath) and robust bodies with short limbs that often allow them to twist and escape from whatever seizes them. The teeth of the half coral snake are unique in that they are hinged and shovel-shaped, an adaptation for seizing and retaining skinks. Other prey, less frequently taken, includes Bourgeau's anole (*Norops bourgeaei*) and teiid lizards.

Courtship among multiple individuals has been observed under natural conditions on two occasions by Eric Smith. Five snakes including a female with ovarian eggs, three males, and an individual of unknown sex that escaped were observed together in courtship on 18 June. An additional four

snakes including two males, a female, and an individual that escaped were found entwined together in courtship on 21 June. The female from this latter group laid two eggs on 23 June that were 33–35 mm long. Guatemalan females appear to lay 1–4 eggs, although there are reports that Chiapan specimens lay 6–10 eggs.

Distribution.—The half coral snake occurs on Atlantic slopes from southern Tamaulipas and on the Pacific versant from the Isthmus of Tehuantepec, Mexico, southward through Central America to northwestern Colombia. It is found throughout most of Petén, Belize, and the northeastern Yucatán Peninsula, occurring from near sea level to about 1,200 m.

Remarks.—Another vernacular name for this snake is *culebra añadida*.

Common Tropical Ratsnake—Ratonera Tropical Común
Senticolis triaspis (Cope, 1866)
Fig. 151

Description.—The head is relatively narrow and the eye is small. There usually are 8 supralabials, 11 infralabials, a single loreal, 1 preocular, 2 postoculars, 3 + 3 or 3 + 4 temporals, 29(31)–33(35)–21(23) dorsal scale rows, 247–281 ventrals, a divided anal plate, and 87–118 divided subcaudals. The dorsal scales are very weakly keeled. This snake reaches about 120 cm in TL; males are smaller than females.

Adults are straw colored, pale olive-green, or grayish tan with brown pale-centered blotches. Juveniles have a

bold pattern of brownish or reddish brown dorsal blotches on an orange-tan background; these blotches persist into adulthood in individuals from the northern and central part of the Yucatán Peninsula. Snakes from southern Petén and the highlands of Guatemala tend to become unicolored as they mature and usually have lost all trace of blotches by the time they reach 600 mm in SVL. There are 42–57 body blotches and 60–85 total blotches, including those on the tail. There is often an intricate head pattern consisting of a curved dark bar across the snout in front of the eyes; a pair of dark bars extending from the supraoculars across the parietals onto the neck, where they often coalesce middorsally; and an irregular median dark bar or series of spots on the frontal, parietals, and scales of the postparietal area. A postorbital bar extends from behind the eye to the angle of the jaw. A poorly defined postorbital bar may persist even in individuals that lose their dorsal pattern as adults. The venter is immaculate white or cream.

Natural History.—The species inhabits tropical and subtropical moist and dry forest. It has particularly large eyes with round pupils. It is often reported to be diurnal, which is true in the Guatemalan highlands. However, in the lowlands of Petén I have found this species active only after dark. I have found it most often in somewhat open, partially cleared areas. This species is a constrictor, feeding mostly on rodents but also sometimes taking shrews, bats, small birds, and lizards.

Females reach maturity at around 625 mm SVL, at not less than 24 months of age. Reproduction appears to be aseasonal, eggs being laid at any time of the year. This snake lays 3–7 eggs, which are 38–42 mm in length.

Distribution.—The common tropical ratsnake is distributed from southeastern Arizona and southwestern New Mexico through central Nuevo León and southern Tamaulipas, Mexico, and southward in lowland and montane environments through the Yucatán Peninsula and Central America to Costa Rica. It occurs throughout most of the northern Yucatán Peninsula. This species is not common in Petén but is probably widespread. It is usually found in relatively dry habitats, including dry pine-oak forest. This snake occurs from near sea level up to about 1,400 m in Guatemala.

Remarks.—The subspecies occurring in northern and central Petén is *Senticolis triaspis triaspis;* the southern portion of Petén is inhabited by *S. t. mutabilis.* This species previously was placed in the genus *Elaphe.*

Coral-backed Snail-eater—Tragababosa Espalda Coral
Sibon dimidiata (Günther, 1872)
Fig. 152

Description.—The head is well differentiated from the slender neck and the snout is short and blunt. The eyes are large with subcircular pupils. There usually are 7–8 supralabials, 9–10 infralabials, 1 scale in the loreal-preocular region, 2 postoculars, 1 + 2 temporals, 15–15–15 smooth dorsal scale rows, 160–206 ventrals, an undivided anal plate, and 95–144 divided subcaudals. The first pair of infralabials are not in contact on the ventral midline and there are usually 1–2 postmentals. The vertebral row of dorsal scales is not enlarged anteriorly and only slightly so posteriorly. This species eaches a maximum of about 70 cm in TL.

The dorsal pattern of this snake consists of alternating pale and darker crossbands. Pale bands have darker mottling and are usually coral or orange dorsally. Laterally, the pale bands tend to be whitish in juveniles but may be pale brown in adults. The 23–31 darker crossbands are deep reddish brown to dark chocolate brown and darkly edged. There are 13–26 dark bands on the tail. The top of the head is whitish, pale brown, or orange with darker mottling or spotting. The labials are mostly white with irregular black spotting. The chin and throat are whitish, with a few dark brown spots, usually with one on the posterior part of the second pair of chinshields and adjacent scales. The venter is cream to pale brown, with pigment from the dorsal blotches extending almost to midventer.

Natural History.—This snake inhabits tropical wet and moist forest and subtropical wet forest. Nocturnal and ar-

boreal, it is most frequently seen in low bushes or on the ground, but there are several records of it in tall trees. Similar to other members in this genus, this species is a gastropod specialist, feeding primarily on tree snails. A female from Belize laid two eggs.

Distribution.—The coral-backed snail-eater occurs from southern Veracruz, Mexico, southward across Petén and eastern Guatemala, southern Belize, northern Honduras and eastern Nicaragua to Costa Rica; it also occurs on the Pacific watershed of southeastern Chiapas, Mexico, and southwestern Guatemala. It is found throughout much of southern and central Petén but is unknown from northern and central Belize and most of the Yucatán Peninsula. In Guatemala, this species is known from near sea level to about 1,000 m.

Remarks.—The subspecies occurring in the Petén region has sometimes been regarded as *Sibon dimidiata dimidiata,* but some authors do not recognize subspecies.

Cloudy Snail-eater—Tragababosa Jaspeada
Sibon nebulata (Linnaeus, 1758)
Fig. 153

Description.—The head is well differentiated from the slender neck and the snout is short and blunt. The eye is large with a subcircular pupil. There usually are 7 supralabials, 8–9 infralabials, 1 scale in the loreal-preocular region, 2–3 postoculars, 1 + 2 temporals, 15–15–15 smooth dorsal scale rows, 159–193 ventrals, an undivided anal

plate, and 70–114 divided subcaudals. Only the first pair of infralabials is in contact behind the mental and there is no postmental; the vertebral row of dorsal scales is slightly enlarged. This species reaches a maximum TL of about 83 cm.

There are about 36–47 black dorsal crossbands on the body and another 30 spots on the tail. The dorsal cross-bands are irregular with jagged edges and are often broken laterally or mid-dorsally. Laterally, the dorsal cross-bands may be edged with pale pink spots distributed in a somewhat irregular fashion. The ground color is gray, punctated with darker spots. The top of the head is gray, heavily mottled with black, and the labials, chin, and throat are cream to pinkish, heavily mottled with dark gray or black. The belly is cream or pink, with the pigment from the dark dorsal crossbands extending to about the ventral midline; these extensions are usually staggered but sometimes may be opposite. The pale ventral interspaces have a few dark spots.

Natural History.—This species occurs in tropical wet, moist, and dry forest and subtropical wet forest. This nocturnal and arboreal snake is most often found at night in low vegetation, either primary or secondary, but it is not uncommon to see individuals active on the ground at night. By day they usually hide on the ground in leaf litter or rotten logs. So far as is known, this species feeds exclusively on slugs and shelled land snails.

A pair of these snakes was found together in a botán palm during late February in Petén, although it is uncertain whether these snakes were courting. A series of juveniles were collected near the Great Plaza of Tikal between mid-March and mid-April. Three to nine eggs are usually laid from May to August and are about 20–26 mm in length, but the reproductive season may be more extensive at certain locations. Six eggs collected in the department of Huehuetenango on 25 July hatched on 4–7 October; these juveniles were 22.2–23.4 cm in TL and weighed 2.77–3.02 g. Juveniles have been collected in March and April, and hatchlings of less than 23 cm TL have been seen in July and August.

This is among the more common of the snail-eaters. I have not usually found more than one during any one night of searching, with the notable exception of a long hike one hot night through the Caribbean lowlands of Costa Rica. We had set out at dusk and had roamed the valleys and hillside just to the north of Turrialba without finding much. At about 3:00 in the morning I sat down to rest beneath a small leafy tree growing on the flood plain of a stream. After a few minutes I noticed a snake in the branches above me. As I was watching it, I spied several other snakes of the same species nearby in the same tree. I ultimately found seven cloudy snail-eaters in that tree, which had several dozen small whitish snails crawling on its limbs and leaves. I continued to search up and down the stream until daybreak without finding any more snakes or trees with snails. During the course of further collecting in the area over the next month, I did not find any other cloudy snail-eaters. Although I am sure there is a perfectly good biological explanation, I still am unaware of why the snails converged on that particular tree or how these snakes were able to find and congregate at this food source.

Distribution.—This snake is distributed from Nayarit and Veracruz, Mexico, through much of Central America and South America to Ecuador and Brazil, also occurring on Trinidad and Tobago. It is found throughout most of Petén, Belize, and the eastern part of the northern Yucatán Peninsula. In Guatemala, it occurs from near sea level to at least 1,350 m.

Remarks.—The subspecies in Petén is presumably *Sibon nebulata nebulata;* however, the validity of subspecies has been called into question by some authors.

Yucatán Snail-eater—Tragababosa Yucateca
Sibon sanniola (Cope, 1866)
Fig. 154

Description.—The head is moderately differentiated from the neck and the snout is short and blunt. The eye is large with a subcircular pupil. There usually are 9 supralabials, 9–10 infralabials, 2–3 preoculars, 2 postoculars, . + 2 temporals, 15–15–15 smooth dorsal scale rows, 143–162 ventrals, an undivided anal plate, and 57–88 divided subcaudals. The first pair of infralabials are not in contact on the ventral midline and there are usually 1–2 postmentals. Although extremely variable in most morphological features, this species is unique among members of the the genus in not having the loreal enter the orbit and in having 9 supralabials. This species reaches a maximum TL of about 43 cm.

The dorsum is pale brown or pale gray-brown, with 35–67 dark brown spots on the body and 17–32 on the tail; usually confined to the vertebral and paravertebral dorsal scale rows, often these spots coalesce to form a zigzag pattern on the back and are narrowly outlined by creamy yellow. Spots in lateral and ventrolateral series are smaller and paler than in the dorsal series; the ventrolateral series extends onto the ventrals. The venter is cream with heavy lateral stippling and mottling, decreasing toward the midline. The top of the head is stippled with dark brown and the labial sutures are brown. A postorbital stripe is often present from just behind the eye to the angle of the jaw. The venter of the head is cream, often with dark brown stippling.

The population in Belize, which may be a distinct species, has a dorsal pattern of about 34 dark brown bands, on the body and 23 bands on the tail alternating with pale bands, and the top of the head has a large dark blotch that extends from the frontal posteriorly to merge with the first dark body band. Individuals from Belize have a relatively high number of ventrals and subcaudals.

Natural History.—This nocturnal snake occurs in tropical wet, moist, and dry forest in a variety of habitats, including dry scrub forest, quasi-rainforest, and more mesic rainforest. Unlike most snail-eaters, which tend to be highly arboreal, two of the snail-eaters occurring in Petén, the Yucatán snail-eater and the ringed snail-eater (*Sibon sartorii*), are terrestrial and do not possess the adaptations to arboreality characteristic of some of their congeners (namely, a laterally compressed, elongate, and attenuate body, an abruptly narrowing neck that dramatically sets apart the head, and a wide row of vertebral scales). The Yucatán snail-eater has a specialized diet, feeding almost exclusively on slugs and snails.

In the northern part of the Yucatán Peninsula, this snake has a seasonal reproductive cycle that is correlated with the rainy season and the species reproduces annually. Females lay 2–5 eggs between June and September; most

eggs hatch during August through November. Eggs are about 26 mm in length. Hatchlings are of about 10 cm in SVL and have a TL of about 13 cm. The young grow quickly, with females attaining a reproductively mature length of 20 cm SVL within eight months after hatching.

Distribution.—This species occurs across the northern portion of the Yucatán Peninsula, including the northern part of Campeche, most of Yucatán, and the eastern half of Quintana Roo, Mexico; in most of Belize; and the extreme eastern part of the Department of Petén. It occurs at low elevations between sea level and 300 m.

Remarks.—Subspecies recognized are *Sibon sanniola sanniola* of the northern Yucatán Peninsula and *S. s. neilli* of Belize and eastern Petén.

Ringed Snail-eater—Tragababosa Anillada
Sibon sartorii (Cope, 1863)
Fig. 155

Description.—Unlike in other Petén snail-eaters, which have heads that are at least moderately set off from the body, the head of this species is scarcely wider than the neck. The body is cylindrical is cross section. The snout is short and blunt and the eyes are relatively small and nonprotruding, with subcircular pupils. There usually are 6–8 supralabials, 7–10 infralabials, a single loreal, 1–2 preoculars, 1 postocular, 1 + 1 or 1 + 2 temporals, 17–17–17 dorsal scale rows, 165–197 ventrals, an undivided anal plate, and 56–73 divided subcaudals. The first pair of infralabials are in contact behind the mental and there is no postmental. The dorsal scales are weakly keeled on top of the body. This species attains a TL of at least 80 cm.

North of Lago Petén Itzá, most individuals are distinctly patterned with alternating reddish orange and black rings on the body; throughout most of its range, however, this snake has yellow and black rings. There are 17–25 black body rings in Petén specimens. The dorsal scales in the pale rings are usually tipped with black. The top of the head is black from the tip of the snout posteriorly, including most of the parietals, and laterally to the supralabials beneath the eye and forward. A yellow collar usually involves the posterior edges of the parietals and extends onto the neck for about 2–4 scale lengths at middorsum. The collar is wider laterally and merges with the yellow of the throat. The mental, first 5–6 pairs of infralabials, and anterior chinshields are mottled with black; the rest of the chin and the throat are yellow.

Natural History.—This nocturnal snake inhabits tropical dry, moist, and wet forest and subtropical wet and moist forest. Most snail-eaters tend to be highly arboreal; the ringed snail-eater, however, is more robust than the other snail-eater species in the region and is almost always found on the ground. This species is common in forested and secondary growth habitats. Slugs and pulmonate land snails are the main, if not the exclusive, prey of this species. Three to five eggs are laid in the late dry season or early part of the rainy season. Adult males have breeding tubercles on the chin and snout.

✔*Distribution.*—This snake is distributed from San Luis Potosí and Oaxaca, Mexico, to Nicaragua. It occurs throughout most of Petén, Belize, and the northern Yucatán Peninsula, ranging in Guatemala from near sea level to about 1,400 m.

Remarks.—The subspecies *Sibon sartorii sartorii* occurs in Petén. Until fairly recently, this species was placed in the genus *Tropidodipsas*.

Tiger Treesnake—Chichicua
Spilotes pullatus (Linnaeus, 1758)
Figs. 156–157

Description.—This slender snake is one of the longest in the Petén, not uncommonly exceeding 250 cm in TL. The head is moderately distinct from the neck and the eye is large and dark brown, with a round pupil. There usually are 7–8 supralabials, 7–8 infralabials, a single loreal, 1 preocular, 2 postoculars, 1 + 1 temporals, 18(16)–18–12 (13–15) dorsal scale rows, 206–220 ventrals, an undivided anal plate, and 121–132 divided subcaudals. Scales on the dorsum of the body are keeled and those on the sides are smooth.

This snake has a handsome black-and-yellow pattern. There are 25–32 dark crossbands on the body, which often tend to be ill-defined on the neck, and 12–16 well-defined dark bands on the tail. The dorsal pattern of crossbands is more distinctive in juveniles. The top of the head is mostly black, but much of the rostral is usually yellow, there may be yellow bars on the internasals and prefrontals, and yellow spots occur more posteriorly on the head; these yellow markings are especially prominent in young specimens. The sides of the head are black and yellow. The venter is yellow with transverse black markings, becoming darker posteriorly.

Natural History.—This species occurs in tropical wet, moist, and dry forest and subtropical wet forest. It may be found on the ground, in low bushes, or in the canopy of tall forest (see "Phantoms in the Night," page 246). This diurnal species is highly arboreal and usually tries to escape by climbing. It is found most frequently in forested areas but will enter adjacent secondary vegetation. When threatened, this species inflates and vertically compresses its neck. Rodents of various kinds, including harvest mice (*Reithrodontomys*), have been most frequently found in its diet, and it also feeds on birds and their eggs. From 7 to 10 eggs are laid during the late dry season or the early rainy season from April to July. Hatchlings about 50 cm in TL have been found from June to November.

✔*Distribution.*—The tiger treesnake is distributed from Tamaulipas and Oaxaca, Mexico, southward through Central America and South America to Argentina. It occurs throughout most of Petén, Belize, and the northern Yucatán Peninsula. In Guatemala, this species is found from near sea level to about 1,200 m.

Remarks.—This conspicuously colored snake is well known to inhabitants of the Guatemalan lowlands. Most people in Petén realize that it is not venomous but nevertheless greatly fear it. The subspecies occurring in Petén is *Spilotes pullatus mexicanus*. Other vernacular names are *mica* and *voladora*.

Phantoms in the Night.—One dark night in the early 1960s, I was hunting for tepezcuintles (*Agouti paca*) with a Guatemalan named Miguel along the shores of Lago de Izabal, near what is known locally as Playa Dorada. Some 35 m above us on a branch of a tall tree, Miguel saw what he thought was a sleeping great curassow (*Crax rubra*). Never having been schooled in the meaning of sport, and not one to miss an opportunity to obtain meat for his family, he shot up into the tree with his 12-gauge shotgun. Immediately, we could see an apparition changing form in our headlights as the "bird" became extended to a considerable length and fell from the tree almost on the head of Miguel, who dropped his shotgun and crashed off through the forest in the dark.

The object falling from the tree turned out to be a tiger treesnake or *mica* about 2 m long, which unfortunately was mortally wounded, and which I dispatched with a machete to end its suffering. The next day, I suppose because he was somewhat ashamed of his flight of the evening before and wanted to justify his actions, Miguel recounted several horror stories of the incredible abilities of the *mica*. A few years later, Miguel failed to return from a hunting trip and was never seen again; his fate remains unknown. Such occurrences in rural Guatemala are common and often are explained by various superstitions about animals—including many species that, like the mica, are harmless.

The only time I have ever been bitten by a snake without having seen it first involved a tiger treesnake. Although I know of no truly aggressive snake, the mica stands its ground and makes clumsy efforts to strike when irritated. I had hiked through a large patch of virgin forest one morning and come upon a small, overgrown clearing with the remains of a hut. The structure had collapsed long before, and the rotting thatched roof lay on the ground. I was standing on the thatch talking to a companion when I felt a sudden sharp jab in the back of my leg. Thinking I had inadvertently backed into a chichicaste plant, a fearsome kind of nettle that grows in many of these cleared areas, I jumped forward. About that time, my companion let loose a series of expletives that roughly translated into advice that the "mother of all snakes" had me in the calf. By the time I realized it was only a mica and that I was not going to die after all, my heart was racing so wildly that I feared that I might die of a heart attack instead. Obviously, I had trodden on this snake as it lay hidden beneath the old thatch. What I find remarkable is that rather than fleeing as most snakes would have, this one chose to emerge and bite me. Perhaps I had its tail pinned beneath my boot, making escape impossible, but in the excitement I lost track of exactly how the snake was situated, so I will never know.

Degenhardt's Scorpion-hunter—Alacranera de Degenhardt
Stenorrhina degenhardtii (Berthold, 1846)
Fig. 158

Description.—The head is scarcely distinct from the neck and the eye is medium sized with a round pupil. There are usually 7 supralabials, 7–9 infralabials, a loreal present or not, 1 preocular, 2 postoculars, 1 + 2 temporals, 17(19–21)–17–17 smooth dorsal scale rows, 136–159 ventrals, a divided anal plate, and 31–48 divided subcaudals. The rostral projects anteriorly and is rounded in dorsal profile. The internasal is fused with the anterior section of the nasal. This species reaches a maximum length of about 80 cm.

The dorsal ground color may be brownish, reddish, or grayish. The dorsum may be uniform or have 24–37 pale-edged dark blotches or transverse bars on the body, some of which may reach the ventrals. Adults sometimes have faint indications of lateral stripes. Juveniles usually are distinctly patterned, but this pattern is lost in many adults. The top of the head is colored similarly to the body and may be uniform or have darker spots or mottling. An ill-defined dark gray postocular stripe extends from the posterior edge of the eye to above the angle of the jaw. The labials, chin, and throat are cream with gray or brownish mottling. The venter is mostly pale cream, salmon, or pink, but the ventrals are heavily marked with rectangular or triangular dark spots, with a series of spots often present along the ventral midline, forming a longitudinal black line.

Natural History.—This terrestrial snake inhabits tropical wet and moist forest and subtropical wet forest. It may be active by day or at night. The diet of this species consists of various invertebrates, mainly spiders but also crickets, grasshoppers, scorpions, and insect larvae. This snake lays eggs and juveniles less than 25 cm in TL with a prominent umbilical scar have been found in March and May.

Distribution.—Degenhardt's scorpion-hunter occurs on the Atlantic watershed from southern Veracruz, Mexico, through Central America to Colombia and Venezuela in northern South America and on the Pacific versant from Honduras to Ecuador. It is found in the southern, humid portion of the Petén region but is absent from the central and northern part of the department, as well as from the Yucatán Peninsula in Mexico. In Guatemala, this species occurs from near sea level to about 1,740 m.

Remarks.—Several subspecies of this variable species have sometimes been recognized; *Stenorrhina degenhardtii mexicana* is the subspecies occurring in Petén.

Freminville's Scorpion-hunter—Alacranera de Freminville
Stenorrhina freminvillii Duméril, Bibron, and Duméril, 1854
Fig. 159

Description.—The head is small and scarcely distinct from the neck. The eye is medium sized with a round pupil. There are usually 7 supralabials, 7 infralabials, a single loreal or none, 1 preocular, 2 postoculars, 1 + 2 temporals, 17–17–17 smooth dorsal scale rows, 162–178 ventrals, a divided anal plate, and 28–38 divided subcaudals. The rostral projects anteriorly and is rounded in dorsal profile. The internasal is fused with the anterior section of the nasal. The posterior nasal is greatly elongate posteriorly or sometimes fragmented, forming a loreal. This species often reaches 70 cm in TL and may be over 80 cm, with males attaining a greater length than females.

The dorsum is yellowish brown, grayish brown, or reddish. The body may be uniformly colored or have one to five thin black lines extending down the body. The pattern, if present, consists of a lateral line on the upper part of scale row 3 and the lower part of row 4, a dorsolateral line on scale row 6 and adjacent parts of rows 5 and 7, and a middorsal line on the vertebral scale row and adjacent portions of the paravertebral rows. The lateral line usually extends only to the level of the vent, the dorsolateral line to about the middle of the tail, and the middorsal line the full length of the tail. The lateral and dorsolateral dark lines are reduced in some specimens to a series of spots on scale rows 4 and 6, respectively, and the middorsal line occupies only the medial portion of the vertebral scale row. I have seen specimens that possess only a thin vertebral line and otherwise are uniformly reddish or grayish. The base of each dorsal scale may be black in some specimens. The top of the head is colored similarly to the dorsum and may be unmarked or have dark spots on the frontal and parietals. The upper part of the iris is reddish bronze. The venter is often colored similarly to the dorsum but much paler, often being yellowish, pale gray, or pinkish. The belly may be immaculate or there may be slight dark mottling posteriorly. Some specimens have a series of midventral dark spots on the posterior three-fourths of the body.

Natural History.—This terrestrial snake occurs in tropical and subtropical moist and dry forest. As with many species of snakes that have considerable elevational ranges, in the highlands of Guatemala this snake is often seen crawling by day, but in the warm Petén lowlands it is active mostly at night. It feeds on insects, spiders, and scorpions, and reportedly is immune to the stings of scorpions.

Females reach maturity at about 448 mm SVL, at about a year of age. They often lay two clutches of eggs annually. Unlike most other species of snakes in the region, this species usually deposits eggs during the dry season between October and April. However, there are also records of Guatemalan specimens laying eggs during the early rainy season. Adult females collected in Petén during April contained 4–6 fully developed eggs; several recently collected specimens laid eggs in May and June. Females lay 5–19 oblong eggs measuring about 20–28 × 10 mm, often in dirt crevices or abandoned ant mounds. Hatchlings collected in March and April were about 15 cm in TL.

Distribution.—Freminville's scorpion-hunter is distributed on the Atlantic versant from the Isthmus of Tehuantepec and on Pacific slopes from Guerrero, Mexico, to Costa Rica. This species occurs throughout much of central Petén, Belize, and the northern Yucatán Peninsula. In central Petén, most specimens have been found near aguadas. In Guatemala, this species occurs from near sea level to about 2,200 m.

Remarks.—Another vernacular name is *sabanera*.

Tropical Brown Snake—Traga-lombriz Café
Storeria dekayi (Holbrook, 1839)
Fig. 160

Description.—The head is only slightly differentiated from the neck and the snout is short and blunt. The eye is moderate in size with a round pupil. There usually are 7 supralabials, 6–7 infralabials, no loreal, 1 preocular, 1–3 (usually 2) postoculars, 1 + 2 temporals, 17–17–17 keeled dorsal scale rows, 129–140 ventrals, a divided anal plate, and 40–53 divided subcaudals. This small species reaches a maximum TL of about 33 cm.

The ground color of adults is variable. Most frequently these snakes are tan or gray-brown, but orangish or cinnamon-colored specimens are not uncommon. The belly is cream or pale tan and the iris is metallic brown in brownish specimens; the venter is pale salmon and the iris is reddish bronze in orangish specimens. Laterally, the ventrals have small black punctations. A pale dorsal stripe occupying the vertebral and paravertebral scale rows extends from the back of the head to the tail. A pale ventrolateral stripe may be present on several of the lower dorsal scale rows, but this stripe is usually vague or absent in large individuals. A series of small, often indistinct, dark spots is present lateral to the dorsal stripe, especially on the anterior part of the body. These black spots are sometimes arranged in several alternating series, forming a checkerboard pattern. The supralabials and the side of the head are paler than the top of the head, and the infralabials and throat are usually white. In juveniles, the ground color usually is gray-brown, the ventrolateral stripes are better defined, both the supralabials and infralabials are white, and there is a black collar, which may be interrupted middorsally.

Natural History.—This snake inhabits mesic forests such as tropical wet forest and subtropical wet and moist forest. I have found individuals actively crawling through wet leaf litter during the early morning in cloudforest. When alarmed, these snakes tend to flatten their bodies, spread their mandibles, and often discharge a foulsmelling substance from their anal scent glands.

They feed mostly on soft-bodied invertebrates such as earthworms, slugs, and certain insects. This species gives birth to live young. One Guatemalan female collected in early March contained nine ova; another collected in late March also had well-formed embryos. A juvenile specimen collected in late May was thought to be only a few days old. These data suggest that young are born near the beginning of the rainy season.

Distribution.—The brown snake occurs from southern Quebec and Ontario, Canada, and southern Maine westward to eastern South Dakota and southward through most of the eastern United States, including peninsular

Florida and eastern Texas; along the Atlantic versant and coast of Mexico from the Río Bravo del Norte to about central Veracruz; and in a disjunct population from eastern Chiapas, Mexico, through central Guatemala to Honduras. Most of the records for this species in Guatemala are from the mountains of Alta and Baja Verapaz. It reportedly occurs at low elevations in tropical forests, but I have not seen specimens in this kind of habitat. In Guatemala, it reportedly occurs at low elevations, although I have never seen it below about 1,200 m. This species ranges in mesic forests up to about 1,710 m.

Remarks.—The subspecies occurring in Guatemala is *Storeria dekayi tropica*.

Mayan Golden-backed Snake—Culebra Maya Dorso Dorado
Symphimus mayae (Gaige, 1936)
Fig. 161

Description.—The head is elongate and narrow but nevertheless wider than the neck. The eye is medium sized with a round pupil. There usually are 6 supralabials, 8 infralabials, a loreal present, a divided anal plate, 1 + 2 temporals, 15–15–15 smooth dorsal scale rows, 123–153 ventrals, and 120–123 divided subcaudals. This small, slender snake grows to about 80 cm.

The dorsum is pale gray-brown on the sides with a darker brown or reddish brown stripe on the three middorsal scale rows and half of the adjacent scales. This stripe begins on the neck and extends posteriorly over most of the body but becomes less distinct, grading into the ground color by the time it reaches the tail. The edges of the scales in the middorsal stripe and the interstitial skin are bright yellow. The tail is uniformly gray-brown dorsally. The gular area and venter of the anterior one-fourth of body are whitish, grading into pale gray. A thin, usually broken, dark brown lateral line is sometimes present, extending from about the anterior one-fourth of the body most of the way onto the tail. An ill-defined dark postocular stripe extends posteriorly from the margin of the eye to above the angle of the jaw; sometimes a dark streak is also present across the canthus from about the nasals to the anterior edge of the eye. The upper lip is mostly white or cream, sharply contrasting with the top and sides of the head, which are medium to dark brown.

Natural History.—This little-known snake inhabits tropical dry forest. It is diurnal and apparently arboreal; it has been found in small trees and bushes. This snake feeds mostly on orthopterans such as grasshoppers, crickets, and katydids. It presumably lays eggs.

Distribution.—The Mayan golden-backed snake occurs in the northern portion of the Yucatán Peninsula in the states of Yucatán and Quintana Roo, Mexico, and in the Belize and Corozal districts of Belize. It has not been found in Petén but probably occurs in the northeastern part of the department. Elevation records for this snake are between sea level and 300 m.

Remarks.—This species was at one time placed in the North American genus *Opheodrys,* to which it appears to be related.

Mayan Black-headed Centipede-eater—Traga-cienpiés Maya Cabeza Negra
Tantilla cuniculator Smith, 1939
Fig. 162

Description.—The head is small and scarcely distinct from the neck. The eye is small with a round pupil. There usually are 7 supralabials, 6 infralabials, no loreal, 1 preocular, 2 postoculars, 1 + 1 temporals, 15–15–15 smooth dorsal scale rows, 140–154 ventrals, a divided anal plate, and 48–58 divided subcaudals. This snake reaches about 25 cm in TL.

The ground color is medium to dark brown. A pale apricot to orangish collar, involving the posterior tips of the parietals or just posterior to these, is about 2–3 dorsal scale lengths wide and is bordered posteriorly with dark brown pigment. The dorsal pattern consists of pale lateral stripes that begin about 2–3 scales behind the collar and extend to the tip of the tail. The lateral stripes involve the upper portion of scale row 3 and the lower part of scale row 4. A middorsal stripe is often absent or may be present beginning about one scale length behind the collar and becoming ill-defined posteriorly. The middorsal stripe, when present, usually involves only the medial portion of the vertebral scale row. All pale stripes are bordered by dark brown pigment. The head is dark brown with small pale flecks. The tip of the snout, including the upper part of the rostral, the internasals, and posterior part of the prefrontals, is pale. A white spot is on the side of the head behind the eye (mostly on supralabial 5). The lingual border of the infralabials is darkly marked. The venter is reddish orange, with dark pigment from the dorsum encroaching on the lateral portions of the ventrals and subcaudals.

Natural History.—This secretive, terrestrial snake inhabits tropical moist and dry forest. It has been seen crawling in leaf litter in primary forest at Tikal by day and after dark. It presumably feeds on invertebrates and lays eggs.

Distribution.—The Mayan blackheaded centipede-eater occurs from northern Petén and northern Belize to the northern portion of the Yucatán Peninsula in Mexico. In Guatemala it is known only from Tikal at about 200 m.

Black-bellied Centipede-eater—Traga-cienpiés Panza Negra
Tantilla moesta (Günther, 1863)
Fig. 163

Description.—The head is only slightly distinct from the neck and the eye is small with a round pupil. There usually are 7 supralabials, 6 infralabials, no loreal, 1 preocular, 2 postoculars, 1 + 1 temporals, 15–15–15 smooth dorsal scale rows, 138–152 ventrals, a divided anal plate, and 52–62 divided subcaudals. This is a large, robust member of the genus, reaching a maximum TL of about 60 cm.

The dorsum of the body is dark gray or black. The top of the head from the tip of the snout to about the anterior part of the parietals, the posterior margin of the eye, and the first three and a half supralabials are black; usually there is some white mottling on the side of the head on the nasals, first two supralabials, and preocular. A broad white collar usually includes most of the parietals, the posterior portion of the postoculars, and supralabials 5–7 and the posterior part of 4; the collar extends posteriorly from the parietals for 2–7 dorsal scale lengths. Sometimes a series of white dots on the vertebral scale row extends posteriorly from the collar for 6–10 dorsal scale lengths. Infralabials 1–4 often have dark mottling along the margin of the mouth and infralabials 5–7 may have dark spotting; otherwise the infralabials, chin, and throat are immaculate white. This white coloration extends posteriorly, at least on the median portion of the ventrals, for up to about 10 scales. The rest of the ventrals and subcaudals are dark gray or black, with the exception of the anal plate and a few adjacent ventrals and subcaudals, which are white.

Natural History.—This secretive, terrestrial snake inhabits tropical moist and dry forest. Specimens were found in secondary growth near Lago Petén Itzá and under a log in forest at Tikal. It presumably feeds on invertebrates and lays eggs.

Distribution.—The black-bellied centipede-eater is found from the vicinity of Lago Petén Itzá in Peten northward through the Yucatán Peninsula. The species is not known from Belize. This lowland snake occurs near sea level to about 200 m.

Remarks.—The common name centipede-eater for the genus *Tantilla* is derived from their unusual habit of including this potentially dangerous prey in their diets.

Lesser Centipede-eater—Traga-cienpiés Pequeña
Tantilla schistosa (Bocourt, 1883)
Fig. 164

Description.—The head is small and scarcely distinct from the neck, the eyes are small and dark, and the pupils are round. The tail is relatively short but robust and easily broken. There usually are 7 supralabials, 6 infralabials, no loreal, 1 preocular, 2 postoculars, 1 + 1 temporals, 15–15–15 smooth dorsal scale rows, 117–147 ventrals, a divided anal plate, and 24–42 divided subcaudals. Adults of this snake reach only about 30 cm in SVL and are usually under 200 mm.

The dorsum is medium brown to almost black; in some specimens most of the dorsal scales, especially laterally, have a vague pale center. The dark dorsal coloration extends onto the ventrals, with dark projections of pigment along the anterolateral edges of the scales. The top of the head is dark, usually with no pale markings except for a pair of white spots on the internasals of some specimens. A whitish or yellowish nuchal band covers the posterior tips of the parietals, usually extending no more than one scale length behind the parietals, and involves the secondary temporal. This pale nuchal band sometimes is continuous with the pale ventral coloration. The dark color of the head extends onto the infralabials, which are mostly smoky gray or black; the mental is pale with a little dark pigment. Ventral coloration is subject to much variation. In some specimens it is uniformly salmon, and the chin and throat sometimes may be heavily suffused with gray. However, in most snakes there is an anterior-posterior progression from white, cream, yellow, or chartreuse to salmon or purplish red. However, where the reddish ventral coloration begins is variable. In a typical snake, the chin and throat are whitish, grading to yellow on the anterior part of the body, chartreuse at about midbody, and finally to a deep purplish red on the posterior quarter of the body and on the tail.

Natural History.—This secretive, terrestrial species occurs in tropical wet and moist forest. I have usually found this snake beneath rotten logs or in leaf litter. Centipedes are the major prey of this diminutive snake; occasionally beetle larvae are also eaten. This species lays eggs and hatchlings have been collected in June.

Distribution.—The lesser centipede-eater is found from central Veracruz, Mexico, southward on the Atlantic watershed through Central America to central Panama, where it also occurs on the Pacific slope. It is known from east-central Petén, and it probably also occurs in the wet forests in the southern part of the department. There are records for the western foothills of the Maya Mountains in Belize, but this snake is absent from all of the Yucatán Peninsula in Mexico. It occurs from about 100 to 1,300 m.

White-striped Centipede-eater—Traga-cienpiés Listado de Amarillo
Tantilla tecta Campbell and Smith, 1997
Fig. 165

Description.—The head is small and scarcely distinct from the neck. The eye is small with a round pupil. There are 7 supralabials, 6 infralabials, no loreal, 1 preocular, 2 postoculars, 1 + 1 temporals, 15–15–15 smooth dorsal scale rows, 148 ventrals, a divided anal plate, and 54 divided subcaudals. On most of the dorsum of the tail, only two longitudinal scale rows cover the area between lateral stripes. This snake is known from a single female specimen 22.2 cm in TL.

The ground color is pale brown (under magnification scales are pale brown finely mottled with dark brown), and the head is dark brown with small pale specks. The snout is pale (upper part of rostral, internasals, and anterior part of the prefrontals); a white spot occurs on the side of the head behind the eye, mostly on supralabial 5; a pale collar about two scales long is present just posterior to the parietals, bordered posteriorly by dark pigment; and there is dark pigment along the lingual border of the infralabials. Pale middorsal and lateral stripes are present. The middorsal stripe begins on the neck one scale length behind the collar, becoming ill-defined posteriorly and absent on about the posterior fourth of the body; this stripe involves only about the medial third of the vertebral scale row. The lateral stripes begin 2–3 scales behind the collar and extend to the tip of the tail; on the body they involve the upper third of scale row 3 and the lower half of scale row 4. All pale stripes are bordered above and below by dark brown pigment. The venter is pale cream with dark pigment encroaching on lateral portions of ventrals and subcaudals.

Natural History.—This secretive, terrestrial snake inhabits tropical moist forest. Nothing is known of its habits; it presumably feeds on invertebrates and lays eggs.

Distribution.—It is known only from one locality, just to the northeast of Laguna Yaxjá in Petén, Guatemala. This site lies at about 220 m.

Remarks.—The single specimen of the *Tantilla taeniata* group known from Petén resembles other members of the group (*T. taeniata, T. jani, T. slavensi*) in certain features but appears to represent an isolated population of a distinct species.

Yucatán Dwarf Centipede-eater—Traga-cienpiés Enana Yucateca
Tantillita canula Cope, 1876
Fig. 166

Description.—The head is small and about as wide as the neck. The eye is small with a round pupil. There usually are 6–7 supralabials, 6 infralabials, no loreal, 1 preocular, 2 postoculars, 1 + 1 temporals, 15–15–15 smooth dorsal scale rows, 103–114 ventrals, a divided anal plate, and 32–44 divided subcaudals. This small snake reaches only about 18 cm in TL.

The dorsum is pale to medium brown. There is usually a vague pale middorsal stripe on the posterior part of the body and tail; in some snakes this stripe extends forward on the body as far as the neck. The top of the head is heavily mottled with dark brown. Usually a pale mark is on the snout at the juncture of the internasals and prefrontals, but pale preocular or postocular spots are absent. The labials and chin are pale with dark brown mottling. The ventrals and subcaudals are whitish and immaculate except for the lateral edges, where dark pigment from the dorsum encroaches on these scales. *Natural History.*—This secretive, terrestrial snake occurs in tropical moist and dry forest. It is somewhat fossorial and I have found individuals under large logs in the forest and under rocks along the edges of clearings. Other specimens of the yucatán dwarf snaileater have been found by workmen who were excavating archaeological ruins or the foundations of new houses. Presumably it feeds chiefly on invertebrates and lays eggs.

🖝*Distribution.*—Found from central Petén and central Belize northward through the Yucatán Peninsula, this species occurs in the lowlands from near sea level to about 300 m.

Remarks.—Until recently this species was placed in the genus *Tantilla.* The diet of snakes of the genus *Tantillita* includes small centipedes, which are usually avoided by most other snakes (exceptions are members of the genus *Tantilla* and some small vipers).

Linton's Dwarf Centipede-eater—Traga-cienpiés Enana de Linton
Tantillita lintoni (Smith, 1940)
Fig. 167

Description.—The head is small and scarcely distinct from the neck. The eye is small and the pupil is round. There are usually 7 supralabials, 6 infralabials, no loreal, 1 preocular, 2 postoculars, 1 + 1 temporals, 15–15–15 smooth dorsal scale rows, 103–115 ventrals, a divided anal plate, and 43–56 divided subcaudals. This diminutive snake reaches only a little over 20 cm in TL.

The dorsum is uniformly brown with the dorsal scales narrowly outlined in dark brown. Dorsal coloration reaches the lateral edges of the ventrals. The top and sides of the head are a little darker than the dorsum except for a few irregular areas on the supralabials, which are whitish. The infralabials (except for the posterior two, which are usually brown), chin, throat, and all but the lateral edges of the ventrals and subcaudals are cream.

Natural History.—This secretive, terrestrial snake inhabits tropical wet and moist forest. Several specimens have been taken in secondary growth and others have been encountered in forest leaf litter. Practically nothing is known about behavior, feeding habits, or reproduction in this species. It presumably feeds on invertebrates and lays eggs.

✔*Distribution.*—Linton's dwarf centipede-eater occurs from northwestern Guatemala to southern Belize and northern Honduras. In Petén, it is known only from near Piedras Negras and Tikal. It is absent from the northern portion of Petén and the Yucatán Peninsula in Mexico. This snake is known from low elevations between sea level and about 200 m.

Checkered Garter Snake—Ranera Cuadriculada
Thamnophis marcianus (Baird and Girard, 1853)
Fig. 168

Description.—The head is slender but is moderately distinct from the neck. The eyes are medium sized with a round pupil. There are usually 8 supralabials, 10 infralabials, a single loreal, 1–2 preoculars, 3 postoculars, 1 + 2 temporals, 19–19–17 keeled dorsal scale rows, 134–150 ventrals, an undivided anal plate, and 58–76 divided subcaudals. This snake reaches about 100 cm in TL.

The dorsum is olive-brown, tan, or reddish brown. A poorly defined, pale tan middorsal stripe occupies the vertebral scale row and most or all of the paravertebral scale rows; it extends from the occipital region for the length of the body and onto the tail and is bordered by large, dark brown or black spots. A lateral stripe is usually vaguely indicated and involves dorsal scale rows 2–3 on the anterior of the body. On the sides of the body there are lateral and ventrolateral series of spots, quadrangular or irregular in shape and usually staggered relative to one another. Vertical black bars or streaks are located along the supralabial sutures, including two below the eye and one or two posterior to the eye. The interspaces between the black streaks near the eye are whitish and often a white crescent-shaped mark is on the side of the head above the angle of the jaw. Paired small yellow spots on the parietals sometimes coalesce. The venter may be immaculate and cream but there usually are two rows of small, rounded spots.

Natural History.—This semiaquatic snake inhabits tropical wet, moist, and dry forest. I have observed it in open situations and along forested streams. It may be active by day or at night. Almost nothing is known about southern populations of this wide-ranging snake. In Guatemala, individuals have been observed in shallow water along the shore of Lago de Izabal and in tributaries flowing into the Río Dulce, Izabal. Frogs, fishes, and crayfish have been recorded as prey in snakes from the United States. The species is viviparous and females from U.S. populations give birth to 5–31 young, which are 20–23.5 cm in TL.

Distribution.—The checkered garter snake ranges from Arizona, southeastern California, and northeastern Mexico (Baja California del Norte and northern Sonora) eastward to Kansas, Oklahoma, and Texas and southward to Zacatecas and northern Veracruz. In southern Mexico and over much of Central America its distribution is disjunct, with populations in southeastern Oaxaca, northern Chiapas, and several widely scattered localities in the northern Yucatán Peninsula, and in Belize, eastern Guatemala, Honduras, Nicaragua, and Costa Rica. This snake is not known from Petén but is known close to the borders of this department and may occur in aquatic habitats in the eastern, southern, or northwestern part of the region. It has been found in Belize, around Lago de Izabal, and in the Río Usumacinta drainage to the northwest of Piedras Negras. In the Yucatán Peninsula and eastern Guatemala, this snake is known from elevations of less than 150m.

Remarks.—The subspecies occurring in the Petén region is *Thamnophis marcianus praeocularis.*

Middle American Ribbon Snake—Ranera Listada
Thamnophis proximus (Say, 1823)
Fig. 169

Description.—The slender head is moderately distinct from the neck and the medium-sized eyes have round pupils. There usually are 7–9 supralabials, 8–11 infralabials, a single loreal, 1–2 preoculars, 2–5 (usually 3) postoculars, 1(2) + 2(3) temporals, 19–19–17 keeled dorsal scale rows, 141–164 ventrals, an undivided anal plate, and 82–104 divided subcaudals. In Guatemala, this species reaches a maximum adult TL of about 75 cm in females; males are somewhat smaller, the largest recorded TL being 62.5 cm.

The dorsum is olive-brown to reddish brown, being paler below the lateral stripe. A pale grayish tan to reddish tan vertebral stripe is often obscure. A narrow yellowish or yellow-orange lateral stripe, located mostly on scale row 3, runs the length of the body. A pair of bright yellow spots (sometimes fused) is present on the parietal scales. A black postorbital streak, if present, is poorly defined, narrow, and confined to the temporals. The supralabials and infralabials are bright yellow-orange or buff. The chinshields, many of the gular scales, and the preventrals are white. The venter of the neck and anterior part of the body is pale tan or orangish, grading to pale green posteriorly. The iris is deep bronze, heavily suffused with brown and with a yellow ring around the pupil.

Natural History.—This snake occurs in tropical moist and dry forest. It usually is found around the edges of ponds, streams, or lakes in open, grassy situations. It may be active by day or at night. I have seen individuals in habitats as divergent as dry savannas and brackish mangrove swamps. It feeds mostly on tadpoles, small frogs, and small fishes. Anuran species that have been recorded from the stomach of this species include the Gulf Coast toad (*Bufo valliceps*), fringe-toed foamfrog (*Leptodactylus melanonotus*), and Baudin's treefrog (*Smilisca baudinii*).

Females mature at about 35–36 cm in SVL and give birth to about half a dozen live young in June–July. Neonates are 16–17 cm in SVL.

Distribution.—The ribbon snake occurs in the United States from Nebraska, Iowa, and Wisconsin southward to Mississippi, Louisiana, Texas, and New Mexico. In Middle America it is found southward along the Atlantic watershed of Mexico, including the Yucatán Peninsula, through northern Guatemala and Belize to Costa Rica.

Along the Pacific lowlands of Mexico and Central America it is distributed disjunctly, with isolated populations in Guerrero, Oaxaca, and Chiapas, Mexico, and in Guatemala, El Salvador, Honduras, Nicaragua, and Costa Rica. In Petén, this species is known only from several localities along the edges of the larger lakes in the northern half of the region. Most records for this snake in Guatemala are from near sea level to 300 m, but it may occur up to about 1,200 m in a few isolated areas such as around Laguna del Pino in the Department of Santa Rosa.

Remarks.—The subspecies occurring in Petén is *Thamnophis proximus rutiloris*.

Middle American Swamp Snake—Buceadora
Tretanorhinus nigroluteus Cope, 1861
Fig. 170

Description.—The head is rather elongate and well differentiated from the neck. The eyes are medium sized and dorsolaterally placed with a subcircular pupil. There usually are 8 supralabials, 10–11 infralabials, a single loreal, 2–3 preoculars, 2 postoculars, 1 + 2 temporals, 21–21(19)–19(17) dorsal scale rows, 129–148 ventrals, a divided anal plate, and 56–80 divided subcaudals. Curiously, the number of internasal scales seems to be sexually dimorphic, at least in some populations. About half of the males from Belize have a single internasal, and the other half have two, whereas all of the females have two internasals. All dorsal scale rows are

keeled except for rows 1–2 on the anterior part of the body. This species reaches about 70 cm in TL. In one study containing a sample of about 40 snakes from Belize, the largest male was 42.3 cm in SVL, and the largest female was 59.7 cm in SVL.

The dorsum is pale brown to grayish brown with small paired, irregular brown spots or blotches on the back; these spots often fuse on the anterior part of the body, sometimes forming a dark brown vertebral stripe. Posteriorly, these dorsal spots become obscure or absent. A dark brown lateral stripe low on the sides of the body is located on scale rows 1–5 anteriorly, decreasing to rows 1–3 posteriorly. A narrow cream or tan longitudinal stripe separates the pale brown dorsal and dark brown lateral coloration. Only the first scale row is dark on the tail and the pale lateral stripe is very narrow or absent. The top of the head is colored similarly to the dorsum of the body, and the supralabials, anterior temporal, and lower secondary temporal are dark brown, similar to the lateral coloration. The infralabials, chinshields, and most of the gulars are also dark brown, but are punctated with clusters of small cream spots. The belly varies from dark grayish brown with cream flecks to mostly pale dingy yellow, with dark mottling confined mostly to the midventer. The dark brown from the lateral stripe encroaches on the lateral ends of the ventrals. The subcaudals are dingy yellow, often with each scale outlined in dark brown or with a midventral dark caudal stripe.

Distinctive tubercles develop in males, presumably in breeding condition, on the infralabials, chinshields, gulars and anterior ventrals, and to a lesser extent on the supralabials, loreal, pre- and postoculars, all of the ventrals, and scales in dorsal rows 1–2. It has been suggested that these tubercles function in stimulating the female during courtship or in positioning the male during mating.

Natural History.—This aquatic species inhabits tropical wet and moist forest. It is always in the vicinity of swamps, marshes, lakes, or sluggish streams. I have never seen a specimen out of the water, but there are records of individuals on banks near streams and lakes. They appear to be most active just before and after dark.

The natural prey of this snake includes small fishes of the families Poeciliidae and Gobiidae, the tadpoles of toads, and small individuals and larvae of frogs of the genus *Rana*. One specimen was caught in a fish net from which it had eaten a cichlid (*Cichlasoma octofasciatum*).

Females with oviducal eggs have been collected in January and July. Six to nine eggs are laid over an apparently extensive breeding season. A closely related species from Cuba was reported to lay eight adherent eggs that hatched after only 35 days.

Distribution.—The Middle American swamp snake occurs from southern Veracruz, Mexico, to Colombia in Atlantic drainages and from Honduras to Nicaragua in the Pacific drainage. It is found throughout most of Petén and Belize, wherever there are streams or lakes, but is absent from all of the Yucatán Peninsula in Mexico except for the flooded coastal swamps of Campeche. This lowland species occurs between sea level and about 200 m.

Remarks.—The subspecies occurring in Petén is *Tretanorhinus nigroluteus lateralis.*

False Barba Amarilla—Engañosa
Xenodon rabdocephalus (Wied, 1824)
Fig. 171

Description.—This snake is easily confused with the dangerously venomous barba amarilla and derives its common names *engañosa* (imposter) and *barba amarilla falsa* from being similar to that species in appearance and in its defense display (see Barba Amarilla). Some of the differences that distinguish the false barba amarilla from the barba amarilla are a rounded versus lanceolate snout, large dorsal head plates versus small, keeled, dorsal head scales, no loreal pit, round versus vertical pupils, and smooth versus keeled scales on the body. In the false barba amarilla the head is moderately large and distinct from the neck and the eye is large with a round pupil. This species has especially long rear fangs on the back of the maxillary bone. There usually are 8 supralabials, 9–11 infralabials, a single loreal, 1 preocular, 2 postoculars, 1 + 2 temporals, 19–19–17 smooth dorsal scale rows, 124–153 ventrals, an undivided anal plate, and 38–67 divided subcaudals. This snake reaches about 80 cm in TL.

The ground color is medium brown to pale gray-brown. The body has 10–16 hourglass-shaped, black-edged, dark brown crossbands that are cream bordered. The dark pigment from the crossbands may extend only to the lateral edges of the ventrals or all the way across the venter, especially in juveniles. There are 3–5 dark bars on the tail. The head is usually blotched with dark brown; postocular stripes are usually present. Often there is a dark bar across the internasals and prefrontals. There may be a bar on the top of the head between the eyes, and this bar may be continuous with a pair of parietal blotches that extend to the nape. The supralabials are cream to tan with darker pigment bordering the vertical sutures. The venter is cream with dark flecks or heavy mottling or, in some specimens, is banded with dark brown or black. The subcaudals are usually mostly pale yellow.

Natural History.—This terrestrial snake occurs in tropical wet, moist, and dry forest. It may be active by day or at night on the forest floor and feeds mostly on toads and, less frequently, frogs. Both the Gulf Coast toad (*Bufo valliceps*) and giant toad (*B. marinus*) are known prey items for this snake. Toads tend to puff up when seized, making them hard to swallow, but this snake uses the enlarged rear teeth to puncture and deflate its prey. Nine to ten eggs are laid in the rainy season. Juveniles have been seen from June through November.

✔*Distribution.*—The false barba amarilla occurs from Veracruz and Guerrero, Mexico, southward through Central America and South America to Bolivia and Brazil. It is found throughout most of Petén and Belize in forested habitats; it is absent, however, from all of the Yucatán Peninsula in Mexico except for eastern Quintana Roo. In Guatemala, this snake is known from near sea level to about 400 m.

CORAL SNAKES—CORALES

FAMILY ELAPIDAE

The distribution of this family includes Africa, southern Asia, Australia, the southern United States, Mexico, and Central and South America. The family contains the cobras, kraits, and mambas as well as the coral snakes, which are the only New World representatives. Coral snakes are slender and those occurring in Guatemala usually do not exceed 1 m in length. The eyes are small with a subcircular pupil. Scalation on their bodies is rather consistent, with 9 large supracephalic plates, 15 unreduced and smooth dorsal scale rows, 7 supralabials, 7 infralabials, a divided anal plate, relatively few subcaudals on a short tail, and no loreal scale. When threatened, coral snakes typically present a display that includes flattening the body, hiding the head beneath their coils, curling and elevating the tail, and jerking the body erratically back and forth. Coral snakes feed heavily on other snakes and lay eggs. Vernacular names include *coral*, *coralillo*, and *gargantilla*.

Coral snakes are extremely venomous and they should never be handled casually (and preferably never handled at all). Their hollow fangs are short compared to those of vipers and are relatively fixed in an erect position. The generally small body size and small head of coral snakes has given rise to a myth that these snakes are incapable of biting humans unless they happen to seize a very small structure such as the little finger or webbing between the fingers. Actually, even small coral snakes are able to deliver a bite to almost any part of the human body. These snakes have a wide gape and anywhere there is skin loose enough to be even slightly pinched, there is a possibility of getting bitten. The parts of the body most commonly receiving bites are the hands, feet, and ankles.

The symptoms of a coral snake bite may include some localized pain or numbness at the site of the bite, but even these symptoms may be absent, and usually there is no swelling. Because of the lack of any immediate severe symptoms, bites from coral snakes sometimes are not taken seriously at the outset. However, alarming symptoms may develop after several hours and these include nausea and vomiting, convulsions, and drowsiness. Coral snake venoms in general act on the nervous system inducing paralysis of various nerves, including those associated with the head (thus, often there may be difficulty in swallowing, twitching of the tongue, and pin-point pupils). In fatal cases of envenomation, death is usually caused by respiratory and cardiac failure. As in the case of all venomous snakebites, victims should be taken as quickly as possible to the nearest hospital. Unfortunately, antivenin for coral snake venoms is rarely available in Central American hospitals.

Variable Coral Snake—Coral Variable
Micrurus diastema (Duméril, Bibron, and Duméril, 1854)
Figs. 172–173

Description.—The head is broadly rounded in dorsal profile and scarcely distinct from the neck. The eye is small with a subcircular pupil. The body is slender and the tail is short. There usually are 7 supralabials, 7 infralabials, 1 preocular, 2 postoculars, 1 + 1 or 1 + 2 temporals, 15–15–15 smooth dorsal scale rows, 188–228 ventrals, a divided anal plate, and 28–62 subcaudals. The loreal is absent. Although most snakes from Petén and the Yucatán have 1 + 2 temporals, snakes from Alta Verapaz and Veracruz, Mexico, usually have 1 + 1 temporals. In some individuals many of the subcaudals may be undivided, with males averaging a dozen or more undivided scales and females about half this number. Males lack supraanal tubercles. This species reaches 80–85 cm in TL.

The pattern usually consists of red, yellow, and black rings in the sequence of black-yellow-red-yellow-black. The number of black rings on the body, exclusive of the tail, is highly variable in snakes from Petén and may be as low as 18 or as high as 50. The average for snakes from Alta Verapaz is 48, those from northern Petén and Belize average between 25 and 30, and snakes from the northern portion of the Yucatán Peninsula average 12–20. Snakes I have examined from Tikal have 24–29 black body bands. The width of the black body rings averages between 1–2 ventral scales in snakes from most of Petén, but it averages more than 2 ventral scales in extreme northern Petén and up to 4 ventrals in the northern Yucatán Peninsula. The same trend is observed in the number of tail rings, with averages ranging from about 11 in Alta Verapaz to about 3 in the northern Yucatán Peninsula. There are 4–9 black rings on the tail of snakes from Tikal. Several features of color pattern vary geographically. Snakes in the southern portion of Petén and Alta Verapaz tend to have red scales that are only scarcely to moderately tipped with black (but black is sometimes concentrated in the middle of a red ring); yellow body rings may be absent or no more than a single scale long, and in about a third of these snakes at least one black body ring is incomplete (fails to encircle the body). In contrast, snakes from the northern portion of Petén have red scales that are more heavily tipped with black, the yellow body rings are 1–2 scales wide, and individuals almost invariably have all of the black body rings complete. In snakes from Petén and Alta Verapaz, the snout usually has a yellow marking on the rostral, internasals, and the anterior part of the prefrontals, but most snakes from the northern Yucatán Peninsula have a uniformly black snout.

Natural History.—This secretive snake inhabits a variety of forests including tropical wet, moist, and dry forest and subtropical wet and moist forest. It is most frequently seen crawling through leaf litter on the forest floor. It may occur in areas of secondary growth or in virgin forest and it may be active at night, during the early morning, or in the late afternoon.

The diet consists mostly of small species of leaf-litter snakes, such as *Adelphicos quadrivirgatus, Ninia sebae,* and *Coniophanes fissidens.* Variable coral snakes also feed occasionally on juvenile snakes of larger species, such as *Dendrophidion vinitor* and *Sibon sartorii,* as well as *Typhlops microstomus,* and lizards of various species, including *Sphenomorphus cherriei* and *Eumeces schwartzei.* Among the more interesting items recovered from their stomachs have been a caecilian

(*Gymnopis syntrema*) and an eel (*Synbranchus marmoratus*).

A gravid female with well-formed eggs was found in Alta Verapaz in April. In Petén, this species probably lays eggs during the rainy season, from about April to August, which hatch about two months later. Juveniles have been seen in June and July.

Distribution.—The variable coral snake occurs from central Veracruz and northern Oaxaca in southern Mexico southward throughout the Yucatán Peninsula in Mexico, Belize, and northern Guatemala to northwestern Honduras. It is found throughout Petén. In Guatemala, this species occurs from near sea level to about 1,250 m.

Remarks.—Seven geographic races of this species of coral snake are sometimes recognized. Some of the characters distinguishing these subspecies may vary clinally, but others are discordant. Two subspecies are sometimes recognized in Petén: *Micrurus diastema alienus* in the central and northern part of the department, with relatively few, wide black rings, and *M. d. sapperi* in the southern part of Petén, with more numerous, narrower black rings. Other vernacular names include *coralillo* and *gargantilla.*

Deceit among Snakes.—New World coral snakes and harmless colubrid snakes provide perhaps the most famous case of mimicry in vertebrates—and highly effective mimicry. My time in graduate school overlapped with that of Harry Greene, who is now a professor at the University of California at Berkeley and is one of the foremost authorities on reptilian antipredator mechanisms. Even when I first met him, Harry was intensely interested in coral snakes and the hypothesis that these snakes are mimicked by certain harmless snakes.

On one of my trips to Guatemala, Harry asked me to pick up any live coral snakes I might find for some experiments he was conducting. Coral snakes, although not rare, are not predictably encountered. I was most fortunate to discover not one but two specimens under a large rotten log in a coffee grove on the Pacific slope of the Volcán de Agua. (Its deep ravines and forested ridges, once among my favorite haunts, are no longer safely accessible owing to the violence that gripped Guatemala in the early 1980s. The region was so heavily mined that its footpaths are now traversed only at considerable risk. A friend of mine stepped on a mine while gathering firewood; at the hospital in Escuintla he was refused treatment because of a strike, and he died outside the building from his horrible wounds about twelve hours later.)

I took great care in collecting the two snakes, and from time to time I cautiously soaked them in a *pila* (a concrete sink) to give them a drink of water. Arriving back at school in the United States, I informed Harry that I had brought him a beautiful pair of Central American coral snakes (*Micrurus nigrocinctus*) and that at that very minute they were down in the laboratory. He hurried to the terrarium where they were housed and carefully lifted the slab of bark under which they were hiding. Harry let out a chuckle and, to my horror and amazement, reached down and lifted both snakes out of their enclosure with his bare hands.

I had grievously erred in my identification of these snakes. The reason for my gaffe were inoffensive long-tailed false corals (*Pliocercus elapoides*, see fig. 147). I use this example to demonstrate how easily even a person who has some experience with snakes can confuse harmless (or in this case only slightly venomous) snakes with venomous species.

In Petén there is only a single, widely distributed species of coral snake, *Micrurus diastema*. However, the species is so variable in patterning that at least seven subspecies are sometimes recognized throughout its range. This has led to a considerable amount of taxonomic confusion and is reflected in the common name *variable* coral snake (see figs. 172–173). A number of other snakes in the Petén region exhibit bright coloration that perhaps warns predators that they may be dealing with a venomous animal. This warning coloration, referred to as aposematism, occurs in the tropical milksnake (*Lampropeltis tri-*

angulum, fig. 136), red coffee snake (*Ninia sebae*, fig. 143), white-bellied false coral (*Oxyrhopus petola*, fig. 146), half coral snake (*Scaphiodontophis annulatus*, fig. 150), and ringed snail-eater (*Sibon sartorii*, fig. 155) as well as in the aforementioned long-tailed false coral. All of these species have some combination of red, yellow, and black disposed in rings or dorsal crossbands. It has been shown that potential predators avoid some brightly colored snakes, whether it be because of learned or innate behavior, although whether all the species listed here are involved in this mimicry system remains to be demonstrated.

Mimicry involves one species (the model) that is closely resembled by another species (the mimic) in color pattern, shape, or behavior. Some of the strongest circumstantial evidence for mimicry among snakes in particular is the strong geographical concordance in color pattern. For example, the long-tailed false coral has a broad geographical distribution that overlaps, at least in part, the distribution of several species of true coral snakes. To a remarkable degree, the long-tailed false coral tends to resemble closely the various *Micrurus* species wherever it occurs sympatrically with them.

Two types of mimicry are recognized in coral snakes. In one, as outlined, a venomous coral snake serves as the model for harmless species, which are the mimics. A mimic derives benefit because potential predators think it is dangerous and avoid it. This kind of mimicry is called Batesian mimicry. However, several species that are dangerous may also resemble one another; in this case the two or more species involved are both or all potentially dangerous to a predator. A good example is provided by the more than 50 species of New World coral snakes. Although there is no doubt that considerable variation in pattern exists among these snakes, there are common elements, such as brightly colored rings of red and/or yellow, that are shared among most of the species. So, in this case, individual species serve as both model and mimic in what is known as Müllerian mimicry. Having common warning coloration and patterning would seem to be a more effective mechanism for warning predators and to place less of a burden on their learning abilities or genetics.

Two other species of coral snakes occur along the periphery of Petén—the Mayan coral snake (*Micrurus hippocrepis*, figs. 174–175) and the Central American coral snake (*M. nigrocinctus*, fig. 176)—and each of these has its harmless mimics. Further, there are several other snakes that are not aposematically colored but seem to be components of a mimicry system. The false barba amarilla (fig. 171) occurs throughout much of the range of the true barba amarilla (figs. 182–183) and the color pattern of these species is very similar.

Mayan Coral Snake—Coral Maya
Micrurus hippocrepis (Peters, 1862)
Figs. 174–175

Description.—The head is broadly rounded in dorsal profile and is scarcely distinct from the neck. The eye is small with a subcircular pupil. There are usually 7 supralabials, 7 infralabials, no loreal, 1 preocular, 2 postoculars, 1 + 1 or 1 + 2 temporals, 15–15–15 smooth dorsal scale rows, 199–226 ventrals, a divided anal plate, and 37–57 mostly divided subcaudals. Supra-anal keels are absent. This snake reaches a TL of 65–70 cm, with females usually larger than males.

The species is tricolored with black, yellow and red rings. There are 0–24 black rings on the body, each are 2–3 scales in width; some of these black rings are incomplete on some snakes. Each black ring is bordered with yellow rings about 1.5–2 scales in width. Scales of the red and yellow rings are dusky, and there may be a few black spots in the red rings, but the red scales are not black tipped. There is a yellow spot on the tip of the snout involving the rostral, the internasals, the anterior portion of the prefrontals, the prenasals, and the first supralabials. A black head cap covers the posterior part of the prefrontals, most or all of the frontal, the supraoculars, the postoculars, and sometimes the anterior edges of the parietals; the lateral extent of the head cap is variable; sometimes it reaches the margin of the lip and in other specimens it may reach only to just below the eye. A yellow parietal ring across the back of the head extends from just posterior to the edge of eye to the posterior tips of the parietals. The black nuchal ring extends from near the posterior edges of the parietals and is 2–4 dorsal scales long. The tail has 4–7 black rings that are separated by yellow rings. Occasionally, specimens may have almost all red bodies, but these individuals usually have a black nape ring and rings on the tail.

Natural History.—This secretive snake occurs in tropical wet and moist forest and subtropical wet forest. I have found this species most active during the early morning and after dark. Not much is known about its biology. Prey items found in stomachs include the mountain caecilian (*Gymnopis syntrema*) and earthworms. This snake lays eggs and juveniles less than 25 cm in TL, probably young-of-the-year, have been seen in July and August.

Distribution.—The Mayan coral snake

occurs from central Belize southward to eastern Guatemala; it probably occurs in extreme southeastern Petén. It is found from near sea level to about 800 m.

Remarks.—Given the variability of *Micrurus diastama*, it is possible that *M. hippocrepis* is nothing more than a color morph of the variable coral snake. Other vernacular names include *coralillo* and *gargantilla.*

Central American Coral Snake—Coral Centro Americano
Micrurus nigrocinctus (Girard, 1854)
Fig. 176

Description.—The head is broadly rounded in dorsal profile and scarcely distinct from the neck. The eye is small with a subcircular pupil. The body is slender and the tail is short. There are usually 7 supralabials, 7 infralabials, no loreal, 1 preocular, 2 postoculars, 1 + 1 or 1 + 2 temporals, 15–15–15 smooth dorsal scale rows, 180–230 ventrals, a divided anal plate, and 31–58 mostly divided subcaudals. Supra-anal tubercles (keels) are present in adult males. This species reaches at least 100 cm in TL.

This is usually a tricolored species, having black, yellow, and red rings; however, in some specimens the yellow is much reduced or even absent. The snout and anterior part of the head are entirely black, followed by a yellow ring across the back of the head; the size and location of this yellow ring are highly variable, but it usually extends from the posterior part of the frontal to the posterior part of the parietals. There are 10–29 black rings on the body and 3–8 black rings on the tail. The yellow rings bordering black rings are usually about two scales in width. The scales of red rings may be dusky or spotted with black. The mental and several pairs of anterior infralabials are mostly black.

Natural History.—This secretive snake occurs in tropical moist and dry forest. It feeds mostly on small snakes and lizards, and it lays eggs during the early part of the rainy season.

Distribution.—The Central American coral snake is distributed from about central Belize on the Atlantic watershed and from southeastern Oaxaca, Mexico, on the Pacific versant, southward through most of Central America on both sides of the Continental Divide into Colombia. This species, if it actually occurs in Petén, might be expected in the eastern part of the department near the Belize border. On the Pacific watershed of Guatemala, this snake ranges from near sea level to about 1,300 m, but on the Atlantic it appears to be restricted to lower elevations, perhaps below 500 m.

Remarks.—The subspecies occurring in Belize and on the Atlantic versant of Honduras is *Micrurus nigrocinctus divaricatus.* Other vernacular names include *coralillo* and *gargantilla.*

Vipers—Víboras

Family Viperidae

Vipers are found practically worldwide, from Canada to Argentina, from Siberia to Arabia, in southeastern Asia, the East Indies, and throughout Africa. All of the New World vipers are pit-vipers, meaning they have a heat-sensitive pit on the side of the head in the loreal region. The pit is able to detect very small differences in temperature and allows the snake to sense its thermal environment, including warm-blooded prey. In pitvipers, the pelvis and the left lung are absent. Half a dozen species of pitvipers occur in Petén, and these belong to an equal number of genera. Pitvipers range from slender to heavy-bodied snakes. In length, they vary from species in which adults often reach no more than about 50 cm to impressive serpents of over 2 m. The head scales vary from small flat or keeled scales, with those of the parietal region little differentiated from those more posterior on the body, to large, flat head plates typical of most colubrid snakes. The dorsal scales are keeled and most of the subcaudals are undivided in most species (the barba amarilla, *Bothrops asper*, is the exception). Most are terrestrial, but the eyelash palm-pitviper (*Bothriechis schlegelii*) is primarily arboreal, and barba amarilla juveniles and subadults readily climb into vegetation. The cantil may be found a long way from water, but it freely enters water and forages along the shores of streams and lakes.

Vipers, like coral snakes, are extremely venomous and direct contact with these snakes should be avoided whenever possible. They have relatively long, hollow fangs that are capable of being erected at the time of a bite. Although the serious nature of envenomation from a viper should never be underestimated—it can be a life-threatening experience—it is worth noting that most viper bites, contrary to public notion, do not result in death and that these snakes are not usually aggressive unless provoked. Most vipers depend on their crypsis for protection, remaining motionless when some large animal such as a human passes by. Most people walking in lowland tropical forests probably approach on a regular basis within several meters of venomous snakes without seeing them. Viper bites most frequently occur when people are careless about where they place their hands and feet. Walking barefoot at night in the lowland tropics in areas where venomous snakes are known to be present is foolhardy.

Viper bites may result in a frightening array of symptoms, but the manifestation and severity of these depend on a variety of factors—most notably the species and size of snake involved. Symptoms may include extreme localized pain at the site of the bite, massive swelling, bleeding from the site of the bite, gums, nose, and urinary tract, drooping eyelids, difficulty in moving the eyes, vomiting, severe headaches, difficulty in breathing, kidney damage, abnormal blood clotting, hypotension, bradycardia, arrhythmia, and finally complete circulatory collapse. Victims should be taken as quickly as possible to the nearest hospital for treatment.

Cantil—Cantil
Agkistrodon bilineatus Günther, 1863
Fig. 177

Description.—This snake has a stout body but the tail is relatively long and slender. The head is large and well differentiated from the neck. The eye is medium sized with a vertical pupil. The top of the head is covered with large, flat head plates, usually nine in number, but the parietals are sometimes fragmented into smaller scales. There are usually 8–9 supralabials, 10–12 infralabials, a single loreal, 2 preoculars, 2 postoculars, 25–23(21)–19 dorsal scale rows, 129–144 ventrals, an undivided anal plate, and 46–68 subcaudals, which may be entire or divided. A lacunolabial is present. The dorsal scales are keeled except for the scale rows 1–2 on the anterior part of body. This heavy-bodied snake reaches a maximum TL of over 100 cm.

The dorsum is pale brown to deep reddish brown, with 12–18 broad, dark brown crossbands incompletely bordered by white spots. These crossbands are separated by areas of paler, often reddish, coloration. On the sides of the body the crossbands usually have paler centers and one or two dark spots. On the tail there are 8–12 dark brown crossbands that become faint distally. One of the most conspicuous features of this snake is a pair of pale yellow stripes on each side of the head. A median vertical white line is present on the rostral and mental. The side of the head between the yellow stripes is dark chestnut brown. The median third of the venter on the posterior two-thirds of the body is essentially unpatterned; the chin and throat are dark with small white lines or spots. The distal portion of the tail is pale gray or greenish gray in adults and bright yellow in juveniles.

Natural History.—This snake inhabits tropical moist and dry forest and is often encountered in dry areas such as along the edges of savannas or other natural clearings. Although this species is usually considered semiaquatic, it is sometimes found far from any body of water. This species is active mainly at night. It is rather pugnacious, readily striking at any perceived aggressor and often lashing its tail from side to side or vibrating the tip. This snake feeds on a wide variety of organisms including mammals, reptiles, amphibians, and some invertebrates.

Females give birth to 5–20 young in June and July. One of the remarkable features of this snake is that the juveniles use their bright yellow tails to lure prey within striking distance.

Distribution.—The cantil occurs along the Pacific lowlands from southern Sonora in northwestern Mexico southward though Central America to northwestern Costa Rica. In the Atlantic lowlands its distribution is disjunct. It occurs in Tamaulipas and Nuevo León in northeastern Mexico; the middle Río Grijalva Valley of Chiapas; the northern portion of the Yucatán Peninsula in Mexico and extreme northeastern Belize; the Río Chixoy (Negro) Valley in central Guatemala; and the savanna area of central Petén, Guatemala. This snake is rare and spottily distributed in the Yucatán Peninsula. It is known from a couple of localities in northern Belize in the Corozal and Orange Walk districts, and it has recently been discovered in the area near La Libertad, Petén. In Guatemala, this species occurs from near sea level to about 600 m.

Remarks.—A small individual about 300 mm in TL reportedly caused the death of a woman within several hours after it bit her. Another vernacular name for this snake is *uolpoch* (sometimes spelled *wolpoch* or *volpochh*). The subspecies occurring in Petén is *Agkistrodon bilineatus russeolus.*

Jumping Pitviper—Chalpate
Atropoides nummifer (Rüppell, 1845)
Figs. 178–179

Description.—The head is large and well differentiated from the neck. The eye is small with a vertical pupil. There are usually 9–12 supralabials, 10–14 infralabials, a single loreal, 3 preoculars, 1–4 postoculars, 25–31 dorsal scale rows at midbody, 114–135 ventrals, an undivided anal plate, and 22–39 subcaudals. There are 7–12 intersupraoculars and the supraoculars are frequently fragmented into small, keeled scales. The dorsal scales have prominent high keels in adults, giving the skin of these snakes an almost rasplike appearance. This keeling is best developed in the vertebral and paravertebral scale rows of the larger specimens. This stout snake reaches a maximum length of a little over 80 cm.

The ground color is usually brown or grayish brown. A series of 15–20 dark brown rhomboidal dorsal blotches is present on the body; some of these may be fused, forming a zigzag pattern. Dark brown lateral blotches coalesce with the dorsal blotches, forming dorsal crossbands. A series of small ventrolateral blotches is on the lateral part of the ventrals and first several dorsal scale rows. The head is pale to medium brown, sometimes with dark spots. A dark brown postocular stripe extends from the eye to the angle of the jaw and sometimes beyond. A pair of dark brown nape blotches may fuse posteriorly. Juveniles usually have a paler ground color and a more vivid pattern than adults. The venter is yellowish around the throat and whitish posteriorly and usually heavily mottled with brown. The subcaudals are mostly dark.

Natural History.—This terrestrial snake inhabits tropical wet, moist, and dry forest and subtropical wet and moist forest. It does not move around much and is probably mainly nocturnal. I have encountered individuals mostly during the day and these were coiled in the leaflitter of the forest floor. On several occasions, I have found one coiled between buttressed roots of a large tree in a small patch of sunlight; these snakes were always quick to try to escape down a burrow at the base of the tree. When threatened, this snake coils and holds its mouth open in a wide gape. It is most common in relatively undisturbed areas of high forest but sometimes occurs in secondary growth and along the edges of clearings.

As an adult, this snake eats mostly rodents. Juveniles are known to feed on orthopterans and skinks (*Sphenomorphus cherriei*). The most remarkable food record of which I am aware is a crayfish.

Females give birth to 13–36 young from August to November. Neonates are 14.5–20.0 cm in TL.

Distribution.—The jumping pitviper occurs from San Luis Potosí in Eastern Mexico in southward through foothills and lowlands of Mexico (exclusive of all but the southern part of the Yucatán Peninsula) and Central America to the Canal Zone of Panama; it occurs on Pacific slopes from Oaxaca, Mexico, to El Salvador, and from Costa Rica to Panama. This snake is widespread in the southern and central portion of Petén but is absent from about the northern third of the region. The northernmost record I have for it in the Petén is Tikal. In Guatemala, this species occurs from about 100 to 1,520 m.

Remarks.—The English common name is derived from the mistaken belief that this snake can strike for distances greater than its body length. These claims are exaggerated and may have arisen because of the very stout, muscular body of this species. In actuality, it can strike no farther relative to its body length than can most other vipers—a distance of probably no more than about half of its body length.

Other vernacular names include *chinchintor*, *mano de piedra*, *víbora saltadora*, and *timbo*.

Eyelash Palm-Pitviper—Víbora de Pestañas
Bothriechis schlegelii (Berthold, 1846)
Figs. 180–181

Description.—The raised, spinelike superciliary scales over the eyes of this species give it its common name. The head is large and well differentiated from the slender neck. The eye is medium sized and has a vertical pupil. The tail is prehensile. There are usually 7–10 supralabials, 8–12 infralabials, several loreals, 3 preoculars, 1–3 postoculars, 21–25 (usually 23) dorsal scale rows at midbody, 137–169 ventrals, an undivided anal plate, and 42–64 mostly undivided subcaudals. There are 5–10 intersupraoculars and lateral to the supraoculars is a series of spinelike superciliary scales. A lacunolabial is present. This species reaches a maximum TL of about 80 cm.

The color and pattern of this snake are subject to extreme variation over its range. In some parts of Central America it may be bright golden yellow and may be referred to locally as *oropel*. Specimens from Guatemala, however, usually have a greenish ground color finely suffused with black. There are dorsolateral rust-colored or reddish spots on the body, arranged either opposite or alternate to one another, and there are paired parietal and occipital spots of the same color. A reddish postocular stripe extends to above the angle of the jaw. The chin, throat, and anterior ventrals are immaculate; posteriorly the venter is marked by many dark quadrangular spots.

Natural History.—This arboreal snake occurs in tropical wet and moist forest and subtropical wet forest. I have never found it to be particularly abundant in Guatemala but have found two or three individuals within a couple of minutes on several occasions. These series of snakes were always encountered at night, coiled on low palms growing along streams. This snake occurs in primary forest, usually in mesic situations such as along streams or in deep, shaded ravines. On a vine tangle about 1 m off the ground, I captured a large specimen sitting in a patch of sunlight that penetrated the canopy. This snake's stomach contained a noticeable bulge, which proved to be a large rodent. Besides rodents, the species feeds on bats, frogs of the genera *Hyla* and *Eleutherodactylus*, lizards (especially anoles), and possibly small birds.

Females give birth to about 12–20 young during the rainy season. A gestation period of 166 days was reported for a captive female from Honduras.

Distribution.—The eyelash palm-pitviper occurs from northern Chiapas, Mexico, southward through Central America to Colombia, Venezuela, and Ecuador. It is found in the southern, humid portion of Petén and also in streamside habitats in the eastern portion of the department. Its distribution in northern Petén appears to be somewhat fragmented; I have seen a single specimen from near Laguna Yaxjá and photographs of an individual from Tikal. In Belize, this species is known from Cayo, Orange Walk, and Toledo districts. In Guatemala, it occurs from near sea level to about 770 m.

Remarks.—Other vernacular names are *rash bolay, nauyaca cornuda*, and in Belize green tommygoff.

Barba Amarilla—Barba Amarilla
Bothrops asper (Garman, 1883)
Figs. 182–183

Description.—It is not unusual to see individuals of this species between 150 and 200 cm in TL. The largest specimen I have seen, killed many years ago on the Pacific coast of Guatemala near Escuintla, measured about 230 cm. The head is large and well differentiated from the neck. The eye is medium sized and has a vertical pupil. There usually are 7–8 supralabials, 8–12 infralabials, a single loreal, 3 preoculars, 2–4 postoculars, 25–29 dorsal scale rows at midbody, 185–221 ventrals, an undivided anal plate, and 56–75 divided subcaudals. The second supralabial is fused with the prelacunal, forming a lacunolabial. There are 5–11 keeled intersupraoculars, and scales in most of the dorsal rows rows are keeled.

The dorsum is brown or reddish brown with a series of 18–25 pale-edged dark brown triangular blotches on each side of the body. Dark brown oval paravertebral blotches are usually present in the interspaces between body blotches, especially in smaller specimens. A dark brown postocular stripe extends from behind the eye to the angle of the mouth. The labials, canthal area, chin, and throat are pale yellow; in juveniles and some females the labial area may be spotted with brown. The venter is cream or whitish with gray mottling that becomes darker on the posterior of the body. In juvenile males, the distal 20–30 mm of the tail is bright yellow, but it is dark in juvenile females.

Natural History.—This large, terrestrial viper occurs in tropical wet, moist, and dry forest and subtropical wet forest. In dry regions, it is usually restricted to riparian habitat. It is mostly nocturnal and I have frequently found it crawling across trails in the forest at dusk or after dark. Juveniles may sometimes be active by day as well, especially in the late afternoon. Large adults, when seen by day, are usually coiled in shallow depressions on a hillside, near large mammal burrows, or under low vegetation. I once found an individual coiled on a large rock in the middle of a small stream. Juveniles often climb up on top of fallen logs or in tangles of vines; I have occasionally found small individuals up to about 2 m above the forest floor.

This snake is not uncommon in primary forest (see "The Tepezcuintle Hunters," page 276), but it is sometimes even more abundant in areas of secondary forest around human habitations, no doubt because of the numerous rodents that are invariably associated with human populations.

When irritated, this snake quickly coils in readiness to strike and vibrates its tail. When smaller specimens are prodded with a stick, they sometimes become tired of striking and are almost timid, hiding the head beneath the coils. Nevertheless, the alertness and agility of this snake should never be underestimated. It is quick and can cover short distances with surpising speed.

Adults feed primarily on small mammals, including spiny pocket mice (*Heteromys*) and four-eyed opossums (*Philander*), whereas juveniles feed on lizards (anoles and skinks), frogs (*Eleutherodactylus*), and various invertebrates (orthopterans and centipedes).

Females are prolific, giving birth to about 8–75 live young. Young juveniles have been seen frequently during the middle and late rainy season; this species is not very active during dry periods. The reproductive season probably extends throughout most of the rainy season and perhaps some of the early dry season as well. Neonates are 27–35 cm in TL. Copulation was observed in a pair from Honduras, with the female giving birth 212 days later. In specimens from the Atlantic versant of Costa Rica, males and females reach sexual maturity at 95 cm and 110–120 cm TL, respectively.

Distribution.—The barba amarilla is distributed on the Atlantic versant and lowlands from south-central Tamaulipas southward though Mexico (exclusive of the northwestern portion of the Yucatán Peninsula) and Central America to Colombia and Venezuela in northern South America; it occurs on the Pacific slopes and lowlands from Chiapas in Mexico to Guatemala and from Costa Rica through Panama to Ecuador. This snake is found throughout Petén and Belize in primary forest and secondary vegetation. In Guatemala it ranges from near sea level to about 1,070 m.

Remarks.—In Guatemala, the most widely applied common name for this species is *barba amarilla,* meaning yellow beard or yellow beard or yellow chin. Although the labial scales and undersurface of the head are cream or pale yellow, this usually does not seem to be a very obvious trait. However, under certain circumstances this coloration may be the only part of this cryptically colored snake that stands out. I have occasionally come across a large individual coiled in leaf litter with its head resting on top of its coils, and the only reason I saw the snakes in these instances was because their pale chin color gave them away.

This snake is one of several species commonly referred to in the popular literature as fer-de-lance. In actuality, this name is not properly applied to any species of viper occurring on the mainland of the Americas, and it is questionable whether it has ever been used by local inhabitants of the two Antillean islands previously of French possession (Martinique and Saint Lucia) for the viper species there. Other vernacular names for the barba amarilla include *cantil devanador, nauyaca real,* and *terciopelo.*

For good reason, this is the most feared snake in the Petén region. I have collected dozens of specimens for various museums over the years, but more recently, unless a specimen is found at a geographically interesting locality, I tend to leave them alone, especially the larger ones. This is a result, in part, of several near misses I have had while trying to collect this species under difficult circumstances. Unless irritated, these snakes are not aggressive and will not attack. However, they are easily excitable and are dangerous if aroused. People walking about, especially by night, should be exceedingly careful never to tread where they cannot see. Many snakebites are the result of people looking too far ahead on the trail and not where they are walking.

Mario Jolón, a student of rodents at Tikal, showed me the materials removed from the cheek pouches of spiny pocket mice. Among these were fragments of a shed skin that clearly came from a barba amarilla. What the rodent was doing with this shed skin is not certain, but perhaps it was nesting material. I was surprised that the mouse would venture so near to the skin, much less collect this in its cheek pouches. The skin must have retained some of the scent of this mortal enemy of the rodent.

The Tepezcuintle Hunters.—One of the most painful accidents to which I have been witness came about indirectly because of a barba amarilla. I had been camped out for a few days in the late 1970s at the end of a dirt road in eastern Izabal, where I had been working along the eastern slopes of the Montañas del Mico. I had barely returned to camp just past midnight one evening when I heard a great commotion up on a nearby trail. I could see the flickering of flashlights through the forest and could hear shouting and the sucking sounds of rubber boots being pulled out of deep mud as a small party of men approached.

As they drew nearer, I recognized some of them as hunters I had run into in the forest over the previous few rainy days. They were half-dragging one of their companions, who was obviously suffering severe paroxysms of pain. They had brought him to me because I had the only vehicle within miles, and they begged me to take him to the hospital. Not wanting to waste time inquiring about the nature of the problem, I quickly loaded up the injured man and two companions in the back of my pickup truck. Two others jumped into the cab with me and we took off hell-bent down the washboard-rutted, slippery road for the nearest hospital, which was in Puerto Barrios about 20 km distant.

On the way I learned that the five hunters had decided to sit out all night along a stream in the forest, where they assured me tepezcuintles (*Agouti paca*) were as abundant as stars in the sky. They had spaced themselves out along this stream and then, as it began to get dark, each had found a tree to climb, partly because they wanted not to be detected by any unsuspecting tepezcuintle that came down to the stream for a drink but mainly, they assured me, because the barba amarilla was even more common in the region than the tepezcuintle, and they were afraid to sit on the ground after dark. One poor fellow, who must not have been much of a woodsman, selected a chechem tree (probably *Metopium brownei* or *Rhus striata*) and had climbed several meters into it, hacking limbs that were in his way, before he realized something was amiss.

These trees are in the family Anacardiaceae, which is the same family that contains the poison ivy and poison sumac of temperate North American regions. Chechem trees present a hazard to people clearing the forest because the sap of these trees flows readily whenever they are cut and is extremely toxic when it comes in contact with human skin. The trees have to be cut with great care, and even once felled remain a hazard, because, I am told, inhalation of the smoke from a burning tree can be fatal. Before he realized what he had done, the poor hunter had managed to anoint his body more or less completely, including his eyes and scrotum, with sap.

The trip to the hospital took only a little over half an hour but seemed much longer because it was punctuated with terrifying screams of agony as the hunter thrashed and bashed his head on the floor and side of the pickup, and ripped at the affected parts of his body in an effort to relieve the pain, which of course only made it worse. Fortunately, there were several nurses awake when we finally arrived at the little regional hospital. By that time the suffering man, still shrieking violently, was bleeding rather profusely from his eyes. I left the area two days later and never was able to find out what became of him.

Rainforest Hognosed Pitviper—Víbora Chatilla de la Selva
Porthidium nasutum (Bocourt, 1868)
Fig. 184

Description.—In this stout-bodied snake, the tip of the snout is turned upward and the rostral scale is considerably higher than it is wide. The head is large and well differentiated from the neck, and the eye is medium sized with a dark brown iris and a vertical pupil. There are 8–11 supralabials, 10–13 infralabials, a single loreal, 3 preoculars, 1–4 suboculars, 1–4 postoculars, 21–25 (usually 23) dorsal scale rows at midbody, 123–145 ventrals, an undivided anal, and 24–41 mostly undivided subcaudals. There are 3–7 intersupraoculars. The dorsal scales are keeled. Males of this species reach a maximum of about 46 cm in TL, but females sometimes exceed 63 cm.

The dorsal ground color is brown, reddish brown, or grayish brown. A thin vertebral orange or tan line usually is bordered by 15–23 triangular or rectangular dark brown blotches. In some large adults the vertebral line and even the dorsal blotches my be somewhat obfuscated. The venter is heavily mottled with brown. In general, females are darker and have a less contrasting pattern than males.

Natural History.—This relatively small pitviper inhabits tropical wet and moist forest and is commonly seen coiled on the forest floor. Although it is usually considered to be nocturnal, I have found it most frequently in the early morning as it crossed jungle paths or roads, or lay coiled in leaf litter in small patches of light coming through the canopy. It has also been found under logs in the forest. I have encountered this species only in primary forest or in small patches of secondary forest within primary forest. It feeds mostly on lizards and frogs and also takes small rodents. Juveniles are known to feed on a variety of invertebrate prey.

From 8 to 18 young are born alive during the rainy season. Neonates are about 12–15 cm in TL.

Distribution.—The rainforest hognosed pitviper occurs in Atlantic lowland forests from northwestern Chiapas in southern Mexico southward through much of northern Guatemala and southern Belize and the rest of Central America to Colombia; in the Pacific lowlands it has a restricted distribution in Costa Rica and Panama and along the west coast of Colombia and northwestern Ecuador. This species occurs in most of southern and central Petén but is absent from about the northern quarter of the region. I have found it to be moderately common at Tikal and on Cerro Cahuí bordering the northern side of Lago Petén Itzá. This snake is recorded from Cayo District in Belize. In Guatemala, it occurs from near sea level to about 900 m.

Neotropical Rattlesnake—Víbora de Cascabel Neotropical
Crotalus durissus Linnaeus, 1758
Fig. 185

Description.—The presence of a rattle on the end of the tail is unique to rattlesnakes and makes this group readily recognizable from all other snakes, although the rattle rarely may be missing owing to an accident. Also, all loose segments of the rattle are lost in certain populations of rattlesnakes inhabiting islands in the Gulf of California, but not the Neotropical rattlesnake. The rattle is composed of a tough structural protein, keratin, which is the same material making up the scales of reptiles, feathers of birds, and our hair and fingernails. There is a general consensus among herpetologists that the rattle serves as a defense mechanism and is used to frighten away animals that might inflict harm on the snake. However, not all individuals rattle before striking in defense.

At birth, young rattlesnakes have a single tiny segment on the tip of the tail known as the prebutton. Only a few days after being born, the juveniles shed their entire skin including the prebutton and a new segment, the button, emerges. Subsequently, every time the snake sheds its skin a new rattle segment is added to the string of rattles. Young, rapidly growing rattlesnakes may shed three or four times a year, whereas old adults may shed only once. Not all segments are retained during the life of a rattlesnake and the distal portion of the rattle breaks from time to time, whenever the series becomes too long. Thus it is rare to see individuals in nature (but not long-term captives) with more than about seven or eight segments.

Despite the many exaggerated local reports of this species reaching great lengths, this robust snake reaches a maximum TL of about 170 cm. There are published reports of the Neotropical rattlesnake exceeding 200 cm, but most of these are probably field estimates, which are notoriously inaccurate. The large triangular head is distinct from the neck and the eye is medium sized with a vertically elliptical pupil. There are usually 14–17 supralabials, 15–19 infralabials, 3–4 loreals, 2–3 preoculars, 1–3 postoculars, 27–29 dorsal scale rows at midbody,
170–191 ventrals, an undivided anal plate, and 20–34 mostly undivided subcaudals followed by a rattle. The dorsal scales are strongly keeled, especially on the middorsal rows of the neck to either side of the vertebral row, where they are raised and tuberculate. The top of the snout is covered by a pair of internasals and a pair of prefrontals.

The overall ground color of this species is pale brown or gray-brown; I have seen a few specimens that were pale blue-gray. Conspicuous dark paravertebral stripes are present on the neck, usually extending posteriorly from about the supraoculars for 2–3 head lengths. The paravertebral stripes are separated from one another by three scales (or more in parietal region). The head has several prominent markings, including a dark crossbar involving the anterior portion of the supraoculars and the posterior part of the canthals, and a postocular stripe from the eye to about the angle of the jaw. The paravertebral stripes are followed by 21–31 dark brown, black, or reddish brown dorsal diamonds. These diamonds are 11–13 scale rows wide at midbody, 4–6 scales long, and separated from one another middorsally by 1–2 scales. Diamonds have pale centers and are edged on the outside by a single row of buff or cream scales. Laterally small blotches are located just below the dorsal blotches and made up of clusters of 4–5 dark scales; posteriorly these blotches often merge with the dorsal blotches to form crossbands. Often smaller lateral blotches are spaced at levels between the lateral blotches; these may involve the outer edges of the ventral scales and usually are only 1–2 dark scales in extent. In juveniles, the dorsal markings are often distinct throughout the body. In large adults, however, the diamond-shaped markings and ground color fade into one another on the posterior of the body, making distinction of posterior blotches difficult. The tail is gray, a little darker above than below, and the proximal rattle segment is gray in adults and buff in juveniles. The venter is cream or pale yellow, becoming darker on the posterior part of the body. *Natural History.*—This terrestrial species occurs in tropical and subtropical moist and dry forest. It seems to prefer the more open, drier areas. This species used to be common in the savanna region around La Libertad but has now become rare (see "Potent Medicine," page 281). It also occurs in drier habitats of northern Belize, including in the Mountain Pine Ridge region at elevations over 700 m. Although it is generally considered a denizen of the savannas and open areas, I have encountered this snake in forested environments, but usually not too far from natural clearings. However, I observed a rattlesnake in Tikal National Park in 1996, the first record for the park, and this specimen came from a transect deep within the forest, many miles from any natural clearing.

This species may be active by day or at night. I often have seen this snake in the evening between about 4:00–6:00 P.M. crawling across roads. It is particularly active on drizzly nights or at other times when the humidity is high.

The defensive posture of this snake is dramatic; almost half of the anterior part of the body is raised off the ground and held vertically, with the neck curved into a sharp crook with the head facing the adversary. The posterior part of the body is in a large, open coil, except for the tail and rattle, which are raised vertically in about the center of this coil.

This snake feeds mostly on rodents and also takes other warm-blooded prey, including ground-nesting birds. Adults also feed on black iguanas (*Ctenosaura similis*). Juveniles feed heavily on lizards and small mice.

Females give birth to 15–47 live young during the middle or late rainy season. Neonates are about 31–32 cm in TL.

Distribution.—The Neotropical rattlesnake is distributed from Nuevo León and Tamaulipas, Mexico, on the Atlantic versant and from Michoacán, Mexico, on the Pacific slopes southward to Costa Rica; and in South America from Colombia to Uruguay and central Argentina. Its distribution is fragmented over much of Latin America. It is known from scattered localities in Petén and western Belize. Over most of its range, this snake occurs in lowland habitats, but near Lago Atitlán (Cerro de Oro) in Guatemala there is an isolated population at about 1,600 m.

Remarks.—There are about 30 species of rattlesnakes, all of them occurring in the New World and all but this one restricted to areas north of the Isthmus of

Tehuantepec in Mexico. Rattlesnakes have evoked fascination in humans, being the subject of many fanciful legends and superstitions. They figure prominently in Mayan and Aztec art. This is a potentially dangerous snake and it is known to have caused human fatalities in Guatemala.

Two subspecies are recognized in Petén; *Crotalus durissus durissus* occurs sporadically over most of the region except in the northern third of the department, which is inhabited by *C. d. tzabcan*. Another vernacular name for this snake is *víbora real* or simply *cascabel*.

Potent Medicine.—In Guatemala there is widely held belief that the rattlesnake provides a potent cure for cancer. Some persons claim that medicine derived from rattlesnakes cures any kind of cancer; others have told me that it is only good for stomach cancer. The head and rattle of the rattlesnake are chopped off, it is skinned and eviscerated, and then the carcass is placed in the sun to dry thoroughly. Subsequently, it is rendered into powder, bones and all, which is then sold in small quantities, usually in encapsulated form, to the infirm and dying.

When opportunity prevails, I often purchase snakes from local collectors to use as scientific specimens. This usually presents no problem, other than that people obviously think I'm crazy for wanting something they are so eager to get rid of. I once encountered on trail a young man who had about a meter-long rattlesnake in his possession. The snake had been killed by decapitation and was tied to the end of a long pole. At the time, I had no specimens of rattlesnake from the immediate area and offered him five *quetzales* for the snake, which I thought perhaps too generous because the snake lacked its head, but I was desirous of at least documenting the existence of the species in this region.

He laughed at my offer and explained that he intended to get many times what I had offered him by pounding the snake into dust and selling it as medicine. He further informed me that he and various of his friends greatly looked forward to doing the same to any rattlesnake they chanced across. It seemed to him that rattlesnakes, for some inexplicable reason, were now becoming rare in this valley so they had recently taken to pulverizing other kinds of snakes and even lizards, which they mixed with rattlesnake dust. The fate of rattlesnakes meeting with humans in Guatemala is not a happy one.

CROCODILIANS—COCODRILOS

These magnificent animals are sometimes called the "last of the ruling reptiles" because they are living representatives of the Archosauria, the group that contained the dinosaurs. Crocodiles are more closely related to birds than they are to other groups of living reptiles, even though they possess a superficial resemblance to lizards. Characteristics that they share with birds include various behavioral traits, such as nest building and parental care of the young, and anatomical features, such as a four-chambered heart. Crocodilians have a complete secondary palate that allows them to breathe while they grasp and hold onto prey on the surface of the water, and they are the only living reptiles to have thecodont teeth; that is, teeth rooted in sockets in the jaws. Other morphological features include an elongate snout with nostrils located at the end, a heavy dorsal armor of bony plates (os-teoderms) raised into a series of ridges, five digits on the front feet, four digits with webbing on the hind feet, and a longitudinal vent.

Many diverse kinds of animals, from small spiders to jaguars, have reflective eyeshine, but perhaps none as dramatic and beautiful as that of crocodiles. No matter how often I witness the bright emberlike glow of crocodile eyes reflecting in my light on the hot, mosquito-infested nights that seem to be typical of their habitat, I will never cease to have a rush of adrenaline and a feeling of awe. Unfortunately this trait has helped lead to their demise; crocodiles are hunted at night, when they can be easily located by their eyeshine. Experienced hunters can severely deplete or even completely exterminate crocodiles from a region in a very short time. Most crocodiles, although wary by day, are remarkably placid at night and can be approached in a boat to within easy range of a harpoon or rifle.

There are 23 living species of crocodilians and most of these are endangered owing to overexploitation. Living species of crocodilians are placed into three groups: the alligators and their allies, the true crocodiles, and the slender-snouted Indian gavial. Various authorities, at one time or another, have recognized each of these groups as a separate family. More recently, however, often only one family has been recognized—the Crocodylidae. Three species of crocodilians occur in Guatemala: the brown caiman of the Pacific lowlands, the American crocodile of both the Atlantic and Pacific coastal regions, and Morelet's crocodile, the only species occurring in the interior of Petén.

American Crocodile—Cocodrilo de Río
Crocodylus acutus Cuvier, 1807
Figs. 186–187

Description.—The snout is relatively more slender and elongate than in Morelet's crocodile, and the top of the head in front of the eyes is distinctly convex. Osteoderms are reduced on the neck, but the dorsal armor is well developed elsewhere on the back and the arrangement of osteoderms is often not bilaterally symmetrical. Adults of this species commonly used to reach lengths of 4–5 m, and there are reliable reports of old individuals exceeding 6 m. Males reach greater lengths than females and have more massive jaw musculature and a more pronounced prefrontal hump. Females are reported to be stouter, with a proportionally shorter tail and a less elongate snout.

The dorsal coloration of adults varies from olive or yellowish brown to gray-brown, and there may be some darker mottling dorsally or large dark splotches on the sides of the body and on the tail. The area around the jaws is yellow, sometimes with an orange tinge. The venter is whitish or cream. The iris has been reported to be silver or blue-green, but its exact color seems to be age dependent and geographically variable. Juveniles are pale yellow or tan with dark crossmarkings on the body and tail; a few individuals may be unicolored.

Natural History.—This species occurs in large, lowland rivers, lakes, and marshes. It also occupies coastal mangrove swamps and may enter brackish or even salt water. This crocodile often lives in large bodies of clear water but is not restricted to such habitats. Females guard their nesting sites and are territorial. Males, also, will defend certain stretches of a river or shoreline against potential rival males.

Females reach sexual maturity at a total length of about 2.8 m and usually make nests near the water's edge, but in some cases nests may be removed somewhat from the water. There is a report of a female that constructed her nest about 30 m from a river and up on a steep bank about 6 m above the water level. Nests are constructed of a combination of sand, mud, and/or dead vegetation. The hole excavated by the female prior to depositing her eggs is usually not vertical but rather dug diagonally; and a typical nest is 70 cm in diameter and 50 cm deep. From 30 to 70 eggs, depending on the size of the female, are laid between March and May, although nest-building activity may begin as early as February. The white, calcareous eggs are about 80 mm long and 54 mm wide and have a number of pores in the brittle shell. The incubation period is 75–80 days. Young hatch at about the time of the first rains of the rainy season, before extensive flooding occurs. Just prior to and at the time of hatching, the young emit soft, grunt-like croaks. These sounds, emanating from the interior of the nest, seem to stimulate the female to excavate it. She gently scoops up the young in her mouth as they hatch and transports them to the water. Hatchlings are 24–27 cm in total length. They are reported to hunt prey actively within four days after hatching. The young are gregarious and may remain together for about five weeks, at which time sibling aggregations begin to disband. Females remain with the young after they hatch. Growth of the young varies with food availability; it has been estimated that under natural conditions young may reach about 1.5 m in about five years.

Juveniles feed on a variety of small animals, including insects, small fish, and frogs and their larvae. Larger specimens eat turtles, birds, and mammals, but their diet consists mostly of fish. One small individual 1.1 m in total length was found to contain a four-eyed opossum (*Philander*). It has been reported that this crocodile hunts most actively during the first hours following nightfall, especially on moonless nights.

Crocodile eggs are preyed on by many animals, including raccoons, coatimundis, foxes, and skunks. The juveniles are eaten by various birds of prey and large water birds as well as by larger fishes.

In areas of Guatemala where these crocodiles had not been severely hunted or disturbed, seeing several individuals basking on a sandbar used to be a common occurrence. They are fond of basking and I used to encounter them frequently during the late morning or early afternoon on the banks of the Río María Linda and the Río Naranjo on the Pacific Coast. Throughout Guatemala, these magnificent animals have been severely persecuted and it is a rare sight to see one these days.

Distribution.—The American crocodile occurs from southern Florida (the Everglades and Florida Keys) across the Greater Antilles (Cuba, the Cayman Islands, Jamaica, Hispaniola); on the mainland from Tabasco and Campeche, Mexico, southward through the Cayos of Belize and coastal Central America to Colombia and Venezuela, including a few islands such as Trinidad and Margarita; and on the Pacific from southern Sinaloa, Mexico, southward through Mexico and Central America to Ecuador and northern Peru. Along the Pacific Coast of Guatemala, this species occurs in major rivers and mangrove swamps. A small population persists in the clear blue waters of the Río Lagartero of western Guatemala. In eastern Guatemala, American crocodiles occur in the Río Motagua at least as far inland as the level of Teculután, and they occur in the Río Polochic, Lago de Izabal, and Río Dulce. The presence of this species has not been confirmed for Petén, but it almost certainly occurs in the Río Usumacinta, which forms the western boundary of the department. The account by the Maudslays in *A Glimpse at Guatemala* of "alligators" seen during the late 1800s along the Río Usumacinta may refer to this species.

Remarks.—American crocodiles can be dangerous, although there are few documented reports of recent attacks on humans. In 1960, I arrived in the town of Iztapa on the Pacific Coast of Guatemala a couple of days after a large individual had seized and killed a woman who was washing clothes in the Canal de Chiquimulilla. This individual was shot by a friend of mine, Victor Printemps, a longtime resident of Iztapa, and was said to have measured over 5 m. I did not see the intact specimen but was given the skull, which seemed gigantic to me. Unfortunately, this skull now has become lost, so I am unable to give its dimensions.

People in Iztapa told me in 1960 that crocodile attacks on humans had not been a rare occurrence several decades previously, but that this was the first such attack in many years.

I saw the injuries inflicted by another crocodile in 1963 and I assume that the species involved was an American crocodile. This attack occurred in Lago de Yojoa in Honduras, reportedly by a crocodile that was a little over 3 m in length. The victim was a Dutch helicopter mechanic who worked for a crop-dusting company based out of Guatemala City. Attacked while snorkling near the shore, he was able to free himself but sustained some formidable lacerations on one shoulder and arm.

The American crocodile is listed on CITES Appendix I, meaning that it is classified as an endangered species. It is protected by law throughout Guatemala, but the hunting laws are almost never enforced. It has now been extirpated from many areas and all remaining populations are probably in decline.

Another common name for this species is *lagarto amarillo*.

Morelet's Crocodile—Cocodrilo de Pantano
Crocodylus moreletii Duméril and Bocourt, 1851
Figs. 188–189

Description.—The snout of Morelet's crocodile is relatively broader than that of the American crocodile. In Guatemala, there are trustworthy records of this crocodile growing to a length of 3 to 3.4 m, but I have not seen specimens much over 2 m. The largest specimen from Guatemala that I am aware of was measured by my friend Santiago Billy. This crocodile, captured 4 October 1995 in a gill net at the confluence of the Río Sacluc with the Río San Pedro, had a total length of 3.4 m from the tip of the snout to the tip of the tail. The cranium reportedly was 50 cm in length from the anterior end of the premaxillae to the posterior end of the quadrate, and was 32 cm wide at the posterior part of the skull. In Mexico, even larger specimens have been reported—individuals of up to 4.25 m in length.

The coloration of large adults is somewhat variable; most of the specimens I have seen, especially the larger males, tend to be rather drab, usually more or less uniformly gray-brown or blackish brown dorsally without much evidence of a pattern. In most individuals more than 1 m in length, the back has already become dark with yellow spots. Some individuals are heavily mottled with yellow and black and with large dark bars or blotches on the sides of the body and tail. The belly is pale and usually yellowish white. Young individuals are yellowish with black spots and bands on the body and tail; moderate-sized specimens generally become darker brown, but some indistinct black markings often persist. The iris of the eye has variously been described as being silver, silver-gray, or golden brown. The snout is relatively wide for a crocodile, being 1.4–1.8 times as long as its width (length is measured from the level of the anterior edge of the eye to the tip of the snout; width is measured at a level just in front of the eyes). There is a moderate amount of dorsal armor on the neck and body. The primary transverse rows of scales on the underside of the proximal part of the tail have a number of small scales inserted between them. The rear teeth are relatively blunt and stout, perhaps an adaptation for cracking the shells of turtles.

Natural History.—This is a species of quiet water, occurring in backwater lagoons, slow-moving streams, lakes, and aguadas. For the most part, it seems to avoid the large, permanently flowing rivers and inhabits the smaller tributaries that feed into the larger rivers. Many of these sluggish streams become fragmented into isolated bodies of water during the dry period. This crocodile appears to prefer bodies of water with dense vegetation around the margins in open areas such as savannas, but I have seen it also in dense forest habitats. It is highly adaptable and may be found in habitats as different as the brackish mangrove lagoons of Belize and the swiftly flowing mountain streams emanating from the Maya Mountains.

Larger individuals tend to be wary but may occasionally be seen basking on the shore, on logs in the water, or on the water's surface near the bank. If you know where and how to look for crocodiles at night, it is still relatively easy to find Morelet's crocodiles, especially juveniles, by their eyeshine.

Adults feed on mud turtles, small mammals, molluscs, fish, aquatic birds, frogs, and other animals. The young eat mostly insects and other small animals that move on or near the surface of the water, including snails, small crustaceans, and small fish.

Morelet's crocodiles build a nest of dead vegetation, green vegetation that has been pulled up, and small sticks and mud. Nesting occurs from April to June, incubation taking from 75 to 80 days. Nests vary in size but often are about 1.5 m in diameter and about 0.9 m tall. From 20 to 42 eggs are laid in the nest, which is guarded by the female. These eggs are approximately 68 × 45 mm, with a hard, smooth shell. At the time of hatching, probably in response to soft croaks emitted by young still in the eggs, the female digs into the nest and scoops up one to several eggs or young at a time. She carries these to the edge of the water, where she gently cracks unhatched eggs and releases the young into their new environment. The female remains with and guards her young for an unknown period. Hatchlings are from 23 to 26 cm in length and weigh from 37 to 50 g. Captives in seminatural conditions averaged 40.7 cm TL after 12 months, 65.7 cm after 24 months, and 82.6 cm after 36 months.

Distribution.—Morelet's crocodile occurs from central Tamaulipas in northeastern Mexico southward through the southern portion of the Yucatán Peninsula and northern Guatemala to central Belize. It is found throughout most of Petén and large individuals can occur in surprisingly small bodies of water. Old reports of this species from northern Honduras are probably erroneous and based on specimens of the American crocodile, *Crocodylus acutus*. At one time this species reportedly ranged into the Central Depression of Chiapas, but it is now apparently extirpated from that portion of the Río Grijalva drainage. There is an old record for the Río Polochic, and more recently Oscar Lara has informed me of specimens from the Canal Inglés in the lower Río Motagua valley, which may represent the southern part of this species' range.

Remarks.—During his travels through Petén in 1847–1848, the French naturalist/explorer Morelet collected several crocodiles at Lago Petén Itzá. These specimens were shipped back to the Paris Museum of Natural History, where they were formally described in 1851 by French herpetologists, who named this new species in honor of the collector. Morelet noted that these crocodiles were known to attack humans who ventured into their watery domain. There are documented cases of this species attacking people in Belize, southern Mexico, and Guatemala (see "Goliath and the Chocolate Maker"). The species of crocodilians that have a reputation of attacking people are generally large species and individuals implicated in attacks are almost always over 3.5 m in length. Morelet's crocodile perhaps has the distinction of being the smallest of the crocodiles known to have caused human fatalities.

This crocodile has been ruthlessly hunted throughout its range, primarily for its hide, and its numbers are now greatly reduced. It is hunted also for its flesh, especially from the tail, which is relished by some persons. Years ago, I sampled Morelet's crocodile—cooked on an open fire and, even better, wrapped in banana leaves and smoked—and can attest that it is better than many of the "bush meats" I have tried.

As recently as the 1960s and 1970s, it was not uncommon to see many Morelet's crocodiles at various places throughout Petén, but they have since suffered a major decline coincident with massive human migrations into the area. However, government protection has been more effective with this species than for the American crocodile, probably because Morelet's crocodile is able to survive in the many small streams and aguadas scattered across Petén. The virtual demise of the *lagartero*, or professional crocodile hunter, in recent years also has been beneficial to this species, and it seems to be making somewhat of a comeback in some areas. During a one-week trip to Petén in 1995, during which no special effort was made to inventory the species, my wife and I saw crocodiles in every major body of water we visited, including Lago Petén Itzá, Laguna Petenchel, and Laguna Yaxjá.

Neverless, the pathetic current status of this crocodile belies its former abundance. In the 1920s, reportedly, an average of 1,000 skins of this species per day passed through the marketplace of Villahermosa in Tabasco. Morelet's crocodile is listed on CITES Appendix I.

Other vernacular names are *lagarto negro* and *cocodrilo pardo*.

Goliath and the Chocolate Maker.—The young crocodile first saw the light of day in about 1955. His mother had constructed on the bank of a river a nest of leaves and mud, which she had guarded for almost three months. The soft croaking of this young crocodile and his siblings had stirred maternal feelings in this old archosaur and she had dug down into the nest to assist in the hatching. She had tenderly carried many of her offspring down to the water's edge within her toothy mouth, behavior seemingly incongruous with her large and fearsome aspect. The young crocodile had thrived for several years hidden under the vegetation overhanging his river home, feeding on insects that happened to move across his field of view as well as on an occasional frog, fish, or other small vertebrate that ventured too close.

The little crocodile had grown to length of a bit over a meter when the coal-red eyeshine typical of his order gave his presence away one night and a fisherman captured him in a cast net. The crocodile was taken to the nearest village and probably would have been killed and skinned had fate not intervened. Hearsay has it that a visiting North American archaeologist purchased this handsome young specimen, probably on a whim, and transported him back to Tikal, where he was released in the main aguada, one of the few bodies of water in the area. There are several aguadas around Tikal. The main one serves as the reservoir for the houses and restaurants near the visitor center and has been subdivided into several smaller ponds in recent years.

There is agreement among most of the old-timers at Tikal that the crocodile inhabiting the main reservoir from the 1950s until 1985 was introduced by University of Pennsylvania personnel who began working at the site in 1956. I was assured by several people that this crocodile was brought to Tikal by the archaeologist Dennis E. Puleston. However, Puleston did not arrive in Petén for the first time until the early 1960s, as an undergraduate, and did not begin his graduate field research there until about 1965, so it seems that the crocodile arrived by other means. Puleston was killed by lightning in the Yucatán of Mexico during the summer of 1978.

Although this new home was somewhat different from the crocodile's initial riverine environment, it was perfectly suitable. His species had become adapted to such habitats throughout the Yucatán Peninsula many tens of thousands of years previously. For many years (from at least 1959, when I first saw him, until 1985), this beautiful specimen of Morelet's crocodile was easily observed in the reservoir at Tikal and provided many tourists with their only glimpse of a crocodile. The only crocodile in the aguada, he was free from intraspecific competition. He flourished, feeding on just about all that moved through or along the edge of his aquatic environment. Sometime in the 1970s, this crocodile had reached a sufficient size to be dubbed Goliad (Goliath). He continued to grow steadily, and when I saw him in 1980 he looked to be about 2 m in length.

Unfortunately, this individual became so tame that he would often quickly rush the bank, looking for a handout from visitors. I had captured him several times in the 1960s while collecting frogs at night, and while Goliad was a little pugnacious in temperament, I never considered him very dangerous. However, life in the Tikal aguada must have been good and he began a reign of terror. For names, dates, and some of the details of these attacks, I am indebted to Luis Savala and Haroldo García. In 1971 the crocodile shredded the forearm of a 10-year-old girl. In 1972 he maimed the lower leg of a 13-year-old boy named Eduardo. Subsequently, this crocodile was responsible for a number of attacks on people, some of which were serious.

It was in 1981 that Goliad caused his first human fatality. Park worker Salvador Garillo was in a shallow part of the aguada at about 3:00 in the afternoon, catching some of the little fish that have been introduced. The crocodile attacked from beneath water, seizing Garillo by both hands and pulling him into deeper water, where the animal released him, grabbed him by the belly, and eviscerated him. This man was still alive when rescued but died shortly thereafter from his terrible wounds. The next fatality was Inocencia García in 1985. While filling a water jug near the edge of the aguada, he was seized directly by the face so that the anterior teeth of the crocodile penetrated his temples, killing him almost instantly.

Several weeks after this last attack, the order came from top administrators to dispatch the crocodile, and he was shot by a park ranger. I heard many exaggerated accounts of his size and had the opportunity to measure the remains during a visit to Tikal in July 1995. The specimen had originally been buried but fortunately was disinterred some time later. The skeleton is shelved in a *bodega* (storeroom) at the Tikal workers' camp, El Corral. Measurements for this crocodile are as follows: skull from tip of mandible to posterior articulating surface of jaw, 39.5 cm; skull from tip of snout to back of occipitals, 37 cm; body length from tip of snout to posterior edge of sacral vertebra, 115 cm; and total length from tip of snout to tip of tail, 226 cm.

In 1995 and 1996, several other small crocodiles were living in the Tikal reservoir. As regards how they reached Tikal, some people say they were brought in from Lago Petén Itzá, whereas others swear they arrived on their own. I tend to favor the former explanation, although this species is sometimes found wandering far from water.

Another case of crocodile attack, documented by various newspaper reports, occurred relatively recently in Laguna Yaxjá. In November 1994, a Dutch tourist, who reportedly was the royal chocolate maker for the queen of Holland, was attacked during the morning while swimming along the southeastern shore of the lake. Several people who witnessed the attack came to the man's rescue by smashing the crocodile with oars, finally causing the animal to release its victim. This man was badly injured but survived and was flown from Flores to Guatemala City for treatment. For details relating to this attack, I thank Eduardo Cofiño, owner of Gringo Perdido near El Remate, Petén. Personnel of the Dutch Embassy in Guatemala City would not provide me with additional information. The crocodile was subsequently hunted down and shot by Juan de la Oz. I have examined the skull of the Yaxjá crocodile, which was an adult but not an impressively large animal. The skull from the tip of the snout to the posterior edge of the occipital bones is only 36 cm. I would estimate the animal's total length not to have exceeded 2.2 m.

Although it is often claimed that this species is not dangerous to humans, there are several earlier reports of Morelet's crocodile's attacking people in Guatemala, including Morelet's original account in the mid-1800s; but the details of these attacks are sketchy. In about 1930, the young daughter of a Belize resident was injured by a crocodile while swimming in Laguna Perdida. In about 1955, another crocodile of unknown size seized and killed a small girl in Laguna Perdida. On 4 April 1980, George Ack was attacked, killed, and partially eaten while he was fishing in a roadside pond near Orange Walk, Belize; the crocodile that killed him was reported to be only seven feet (2.1 m) in length. In 1994, an adult man was seized and drowned by a crocodile in a tributary of the Río San Pedro in northwestern Petén.

It is worth noting that all of the attacks described above occurred during the day, even though crocodiles are known to be more active at night. Although I hardly consider crocodile attacks to be of major concern in Petén, I would think twice before swimming in some of the more remote and isolated lagunas, and swimming after dark anywhere that crocodiles are known to exist is probably not a good idea.

APPENDICES: IDENTIFICATION KEYS

Appendix A

KEY TO MAJOR GROUPS OF AMPHIBIANS AND REPTILES

1. Skin smooth or with tubercles but never with epidermal scales (amphibians) 2
   Skin with conspicuous epidermal scales, scutes, or plates (reptiles) 4
2. Limbs absent; eyes vestigial without eyelids . . . . .Caecilians
   Limbs present; eyes with eyelids 3
3. Tail present . . . . .Salamanders
   Tail absent . . . . .Frogs and Toads
4. Body encased by a shell; no teeth on jaws . . . . .Turtles
   Body not encased by a shell; teeth present on jaws 5
5. Vent longitudinal; scutes on back raised into series of ridges;
   toes webbed . . . . .Crocodiles
   Vent transverse; scales on back not modified into ridges;
   toes, if present, not webbed 6
6. Fore and hind limbs clearly evident; ear opening present . . . . .Lizards
   Fore and hind limbs usually absent (hind limbs, if present,
   vestigial and not extending past the contour of the body);
   ear opening absent . . . . .Snakes

CLAVE PARA LOS GRUPOS MAYORES DE ANFIBIOS Y REPTILES

1. Piel lisa o con tubérculos, pero nunca con escamas epidérmicas (anfibios) 2
   Piel con escamas epidérmicas conspicuas, escudos, o placas (reptiles) . . .4
2. Sin patas; ojos vestigiales sin párpados . . . . .Cecílidos
   Con patas; ojos con párpados 3
3. Con cola . . . . .Salamandras
   Sin cola . . . . .Ranas y Sapos
4. Cuerpo rodeado por una caparazón; mandíbulas sin dientes . . . . . . .Tortugas
   Cuerpo no rodeado por una caparazón; mandíbulas con dientes 5
5. Abertura cloacal longitudinal; escudos en dorso alzados en series de crestas; membranas entre dedos de los pies . . . . .Cocodrilos
   Abertura cloacal transversal; escudos en dorso no alzados en series de crestas; dedos de los pies, si están presentes, sin membranas 6
6. Patas delanteras y traseras claramente evidentes; con orificio auditivo . . . . .Lagartijas
   Patas delanteras y traseras usualmente ausentes (patas traseras, si presentes, vestigiales y no se extienden más allá del contorno corporal); sin orificio auditivo . . . . .Culebras

Appendix B

KEY TO SPECIES OF CAECILIANS AND SALAMANDERS

1. Limbs absent; eyes vestigial without eyelids (caecilians) 2
   Limbs present; eyes with eyelids (salamanders) 3
2. Primary body annuli fewer than 120; head and anterior part of
   body grayish ....*Dermophis mexicana* (fig. 14)
   Primary body annuli more than 120; head and anterior part of
   body pinkish ....*Gymnopis syntrema* (fig. 15)
3. Elongate, vermiform salamanders; more than 15 costal grooves between
   axilla and groin; body grayish with small white dots, a distinctive
   white blotch on top of head ....*Oedipina elongata* (fig. 21)
   Robust to slender salamanders but never vermiform; fewer
   than 15 costal grooves between axilla and groin; color variable 4
4. Dorsal pattern of dark flecks, peppering, or streaks on a pale
   background; adults less than 40 mm in snout-vent
   length ....*Bolitoglossa rufescens* (fig. 20)
   Body dark, at least on sides and venter, with or without
   pale dorsal markings; adults greatly exceeding 40 mm in
   snout-vent length 5
5. Robust body and tail; dorsal coloration dark brown with or without paler
   brown mottling ....*Bolitoglossa dofleini* (fig. 16)
   Body relatively slender; dorsum uniformly dark or
   with a pattern of yellow or orange markings 6
6. Body entirely black except usually for a narrow yellow or orange
   middorsal stripe on body and tail ....*Bolitoglossa mulleri* (fig. 18)

Yellow paravertebral markings on body, *or* dorsum of head, body, and
tail mostly pale, broken with black longitudinal stripes or spots 7
7. Yellow or cream dorsolateral markings on body
. . . .*Bolitoglossa odonnelli* (fig. 19)
Dorsum of head, body, and tail dark with yellowish
spots or blotches . . . .*Bolitoglossa mexicana* (fig. 17)

CLAVE PARA LAS ESPECIES DE CECÍLIDOS Y SALAMANDRAS

1. Sin patas; ojos vestigiales y sin párpados (cecílidos) 2
   Con patas; ojos con párpados (salamandras) 3
2. Menos de 120 anillos primarios en el cuerpo; cabeza y parte anterior del
   cuerpo de color gris . . . .*Dermophis mexicana* (fig. 14)
   Mas de 120 anillos primarios en el cuerpo; cabeza y parte
   anterior del cuerpo de color rosa . . . .*Gymnopis syntrema* (fig. 15)
3. Salamandras alargadas y vermiformes; más de 15 surcos costales entre
   la axila y la ingle; cuerpo grisaceo con pequeños puntos blancos,
   con mancha blanca en la parte dorsal de la cabeza
   . . . .*Oedipina elongata* (fig. 21)
   Salamandras robustas, nunca vermiformes; con menos
   de 15 surcos costales entre la axila y la ingle; color variable 4
4. Patrón dorsal de vetas, motas o jaspeaduras oscuras sobre un
   color claro como fondo; adultos menos de 40 mm de largo
   entre el hocico y la cloaca . . . .*Bolitoglossa rufescens* (fig. 20)
   Cuerpo oscuro, por lo menos a los lados o en el vientre, con o sin
   marcas claras en el dorso; adultos con mucho más de 40 mm
   de largo entre el hocico y la cloaca 5
5. Robusto de cuerpo y cola; coloracion dorsal café oscuro
   con o sin motas café claro . . . .*Bolitoglossa dofleini* (fig. 16)
   Cuerpo relativamente delgado; dorso uniformemente oscuro
   o con un patrón de marcas amarillas o anaranjadas 6

6. Cuerpo completamente negro, excepto por una sola línea
    delgada de color amarillo o anaranjado en el dorso del
    cuerpo y la cola .... *Bolitoglossa mulleri* (fig. 18)
    Marcas amarillas paravertebrales en el cuerpo, o el dorso de la cabeza,
    cuerpo y cola mayormente palidas, partidas por líneas longitudinales
    o puntos negros 7
7. Marcas dorsolaterales en el cuerpo de color amarillo o de crema
    .... *Bolitoglossa odonnelli* (fig. 19)
    Dorso de la cabeza, cuerpo y cola oscuro con puntos
    o manchas amarillentas .... *Bolitoglossa mexicana* (Fig. 17)

Appendix C

KEY TO SPECIES OF TOADS AND FROGS

1. Body nearly round in dorsal view; dorsum dark with pale reddish or sometimes yellow vertebral stripe and spots on the sides; head small and
   limbs short; hind foot with 4 digits; inner side of hind limb with 2
   distinctive spadelike tubercles ....*Rhinophrynus dorsalis* (fig. 22)
   Body shape and color variable; hind foot with 5 digits; no spadelike
   tubercles on hind limbs 2
2. A conspicuous parotoid gland on side of neck behind eye; skin
   dry and warty 3
   No parotoid glands; skin may be smooth or tubercular but is usually wet
   to the touch 6
3. No cranial crests; small anurans (< 35 mm SVL)
   ....*Physalaemus pustulosus* (fig. 32)
   Cranial crests present; usually > 35 mm SVL (true toads) 4
4. Parotoid gland huge, at least 3–4 times as large as upper eyelid; no
   prominent row of lateral tubercles or, if some are present, these
   not larger than those on dorsum; cranial crests without or with
   a poorly defined parietal spur ....*Bufo marinus* (fig. 35)
   Parotoid gland smaller, usually about the size of upper eyelid; a
   prominent lateral row of enlarged, conical tubercles extending
   from posterior of parotoid gland to groin; cranial crests including
   a long, distinct parietal spur 5
5. Legs long, tibia more than 45 percent of SVL; tympanum width less than
   half that of orbit; cranial crests are narrow ridges; preorbital and
   pretympanic crests absent or poorly developed ...*Bufo campbelli* (fig. 34)

Legs shorter, tibia less than 45 percent of SVL; tympanum width more than half that of orbit; cranial crests knobby and rounded; preorbital and pretympanic crests well developed . . . .*Bufo valliceps* (fig. 36)

6. Small fat frogs with narrow, pointed heads; a distinct transverse fold across top of head just posterior to the level of eyes (microhylid frogs) . .7

    Shape of body and head variable; no transverse fold across top of head just posterior to the level of eyes 8

7. Dorsum grayish or gray-brown without distinctive pale middorsal line; toes without any webbing; tips of toes slightly expanded; adults usually less than 25 mm in SVL . . . .*Gastrophryne elegans* (fig. 52)

    Dorsum orange or reddish brown with distinctive pale middorsal line; toes with a basal web; tips of toes not expanded; adults exceeding 30 mm in SVL . . . .*Hypopachus variolosus* (fig. 53)

8. Webbing between outer two toes (Toes IV–V) relatively prominent, incised no more deeply than midway between proximal and distal tubercles of outer toe 9

    Webbing between outer two toes (Toes IV–V) absent or reduced to below midpoint between proximal and distal tubercles of outer toe (leptodactylid frogs) 26

9. Tips of fingers and toes expanded into definite discs; no dorsolateral ridges; webbing between toes moderate to extensive (treefrogs and glassfrogs) 10

    Tips of fingers and toes not expanded into discs; conspicuous dorsolateral ridges; webbing between toes extensive (true frogs) 23

10. Skin covering belly transparent; small pale green frog
    . . . .*Hyalinobatrachium fleischmanni* (fig. 37)

    Skin covering belly opaque; size and color variable 11

11. Sides of head flared . . . .*Triprion petasatus* (fig. 51)

    Sides of head not modified 12

12. Skin of dorsum glandular with many large, scattered tubercles
    . . . .*Phrynohyas venulosa* (fig. 46)

    Skin of dorsum smooth with few or no tubercles 13

13. Pupil of eye vertical; green frogs with brightly colored concealed surfaces 14

    Pupil of eye horizontal 15

14. Bright red eyes; flanks bluish with yellow or cream vertical bars
    . . . .*Agalychnis callidryas* (fig. 38)

    Eyes appear black (in bright light deep purple); flanks orange
    . . . .*Agalychnis moreletii* (fig. 39)

15. A distinctive axillary web extending on arm almost to elbow 16

    Axillary web absent or poorly developed 17

16. Dorsum variable, but usually tan to reddish brown with a little
mottling or dark flecking; hidden surfaces of hind limbs bright
orange . . . .*Hyla loquax* (fig. 42)
Dorsum yellow or yellowish tan, usually with a bold dark
brown pattern; hidden surfaces of hind limbs mostly yellowish
or pale orange . . . .*Hyla ebraccata* (fig. 41)
17. Snout pointed and protruding; dark longitudinal markings on back,
transverse bars on shanks; small frog (< 32 mm in SVL)
. . . .*Scinax staufferi* (fig. 47)
Snout truncate or broadly rounded; variable in size and color pattern . .18
18. Small frogs (< 30 mm in SVL); dorsum yellowish with or without darker
flecks or streaks 19
Larger frogs (body length of 45 mm or more); dorsum variable, often
with large dark blotches 21
19. Dorsum usually with dark X-shaped or reticulate pattern
. . . .*Hyla microcephala* (fig. 43)
Dorsum usually immaculate or with only dark flecking 20
20. A dark stripe, pale bordered above, extending posteriorly from
eye onto sides . . . .*Hyla picta* (fig. 44)
No dark stripe extending posteriorly from eye . .*Hyla bromeliacia* (fig. 40)
21. Outer edge of tarsus with series of conical tubercles; hands more
than three-fourths webbed; skin on dorsum tuberculate; dorsal
pattern lichenose; skin on top of head co-ossified with skull
in adults . . . .*Hyla valancifer* (fig. 45)
Outer edge of tarsus smooth; hands less than one-third webbed; skin on
dorsum smooth; dorsal pattern blotched or unicolor; skin on top of head
not co-ossified with skull 22
22. Posterior surface of thigh with blue spotting; side of body, especially
posteriorly, with fine black reticulations; upper lip with pale margin
. . . .*Smilisca cyanosticta* (fig. 50)
Posterior surface of thigh usually darkly mottled or unicolored; sides
of body usually with spotting; upper lip with a distinctive spot (pale
or dark) just below eye . . . .*Smilisca baudinii* (figs. 48–49)
23. Dorsal pattern between dorsolateral ridges usually a double series
of large spots (these sometimes irregular or absent); skin not
denticulate; toe tips not expanded . . . .*Rana berlandieri* (fig. 54)
Dorsal pattern between dorsolateral ridges usually scattered small
dark spots, especially posteriorly, or uniformly colored; skin
denticulate; toe tips expanded 24

24. Tympanum large (greater than eye diameter); no distinct face mask; no distinct supralabial stripe ....*Rana vaillanti* (fig. 57)
    Tympanum small (less than eye diameter); dark face mask present; pale supralabial stripe present 25
25. Tympanum nearly as large as eye; vocal sacs and slits absent in adult males; occurring in the Maya Mountains ....*Rana juliani* (fig. 55)
    Tympanum about half the diameter of eye or less; vocal sacs and slits present in adult males; occurring in the foothills of Alta Verapaz and eastern Guatemala ....*Rana maculata* (fig. 56)
26. Legs short, tibial segment no longer than distance from tip of snout to level of insertion of forelimb; distal tips of digits not expanded 27
    Legs longer, tibial segment longer than distance from tip of snout to level of insertion of forelimb; distal tips of digits expanded or not 28
27. Lateral dermal fringes folding downward around toes; males with two black keratinized spines on pollex ....*Leptodactylus melanonotus* (fig. 31)
    Lateral dermal fringe absent from toes; males without black, keratinized spines on pollex ....*Leptodactylus labialis* (fig. 30)
28. Small frogs (usually < 28 mm SVL); without inner tarsal fold or tubercle; tips of fingers expanded 1.5–4 times width of digit 29
    Larger frogs (usually > 28 mm SVL); with either inner tarsal fold or tubercle; tips of fingers expanded or not 30
29. Tips of fingers expanded no more than about 1.5 times digit width; vomerine teeth absent; dorsal color pattern greenish with black mottling or reticulations ....*Syrrhophus leprus* (fig. 33)
    Tips of fingers expanded about 3–4 times digit width; vomerine teeth present; dorsal color pattern brown with dark brown mottling ....*Eleutherodactylus alfredi* (fig. 23)
30. Tips of fingers expanded at least 1.5–2 times digit width 31
    Tips of fingers sometimes slightly swollen but about same width as digit 33
31. Skin covering lower belly with numerous dark melanophores; skin of dorsum rugose with many large tubercles; webbing between toes III and IV not extending to level of proximal subarticular tubercles ....*Eleutherodactylus psephosypharus* (fig. 26)
    Skin covering lower belly unpigmented; skin of dorsum with many small, scattered tubercles but not noticeably rugose; webbing between toes III and IV extending to or past proximal subarticular tubercles ...32
32. Hind limbs relatively short, heel reaching to about level of eye; webbing between toes III and IV extending well past proximal subarticular tubercles ....*Eleutherodactylus sandersoni* (fig. 28)

Hind limbs relatively long, heel reaching to about tip of snout; webbing between toes III and IV extending to about level of subarticular tubercles
. . . .*Eleutherodactylus* sp. (*rugulosus* group) (fig. 29)
33. No inner tarsal fold; a tarsal tubercle about a third of the distance from the inner metatarsal tubercle to the heel; small frogs (<32 mm SVL)
. . . .*Eleutherodactylus rhodopis* (fig. 27)
A well-developed inner tarsal fold extending about half the length of the tarsus 34
34. No dark face mask usually present, but usually a dark subocular spot and often a dark canthal stripe; usually lacking a triangular dark anal patch; large frogs (males > 40 mm in SVL, females > 65 mm SVL)
. . . .*Eleutherodactylus laticeps* (fig. 25)
Dark face mask usually present; usually having a distinctive triangular dark anal patch; smaller frogs (males < 27 mm in SVL, females < 39 mm SVL) . . . .*Eleutherodactylus chac* (fig. 24)

CLAVE PARA LAS ESPECIES DE SAPOS Y RANAS

1. Cuerpo casi redondo en vista dorsal; dorso oscuro con línea vertebral y
   puntos laterales de color rojizo pálido o algunas veces amarillos;
   cabeza pequeña y extremidades cortas; pata trasera con 4 dedos;
   parte interior de la pata trasera con 2 tubérculos distintivos en
   forma de pala . . . .*Rhinophrynus dorsalis* (fig. 22)
   Forma del cuerpo y color variable; pata trasera con 5 dedos;
   pata trasera sin tubérculos en forma de pala 2
2. Con glándula parotoidea conspicua al lado del cuello y posterior
   al ojo; piel seca y verrugosa 3
   Sin glandulas parotoideas; piel puede ser suave o con tubérculos,
   pero usualmete humeda al tacto 6
3. Dorso de la cabeza sin crestas craniales; sapillo pequeño (< 35 mm)
   . . . .*Physalaemus pustulosus* (fig. 32)
   Dorso de la cabeza con crestas craniales; sapos grandes,
   usualmente > 35 mm (verdaderos sapos) 4
4. Glándula parotoidea enorme, por lo menos 3 o 4 veces el tamaño del párpado
   superior; sin hilera prominente de tubérculos laterales, pero si estas se
   encuentran presentes, sus tubérculos no son mas elevados que los del
   dorso; cresta cranial sin espolón parietal . . . .*Bufo marinus* (fig. 35)
   Glándula parotoidea mas pequeña, usualmente del tamaño del párpado
   superior; con línea lateral prominente de tubérculos cónicos agrandados
   extendiendose desde la parte posterior de la glándula parotoidea hasta la
   ingle; cresta cranial incluyendo un espolón parietal 5

5. Patas largas, tibia mas del 45 porciento del largo entre el hocico y la
cloaca; ancho del tímpano menor que la mitad del ancho orbital;
crestas craniales en forma de aristas angostas; crestas preorbitales
y pretimpánicas ausentes o poco desarrolladas . . .*Bufo campbelli* (fig. 34)
Patas mas cortas, tibia menor del 45 porciento del largo entre el
hocico y la cloaca; ancho del tímpano mayor que la midad del
ancho orbital; crestas craniales no finas, con pequeñas borlas y
contornos redondos; crestas preorbital y pretimpática bién
desarrolladas . . . .*Bufo valliceps* (fig. 36)
6. Pequeñas ranas gordas de cabeza puntiaguda y delgada; con un pliegue
transversal distinctivo en la parte dorsal de la cabeza inmediatamente
detrás del nivel en que se encuentran los ojos (ranas microhylidas) 7
Forma del cuerpo y cabeza variable; sin un pliege transversal en la
parte dorsal de la cabeza inmediatamente detrás del nivel en que se
encuentran los ojos 8
7. Dorso pardusco o café-gríseo sin una linea pálida dorsovertebral distintiva;
dedos de los pies sin ninguna membrana interdigital; punta de los dedos
de los piesligeramente expandidos; adultos usualmente menos de 25 mm
de largo hocico–cloaca . . . .*Gastrophryne elegans* (fig. 52)
Dorso anaranjado o café-rojizo con una linea pálida dorsovertebral
dintintinva; dedos de los pies con membrana basal; punta de los
dedos de los pies no expandidos; adultos mas de 30 mm de largo
hocico–cloaca . . . .*Hypopachus variolosus* (fig. 53)
8. Membrana entre los dos dedos exteriores del pie (dedos IV–V) relativamente
prominente, añadiendose al dedo externo del pie no mas profundamente
que la mitad entre los tubérculos próximal y distal 9
Membrana entre los dos dedos exteriores del pie (dedos IV–V)
ausente o reducida a un punto por debajo de la mitad entre los
tubérculos próximal y distal del dedo externo (ranas leptodactylidas)   26
9. Puntas de los dedos de los pies y las manos expandidas formando discos
bién definidos; sin aristas dorsolaterales; membrana entre los dedos
de los pies moderada a extensa (ranas arborícolas y de vidrio) 10
Punta de los dedos no expandida en forma de disco; con aristas
dorsolaterales conspicuas; membrana entre los dedos de los pies
extensa (ranas verdaderas) 23
10. Vientre cubierto por piel transparente; rana pequeña de color verde
pálido . . . .*Hyalinobatrachium fleischmanni* (fig. 37)
Vientre cubierto por piel opaca; tamaño y color variable 11
11. Lados de la cabeza con vuelillo . . . .*Triprion petasatus* (fig. 51)
Sin modificaciones al lado de la cabeza 12

12. Piel en el dorso glandular, con muchos tubérculos grandes esparcidos
......................................*Phrynohyas venulosa* (fig. 46)
  Piel en el dorso lisa con pocos o ningún tubérculo 13
13. Pupila del ojo vertical, ranas verdes con superficies ocultas de colores
  brillantes 14
  Pupila del ojo horizontal 15
14. Ojos rojo brillante; flancos azulados con barras verticales amarillas
  o color crema ....*Agalychnis callidryas* (fig. 38)
  Ojos parecen negros (en luz brillante morado oscuro);
  flancos anaranjados ....*Agalychnis moreletii* (fig. 39)
15. Una membrana axilar distintiva en el brazo extendiéndose casi
  hasta el codo 16
  Membrana axilar ausente o pobremente desarrollada 17
16. Dorso variable, usualmente color café-bronce a café-rojizo con ligero
  moteado o veteado oscuro; superficies ocultas de las extremidades
  traseras color naranja brillante ....*Hyla loquax* (fig. 42)
  Dorso color amarillo o canela amarillenta, usualmente con patrón
  café oscuro bién definido; superficies ocultas de las extremidades
  traseras en su mayor parte amarillentas o un color naranja pálida
  ....*Hyla ebraccata* (fig. 41)
17. Hocico puntiagudo y prominente; marcas longitudinales oscuras en el
  dorso, barras transversales en las canillas; ranas pequeñas (< 32 mm
  de longitud de cuerpo) ....*Scinax staufferi* (fig. 47)
  Hocico truncado o ampliamente redondeado; patrón variable
  en tamaño y color 18
18. Ranas pequeñas (> 30 mm de longitud de cuerpo); dorso amarillento
  con o sin vetas o jaspeaduras más oscuras 19
  Ranas más grandes (longitud del cuerpo de 45 mm o más; dorso
  variable, a menudo con manchas grandes oscuras 21
19. Dorso usualmente con patrón oscuro en forma de X o reticular
  ....*Hyla microcephala* (fig. 43)
  Dorso usualmente inmaculado o solamente con vetas oscuras 20
20. Una raya oscura, con borde pálido arriba, extendiéndose posteriormente
  desde el ojo a los lados ....*Hyla picta* (fig. 44)
  Sin raya oscura que se extiende posteriormente desde
  el ojo ....*Hyla bromeliacia* (fig. 40)
21. La orilla exterior del tarso con una serie de tubérculos cónicos; manos
  más de tres cuartas partes con membrana; piel del dorso tuberculada;
  patrón dorsal como liquen; piel arriba de la cabeza co-osificada con
  el cráneo en adultos ....*Hyla valancifer* (fig. 45)

Orilla exterior del tarso liso; manos menos de un tercio con membrana; piel del dorso lisa; patrón dorsal de manchas o unicolor; piel arriba de la cabeza no co-osificada con el cráneo 22

22. La superficie posterior del muslo con manchas azules; lados del cuerpo, especialmente en la parte posterior, con reticulación fina de color negro; labio superior con margen pálido . . . .*Smilisca cyanosticta* (fig. 50)
Superficie posterior del muslo usualmente oscuramente moteada o unicolor; los lados del cuerpo usualmente con manchas; labio superior con mancha distintiva (pálida u oscura) justo abajo del ojo . . . . *Smilisca baudinii* (figs. 48–49)

23. Patrón dorsal entre aristas dorsolaterales usualmente una doble serie de manchas grandes (éstas son algunas veces irregulares o ausentes); piel no denticulada; la punta de los dedos no expandida
. . . .*Rana berlandieri* (fig. 54)
Patrón dorsal entre aristas dorsolaterales usualmente de pequeñas manchas oscuras esparcidas, especialmente en la parte posterior, o coloreado uniformemente; piel denticulada; la punta de los dedos expandida 24

24. Tímpano grande (más grande que el diámetro del ojo); sin máscara facial notable; sin raya supralabial notable . . . .*Rana vaillanti* (fig. 57)
Tímpano pequeño (menor que el diámetro del ojo); con máscara oscura; con raya supralabial pálida 25

25. Tímpano casi tan grande como el ojo; sacos y hendiduras vocales ausentes en los machos adultos; habitan las Montañas Maya
. . . .*Rana juliani* (fig. 55)
Tímpano como la mitad o menos del diámetro del ojo; sacos y hendiduras vocales presentes en machos adultos; habitan las montañas de Alta Verapáz y oriente de Guatemala . . . .*Rana maculata* (fig. 56)

26. Piernas cortas, segmento de la tibia no más largo que la distancia de la punta del hocico al nivel de inserción del miembro delantero; la punta distal de los dígitos no expandida 27
Piernas más largas, segmento tibial más largo que la distancia de la punta del hocico al nivel de inserción del miembro delantero; la punta distal de los dígitos expandida o no 28

27. Dedos de pie con flequillos dérmicos laterales extendiéndose hacia abajo; machos con dos espinas queratinizadas en el dedo pulgar
. . . .*Leptodactylus melanonotus* (fig. 31)
Dedos de pie sin flequillos dérmicos laterales; machos sin espinas queratinizadas en el dedo pulgar . . . .*Leptodactylus labialis* (fig. 30)

28. Ranas pequeñas (usualmente < 28 mm de longitud de cuerpo); no tienen pliegue o tubérculo proximal en el tarso; puntas de los dedos de las manos expandidas 1.5–4 veces el ancho del dígito 29

Ranas más grandes (usualmente > 28 mm de longitud de cuerpo); con pliegue o tubérculo proximal en el tarso; puntas de los dedos de las manos expandidas o no 30

29. Puntas de los dedos de las manos expandidos no más de como 1.5 veces el ancho del dígito; dientes vomerinos ausentes; patrón dorsal verdoso con motas o reticulaciones negras . . . .*Syrrhophus leprus* (fig. 33)
Puntas de los dedos de las manos expandidas como 3–4 veces el ancho del dígito; con dientes vomerinos; patrón dorsal café con motas café oscuro . . . .*Eleutherodactylus alfredi* (fig. 23)

30. Puntas de los dedos de las manos expandidos por lo menos 1.5–2 veces el ancho del dígito 31
Puntas de los dedos de las manos algunas veces ligeramente anchas, pero como del mismo ancho que el dígito 33

31. La piel que cubre la parte baja del vientre con numerosos melanóforos os-curos; la piel del dorso rugosa con muchos tubérculos grandes; membrana entre los dedos II y IV de los pies no extendiéndose a nivel del tubérculo subaticular proximal . . . .*Eleutherodactylus psephosypharus* (fig. 26)
La piel que cubre la parte baja del vientre sin pigmentación; la piel del dorso con muchos tubérculos pequeños diseminados, pero sin rugosidad notable; membrana entre los dedos III y IV de los pies extendiéndose hasta o mas alla del nivel de los tubérculos subarticulares proximales 32

32. Miembros traseros relativamente cortos, talón llegando como al nivel del ojo; membrana entre los dedos III y IV de los pies se extiende mas alla de los tubérculos subarticulares proximales
. . . .*Eleutherodactylus sandersoni* (fig. 28)
Miembros traseros relativamente largos, talón alcanzando un nivel cer-cano a la punta del hocico; membrana entre los dedos III y IV de los pies se extienden hasta el nivel de los tubérculos subarticulares
. . . .*Eleutherodactylus* sp. (rugulosus group) (fig. 29)

33. Sin pliegue tarsal proximal; un tubérculo tarsal como una tercera parte de la distancia entre el tubérculo metatarsal proximal y el talón; ranas pe-queñas (< 32 mm SVL) . . . .*Eleutherodactylus rhodopis* (fig. 27)
Con pliegue tarsal proximal bién desarrollado extendiéndose como a la mitad del largo del tarso; tamaño variable 34

34. Usualmente sin máscara oscura, pero usualmente con una mancha oscura subocular y a menudo una banda oscura cantal; usualmente sin mancha triangular oscura cloacal distintiva; ranas grandes (machos > 40 mm de longitud de cuerpo, hembras > 65 mm) .*Eleutherodactylus laticeps* (fig. 25)
Usualmente con máscara oscura; usualmente con mancha cloacal triangu-lar oscura bién definida; ranas pequeñas (machos < 27 mm en de longitud de cuerpo, hembras < 39 mm) . . . .*Eleutherodactylus chac* (fig. 24)

Appendix D

KEY TO SPECIES OF TURTLES AND CROCODILIANS

1. Body encased by a shell; no teeth on jaws (turtles) .3
   Body not encased by a shell; teeth present on jaws 2
2. Width of snout at level of tenth maxillary tooth ≥ 75 percent of distance
   from base of tenth maxillary tooth to tip of snout; primary caudal
   whorls of scales interrupted ventrally by incomplete secondary whorls
   . . . .*Crocodylus moreletii* (figs. 188–189)
   Width of snout at level of tenth maxillary tooth ≤ 70 percent of distance
   from base of tenth maxillary tooth to tip of snout; no secondary caudal
   whorls of scales, primary caudal whorls usually in contact ventrally
   . . . .*Crocodylus acutus* (figs. 186–187)
3. Plastron hinged, capable of closing tightly against carapace (mud turtles) . .4
   Plastron without hinges 6
4. Tenth marginal scute considerably higher than supracaudal scute
   . . . .*Kinosternon scorpioides* (fig. 63)
   Tenth marginal and supracaudal scutes about the same height 5
5. Anterior lobe of plastron not longer than middle section of plastron
   . . . .*Kinosternon acutum* (fig. 61)
   Anterior lobe of plastron longer than middle section of plastron
   . . . .*Kinosternon leucostomum* (fig. 62)
6. At least four inframarginal scutes present; jaws margins serrated; seams
   between scutes on carapace absent in adults
   . . . .*Dermatemys mawii* (figs. 64–65)
   No inframarginal scutes; jaw margins not serrated; seams between
   scutes on carapace 7

7. Plastron cruciform and comprising 8–10 scutes 8

    Plastron more or less ovate, comprising 12 scutes (pond and tropical wood turtles) 10

8. Posterior edge of carapace strongly serrate; tail long, more than half the length of carapace (snapping turtle) .... *Chelydra serpentina* (fig. 58)

    Posterior edge of carapace rounded and smooth; tail short, much less than half the length of carapace (musk turtles) 9

9. Three high keels on carapace; plastron and carapace separated by a bridge of scutes; top of head dark gray with white spots or mottling .... *Staurotypus triporcatus* (fig. 60)

    Keels on carapace, if present, not strongly developed; plastron and carapace separated by a bridge of ligament; top of head dark without pale markings .... *Claudius angustatus* (fig. 59)

10. Ventral surfaces of neck and hind limbs with longitudinal pale and dark stripes; toes widely separated with a well-developed web .... *Trachemys scripta* (figs. 66–67)

    Ventral surfaces of neck and hind limbs immaculate yellow or with a little dark spotting; toes narrowly separated with little webbing .... *Rhinoclemmys areolata* (fig. 68–69)

CLAVE PARA LAS ESPECIES DE TORTUGAS Y COCODRILOS

1. Cuerpo cubierto por una caparazón; sin dientes en las mandíbulas
   (tortugas) 3
   Cuerpo sin caparazón; con dientes en las mandíbulas 2
2. Ancho del hocico a nivel del décimo diente maxilar ≥ 75 porciento de la
   distancia desde el base del décimo diente maxilar a la punta del
   hocico; anillos primarios de escamas caudales interrumpidos
   ventralmente por anillos segundarios de escamas incompletos
   . . . . *Crocodylus moreletii* (figs. 188–189)
   Ancho del hocico a nivel del décimo diente maxilar ≤ 70 porciento de la
   distancia desde el base del décimo diente maxilar a la punta del hocico;
   sin anillos segundarios de escamas caudales, anillos primarios usualmente en contacto ventralmente . . . . . . *Crocodylus acutus* (figs. 186–187)
3. Plastrón articulado, capaz de cerrarse apretadamente contra el carapacho
   (pochitoques) 4
   Plastrón inarticulado 6
4. Décimo escudo marginal considerablemente más alto que el escudo
   supracaudal . . . . *Kinosternon scorpioides* (fig. 63)
   Escudos décimo marginal y supracaudal como a la misma altura 5
5. Lóbulo anterior del plastrón no más largo que la sección media del
   plastrón . . . . *Kinosternon acutum* (fig. 61)
   Lóbulo anterior del plastrón más largo que la sección media del
   plastrón . . . . *Kinosternon leucostomum* (fig. 62)
6. Con por lo menos cuatro escudos inframarginales; margenes de la
   boca serrados; sin suturas entre los escudos del carapacho en
   adultos . . . . *Dermatemys mawii* (figs. 64–65)

Sin escudos inframarginales; margenes de la boca no serrados; con suturas entre los escudos del carapacho 7

7. Plastrón cruciforme y compuesto de 8–10 escudos 8

Plastrón más o menos aovado, compuesto de 12 escudos (tortugas de laguna y de bosque tropical) 10

8. Orilla posterior del carapacho fuertemente aserrada; cola larga, más de la mitad de la longitud del carapacho (zambundango)
........................*Chelydra serpentina* (fig. 58)

Orilla posterior del carapacho redondeado y liso; cola corta, mucho menor que la mitad del largo del carapacho (chiquiguao y guao) 9

9. Tres quillas altas en el carapacho; plastrón y carapacho separados por un puente compuesto de escudos; parte superior de la cabeza color gris oscuro con manchas o motas blancas ....*Staurotypus triporcatus* (fig. 60)

Quillas en el carapacho, si presentes, no fuertemente desarrolladas; plastrón y carapacho separados por un puente compuesto de un ligamento; parte superior de la cabeza oscura sin marcas pálidas
........................*Claudius angustatus* (fig. 59)

10. Superficies ventrales del cuello y patas traseras con rayas longitudinales pálidas y oscuras; dedos de los pies ampliamente separados, con una membrana bién desarrollada ....*Trachemys scripta* (figs. 66–67)

Superficies ventrales del cuello y patas traseras color amarillo impecable o con pequeñas manchas oscuras; dedos poco separados, con pequeña membrana ....*Rhinoclemmys areolata* (figs. 68–69)

Appendix E

KEY TO SPECIES OF LIZARDS

1. No moveable eyelids 2
   Moveable eyelids present 6
2. Top of head covered with large, smooth plates; subdigital scales not ex-
   panded (night lizards) 3
   Top of head covered with granular scales; one or more subdigital scales
   expanded (geckos, in part) 4
3. Belly with a dark checkerboard pattern; enlarged tubercular scales on sides
   of body evenly arranged in vertical series, separated from each other by
   no more than 1–2 granular scales . . . .*Lepidophyma mayae* (fig. 75)
   Belly without a distinctive pattern; enlarged tubercular scales on sides of
   body irregularly arranged in vertical series, separated from each other by
   2–3 or more granular scales . . . . . .*Lepidophyma flavimaculatum* (fig. 74)
4. A double series of enlarged subdigital scales; adults > 60 mm SVL
   . . . .*Thecadactylus rapicaudus* (fig. 73)
   A single terminal expanded subdigital scale (bark geckos);
   adults < 35 mm SVL 5
5. Dorsal scales flat and smooth . . . .*Sphaerodactylus glaucus* (fig. 71)
   Dorsal scales granular and keeled
   . . . .*Sphaerodactylus millepunctatus* (fig. 72)
6. Belly covered with large, rectangular scales; snout acutely pointed (ameivas
   and whiptails) 7
   Belly covered with granular, cycloid, or sharply pointed scales; snout
   acutely pointed or not 11
7. A single row of enlarged antebrachial scales on upper arm (ameivas) 8

Three or more rows of enlarged antebrachial scales on upper arm
(whiptails) 10
8. Median gular scales not conspicuously enlarged, or if so, grading gradually
into smaller gular scales . . . .*Ameiva undulata* (figs. 107–108)
Median gular scales distinctly and abruptly enlarged 9
9. Two interparietal scales . . . .*Ameiva chaitzami*
A single interparietal scale . . . .*Ameiva festiva* (fig. 106)
10. Supraoculars usually 4 . . . .*Cnemidophorus angusticeps* (fig. 109)
Supraoculars usually 3 . . . .*Cnemidophorus maslini* (fig. 110)
11. Cycloid scales covering dorsum and venter 12
Dorsum and venter not covered with cycloid scales 16
12. Frontonasal scales paired . . . .*Diploglossus rozellae* (fig. 111)
Frontonasal scale single (skinks) 13
13. No supranasal scales; a single frontoparietal *Sphenomorphus cherriei* (fig. 105)
Supranasal scales present; two frontoparietals .14
14. Lower eyelid with a transparent disc; scales between eye and ear about
the same size as dorsal scales . . . .*Mabuya brachypoda* (fig. 104)
Lower eyelid without transparent disc; scales between eye and ear
larger than dorsal scales 15
15. Middorsal scales much broader than those of adjacent regions on
back . . . .*Eumeces schwartzei* (figs. 100–101)
Middorsal scales about the same size as those of adjacent regions
on back . . . .*Eumeces sumichrasti* (figs. 102–103)
16. A distinctive dorsal crest or casque on back of head and neck 17
No dorsal crest on back of head and neck 21
17. A horizontally flattened head casque 18
A vertically projecting crest on back of head and neck 19
18. Posterior margin of head casque without a fringe of spinelike scales;
middorsal scales not enlarged . . . .*Laemanctus longipes* (fig. 94)
Posterior margin of head casque fringed with spinelike scales;
middorsal scale row enlarged, forming a serrate dorsal crest
. . . .*Laemanctus serratus* (fig. 95)
19. A pair of distinctive pale dorsolateral stripes on body; dorsal margin
of head crest in adults (small in females) supported by cartilage,
flexible . . . .*Basiliscus vittatus* (figs. 90–91)
No dorsolateral stripes on body; dorsal margin of head crest
supported by bone, rigid 20
20. Posterior margin of head crest incised and not continuous with body
crest; a sharply protruding temporal spine above tympanum
. . . .*Corytophanes hernandezii* (fig. 93)

Posterior margin of head crest relatively straight and continuous
with body crest; no temporal spine above tympanum
. . . .*Corytophanes cristatus* (fig. 92)
21. A distinctive middorsal row of spinelike scales (iguanas) 22
    Middorsal scales enlarged or not but never spinelike 23
22. Greenish, yellow, or orange in color; an enlarged scale on side of head;
    scales on side of tail about the same in size . . . . . .*Iguana iguana* (fig. 89)
    Gray to brownish in color; no enlarged scale on side of head; tail
    with whorls of enlarged scales separated by whorls of smaller scales
    . . . .*Ctenosaura similis* (fig. 88)
23. Pupils vertical; dorsal scales consisting of regularly spaced large tubercular
    scales surrounded by smaller granular scales; a distinctive U-shaped
    band extending posteriorly from eyes and across back of head
    . . . .*Coleonyx elegans* (fig. 70)
    Pupils round; dorsal scales not tuberculate and no U-shaped band
    on head 24
24. Femoral pores absent; dewlap present, small in females; lateral body
    scales granular and non-imbricate (anoles) 25
    Femoral pores present; dewlap absent; lateral body scales pointed
    and imbricate (spiny lizards) 33
25. Shank relatively long and snout short; length of tibia longer than distance
    from tip of snout to ear . . . .*Norops capito* (fig. 80)
    Shank short and snout usually more elongate; length of tibia equal to or
    shorter than distance from tip of snout to ear .26
26. Scales covering belly and chest smooth, or only weakly keeled on chest 27
    Scales covering belly and chest distinctly keeled 28
27. Shank shorter than distance from tip of snout to posterior edge of eye
    . . . .*Norops beckeri* (fig. 76)
    Shank longer than distance from tip of snout to posterior edge of eye
    . . . .*Norops rodriguezi* (fig. 81)
28. Longitudinal rows of enlarged dorsal scales 8–12, these scales abruptly
    differentiated from scales on sides of body 29
    Enlarged rows of dorsal scales, if present, limited to 2–4 longitudinal
    rows and grading into laterals 30
29. Shank about as long as distance from tip of snout to ear
    . . . .*Norops tropidonotus* (fig. 85)
    Shank shorter than distance from tip of snout to ear
    . . . .*Norops uniformis* (figs. 86–87)
30. Usually 6 or more enlarged dorsal scales grading into laterals
    . . . .*Norops sericeus* (figs. 83–84)
    Enlarged dorsal scales, if present, confined to 2–4 middorsal rows 31

31. Tail laterally compressed; middorsal scale rows of tail enlarged and
forming a low crest ....*Norops sagrei* (fig. 82)
Tail round or ovoid in cross section; middorsal scale rows of tail not
enlarged or forming a low crest 32
32. Shank equal to or barely exceeding distance from tip of snout to posterior
edge of eye ....*Norops biporcatus* (fig. 77)
Shank greatly exceeding distance from tip of snout to posterior edge
of eye ....*Norops bourgeaei* (figs. 78–79)
33. Postfemoral dermal pocket present ....*Sceloporus teapensis* (fig. 99)
No postfemoral dermal pocket 34
34. Dorsal pattern of dorsolateral pale stripes *Sceloporus chrysostictus* (fig. 96)
Dorsal pattern without dorsolateral pale stripes 35
35. No dark nuchal collar ....*Sceloporus lundelli* (fig. 97)
A pale-bordered black nuchal collar present ...*Sceloporus serrifer* (fig. 98)

CLAVE PARA LAS ESPECIES DE LAGARTIJAS

7. Una sola fila de escamas antebraquiales agrandadas en el parte superior del brazo (ameivas) 8
   Tres o más filas de escamas antebraquiales agrandadas en el parte superior del bazo (murishcas) 10
8. Escamas gulares que están situado en medio no conspicuamente agrandadas, o si las tienen, disminuyen en tamaño gradualmente hacia los lados . . . .*Ameiva undulata* (figs. 107–108)
   Escamas gulares que están situado en medio distintiva y abruptamente agrandadas 9
9. Dos escamas interparietales . . . .*Ameiva chaitzami*
   Una única escama interparietal . . . .*Ameiva festiva* (fig. 106)
10. Usualmente 4 supraoculares . . . .*Cnemidophorus angusticeps* (fig. 109)
    Usualmente 3 supraoculares . . . .*Cnemidophorus maslini* (fig. 110)
11. Escamas cicloides cubriendo el dorso y el vientre 12
    Dorso y vientre no cubierto con escamas cicloides 16
12. Escamas frontonasales apareadas . . . .*Diploglossus rozellae* (fig. 111)
    Escama frontonasal unica (salamanquezas) 13
13. Sin escamas supranasales; una unica frontoparietal . . . .*Sphenomorphus cherriei* (fig. 105)
    Escamas supranasales presentes; dos frontoparietales 14
14. Párpado inferior con un disco transparente; escamas entre el ojo y el oído como del mismo tamaño que las escamas dorsales . . . .*Mabuya brachypoda* (fig. 104)
    Párpado inferior sin disco transparente; escamas entre el ojo y el oído más grandes que las escamas dorsales 15
15. Escamas vertebrales mucho más anchas que las de regiones adyacentes en el dorso . . . .*Eumeces schwartzei* (figs. 100–101)
    Escamas vertebrales como del mismo tamaño que las de las regiones adyacentes en el dorso . . . .*Eumeces sumichrasti* (figs. 102–103)
16. Cresta o casco dorsal distintivo atrás de la cabeza y el cuello 17
    Sin cresta dorsal atrás de la cabeza y el cuello 21
17. Cabeza con casco horizontal aplanado 18
    Cresta que se proyecta verticalmente atrás de la cabeza y el cuello 19
18. Margen posterior del casco de la cabeza sin borde de escamas que parecen espinas; escamas dorsovertebrales no agrandadas . . . .*Laemanctus longipes* (fig. 94)
    Margen posterior del casco de la cabeza con borde de escamas con apariencia de espinas; hilera de escamas dorsovertebrales agrandadas, formando una cresta dorsal aserrada . . . .*Laemanctus serratus* (fig. 95)

19. Rayas pálidas dorsolaterales en el cuerpo; margen dorsal de la cresta de la cabeza sostenida por cartílago, flexible ...*Basiliscus vittatus* (figs. 90–91)
    Sin rayas dorsolaterales en el cuerpo; margen dorsal de la cresta de la cabeza sostenida por hueso, rígido 20
20. Margen posterior de la cresta de la cabeza con incisión y sin continuidad con la cresta del cuerpo; con espina temporal aguda arriba del tímpano ....*Corytophanes hernandezii* (fig. 93)
    Margen posterior de la cresta de la cabeza más o menos recta y con continuidad con la cresta del cuerpo; sin espina temporal arriba del tímpano ....*Corytophanes cristatus* (fig. 92)
21. Hilera dorsovertebral distintiva de escamas con apariencia de espinas (iguanas) 22
    Escamas agrandadas dorsovertebrales presentes o no, pero nunca con apariencia de espinas 23
22. Verde, amarillla naranjo; con una escama agrandada a un lado de la cabeza; escamas a los lados de la cola como del mismo tamaño ....*Iguana iguana* (fig. 89)
    Color de gris o pardo castaño; sin escama agrandada al lado de la cabeza; cola con anillos formados de escamas agrandadas separados por anillos de escamas más pequeñas ....*Ctenosaura similis* (fig. 88)
23. Pupilas verticales; dorso consistente de escamas tuberculares espaciadas regularmente y rodeadas por escamas menores granulares; una banda distintiva en forma de U extendiéndose posteriormente desde los ojos y a través de la parte de atrás de la cabeza ....*Coleonyx elegans* (fig. 70)
    Pupilas redondas; escamas dorsales no son tuberculares y sin una banda en forma de U en la cabeza 24
24. Poros femorales ausentes; abaniquillo (saco gular) presente, pequeño en las hembras; escamas laterales del cuerpo granulares y no imbricadas (abaniquillos) 25
    Poros femorales presentes; abaniquillo ausente; escamas laterales del cuerpo puntiagudas e .. imbricadas (lagartijas espinozas) 33
25. Canilla relativamente larga y hocico corto; largo de la tibia mayor que la distancia de la punta del hocico al oído ....*Norops capito* (fig. 80)
    Canilla corta y hocico usualmente más largo; largo de la tibia igual o más corto que la distancia desde la punta del hocico al oído 26
26. Escamas que cubren el abdomen y pecho son lisas o aquilladas debilmente sobre el pecho 27
    Escamas cubriendo el abdomen y pecho distintivamente aquilladas ...28
27. Canilla más corta que la distancia entre la punta del hocico y la orilla posterior del ojo ....*Norops beckeri* (fig. 76)

Canilla más larga que la distancia de la punta del hocico y la orilla posterior del ojo . . . .*Norops rodriguezi* (fig. 81)

28. Filas longitudinales de escamas dorsales agrandadas ocho a doce, abruptamente diferenciadas de las escamas de los lados del cuerpo 29

    Filas ensanchadas de escamas dorsales, si presentes, limitadas a 2–4 filas longitudinales que disminuyen gradualmente en tamaño hacia los lados 30

29. Canilla como del largo de la distancia entre la punta del hocico y el oído . . . .*Norops tropidonotus* (fig. 85)

    Canilla más corta que la distancia entre la punta del hocico y el oído . . . .*Norops uniformis* (figs. 86–87)

30. Usualmente seis o más escamas dorsales agrandadas disminuyendo gradualmente en tamaño hacia los lados . . . .*Norops sericeus* (figs. 83–84)

    Escamas dorsales agrandadas, si presentes, limitadas a dos o cuatro filas dorso-vertebrales 31

31. Cola comprimida lateralmente; filas de escamas dorso-medias de la cola agrandadas y formando una pequeña cresta . . . .*Norops sagrei* (fig. 82)

    Cola redonda u ovoide en sección transversal; filas de escamas dorso-medias de la cola no agrandadas ni formando una pequeña cresta 32

32. Canilla igual o escasamente excediendo la distancia desde la punta del hocico a la orilla posterior del ojo . . . .*Norops biporcatus* (fig. 77)

    Canilla excediendo grandemente la distancia desde la punta del hocico a la orilla posterior del ojo . . . .*Norops bourgeaei* (figs. 78–79)

33. Bolsa dermal postfemoral presente . . . .*Sceloporus teapensis* (fig. 99)

    Sin bolsa dermal postfemoral 34

34. Patrón dorsal de rayas pálidas dorsolaterales . . . .*Sceloporus chrysostictus* (fig. 96)

    Patrón dorsal sin rayas pálidas dorsolaterales .35

35. Sin collar nucal . . . .*Sceloporus lundelli* (fig. 97)

    Con un collar negro marginado con blanco o amarillo . . . .*Sceloporus serrifer* (fig. 98)

Appendix F

KEY TO SPECIES OF SNAKES

1. Ventral scales about equal in size to dorsal scales; eyes vestigial (blind snakes and thread snakes) 2
   Ventral scales enlarged, straplike; eyes not vestigial 3
2. Dorsal scale rows at midbody 14 ....*Leptotyphlops goudotii* (fig. 113)
   Dorsal scale rows at midbody 18 ....*Typhlops microstomus* (fig. 112)
3. No loreal pit 4
   A loreal pit present 63
4. Midbody dorsal scale rows more than 30 5
   Midbody dorsal scale rows fewer than 30 8
5. Dorsum of head covered by small scales 6
   Dorsum of head covered by large plates 7
6. Body pattern of dark dorsal saddles (present also in juveniles); moderately robust body; fewer than 70 subcaudals ....*Boa constrictor* (fig. 114)
   Body pattern of dark lateral ocelli (juveniles may be uniformly orange); slender body; more than 70 subcaudals .....*Corallus annulatus* (fig. 115)
7. Dorsal blotches reddish; usually 9 supralabials ....*Elaphe flavirufa* (fig. 132)
   Dorsal blotches, if present, grayish to tan; usually 8 supralabials
   ....*Senticolis triaspis* (fig. 151)
8. Number of dorsal scale rows about one head length anterior to vent at least two less than number at midbody 9
   Number of dorsal scale rows unreduced between midbody and level about one head length anterior to vent 36
9. An even number of dorsal scale rows at midbody (dorsal scale row formula usually 18–14); black with diagonal yellow markings
   ....*Spilotes pullatus* (figs. 156–157)

An odd number of dorsal scale rows at midbody; color pattern not black
with diagonal yellow markings 10
10. Head very narrow, snout strongly acuminate 11
     Head narrow or not, snout blunt or rounded 12
11. Mostly brown; dorsal scales mostly smooth, except for a few posterior
     middorsal scales, which may be very weakly keeled
     . . . .*Oxybelis aeneus* (fig. 144)
          Mostly green; middorsal scales keeled . . . .*Oxybelis fulgidus* (fig. 145)
12. Anal scale divided 13
     Anal scale entire 28
13. Dorsal scales keeled, at least on back 14
     Dorsal scales smooth 17
14. Dorsal scale rows more than 15 at midbody 15
     Number of dorsal scale rows at midbody 15, reduced to 11 posteriorly . .16
15. Dorsal scale row formula 21–17; a broad, dark, lateral stripe
     . . . .*Tretanorhinus nigroluteus* (fig. 170)
          Dorsal scale row formula 17–15; turquoise with orange or yellow spots on
          most of dorsal scales . . . .*Drymobius margaritiferus* (fig. 131)
16. More or less uniformly green; loreal absent . .*Leptophis ahaetulla* (fig. 139)
     Body with distinct lateral stripes; loreal present
     . . . .*Leptophis mexicanus* (fig. 140)
17. Dorsal scale rows 17 18
     Dorsal scale rows more than 17 20
18. No presubocular below preocular . . . . .*Dryadophis melanolomus* (fig. 129)
     Small presubocular below preocular 19
19. Ventrals more than 180 . . . .*Masticophis mentovarius* (fig. 141)
     Ventrals fewer than 180 . . . .*Coluber constrictor* (fig. 119)
20. Pupil a vertical slit; body pattern spotted or with large blotches 21
     Pupil round or a broad ellipse; body pattern striped, unicolor, or
     blotched 22
21. Dorsal scale row formula 23–17; postocular stripe, if present, poorly defined
     and not merging with first dorsal blotch . .*Leptodeira polysticta* (fig. 138)
     Dorsal scale row formula 21–15; dark postocular stripe merging with first
     dorsal blotch . . . .*Leptodeira frenata* (fig. 137)
22. Body pattern blotched or banded; dorsal scales arranged in oblique rows
     . . . .*Xenodon rabdocephalus* (fig. 171)
          Body pattern striped or unicolor 23
23. Temporals 2 + 3 . . . .*Conophis lineatus* (fig. 125)
     Temporals 1 + 2 24
24. Dorsal scale rows 23 or 25 at midbody . . . .*Coniophanes schmidti* (fig. 124)
     Dorsal scale rows 21 or fewer 25

25. Dorsal scale rows 19 . . . .*Coniophanes imperialis* (fig. 122)
    Dorsal scale rows 21 26
26. Spotting on venter, if present, consisting of small punctations
    . . . .*Coniophanes fissidens* (fig. 121)
    A series of large, bold, dark spots on lateral portions of ventrals 27
27. Ventrals fewer than 150 . . . .*Coniophanes bipunctatus* (fig. 120)
    Ventrals more than 150 . . . .*Coniophanes quinquevittatus* (fig. 123)
28. Dorsal scales keeled, at least middorsally 29
    Dorsal scales smooth 33
29. Body pattern of stripes; 1 + 2 temporals 30
    Body pattern of crossbars or mottled, never striped; temporals variable   31
30. Dark vertical streaks on supralabials below eye
    . . . .*Thamnophis marcianus* (fig. 168)
    Supralabials without dark vertical streaks *Thamnophis proximus* (fig. 169)
31. Dorsal scale row formula 17–15 32
    Dorsal scale rows at midbody 23 or 25   . . .*Pseustes poecilonotus* (fig. 148)
32. Subcaudals more than 130; dark-edged pale crossbands on neck one-half
    scale row wide or less, or absent; venter with suffusions of dark pigment
    on ventral scales in adults . . . .*Dendrophidion nuchale* (fig. 126)
    Subcaudals fewer than 130; dark-edged pale crossbands on neck more
    than one-half scale row wide; venter immaculate white or pale yellow
    . . . .*Dendrophidion vinitor* (fig. 127)
33. Dorsal pattern of red and black rings or crossbands 34
    Dorsum mostly dark brown or black; if red, mostly unicolor
    with pale collar 35
34. Dorsal pattern of rings completely encircling the body; dorsal scale
    row formula 23–19 . . . .*Lampropeltis triangulum* (fig. 136)
    Dorsal pattern of crossbands on back and sides of body, venter white
    . . . .*Oxyrhopus petola* (fig. 146)
35. Dorsal scale row formula 17–15; dorsum brownish with small black mark-
    ings; a series of bold vertical or diagonal dark streaks extending from
    under or behind eye to margin of upper lip   . .*Drymarchon corais* (fig. 130)
    Dorsal scale row formula 19–17; in adults, dorsum uniformly black,
    venter immaculate; area along supralabial sutures often dark but no
    bold streaks on upper jaw (in juveniles, dorsum of body red, head black;
    in subadults, dorsum of body brown, head black) . . .*Clelia clelia* (fig. 118)
36. Anal plate entire 37
    Anal plate divided 43
37. Dorsal scale rows 19 throughout body 38
    Dorsal scale rows fewer than 19 throughout body 39

38. Dorsum of body dark gray; venter with one or two series of dark spots
. . . .*Ninia diademata* (fig. 142)
    Dorsum of body red, with or without darker spots or crossbands; venter
    mostly immaculate . . . .*Ninia sebae* (fig. 143)
39. Loreal present; dorsal scale rows 17 throughout body; dorsal scales weakly
    keeled posteriorly . . . .*Sibon sartorii* (fig. 55)
    No loreal; dorsal scale rows 15 throughout body; dorsal scales
    all smooth 40
40. First pair of infralabials not in contact with each other behind mental;
    usually one or two postmentals 41
    First pair of infralabials in contact with each other behind mental; no
    postmental 44
41. Ventrals 143–162, subcaudals 57–86 . . . .*Sibon sanniola* (fig. 154)
    Ventrals 160–206, subcaudals 95–144 . . . .*Sibon dimidiata* (fig. 152)
42. Body pattern of 9–15 alternating, sharply contrasting black and pink,
    orange, or white rings; pale rings usually immaculate
. . . .*Dipsas brevifacies* (fig. 128)
    Body pattern of more than 20 dark rings on a brownish or grayish
    background; rings may not be complete ventrally; background mottled
    or spotted with dark pigment . . . .*Sibon nebulata* (fig. 153)
43. Dorsal scale rows 15 throughout body 44
    Dorsal scale rows 17 throughout body 53
44. Body pattern of red, yellow, and black rings, or dorsum uniformly red; tail
    with only black and yellow rings; short front fangs 45
    Dorsum unicolored (never red), spotted, or striped; front teeth all about
    equal in size 47
45. Tip of snout uniformly black . . . .*Micrurus nigrocinctus* (fig. 176)
    Tip of snout pale 46
46. Red scales may be dusky, but not tipped or marked with black; 0–24
    black rings on body, some of these often incomplete dorsally
. . . .*Micrurus hippocrepis* (figs. 174–175)
    Red scales may be mottled with black, but not uniformly; black rings
    25 or more, these usually complete dorsally
. . . .*Micrurus diastema* (figs. 172–173)
47. One or two infralabials lateral to chinshields reduced in width and very nar-
    row, being confined to margin of lip *Adelphicos quadrivirgatus* (fig. 116)
    No infralabial reduced in width 48
48. Loreal present; tail long, with more than 100 subcaudals
. . . .*Symphimus mayae* (fig. 161)
    Loreal absent; tail shorter, fewer than 60 subcaudals 49

49. Distinctive pale spot on side of head behind eye; pale lateral stripes on
    body ....*Tantilla cuniculator* (fig. 162)
        No pale spot on side of head; no pale lateral stripes on body 50
50. Body and venter dark gray to black; a long pale collar on neck
    ....*Tantilla moesta* (fig. 163)
        Dorsum pale brown, venter pale yellow, pinkish, or tan; pale collar on
        neck present or not 51
51. A pale collar on back of head ....*Tantilla shistosa* (fig. 164)
        No pale collar on back of head 52
52. Ventrals more than 120; usually a pale vertebral stripe on tail
    ....*Tantillita canula* (fig. 166)
        Ventrals fewer than 120; no pale vertebral stripe on tail
    ....*Tantillita lintoni* (fig. 167)
53. Dorsal scales keeled throughout or on posterior part of body 54
        Dorsal scales smooth throughout 55
54. Loreal present; dorsal scales weakly keeled on posterior of body; 77–86
    subcaudals; dorsum usually dark gray to black
    ....*Amastridium veliferum* (fig. 117)
        Loreal absent; dorsal scales keeled throughout body; 40–53 subcaudals;
        dorsum tan, brownish, or orangish ....*Storeria dekayi* (fig. 160)
55. Rostral upturned and pointed in contact with frontal
    ....*Ficimia publia* (fig. 133)
        Rostral normal or slightly pointed, but not upturned or in contact
        with frontal 56
56. Body pattern consisting of red, yellow, and black rings or bands, at least
    anteriorly 57
        Body pattern of spots, blotches, stripes, or unicolor 58
57. Crossbands confined to anterior part of body (rarely on all of body); red
    bands bordered with black ....*Scaphiodontophis annulatus* (fig. 150)
        Rings throughout body; red rings bordered with yellow
    ....*Pliocercus elapoides* (fig. 147)
58. Body extremely gracile and attenuate; head much broader than neck; pupils
    vertical; ventrals more than 215, subcaudals more than 120 59
        Body more robust; head not much broader than neck; pupils round or
        subcircular; ventrals fewer than 215; subcaudals fewer than 120 60
59. Vertebral scales three to four times larger than adjacent scales; more than
    140 subcaudals ....*Imantodes cenchoa* (fig. 134)
        Vertebral scales less than three times the size of adjacent scales; fewer
        than 140 subcaudals ....*Imantodes gemmistratus* (fig. 135)
60. Tail relatively long with more than 50 subcaudals; a pale postocular streak 61

Tail relatively short with fewer than 50 subcaudals; no pale postocular
streak 62
61. Pale postocular streak extending from *upper* posterior border of orbit; no
nuchal collar; fewer than 135 ventrals; 2 postoculars
. . . .*Rhadinaea decorata* (fig. 149)
Pale postocular streak extending from *lower* posterior border or orbit;
nuchal collar present (interrupted middorsally); more than 135 ventrals;
a single postocular . . . .*Rhadinaea anachoreta*
62. Dorsal body pattern striped or unicolor; more than 160 ventrals
. . . .*Stenorrhina freminvillii* (fig. 159)
Dorsal body pattern spotted or mottled; fewer than 160 ventrals
. . . .*Stenorrhina degenhardtii* (fig. 158)
63. Tail terminating in a rattle or button . . . .*Crotalus durissus* (fig. 185)
Tail not terminating in a rattle or button 64
64. Dorsum of head covered with 9–15 mostly flat scales; distinctive pair of
yellow stripes on side of head . . . .*Agkistrodon bilineatus* (fig. 177)
Dorsum of head covered with more than 15 mostly keeled scales; pattern
on side of head not consisting of a pair of yellow stripes 65
65. Subcaudals mostly paired . . . .*Bothrops asper* (Figs. 182–183)
Subcaudals mostly single 66
66. Raised superciliary scales giving appearance of eyelashes; color pattern
greenish with reddish markings; arboreal, with prehensile tail
. . . .*Bothriechis schlegelii* (Figs. 180–181)
No superciliary scales; color pattern tan, brownish, or grayish; terrestrial,
without prehensile tail 67
67. Tip of snout strongly upturned, forming a free flap; supraoculars large and
well differentiated from other head scales; usually 7 or fewer intersupraoculars; body scales keeled, but not rugose; a pale middorsal line
. . . .*Porthidium nasutum* (fig. 184)
Tip of snout not strongly upturned; more than 9 scales between orbits;
body scales rugose; no pale middorsal line
. . . .*Atropoides nummifer* (figs. 178–179)

CLAVE PARA LAS ESPECIES DE SERPIENTES

1. Escamas ventrales como del mismo tamaño que las escamas dorsales; ojos vestigiales (serpientes ciegas) 2
   Escamas ventrales agrandadas, como bandas; ojos no vestigiales 3
2. Con 14 hileras de escamas dorsales a mitad del cuerpo
   . . . . *Leptotyphlops goudotii* (fig. 113)
   Con 18 hileras de escamas dorsales a mitad del cuerpo
   . . . . *Typhlops microstomus* (fig. 112)
3. Sin fosa loreal 4
   Con fosa loreal 63
4. Más de 30 hileras de escamas dorsales a mitad del cuerpo 5
   Menos de 30 hileras de escamas dorsales a mitad del cuerpo 8
5. Dorso de la cabeza cubierto de escamas pequeñas 6
   Dorso de la cabeza cubierto de placas grandes 7
6. Patrón del cuerpo de manchas oscuras en forma de monturas ecuestres (presentes también en los juveniles); cuerpo moderadamente robusto; menos de 70 subcaudales . . . . *Boa constrictor* (fig. 114)
   Patrón del cuerpo de ocelos laterales oscuros (juveniles pueden ser uniformemente color naranja); cuerpo delgado; con más de 70 subcaudales . . . . *Corallus annulatus* (fig. 115)
7. Manchas dorsales rojizas; usualmente 9 supralabiales *Elaphe flavirufa* (fig. 132)
   Manchas dorsales, si presentes, grisáceas a castañas; usualmente 8 supralabiales . . . . *Senticolis triaspis* (fig. 151)
8. Número de hileras de escamas dorsales como a una cabeza de distancia antes de la cloaca por lo menos dos menos que en el centro del cuerpo 9

Número de hileras de escamas dorsales no reducidas entre el centro del cuerpo y el nivel como a una cabeza de distancia antes de la cloaca 36

9. Con número par de hileras de escamas dorsales a mitad del cuerpo (fórmula de hileras de escamas dorsales usualmente 18–14); negra con marcas diagonales amarillas . . . .*Spilotes pullatus* (Figs. 156–157)
Con número impar de hileras de escamas dorsales a mitad del cuerpo; patrón no negra con marcas diagonales amarillas 10

10. Cabeza muy angosta, trompa fuertemente acuminada 11
Con cabeza angosta o no, trompa obtusa o ampliamente redondeada . . .12

11. Principalmente café; escamas dorsales en su mayor parte lisas, a excepción de unas pocas escamas posteriores dorso-medias que pueden ser debilmente aquilladas . . . .*Oxybelis aeneus* (fig. 144)
Principalmente verdes, escamas dorso-medias aquilladas
. . . .*Oxybelis fulgidus* (fig. 145)

12. Escama anal dividida 13
Escama anal entera 28

13. Escamas dorsales aquilladas, por lo menos atras 14
Escamas dorsales lisas 17

14. Hileras de escamas dorsales más de 15 a mitad del cuerpo 15
Número de hileras de escamas dorsales 15, reducidas a 11 posteriormente 16

15. Fórmula de hileras de escamas dorsales 21–17; con amplia y oscura raya lateral . . . .*Tretanorhinus nigroluteus* (fig. 170)
Fórmula de hileras de escamas dorsales 17–15; turquesa con manchas naranjas o amarillas en la mayoría de las escamas dorsales
. . . .*Drymobius margaritiferus* (fig. 131)

16. Más o menos uniformemente verde; loreal ausente
. . . .*Leptophis ahaetulla* (fig. 139)
Cuerpo con rayas laterales distintivas; loreal presente
. . . .*Leptophis mexicanus* (fig. 140)

17. Con 17 hileras de escamas dorsales 18
Con más de 17 hileras de escamas dorsales 20

18. Sin presubocular abajo de preocular . . . .*Dryadophis melanolomus* (fig. 129)
Pequeña presubocular abajo de preocular 19

19. Más de 180 ventrales . . . .*Masticophis mentovarius* (fig. 141)
Menos de 180 ventrales . . . .*Coluber constrictor* (fig. 119)

20. Pupila en forma de hendidura vertical; patrón del cuerpo moteado o con grandes manchas 21
Pupila redonda o como una elipse ancha; patrón del cuerpo rayado, unicolor o manchado 22

21. Fórmula de hileras de escamas dorsales 23–17; raya postocular, si presente, pobremente definida y no fusionandose con la primer mancha dorsal
. . . .*Leptodeira polysticta* (fig. 138)
Fórmula de hileras de escamas dorsales 21–15; raya postocular oscura, fusionandose con la primer mancha dorsal . . .*Leptodeira frenata* (fig. 137)
22. Patrón del cuerpo manchado o con franjas; escamas dorsales ordenadas en hileras oblicuas . . . .*Xenodon rabdocephalus* (fig. 171)
Patrón del cuerpo rayado o unicolor 23
23. Temporales 2 + 3 . . . .*Conophis lineatus* (fig. 125)
Temporales 1 + 2 24
24. Con 23 o 25 hileras de escamas dorsales a mitad del cuerpo
. . . .*Coniophanes schmidti* (fig. 124)
Con 21 o menos hileras de escamas dorsales 25
25. Con 19 hileras de escamas dorsales . . . . .*Coniophanes imperialis* (fig. 122)
Con 21 hileras de escamas dorsales 26
26. Vientre moteado consistente de finos puntos *Coniophanes fissidens* (fig. 121)
Una serie de manchas oscuras, grandes, bién delineadas en porciones laterales de las ventrales 27
27. Menos de 150 ventrales . . . .*Coniophanes bipunctatus* (fig. 120)
Más de 150 ventrales . . . .*Coniophanes quinquevittatus* (fig. 123)
28. Escamas dorsales aquilladas, por lo menos atras 29
Escamas dorsales lisas 33
29. Patrón de rayas en el cuerpo; 1 + 2 temporales 30
Patrón de barras transversales o motas en el cuerpo, nunca rayas; temporales variables 31
30. Jaspeado vertical oscuro en supralabiales abajo del ojo
. . . .*Thammophis marcianus* (fig. 168)
Supralabiales sin jaspeado vertical oscuro *Thammophis proximus* (fig. 169)
31. Fórmula de hilera de escamas dorsales 17–15 32
Con 23 o 25 hileras de escamas dorsales a mitad del cuerpo
. . . .*Pseustes poecilonotus* (fig. 148)
32. Más de 130 subcaudales; bandas transversales pálidas con borde oscuro en el cuello de media escama de ancho o menos, o ausentes; vientre con sufusiones de pigmento oscuro en las escamas ventrales, en adultos
. . . .*Dendrophidion nuchale* (fig. 126)
Menos de 130 subcaudales; bandas transversales pálidas con borde oscuro en el cuello de más de media escama de ancho; vientre inmaculadamente blanco o amarillo pálido . . . .*Dendrophidion vinitor* (fig. 127)
33. Patrón dorsal de anillos rojos y negros o bandas transversales de estos colores 34

Dorso principalmente café oscuro o negro; si es rojo, principalmente uni-
color con collar pálido 35

34. Patrón de anillos dorsales circundando completamente el cuerpo; fórmula
de hileras de escamas dorsales 23–19 . .*Lampropeltis triangulum* (fig. 136)
Patrón de bandas transversales en dorso y lados del cuerpo, vientre
blanco . . . .*Oxyrhopus petola* (fig. 146)

35. Fórmula de hileras de escamas dorsales 17–15; dorso pardusco castaño
con pequeñas marcas negras; con una serie de jaspeados verticales o
diagonales oscuros bién definidos extendiéndose desde debajo o atrás
del ojo hasta el margen del labio superior . . .*Drymarchon corais* (fig. 130)
Fórmula de hileras de escamas dorales 19–17; adultos con el dorso
uniformemente negro, vientre inmaculado; área a lo largo de las
suturas supralabiales a menudo oscura, pero sin jaspeado definido
en la mandíbula superior (en juveniles, dorso rojo, cabeza negra; en
subadultos, dorso café oscuro, cabeza negra) . . . .*Clelia clelia* (fig. 118)

36. Placa anal entera 37
Placa anal dividida 43

37. Con 19 hileras de escamas dorsales a lo largo del cuerpo 38
Con menos de 19 hileras de escamas dorsales a lo largo del cuerpo 39

38. Dorso del cuerpo gris oscuro; vientre con una o dos series de manchas
oscuras . . . .*Ninia diademata* (fig. 142)
Dorso del cuerpo rojo, con o sin manchas o bandas transversales más
oscuras; vientre mayormente inmaculado . . . .*Ninia sebae* (fig. 143)

39. Loreal presente; 17 hileras de escamas dorsales a lo largo del cuerpo;
escamas dorsales debilmente aquilladas posteriormente
. . . .*Sibon sartorii* (fig. 155)
Sin loreal; 15 hileras de escamas dorsales a lo largo del cuerpo; escamas
dorsales todas lisas 40

40. Primer par de infralabiales no hacen contacto entre si atrás de la escama
mental; usualmente una o dos postmentales 41
Primer par de infralabiales en contacto entre si atrás de la escama mental;
sin postmental 42

41. Con 143–162 ventrales y 57–86 subcaudales . . . . . .*Sibon sanniola* (fig. 154)
Con 160–206 ventrales y 95–144 subcaudales . .*Sibon dimidiata* (fig. 152)

42. Patrón del cuerpo de 9–16 anillos contrastantes alternados, negro con
rosado, naranja o blanco; los anillo pálidos usualmente inmaculados
. . . .*Dipsas brevifacies* (fig. 128)
Patrón del cuerpo de más de 20 anillos oscuros sobre fondo pardusco
castaño o grisáceo, los anillos pueden ser incompletos en el vientre; fondo
moteado o manchado con pigmento oscuro . . . . .*Sibon nebulata* (fig. 153)

43. Con 15 hileras de escamas dorsales a lo largo del cuerpo 44
   Con 17 hileras de escamas dorsales a lo largo del cuerpo 53
44. Patrón del cuerpo de anillos rojos, amarillos, y negros, o dorso
   uniformemente rojo; cola solamente con anillos negros y amarillos;
   colmillos delanteros cortos 45
   Dorso unicolor (nunca rojo), manchado, o rayado; dientes delanteros casi
   todos del mismo tamaño 47
45. Punta del hocico uniformemente negro . . . .*Micrurus nigrocinctus* (fig. 176)
   Punta del hocico pálido 46
46. Escamas rojas pueden ser negruzcas, pero sin puntas o marcas negras; 0–24
   anillos negros en el cuerpo, algunos de ellos a menudo incompletos
   dorsalmente . . . .*Micrurus hippocrepis* (figs. 174–175)
   Escamas rojas pueden ser moteadas con negro, pero no uniformemente; 25
   o más anillos negros en el cuerpo, estos usualmente completos
   dorsalmente . . . .*Micrurus diastema* (figs. 172–173)
47. Una o dos infralabiales laterales a escudos de la barbilla reducidas en ancho
   y muy angostas, estando limitadas al margen del labio
   . . . .*Adelphicos quadrivirgatus* (fig. 116)
   Sin infralabial reducida en ancho 48
48. Loreal presente; cola larga, con más de 100 subcaudales
   . . . .*Symphimus mayae* (fig. 161)
   Loreal ausente; cola más corta, menos de 60 subcaudales 49
49. Mancha pálida distintiva al lado de la cabeza y atrás del ojo; rayas pálidas
   laterales en el cuerpo . . . .*Tantilla cuniculator* (fig. 162)
   Sin mancha pálida al lado de la cabeza; sin rayas pálidas laterales en el
   cuerpo 50
50. Cuerpo y vientre gris oscuro a negro; con collar ancho y pálido en el cuello
   . . . .*Tantilla moesta* (fig. 163)
   Dorso café claro, vientre amarillo claro, rosado, o canela; con o sin collar
   pálido en el cuello 51
51. Collar pálido atrás de la cabeza . . . .*Tantilla shistosa* (fig. 164)
   Sin collar pálido atrás de la cabeza 52
52. Más de 120 ventrales; usualmente una raya vertebral pálida en la cola
   . . . .*Tantillita canula* (fig. 166)
   Menos de 120 ventrales; sin raya vertebral pálida en la cola
   . . . .*Tantillita lintoni* (fig. 167)
53. Escamas dorsales aquilladas a lo largo de o en la parte posterior
   del cuerpo 54
   Escamas dorsales lisas a lo largo del cuerpo .55
54. Escama loreal presente; escamas dorsales debilmente aquilladas en la parte

posterior del cuerpo; 77–86 subcaudales; dorso gris oscuro o negro
. . . .*Amastridium veliferum* (fig. 117)
Sin escama loreal; escamas dorsales aquilladas en todo el cuerpo;
40–53 subcaudales; dorso color de canela, café, o anaranjado
. . . .*Storeria dekayi* (fig. 160)
55. Rostral doblada hacia arriba y puntiaguda, en contacto con frontal
. . . .*Ficimia publia* (fig. 133)
Rostral normal o ligeramente puntiaguda, pero no doblada hacia arriba o
en contacto con frontal 56
56. Patrón del cuerpo consistente de anillos o bandas rojas, amarillas y negras,
por lo menos anteriormente 57
Patrón del cuerpo con manchas redondas o irregulares, rayas, o unicolor
. 58
57. Bandas transversales confinadas a la parte anterior del cuerpo (rara vez a lo
largo de todo el cuerpo); bandas rojas con borde negro
. . . .*Scaphiodontophis annulatus* (fig. 150)
Anillos a lo largo de todo el cuerpo; anillos rojos con borde amarillo
. . . .*Pliocercus elapoides* (fig. 147)
58. Cuerpo extremadamente delgado; cabeza mucho más ancha que el cuello;
pupilas verticales; más de 215 ventrales, más de 120 subcaudales 59
Cuerpo más robusto; cabeza no mucho más ancha que el cuello; pupilas
redondas; menos de 215 ventrales; menos de 120 subcudales 60
59. Escamas vertebrales tres o cuatro veces más grandes que las escamas
adyacentes; más de 140 subcaudales . . . .*Imantodes cenchoa* (fig. 134)
Escamas vertebrales menos de tres veces el tamaño de las escamas adyacentes; menos de 140 subcaudales . . . .*Imantodes gemmistratus* (fig. 135)
60. Cola relativamente larga, con más de 50 subcaudales; con una lista pálida
postocular 61
Cola relativamente corta, con menos de 50 subcudales; sin una lista pálida
postocular 62
61. Una lista pálida postocular extendiendose desde la parte *superior* del
margen posterior del ojo; sin collar nucal; menos de 135 ventrales; 2
postoculares . . . .*Rhadinaea decorata* (fig. 149)
Una lista pálida postocular extendiendose desde la parte *inferior* del
margen posterior del ojo; con un collar nucal; más de 135 ventrales; 1
postoculare . . . .*Rhadinaea anachoreta*
62. Patrón dorsal del cuerpo rayado o unicolor; más de 160 ventrales
. . . .*Stenorrhina freminvillii* (fig. 159)
Patrón dorsal del cuerpo manchado o moteado; menos de 160 ventrales
. . . .*Stenorrhina degenhardtii* (fig. 158)

63. Cola terminada en cascabel o botón . . . .*Crotalus durissus* (fig. 185)
    Cola no terminada en cascabel o botón 64
64. Dorso de la cabeza cubierto con 9–15 escamas, la mayoría lisas; con par de
    rayas amarillas al lado de la cabeza . . . . .*Agkistrodon bilineatus* (fig. 177)
    Dorso de la cabeza cubierto con más de 15 escamas, la mayoría aquilladas;
    sin un par de rayas amarillas al lado de la cabeza 65
65. Subcaudales principalmente en pares . . . .*Bothrops asper* (figs. 182–183)
    Subcaudales principalmente individuales 66
66. Escamas superciliares elevadas dando la apariencia de pestañas; patrón de
    color verdoso con marcas rojizas; arborícola, con cola prensil
    . . . .*Bothriechis schlegelii* (figs. 180–181)
    Sin escamas superciliares; patrón del color canela, pardusco castaño o
    grisáceo; terrestre, sin cola prensil 67
67. La punta del hocico fuertemente volteada hacia arriba; supraoculares
    grandes y bién diferenciadas de otras escmas de la cabeza; usualmente
    7 o menos intersupraoculares; escamas del cuerpo aquilladas, pero no
    rugosas; una linea pálida dorso-vertebral . .*Porthidium nasutum* (fig. 184)
    Punta del hocico no fuertemente volteada hacia arriba; más de 9 escamas
    entre las orbitas; escamas del cuerpo rugosas; sin una línea pálida
    dorso-vertebral . . . .*Atropoides nummifer* (figs. 178–179)

GLOSSARY

Acahual.—An area consisting mostly of low brush or scrubby trees, usually secondary growth, associated with savanna regions.

Acuminate.—Pointed.

Adpressed limbs.—In salamanders or lizards, the forelimb is folded posteriorly and the hind limb is folded anteriorly and the limbs are held closely against the body. The number of scales or costal grooves or the amount of overlaps that are present between adpressed limbs are diagnostic characters useful in recognizing certain species.

Aglyph.—A snake with dentition consisting of a series of teeth of subequal size attached to the maxillary bone; there are no conspicuously enlarged fanglike teeth.

Aguada.—A shallow surface depression that may be a permanent pond of water or may become mostly dry during the dry season

Akalché.—A low-lying region usually covered with low forest (15–20 m in height) and becoming seasonally flooded but drying out in the dry season.

Allantois.—The extraembryonic membrane of reptiles, birds, and mammals that develops as an outgrowth of the hindgut; it serves for respiration and excretion in reptiles.

Allopatric.—Living apart; two species for which distributions do not overlap at any geographical point are said to be allopatric.

Amnion.—The extraembryonic membrane of reptiles, birds, and mammals that surrounds the embryo in a sac of fluid.

Amplexus.—The sexual embrace of anurans.

Anal.—The ventrally located plate immediately preceding the vent. In snakes, it is larger than other scales of the ventral series and may be single or divided by a diagonal suture. This scale is not included in the ventral series.

Annuli (primary and secondary).—Applied to caecilians, meaning the series of integumentary grooves that encircle the body; primary annuli completely encircle the body, whereas secondary annuli only partially encircle it.

Antebrachial.—Scales lying on the anterior surface of the forelimb. The upper antebrachials are located on the upper arm.

Anuran.—The order of amphibians (Anura) that contains frogs and toads.

Apical.—At the apex or tip.

Arboreal.—Inhabiting trees.

Auricular.—Pertaining to the ear.

Autotomy.—Tail breakage; many lizards are able to break their tails by convulsive contractions of the tail muscles.

Axilla.—The cavity beneath the junction of the forelimb and shoulder; the armpit.

Axillary.—Pertaining to the armpit; some turtles may have a scale referred to by this name in the axillary region; during axillary amplexus, male anurans grasp females just behind the forelimbs.

Bajo.—A relatively large *Akalché* (see definition) or low-lying region.

Band.—An element of color pattern that is darker or paler than the ground color and that runs transversly across the middorsum but does not completely encircle the body (see also *Ring*). Synonymous with crossband.

Bicarinate.—Having two keels.

Bicho.—In Guatemala, a general term that is used for any small animal; as in "critter."

Blotch.—A discrete area that differs from the ground color, being either darker or paler; that is generally as long as or longer than it is wide; and that is not transversely widened to form a band or ring.

Button.—The first and smallest permanent rattle segment acquired by a young rattlesnake. As a rattlesnake matures, the button usually breaks off. At birth rattlesnakes possess a prebutton, which is lost at the time of the first shedding, exposing the button.

Canthal.—Referring to an area or scale lying between the supraocular and the rostral, where the dorsum of the snout turns downward on the side. The *canthus rostralis* is delimited as a sharp ridge in some snakes, such as the barba amarilla (*Bothrops asper*).

Capitalino.—A person from a capital city, such as Guatemala City.

Carapace.—The dorsal part of the shell in turtles.

Casque.—A process or structure suggestive of a helmet. Frogs of the genus *Triprion* are commonly called casque-headed treefrogs and lizards of the genus *Laemanctus* are commonly referred to as casqueheaded basilisks in allusion to the distinctive shape and structure of the heads of these species.

Chinshield.—A large, elongate scale lying directly behind the first pair of infralabials along either side of the midline on the ventral surface of the head in most snakes. Chinshields are always arranged in pairs, a single pair being most frequent.

Chorion.—The outermost extraembryonic membrane of reptiles, birds, and mammals.

Cleidoic egg.—The self-contained egg of most reptiles and all birds, in which a free larval stage is absent.

Cloaca.—The posterior chamber of amphibians and reptiles, into which the digestive tract and urogenital passages open.

Colubrid.—A snake in the family Colubridae. Most members of this family are considered harmless, although many species have enlarged teeth on the rear of the maxilla (opisthoglyphic dentition) and a few Guatemalan species produce a venom capable of causing swelling and discomfort in humans.

Co-ossified.—The fusion of two bony elements.

Costal groove.—One of the vertical grooves on the side of a salamander's body.

Cranial crest.—Any of the raised, bony ridges on the top or side of the head in many toads (Bufonidae).

Crepuscular.—Active in the twilight.

Cruciform.—Shaped in the form of a cross.

Cycloid.—In relation to scales, with a rounded posterior end.

Denticulate.—With reference to amphibian skin, having a rough, sandpapery feel and covered with numrous small, sharp, keratinous projections. Examples of anurans having a denticulate skin are certain bufonids and ranids.

Dermal.—Relating to the skin; or superficial bones that lie in or just beneath the skin and develop by the direct deposition of bone in connective tissue (e.g., the osteoderms of some lizards and crocodilians).

Dewlap.—A laterally compressed fold of skin at the throat. In adult male anoles the dewlap is extensible and usually brightly colored; that of females is usually smaller and duller in color.

Disc.—The flat, circular, platelike expansion on the tips of the digits. Many anurans, such as most hylids, have distinctive discs on their fingers and toes.

Dimorphic.—Occurring in two distinct forms.

Disjunct.—Discontinuous or separated.

Distal.—Pertaining to a part of the body that is farther removed from the center of the body than some other part.

Diurnal.—Active by day.

Dorsolateral ridge.—The glandular ridge extending from behind the eye down the dorsolateral surface of the body of some frogs, such as many ranids.

Dorsal scale rows.—The number of longitudinal scale rows, exclusive of the enlarged ventral series, encircling the body of a snake at a certain point. Often counts are made at three points along a snake's body: a head's length behind the head, at midbody, and a head's length in front of the vent. A dorsal scale formula (e.g., 23–21–19) reflects these three counts, respectively. Numbers in parentheses, as in 17(15)–15(17)–15(13), indicate variability.

Dorsum.—The upper surface of an animal or part of an animal.

Emarginate.—Pertaining to a margin that is notched or scalloped in outline.

Endemic.—Confined to; occurring nowhere except the place in question.

Epidermal.—Relating to the epithelial layer that forms the surface of the skin.

Epidermal lamellae.—The large plates covering the shell of turtles; sometimes also referred to as scutes or shields.

Epiphyte.—A plant such as an orchid or bromeliad that grows on a tree.

Extirpate.—To destroy totally; to wipe out locally.

Face mask.—Present when the side of the head below the canthus through the eye to the tympanum is conspicuously darkened and sharply delimited from more dorsal coloration. A face mask is present in many leptodactylid and some ranid frogs.

Fang.—Any hollow or grooved tooth borne on the maxillary bone in snakes that is longer than other teeth and functions in the conduction of venom. Both coral snakes and vipers have hollow, hypodermic-like fangs, whereas some colubrids have grooved, enlarged teeth on the posterior of the maxillary that are sometimes referred to as "rear fangs."

Fecundity.—The potential reproductive capacity as measured by the individual production of eggs or offspring.

Femoral pore.—A pit or hole in about the center of a single scale on the ventral surface of the thigh in many species of lizards. Femoral pores usually occur in a single linear series for at least part of the length of the thigh.

Foramen.—A small opening or perforation.

Fossorial.—Adapted to digging or living below ground.

Frontal.—The region or scale lying on top of the head between the eyes

Frontonasal.—Scale(s) in lizards located on top of the head between the internasals and prefrontals.

Ground color.—The color between the various elements of pattern; the background color.

Gular.—Pertaining to the throat region or ventral surface of the neck; or a scale in this region not having other designations.

Hemipenis.—One of the pair of copulatory organs in male snakes or lizards; when retracted they lie ventrolaterally in the base of the tail. *Hemipenes* (plural) tend to be ornate, with spines and calyces, thereby providing useful taxonomic characteristics.

Homodont.—A kind of dentition in which the teeth are fundamentally similar in shape and usually in size.

Hybridization.—The act or process of two different species interbreeding with each other.

Hypertrophied.—The excessive development of a part.

Imbricate.—Overlapping, as the shingles of a roof. Used in reference to the scales in reptiles that have their posterior margins overlapping adjacent scales.

Infralabials.—A series of scales along the lip of the lower jaw exclusive of the anterior median mental.

Inframarginal.—In turtles, a scute lying between the marginals of the carapace and the lateral margin of the plastral scutes.

Inguinal.—Pertaining to the groin; some turtles may have a scale referred to by this name in the inguinal region; during inguinal amplexus, male anurans grasp females just before the hind limbs.

Inner metatarsal tubercle.—A large tubercle on the sole of the hind foot at the base of the first digit.

Inner tarsal fold.—A distinct ridge or fold of skin extending along the inner tarsus in many frogs.

Intercalary cartilage.—A cartilaginous element located between the ultimate and penultimate phalanges in the digits of several frog families, including Hylidae and Centrolenidae.

Internasal.—The scales or plates in snakes and lizards that extend across the top of the front of the snout between the prenasals and make contact with the prenasals and/or the rostral. Most frequently there are two internasals in snakes.

Interparietal.—A medial scale lying on the back of the head between the parietal scales in lizards.

Interspecific.—Between different species.

Intraspecific.—Between individuals of the same species.

Karst.—A limestone region marked by sinks and interspersed with abrupt ridges, irregular protuberant rocks, caverns, and underground streams.

Keeled.—With reference to scales, a median ridge; the ridge may or may not extend to the tip of the scale. The carapace of some species of turtles may have one or more prominent ridges, also called keels.

Kekchí.—The Mayan language of the Kekchí people of north-central Guatemala (also sometimes spelled Quekchí).

Keratin.—A horny protein synthesized by the epidermal cells of many vertebrates. The outer layer of skin in reptiles consists mainly of keratin.

Lacunolabial.—The single large scale that is formed in some pitvipers from the fusion of the prelacunal and the second supralabial.

Lateral.—Pertaining to a postion away from the midline of the body.

Law of Priority.—The scientific name of a particular oganism shall be the name proposed by Linnaeus in *Systema Naturae*, 10th edition (1758), or the first name proposed after that date.

Lichenose (also Lichenous).—Resembling lichens, such as certain color patterns with irregular and diffuse blotches or mottling.

Loreal.—The region or scales lying on the side of the head between the nasal and preocular regions. In snakes, there is much variation in the location and number of scales in this region. In Coral snakes, loreals are absent; most vipers have at least one per side; and colubrids are variable.

Loreal Pit.—A deep depression on the side of the head of pitvipers. The pit is located behind the nostril and in front of the eye, but most of it lies below a line drawn from the nostril to the center of the eye. The loreal pit is the external opening of an extremely sensitive infrared-detecting organ.

Marginal.—In turtles, one of a series of scutes forming the outer edge of the carapace, visible from above and below.

Marginal teeth.—In certain tadpoles, the short toothrows lateral to the beaks.

Maxillary.—One of the principal bones of the upper jaw in amphibians and reptiles. The maxillary usually bears teeth.

Medial (also Median).—Pertaining to a position toward the midline of the body.

Melanophore.—A pigment cell that contains a dark brown or black melanin.

Mental.—The median triangular scale at the anterior edge of the lower jaw in snakes in lizards; this scale is bordered on both sides by the first infralabials.

Mesic.—Characterized by a moderate to great amount of moisture.

Mesoptychial.—The scales between the pregular and gular folds, or, in the absence of a pregular fold, immediately preceding the gular fold.

Metachrosis.—The ability to change color.

Microsympatric.—The co-occurrence of two or more species in the same geographical region and also the same specific habitat.

Monotypic.—Consisting of a single species or taxon. For example, the family Dermatemydidae is monotypic because there is only one species in the family, the Central American river turtle (*Dermatemys mawii*).

Montane.—Relating to a mountain or mountainous region.

Mottled.—Marked with many spots or blotches that often run together.

Mucronate.—Terminating in a sharp spine.

Nape.—The dorsal part of the neck. In snakes, this term generally refers to the part of the neck just behind the head and may be used as an adjective (e.g., nape blotch).

Naris.—An external nostril; plural = nares.

Nasolabial groove.—The groove extending from the lower margin of the external naris to the edge of the upper lip in plethodontid salamanders.

Nocturnal.—Active at night.

Norte.—A cold front that arrives in Middle America during the Northern Hemisphere winter months.

Ocellus.—An eyelike spot.

Occiput.—The back part of the head.

Ontogenetic.—Relating to the course of development of an individual organism.

Opisthoglyph.—A snake in which the dentition includes several enlarged, often grooved, teeth on the posterior of the maxillary.

Osteoderm.—A small dermal bone that is located under the epidermal scales of certain lizards and crocodilians.

Oviparous.—Producing eggs that hatch outside of the maternal body.

Palmar.—The ventral surface of the forefoot; the palm of the hand.

Palpebral.—Relating to the eyelids.

Parotoid gland.—A large glandular area lying behind the eye on the side of the neck. This gland is present in Guatemalan species of toads (*Bufo*) and the Túngara frog (*Physalaemus pustulosus*).

Paraventrals.—The lowermost row of dorsal scales; the scales composing the longitudinal series situated on either side of the ventrals. The paraventrals are usually slightly larger than the scales more dorsally located. In snakes in which most of the dorsal scales are keeled, the paraventrals are usually smooth or weakly keeled. Paraventral also refers to the area on either side of the ventrals.

Paravertebral.—Lying to either side of the vertebral line; often used in reference to the rows of dorsal scales on either side of the vertebral row.

Parietal.—The region or scales located on the back of the head posterior to the frontal and supraocular region. Snakes typically have a single pair of large scales in this region.

Parthenogenesis.—A kind of reproduction that involves the development of offspring (all female) without fertilization by a male parent. The Maslin's whiptail (*Cnemidophorus maslini*) is a species consisting of only females that reproduce parthenogenetically.

Phragmosis.—The act of plugging the entrance to a burrow or hole by using a body part. This body part is usually specifically adapted for this use and is bony or has spines. The Yucatán casque-headed treefrog (*Triprion petasatus*) is thought to block the entrance to tree holes by using the bony casque on the top of its head.

Pineal eye.—A light-sensitive "third" eye present in some lizards; it is medially located on the back of the head.

Placenta.—The structure through which exchanges between mother and embryo occur.

Plantar.—The ventral part of the hind foot (e.g., the sole of the foot).

Plastron.—The ventral part of the shell in turtles.

Plate.—Large, usually flat scales; typically used in reference to the enlarged scales on top of the head or on the belly in lizards or snakes.

Pole.—Either of two morphologically or physiologically differentiated areas that are opposite ends of an axis of an egg during the early stages of development.

Pollex.—The first or innermost digit on the hand; the thumb is a pollex.

Postanal spur.—One of the large tubercular scales found dorsolateral to and usually slightly behind the vent in males of some lizard species.

Postfemoral dermal pocket.—A shallow pocket formed by the skin on the posterior of the thigh at the point where the thigh joins the body; this pocket is present in some spiny lizards.

Postocular.—The region or scales lying behind the eye.

Postorbital.—Behind the eye.

Prefrontal.—The region or scales on top of the snout behind the internasals and in front of the frontal scale(s) or region. In squamates, the scales in this region may be paired and meet at the midline or may be fragmented into numerous smaller scales, including the canthals and intercanthals.

Prehensile.—Adapted for seizing by wrapping around; arboreal snakes often have a prehensile tail.

Preocular.—The scale(s) or region bordering the anterior margin of the eye.

Proteroglyph.—A snake with dentition consisting of fangs attached to a relatively immobile maxillary bone that is located in the front of the mouth. At rest, the fangs are not folded against the roof of the mouth.

Proximal.—Pertaining to a part of the body that is closer to the center of the body than is some other part.

Punctate.—Marked with small spots; dotted.

Ramus.—The right or left half or the lower jaw.

Ring.—An element of pattern consisting of a solid color that completely encircles the body. Rings have been described as broad, wide, narrow, short, or long; because of their orientation around the long axis of the body, it is preferable to use the last two terms. The term annulus can be synonymous with ring.

Rostral.—The region covering the anterior tip of the snout; in snakes or lizards this is the median scale in that area.

Rugose.—Covered with wrinkles or tubercles.

Sacral.—Relating to the region near the sacral vertebrae (e.g., those that articulate with the pelvic girdle).

Scansorial.—Adapted for climbing.

Scute.—A large scale; sometime also referred to as a plate, lamella, lamina, or shield.

Serrate.—Resembling the teeth of a saw.

Shank.—A lower sement of the hind leg of a frog or lizard, extending from the knee for the length of the tibia and fibula or tibio-fibula (if fused).

Sinistral.—Relating to the left side.

Snout-vent length.—See *SVL*.

Solenoglyph.—A snake with dentition consisting of fangs attached to a relatively mobile maxillary bone that is located in the front of the mouth. At rest, the fangs are folded against the roof of the mouth.

Spermatophore.—A packet of sperm deposited by male salamanders.

Spiracle.—A small opening to the outside from the gill chamber in anuran tadpoles.

Splenial.—One of the dermal bones of the lower jaw in some vertebrates, including caecilians.

Squamate.—Any member of the order of reptiles, Squamata, containing lizards and snakes.

Squamosal.—A cranial bone located on the posterior part of the side of the head.

Striated.—Marked with many minute parallel grooves or channels.

Striped.—Marked with streaks or lines that are parallel to the long axis of the body.

Subarticular.—Located below the joint between two of the bony phalanges.

Subcaudal.—The region or scales lying on the ventral side of the tail. In snakes, subcaudal scales extend from immediately behind the anal plate to (but not including) the tail spine. In some snakes these scales are entire (undivided), whereas in other species they are paired (divided).

Subequal.—Approximately but not exactly equal.

Superciliary.—Any one in a small series of scales lying above the eye and along the outer edge of the supraocular. In the eyelash palm-pitviper (*Bothriechis schlegelii*), some of these scales are raised into spinelike projections.

Supra-anal keels.—Well-developed keels on the scales covering the lateral portion of the body above the vent. These keels occur in certain species of coral snakes and colubrids. Typically, supra-anal keels occur only in males, however, in some species large females also develop keels in this region. Sometimes called supra-anal tubercles.

Supra-anal tubercles.—See Supra-anal keels.

Supralabials.—The series of scales along the lip of the upper jaw, exclusive of the anterior median rostral.

Supranasal.—Pertaining to the region or scale(s) lying above the nares or nasal scales.

Supraocular.—The region or scale lying on top of the head over either eye. In snakes, usually there is a single large plate on either side.

Suprascapular.—That part of the dorsum lying above the scapula; the shoulder region.

SVL.—Abbreviation for snout-vent length. This measurement is taken from the anterior surface of the snout to the posterior edge of the vent or, in the case of lizards and snakes, the anal scale.

Sympatric.—Coexistent; two species living in the same general region are said to be sympatric.

Symphysis.—A joint between bones that permits limited movement.

Tarsus.—The segment of the hind limb lying just distal to the tibia and fibula (or tibio-fibula, if these bones are fused) and the metatarsus.

Temporal.—The region or scales lying behind the postoculars, above the supralabials or mouth, and below the parietal region. In snakes, the temporals are often arranged in several vertical rows, including the primary and secondary temporals, according to their location. The notation 1 + 2 indicates that a snake has 1 primary and 2 secondary temporals on each side of the head.

Tentacle.—In caecilians, the chemosensory protrusible structure lying somewhere between and below the level of the eye and the naris.

Terrestrial.—Adapted for life on the surface of the ground.

Tessellated.—Having a checkered appearance.

Tetrapod.—All vertebrates above fishes, i.e. amphibians, reptiles, birds, and mammals. Most tetrapods are characterized by four limbs but a few, such as snakes, have secondarily lost these appendages.

Thecodont.—A type of dentition where teeth are rooted in sockets in the jaw.

Thigh.—The proximal segment of the tetrapod hind limb, extending from the hip to the knee and supported by a single long bone, the femur.

Tienda.—A small store.

TL.—Abbreviation for total length; the distance from the tip of the snout to the tip of the tail.

Total length.—See *TL*.

Truncate.—Blunt or square at the end.

Tubercle.—A small, discrete bump or knob on the skin. Most anurans have a distinctive, large inner metatarsal tubercle on the inner side of the hind foot; in the case of the Middle American burrowing toad (*Rhinophrynus dorsalis*), there are two of these tubercles. Some lizards have distinctive knoblike scales that are referred to as tubercular.

Tympanum.—The eardrum.

Unicarinate.—Having one keel.

Vent.—The posterior cloacal aperture.

Venter.—The undersurface of an animal.

Ventral.—Pertaining to the undersurface or scales on the undersurface of an animal. In snakes, there is a series of large, transversely elongated plates on the belly extending from the neck to the anal plate.

Vermiform.—Referring to bodyform, having a wormlike shape; referring to color pattern, a number of wavy or wormlike markings.

Versant.—The side of a mountain range or slope of a region.

Vestigial.—A small and degenerate bodily part that remains from one more fully developed in an earlier state of the individual or of evolution.

Vicariance.—The disruption of a taxon's continuous geographic range owing to the formation of a barrier.

Viviparous.—Producing living young instead of eggs from within the maternal body.

Vomerine teeth.—With reference to amphibians, the teeth that are located on posterior ventral part of the vomer, a paired dermal palatal bone; this bone is perhaps more appropriately considered the "prevomer" rather than the vomer.

Whorl.—A single series of scales encircling the tail in lizards.

Xeric.—Characterized by a low amount of moisture.

Yolk Sac.—The yolk-containing sac attached to the ventral surface of vertebrate embryos.

REFERENCES

Abercrombie, C. L., C. A. Hope, J. M. Holms, D. Scott, and J. E. Lane. 1982. Investigations into the status of Morelet's crocodile (*Crocodylus moreletii*) in Belize, 1980. Pp. 11–27 in Proc. 5th Work. Meet. Croc. Spec. Group Species Surv. Comm. Intern. Union Cons. Nature Nat. Res. Conv., Florida St. Mus.

Ahl, E. 1930. Reptilia (Kriechetiere). Tabulae Biol. 6:625–715.

Alarcón-Pardo, H. 1978. Primer registro de *Tretanorhinus nigroluteus nigroluteus* Cope (Reptilia: Serpentes: Colubridae) para Colombia. Lozania 27:1–4.

Alberch, P. 1981. Convergence and parallelism in foot morphology in the neotropical salamander genus *Bolitoglossa*. I. Function. Evolution 35:84–100.

Allen, E. R. 1949. Observations on the feeding habits of the juvenile cantil. Copeia 1949:225–226.

Allen, E. R., and W. T. Neill. 1959. Doubtful locality records in British Honduras. Herpetologica 15:227–233.

Altig, R. 1987. Key to the anuran tadpoles of Mexico. Southwest. Nat. 32:75–84.

Alvarez del Toro, M. 1960. Los Reptiles de Chiapas. Tuxtla Gutiérrez, Chiapas, México, Instituto Zoológico del Estado. 204 pp. (2nd edition [1972] Gobierho del Estado, 178 pp.; 3rd edition [1983, dated 1982] Publicación del Instituto de Historia Natural, 248 pp.)

———. 1974. Los Crocodylia de México. Inst. Mex. Rec. Nat. Renov., México, D. F. 70 pp.

Alvarez del Toro, M., R. A. Mittermeier, and J. B. Iverson. 1979. River turtle in danger. Oryx 15:170–173.

Anderson, P. K. 1961. Variation in populations of brown snakes, genus *Storeria*, bordering the Gulf of Mexico. Am. Midl. Nat. 66:235–249.

Andrews, E. W. 1937. Notes on snakes from the Yucatan Peninsula. Field Mus. Nat. Hist., Zool. Ser. 20:355–359.

Andrews, R. M. 1979. The lizard *Corytophanes cristatus:* An extreme "sit-and-wait" predator. Biotropica 11: 136–139.

Antonio, F. B. 1980. Mating behavior and reproduction in the eyelash viper (*Bothrops schlegeli*) in captivity. Herpetologica 36:231–233.

Arnold, E. N. 1988. Caudal autotomy as a defense. Pp. 235–273 *in* C. Gans and R. B. Huey (eds.), Biology of the Reptilia, vol. 16, Ecology B: Defense and Life History. Alan R. Liss, New York.

Bailey, J. R. 1937. New forms of *Coniophanes* Hallowell, and the status of *Dromicus clavatus* Peters. Occas. Pap. Mus. Zool. Univ. Michigan 362:1–6.

———. 1939. A systematic revision of the snakes of the genus *Coniophanes.* Pap. Michigan Acad. Sci. Arts Let. 24:1–48.

———. 1940. The Mexican snakes of the genus *Rhadinaea.* Occas. Pap. Mus. Zool. Univ. Michigan 412:1–23.

Barbour, T., and G. K. Noble. 1915. A revision of the lizards of the genus *Ameiva.* Bull. Mus. Comp. Zool. 59:417–479.

Beargie, K., and C. J. McCoy, Jr. 1964. Variation and relationships of the teiid lizard *Cnemidophorus angusticeps.* Copeia 1964:561–570.

Beebe, W. 1944. Field notes on the lizards of Kartabo, British Guiana, and Caripito, Venezuela. Part 1: Gekkonidae. Zoologica 29:145–160.

Bezy, R. L. 1973. A new species of the genus *Lepidophyma* (Reptilia: Xantusiidae) from Guatemala. Contrib. Sci. Los Angeles Co. Mus. 239:1–7.

———. 1989a. Morphological differentiation in unisexual and bisexual xantusiid lizards of the genus *Lepidophyma* in Central America. Herpetol. Monogr. 3:61–80.

———. 1989b. Night lizards: The evolution of habitat specialists. Terra 28:29–34.

Blaney, R. M., and P. K. Blaney. 1978a. Notes on three species of *Micrurus* (Serpentes: Elapidae). Herpetol. Rev. 9:92.

———. 1978b. Additional specimens of *Amastridium veliferum* Cope (Serpentes: Colubridae) from Chiapas, México. Southwest. Nat. 23:692.

Bock, B. C. 1987. Life history notes: *Corytophanes cristatus,* nesting. Herp. Rev. 18:35.

Bohuslavek, J. 1996. *Ninia sebae sebae* (red coffee snake): Reproduction. Herp. Rev. 27:146.

Brame, A. H., Jr. 1968. Systematics and evolution of the Mesoamerican salamander genus *Oedipina.* J. Herpetol. 2:1–64.

Brattstrom, B. H., and R. M. Yarnell. 1968. Aggressive behavior in two species of leptodactylid frogs. Herpetologica 24:222–228.

Brocchi, P. 1881–1883. Études des batraciens de l'Amérique Centrale. Mission Scientifique au Mexique et dans l'Amérique Centrale, Recherches Zoologiques. Paris, Imprimerie Nationale. 122 pp., 21 pls.

Brown, B. C. 1937. Notes on *Coniophanes imperialis* (Baird). Copeia 1937:234.

Brown, K. M., and O. J. Sexton. 1973. Stimulation of reproductive activity of female *Anolis sagrei* by moisture. Physiol. Zool. 46:168–172.

Burger, W. L. 1950. A preliminary study of the subspecies of the jumping viper, *Bothrops nummifer.* Bull. Chicago Acad. Sci. 9:59–67.

Burger, W. L., and P. W. Smith. 1950. The coloration of the tail tip of young fer-de-lances: Sexual dimorphism rather than adaptive coloration. Science 112:431–433.

Burger, W. L., and J. E. Werler. 1954. The subspecies of the ring-necked coffee snake, *Ninia diademata,* and a short biological and taxonomic account of the genus. Univ. Kansas Sci. Bull. 36:643–672.

Burt, C. E. 1931. A study of the teiid lizards of the genus *Cnemidophorus* with special reference to their phylogenetic relationships. Bull. U.S. Natl. Mus. 154:1–286.

Campbell, J. A., and J. L. Camarillo R. 1994. A new lizard of the genus *Diploglossus* (Anguidae: Diploglossinae) from Mexico, with a review of the Mexican and northern Central American species. Herpetologica 50:193–209.

Campbell, J. A., D. R. Formanowicz, and P. B. Medley. 1989. The reproductive cycle of *Norops uniformis* (Sauria: Iguanidae) in Veracruz, México. Biotropica 21:237–243.

Campbell, J. A., and W. W. Lamar. 1989. The Venomous Reptiles of Latin America. Cornell University Press, Ithaca, New York. 425 pp.

Campbell, J. A., W. W. Lamar, and D. M. Hillis. 1989. A new species of diminutive *Eleutherodactylus* (Leptodactylidae) from Oaxaca, Mexico. Proc. Biol. Soc. Washington 102:491–499.

Campbell, J. A., J. M. Savage, and J. R. Meyer. 1994. A new species of *Eleutherodactylus* (Anura: Leptodactylidae) of the *rugulosus* group from Guatemala and Belize. Herpetologica 50:412–419.

Campbell, J. A., and E. N. Smith. 1997. A new species of *Tantilla* from northeastern Guatemala. Proc. Biol. Soc. Washington 110: 332–337.

Campbell, J. A., and J. P. Vannini. 1989. Distribution of amphibians and reptiles in Guatemala and Belize. Proc. Western Found. Vert. Zool. 4:1–21.

Casas-Andreu, G. 1965. Estudio preliminar sobre las tortugas de agua dulce en México. Anal. Inst. Nac. Invest. Biol. Pesq. 1:360–401.

Censky, E. J., and C. J. McCoy. 1988. Female reproductive cycles of five species of snakes (Reptilia: Colubridae) from the Yucatan Peninsula, Mexico. Biotropica 20:326–333.

Christman, S. P. 1982. *Storeria dekayi* (Holbrook): Brown snake. Cat. Am. Amph. Rept. 306.1–4.

Conant, R. 1965. Miscellaneous notes and comments on toads, lizards, and snakes from Mexico. Amer. Mus. Novit. 2205:1–38.

Conners, J. S. 1989. *Oxybelis fulgidus* (green vine snake): Reproduction. Herp. Rev. 20:73.

Cook, D. G. 1984. A case of envenomation by the Neotropical colubrid snake *Stenorrhina freminvillei.* Toxicon 22:823–827.

Crimmins, M. L. 1937. A case of *Oxybelis* poisoning in man. Copeia 1937: 233.

Cruz, G. A., A. Soto, and R. V. Bermúdez. 1989. Reproducción de *Bothrops asper* y *B. nummifer* en Honduras (Serpientes, Viperidae). Rev. Biol. Tropical 37:201–202.

Darevsky, I. S. 1958. Natural parthenogenesis in certain subspecies of rock lizard, *Lacerta saxicola* Eversmann. Doklady Akad. Nauk. Ukr. SSR, Biol. Sci. Sect. 122:877–879.

Darevsky, I. S., L. A. Kupriyanova, and T. Uzzel. 1985. Parthenogenesis in reptiles. Pp. 411–526 in C. Gans and F. Billett (eds.), Biology of the Reptilia, John Wiley and Sons, New York.

Davis, D. D. 1953. Behavior of the lizard, *Corythophanes cristatus*. Fieldiana: Zool. 35:1–8.

Dixon, J. R., and F. S. Hendricks. 1979. The wormsnakes (family Typhlopidae) of the Neotropics, exclusive of the Antilles. Zool. Verh. 173:1–39.

Dodd, C. K., Jr. 1978. A note on the defensive posturing of turtles from Belize, Central America. Herpetol. Rev. 9:11–12.

Dowling, H. G. 1952. A taxonomic study of the ratsnakes, genus *Elaphe* Fitzinger. II. The subspecies of *Elaphe flavirufa* (Cope). Occas. Pap. Mus. Zool. Univ. Michigan 540:1–15.

———. 1960. A taxonomic study of the ratsnakes, genus *Elaphe* Fitzinger. VII. The *triaspis* section. Zoologica (New York) 45:53–81.

Dowling, H. G., and I. Fries. 1987. A taxonomic study of the ratsnakes. VIII. A proposed new genus for *Elaphe triaspis* (Cope). Herpetologica 43:200–207.

Downie, J. R. 1988. Functions of the foam in the foam-nesting leptodactylid *Physalaemus pustulosus*. Herpetol. J. 1:302–307.

———. 1990. Functions of the foam in the foam-nesting leptodactylids: Antipredator effects of *Physalaemus pustulosus* foam. Herpetol. J. 1:501–503.

Dubois, A., and W. R. Heyer. 1992. *Leptodactylus labialis*, a valid name for the American white-lipped frog (Amphibia: Leptodactylidae). Copeia 1992:584–585.

Duellman, W. E. 1956. The frogs of the hylid genus *Phrynohyas* Fitzinger, 1843. Misc. Publ. Mus. Zool. Univ. Michigan 96:1–47.

———. 1958. A monographic study of the colubrid snake genus *Leptodeira*. Bull. Am. Mus. Nat. Hist. 114:1–152.

———. 1960. A distributional study of the amphibians of the Isthmus of Tehuantepec, Mexico. Univ. Kansas Publ. Mus. Nat. Hist. 13:19–72.

———. 1961. A record size for *Drymarchon corais melanurus*. Copeia 1960: 367–368.

———. 1963. Amphibians and reptiles of the rainforests of southern El Petén, Guatemala. Univ. Kansas Publ. Mus. Nat. Hist. 15:205–249.

———. 1965. Amphibians and reptiles from the Yucatan Peninsula, Mexico. Univ. Kansas Publ. Mus. Nat. Hist. 15:577–614.

———. 1970. The Hylid Frogs of Middle America. 2 vols. Monogr. Mus. Nat. Hist. Univ. Kansas 1:1–753.

———. 1971. The burrowing toad, *Rhinophrynus dorsalis*, on the Caribbean lowlands of Central America. Herpetologica 27:55–56.

———. 1978. The fringe-limbed tree frog, *Hyla valancifer* (Amphibia, Anura, Hylidae) in Guatemala. J. Herpetol. 12:407.

Duellman, W. E., and D. C. Cannatella. 1984. Leptodactylid frogs of the *Physalaemus pustulosus* group. Copeia 1984:902–921.

Duellman, W. E., and M. J. Fouquette, Jr. 1968. Middle American hylid frogs of the *Hyla microcephala* group. Univ. Kansas Publ. Mus. Nat. Hist. 17:517–557.

Duellman, W. E., and Klaas, L. T. 1964. The

biology of the hylid frog *Triprion petasatus*. Copeia 1964:308–321.

Duellman, W. E., and L. Trueb. 1966. Neotropical hylid frogs, genus *Smilisca*. Univ. Kansas Publ. Mus. Nat. Hist. 17:281–375.

———. 1986. Biology of Amphibians. McGraw-Hill, New York. 670 pp.

Duellman, W. E., and J. B. Tulecke. 1960. The distribution, variation and life history of the frog *Cochranella viridissima* in Mexico. Am. Midl. Nat. 63:392–397.

Duellman, W. E., and J. Wellman. 1960. A systematic study of the lizards of the *deppei* group (Genus *Cnemidophorus*) in Mexico and Guatemala. Misc. Publ. Mus. Zool. Univ. Michigan 111:1–80.

Duellman, W. E., and J. E. Werler. 1955. Variation and relationships of the colubrid snake *Leptodeira frenata*. Occas. Pap. Mus. Zool. Univ. Michigan 570:1–9.

Duellman, W. E., and J. Wiens. 1992. The status of the hylid frog genus *Ololygon* and the recognition of *Scinax* Wagler, 1830. Occas. Pap. Mus. Nat. Hist. Univ. Kansas 151:1–23.

Duellman, W. E., and R. G. Zweifel. 1962. A synopsis of the lizards of the *sexlineatus* group (genus *Cnemidophorus*). Bull. Am. Mus. Nat. Hist. 123:157–210.

Duméril, A., M. Bocourt, and F. Mocquard. 1870–1909. Études sur les reptiles. Mission Scientifique au Mexique et dans l'Amérique Centrale, Recherches Zoologiques. Imprimerie Nationale, Paris. 1,012 pp., 77 pls.

Dundee, H. A. 1989. Inconsistencies, inaccuracies, and inadequacies in herpetological methodology and terminology, with suggestions for conformity. Herp. Rev. 20:62–64.

Dundee, H. A., and E. A. Liner. 1985. *Phrynohyas venulosa* (veined treefrog): Food. Herpetol. Rev. 16:109.

———. 1985. *Phrynohyas venulosa* (veined treefrog): Reproduction and size. Herpetol. Rev. 16:109.

Dundee, H. A., D. A. White, and V. Rico-Gray. 1986. Observations on the distribution and biology of some Yucatán amphibians and reptiles. Bull. Maryland Herp. Soc. 22:37–50.

Dunn, E. R. 1935. The snakes of the genus *Ninia*. Proc. Natl. Acad. Sci. 21:9–12.

———. 1939. Mainland forms of the snake genus *Tretanorhinus*. Copeia 1939:212–217.

Echelle, A. F., A. A. Echelle, and H. S. Fitch. 1978. Behavioral evidence for species status of *Anolis uniformis*. Herpetologica 34:205–207.

Echternacht, A. C. 1971. Middle American lizards of the genus *Ameiva* (Teiidae) with emphasis on geographical variation. Misc. Publ. Univ. Kansas Mus. Nat. Hist. 55:1–86.

Ernst, C. H. 1978. A revision of the neotropical turtle genus *Callopsis* (Testudines: Emydidae: Batagurinae). Herpetologica 34:113–134.

———. 1980. *Rhinoclemmys areolata* (Duméril and Bibron). Cat. Am. Amph. Rept. 251.1–2.

———. 1990. Systematics, taxonomy, variation, and geographic distribution of the slider turtle. Pp. 57–67 *in* J. W. Gibbons (ed.), Life History and Ecology of the Slider Turtle. Smithsonian Inst. Press, Washington, D.C.

Ernst, C. H., and R. W. Barbour. 1989. Turtles of the World. Smithsonian Inst. Press. Washington, D.C.

Ewert, M. A. 1979. The embryo and its egg: Development and natural history. Pp. 333–413 in M. Harless and H. Morlock (eds.), Turtles: Perspectives and Research. John Wiley and Sons, New York.

———. 1985. Embryology of turtles. Pp. 75–267 in C. Gans, F. Billett, and P. F. A. Maderson (eds.), Biology of the Reptilia, vol. 14, Development A. John Wiley and Sons, New York.

Firschein, I. L. 1951. Rediscovery of the broad-headed frog *Eleutherodactylus laticeps* (Duméril) of Mexico. Copeia 1951:268–274.

Firschein, I. L., and H. M. Smith. 1956. A new fringe-limbed *Hyla* (Amphibia: Anura) from a new faunal district of Mexico. Herpetologica 12:17–21.

Fitch, H. S. 1983. *Sphenomorphus cherriei* (Escincela Parda, Skink). Pp. 422–425 in D. H. Janzen (ed.), Costa Rican Natural History. Univ. Chicago Press, Chicago.

———. 1985. Variation in clutch and litter size in New World reptiles. Univ. Kansas Mus. Nat. Hist. Misc. Publ. 76:1–76.

Fitch, H. S., and J. Hackforth-Jones. 1983. *Ctenosaura similis* (garrobo, iguana negra, ctenosaur). Pp. 394–396 in D. H. Janzen (ed.), Costa Rican Natural History. Univ. Chicago Press, Chicago.

Fitch, H. S., and R. W. Henderson. 1978. Ecology and exploitation of *Ctenosaura similis*. Univ. Kansas Sci. Bull. 51:483–500.

Fitch, H. S., R. W. Henderson, and D. M. Hillis. 1982. Exploitation of iguanas in Central America. Pp. 397–417 in G. M. Burghardt and A. S. Rand (eds.), Iguanas of the World: Their Behavior, Ecology, and Conservation. Noyes Publ., Park Ridge, N. J.

Flores-Villela, O., and G. R. Zug. 1995. Reproductive biology of the chopontil, *Claudius angustatus* (Testudines: Kinosternidae), in southern Veracruz, México. Chelonian Conserv. Biol. 1:181–186.

Foster, M. S., and R. W. McDiarmid. 1982. Study of aggregative behavior of *Rhinophrynus dorsalis* tadpoles: Design and analysis. Herpetologica 38:395–404.

———. 1983. *Rhinophrynus dorsalis* (alma de vaca, sapo borracho, Mexican burrowing toad). Pp. 419–421 in D. H. Janzen (ed.), Costa Rican Natural History. Univ. Chicago Press, Chicago.

Fraser, D. F. 1973. Variation in the coral snake *Micrurus diastema*. Copeia 1973:1–17.

Fritts, T. H. 1969. The systematics of the parthenogenetic lizards of the *Cnemidophorus cozumela* complex. Copeia 1969:519–535.

Frost, D. R., and J. W. Wright. 1988. The taxonomy of uniparental species, with special reference to parthenogenetic *Cnemidophorus* (Squamata: Teiidae). Syst. Zool. 37:200–207.

Fugler, C. M. 1960. New herpetological records for British Honduras. Texas J. Sci. 12:8–13.

Gaige, H. T. 1936. Some reptiles and amphibians from Yucatan and Campeche, Mexico. Carnegie Inst. Washington Publ. 457:289–304.

Gaige, H. T., and L. C. Stuart. 1934. A new *Hyla* from Guatemala. Occas. Pap. Mus. Zool. Univ. Michigan 281:1–3.

Gloyd, H. K., and R. Conant. 1990. Snakes of the *Agkistrodon* complex: A monographic review. Soc. Stud. Amphib. Rept., Contrib. Herpetol. No. 6:1–614.

Gradstein, S. R., and C. Equihua. 1995. An epizoic bryophyte and algae growing on the lizard *Corytophanes cristatus* in Mexican rain forest. Biotropica 27:265–268.

Greding, E. J., Jr. 1972. Call specificity and hybrid compatibility between *Rana pipiens* and three other *Rana* species in Central America. Copeia 1972: 383–385.

———. 1976. Call of the tropical American frog *Rana palmipes* Spix (Amphibia, Anura, Ranidae). J. Herpetol. 10: 263–264.

Green, D. M., and P. Alberch. 1981. Interdigital webbing and skin morphology in the neotropical salamander genus *Bolitoglossa* (Amphibia; Plethodontidae). J. Morphol. 170:273–282.

Greene, H. W. 1969. Reproduction in a Middle American skink, *Leiolopisma cherriei* (Cope). Herpetologica 25: 55–56.

———. 1970. Reproduction in a Mexican xantusiid lizard, *Lepidophyma tuxtlae.* J. Herpetol. 4:85–87.

———. 1975. Ecological observations on the red coffee snake, *Ninia sebae*, in southern Veracruz, Mexico. Am. Midl. Nat. 93:478–484.

———. 1983. *Boa constrictor* (boa, bequer, boa constrictor). Pp. 380–382 *in* D. H. Janzen (ed.), Costa Rican Natural History. Univ. Chicago Press, Chicago.

Greene, H. W., and R. W. McDiarmid. 1981. Coral snake mimicry: Does it occur? Science 213:1207–1212.

Greene, H. W., and W. F. Pyburn. 1973.

Comments on aposematism and mimicry among coral snakes. Biologist 55:144–148.

Greer, A. E. 1966. Viviparity and oviparity in the snake genera *Conopsis, Toluca, Gyalopion* and *Ficimia*, with comments on *Tomodon* and *Helicops.* Copeia 1966:371–373.

Greer, B. J., and F. D. Wells. 1980. Territorial and reproductive behavior of the tropical American frog *Centrolenella fleischmanni.* Herpetologica 36:318–326.

Grismer, L. L. 1988. Phylogeny, taxonomy, classification, and biogeography of eublepharid geckos. Pp. 369–469 *in* R. Estes and G. Pregill (eds.), Phylogenetic Relationships of the Lizard Families: Essays Commemorating Charles L. Camp. Stanford Univ. Press, Stanford, Calif.

Günther, A. C. L. G. 1885–1902. Reptilia and Batrachia. Biologia Centrali-Americana. Taylor and Francis, London. 326 pp., 76 pls.

Guyer, C., and J. M. Savage. 1986. Cladistic relationships among anoles (Sauria: Iguanidae). Syst. Zool. 35:509–531.

Haines, T. P. 1940. Delayed fertilization in *Leptodeira annulata polysticta.* Copeia 1940:116–118.

Hardy, L. M. 1975. A systematic revision of the colubrid snake genus *Ficimia*. J. Herpetol. 9:133–168.

———. 1980. *Ficimia publia.* Cat. Am. Amph. Rept. 254.1–2.

Harris, D. M., and A. G. Kluge. 1984. The *Sphaerodactylus* (Sauria: Gekkonidae) of Middle America. Occas. Pap. Mus. Zoology Univ. Michigan 706: 1–59.

Henderson, R. W. 1972. Notes on the reproduction of a giant anole, *Anolis biporcatus* (Sauria, Igaunidae). J. Herpetol. 6:239–240.

———. 1973. Ethoecological observations of *Ctenosaura similis* (Sauria: Iguanidae) in British Honduras. J. Herpetol. 7:27–33.

———. 1974a. Aspects of the ecology of the neotropical vine snake, *Oxybelis aeneus* (Wagler). Herpetologica 30: 19–24.

———. 1974b. Aspects of the ecology of the juvenile common iguana (*Iguana iguana*). Herpetologica 30:327–332.

———. 1976. Notes on reptiles in the Belize City, Belize, area. J. Herpetol. 10:143–146.

———. 1978. Notes on *Agkistrodon bilineatus* (Reptilia, Serpentes, Viperidae) in Belize. J. Herpetol. 12: 412–413.

———. 1984. *Scaphiodontophis* (Serpentes: Colubridae): Natural history and test of mimicry-related hypotheses. Pp. 185–194 *in* R. A. Seigel, L. E. Hunt, J. L. Knight, L. Malaret, and N. L. Zuschlag (eds.), Vertebrate Ecology and Systematics: A Tribute to Henry S. Fitch. Mus. Nat. Hist., Univ. Kansas, Lawrence.

Henderson, R. W., and M. H. Binder. 1980. The ecology and behavior of vine snakes (*Ahaetulla, Oxybelis, Thelotornis, Uromacer*): A review. Milwaukee Pub. Mus. Contrib. Biol. Geol. 37:1–38.

Henderson, R. W., and H. S. Fitch. 1975. A comparative study of the structural and climatic habitats of *Anolis sericeus* (Reptilia: Iguanidae) and its syntopic congeners at four localities in southern Mexico. Herpetologica 31:459–471.

Henderson, R. W., and L. G. Hoevers. 1975. A checklist and key to the amphibians and reptiles of Belize, Central America. Milwaukee Publ. Mus. Contrib. Biol. Geol. 5:1–63.

———. 1977a. The head-neck display of *Ninia s. sebae* (Reptilia, Serpentes, Colubridae) in northern Belize. J. Herpetol. 11:106–108.

———. 1977b. The seasonal incidence of snakes at a locality in northern Belize. Copeia 1977:349–355.

———. 1979. Variation in the snake *Tretanorhinus nigroluteus lateralis* in Belize, with notes on breeding tubercles. Herpetologica 35:245–248.

Henderson, R. W., L. G. Hoevers, and L. D. Wilson. 1977. A new species of *Sibon* (Reptilia, Serpentes, Colubridae) from Belize, Central America. J. Herpetol. 11:77–79.

Henderson, R. W., and M. A. Nickerson. 1976. Observations on the behavioral ecology of three species of *Imantodes* (Reptilia, Serpentes, Colubridae). J. Herpetol. 10:205–210.

———. 1977. Observations on the feeding behavior and movements of *Oxybelis aeneus* and *O. fulgidus* (Serpentes: Colubridae). Brit. J. Herpetol. 5:663–667.

Henderson, R. W., M. A. Nickerson, and L. G. Hoevers. 1977. Observations and comments on the feeding behavior of *Leptophis* (Reptilia, Serpentes, Colubridae). J. Herpetol. 11:231–232.

Heyer, R. W. 1970. Studies on the frogs of the genus *Leptodactylus* (Amphibia: Leptodactylidae). IV. Biosystematics of the *melanonotus* group. Contrib. Sci. Los Angeles Co. Mus. 191:1–48.

———. 1971. *Leptodactylus labialis*. Cat. Am. Amph. Rept. 104.1–2.

Heyer, W. R., and A. S. Rand. 1977. Foam nest construction in the leptodactylid frogs *Leptodactylus pentadactylus* and *Physalaemus pustulosus* (Amphibia, Anura, Leptodactylidae). J. Herpetol. 11:225–228.

Hillis, D. M., and R. de Sá. 1988. Phylogeny and taxonomy of the *Rana palmipes* group (Salientia: Ranidae). Herpetol. Monogr. 2:1–26.

Himmelstein, J. 1980. Observations and distributions of amphibians and reptiles in the state of Quintana Roo, Mexico. Bull. New York Herp. Soc. 16:18–34.

Hirth, H. F. 1963. Some aspects of the natural history of *Iguana iguana* on a tropical stand. Ecology 44:613–615.

———. 1963. The ecology of two lizards on a tropical beach. Ecol. Monogr. 33: 80–112.

Holdridge, L. R. 1964. Life Zone Ecology. Trop. Sci. Center, San José, Costa Rica.

Holdridge, L. R., P. B. Lamb, and B. Mason. 1950. The forests of Guatemala. (Translated from the Spanish Los Bosques de Guatemala.) Turrialba, Costa Rica, unnumbered, 1 map in original publication.

Holman, J. A. 1964. Observations on dermatemyid and staurotypine turtles from Veracruz, Mexico. Herpetologica 19:277–279.

Hotton, N., III. 1955. A survey of adaptive relationships of dentition to diet in the North American Iguanidae. Am. Midl. Nat. 53:88–114.

Hunt, R. H. 1975. Maternal behavior in the Morelet's crocodile, *Crocodylus moreleti*. Copeia 1975:763–764.

———. 1977. Aggressive behavior by adult Morelet's crocodiles toward young. Herpetologica 33:195–201.

———. 1987. [Morelet's crocodiles in Belize, Central America]. Crocodile Specialist Group Newsletter 6:8.

Instituto Nacional de Sismología, Vulcanología, Meteorología e Hidrología (INSIVUMEH). 1992. Datos Meteorológicos de las Cabeceras Departamentales. 195 pp.

———. 1994. Datos climáticos de la estación Tikal, clave 110108: registro de 1988–1994. Sección de climatología.

Iverson, J. B. 1976. The genus *Kinosternon* in Belize (Testudines: Kinosternidae). Herpetologica 32:258–262.

———. 1980. *Kinosternon acutum* Gray, Tabasco mud turtle. Cat. Am. Amph. Rept. 261.1–2.

———. 1982. Adaptation to herbivory in iguanine lizards. Pp. 60–78 *in* G. M. Burghardt and A. S. Rand (eds.), Iguanas of the World: Their Behavior, Ecology, and Conservation. Noyes Pub., Park Ridge, N. J.

———. 1983. *Staurotypus triporcatus* (Wiegmann). Cat. Am. Amph. Rept. 328.1–2.

———. 1985. *Staurotypus* Wagler, Mexican musk turtles. Cat. Am. Amph. Rept. 362.1–2.

———. 1992. A Revised Checklist with Distribution Maps of the Turtles of the World. Privately printed. Richmond, Ind. 363 pp.

Iverson, J. B., and J. F. Berry. 1980. *Claudius angustatus* Cope, narrow-bridged musk turtle. Cat. Am. Amph. Rept. 236.1–2.

Iverson, J. B., and R. A. Mittermeier. 1980. *Dermatemys mawii*. Cat. Am. Amph. Rept. 237.1–4.

Janzen, D. H. 1962. Injury caused by toxic secretions of *Phrynohyas spilomma* Cope. Copeia 1962:651.

Janzen, F. J., and E. D. Brodie, III. 1995. Visually-oriented foraging in a natural population of herbivorous lizards (*Ctenosaura similis*). J. Herpetol. 29:132–136.

Johnson, J. D. 1977. The taxonomy and distribution of the neotropical whipsnake *Masticophis mentovarius* (Reptilia, Serpentes, Colubridae). J. Herpetol. 11:287–309.

———. 1982. *Masticophis mentovarius*. Cat. Am. Amph. Rept. 295.1–4.

———. 1988. Comments on the report of envenomation by the colubrid snake *Stenorrhina freminvillei*. Toxicon 26:519–521.

Jolón-Morales, M. R. 1996. Ecología poblacional del ratón espinoso de bolsas, *Heteromys desmarestianus* (Rodentia: Heteromyidae) en el Parque Nacional Tikal, Petén, Guatemala. Universidad de San Carlos de Guatemala, Facultad de Ciencias Químicas y Farmacia, Escuela de Biología. 82 pp.

Keiser, E. D., Jr. [1974]. A systematic study of the neotropical vine snake *Oxybelis aeneus* (Wagler). Bull. Texas Mem. Mus. 22:1–51.

———. 1975. Observations on tongue extension of vine snakes (genus *Oxybelis*) with suggested behavioral hypotheses. Herpetologica 31:131–133.

Kennedy, J. P. 1965. Notes on the habitat and behavior of a snake, *Oxybelis aeneus* Wagler, in Veracruz. Southwest. Nat. 10:136–139.

Klauber, L. M. 1945. The geckos of the genus *Coleonyx* with description of new subspecies. Trans. San Diego Soc. Nat. Hist. 10: 311–393.

———. 1952. Taxonomic studies of the rattlesnakes of mainland Mexico. Bull. Zool. Soc. San Diego 26:1–143.

———. 1972. Rattlesnakes: Their habits, life histories, and influence on mankind. 2nd ed., 2 vols. Berkeley and Los Angeles, Univ. California Press. 1,533 pp.

Kofron, C. P. 1982. A review of the Mexican snail-eating snakes, *Dipsas brevifacies* and *Dipsas gaigeae*. J. Herpetol. 16:270–286.

———. 1983. Female reproductive cycle of the neotropical snail-eating snake *Sibon sanniola* in northern Yucatan, Mexico. Copeia 1983:963–969.

———. 1985. Systematics of the neotropical gastropod-eating snake genera, *Tropidodipsas and Sibon*. J. Herpetol. 19:84–92.

———. 1988. Systematics of neotropical gastropod-eating snakes: The *sartorii* group of the genus *Sibon*. Amph.-Rept. 9:145–168.

———. 1990. Systematics of neotropical gastropod-eating snakes: the *dimidiata* group of the genus *Sibon*, with comments on the *nebulata* group. Amph.-Rept. 11:207–223.

Lang, M. 1989. Phylogenetic and biogeographic patterns of basiliscine iguanians (Reptilia: Squamata: Iguanidae). Bonner Zool. Monogr. 28:1–172.

Lazcano-Barrero, M. A. 1992a. First record of *Bolitoglossa mulleri* (Caudata: Plethodontidae) from Mexico. Southw. Nat. 37:315–316.

———. 1992b. *Bolitoglossa mulleri* (Brocchi), Müller's salamander. Cat. Am. Amph. Rept. 533.1–2.

Lazcano-Barrero, M. A., and E. Gongora-Arones. 1993. Observations and review of the nesting and egg-laying of

Corytophanes cristatus (Iguanidae). Bull. Maryland Herp. Soc. 29:67–75.

Lazcano-Barrero, M. A., E. Gongora-Arones, and R. C. Vogt. 1992. Anfibios y reptiles de la Selva Lacandona. *In* Vásquez-Sánchez, M. A., and M. A. Ramos (eds.), Reserva de la Biosfera Montes Azules, Selva Lacandona: Investigación para su Conservación. Publ. Esp. Ecosfera 1: 145–171.

Lee, J. C. 1976. *Rana maculata* Brocchi, an addition to the herpetofauna of Belize. Herpetologica 32:211–214.

———. 1980a. An ecogeographic analysis of the herpetofauna of the Yucatan Peninsula. Misc. Publ. Univ. Kansas Mus. Nat. Hist. 67:1–75.

———. 1980b. Variation and systematics of the *Anolis sericeus* complex (Sauria: Iguanidae). Copeia 1980:310–320.

———. 1990. Creatures of the Maya. Nat. Hist. 1990:44–51.

———. 1996. The amphibians and reptiles of the Yucatán Peninsula. Cornell Univ. Press, Ithaca, N. Y. 500 pp.

Lee, J. C., and M. A. Salzburg. 1989. Mating success and pairing patterns in *Bufo valliceps* (Anura: Bufonidae). Southwest. Nat. 34:155–157.

Lieb, C. S. 1988. Systematic status of the neotropical snakes *Dendrophidion dendrophis* and *D. nuchalis* (Colubridae). Herpetologica 44:162–175.

———. 1991a. *Dendrophidion nuchale.* Cat. Am. Amph. Rept. 520.1–2.

———. 1991b. *Dendrophidion vinitor.* Cat. Am. Amph. Rept. 522.1–2.

Lowe, C. H. 1993. Introduction to the biology of whiptail lizards (genus *Cnemidophorus*). Pp. 1–25 *in* J. W. Wright and L. J. Vitt (eds.), Biology of whiptail lizards (Genus *Cnemidophorus*). Oklahoma Mus. Nat. Hist., Norman.

Lundell, C. L. 1937. The vegetation of Petén. Carnegie Inst. Washington 478:1–244.

Lynch, J. D. 1970. A taxonomic revision of the leptodactylid frog genus *Syrrhophus* Cope. Publ. Univ. Kansas Mus. Nat. Hist. 20:1–45.

Manjarrez, J., and C. Macías-García. 1992. *Thamnophis proximus rutiloris.* Herpetol. Rev. 23:61–62.

Marlin, J. A., K. K. Marlin, and S. G. Platt. 1995. A documented case of an attack by Morelet's crocodile (*Crocodylus moreletii*) on man. Bull. Chicago Herp. Soc. 30:165–167.

Martin, P. S. 1955. Herpetological records from the Gómez Farías region of southwestern Tamaulipas, Mexico. Copeia 1955:173–180.

Maslin, T. P. 1962. All-female species of the lizard genus *Cnemidophorus*, Teiidae. Science 135:212–213.

———. 1963a. Notes on a collection of herpetozoa from the Yucatan Peninsula of Mexico. Univ. Colorado Stud., Biol. Ser. 9:1–20.

———. 1963b. Notes on some anuran tadpoles from Yucatán, Mexico. Herpetologica 19:122–128.

———. 1968. Taxonomic problems in parthenogenetic vertebrates. Syst. Zool. 17:219–231.

———. 1971. Parthenogenesis in reptiles. Am. Zool. 11:361–380.

Maudslay, A. C., and A. P. Maudslay. 1899. A Glimpse at Guatemala and Some Notes on the Ancient Monuments of Central America. Taylor and Francis, London. 289 pp.

McCarthy, T. J. 1982. A note on the reproduction in *Laemanctus longipes* in Belize (Sauria: Iguanidae). Caribbean J. Sci. 18:133.

McCoy, C. J., Jr. 1966. Additions to the herpetofauna of southern El Petén, Guatemala. Herpetologica 22:306–308.

———. 1968. A review of the genus *Laemanctus* (Reptilia, Iguanidae). Copeia 1968:665–678.

———. 1969. Snakes of the genus *Coniophanes* (Colubridae) from the Yucatan Peninsula, México. Copeia 1969: 847–849.

———. 1970. The snake fauna of Middlesex, British Honduras. J. Herpetol. 4:135–140.

———. 1975. Reproduction in Guatemalan *Anolis biporcatus* (Sauria: Iguanidae). Herpetologica 31:65–66.

———. 1986. Results of the Carnegie Museum of Natural History expeditions to Belize. I. Systematic status and geographic distribution of *Sibon neilli* (Reptilia, Serpentes). Ann. Carnegie Mus. 55:117–123.

———. 1990. Additions to the herpetofauna of Belize, Central America. Caribbean J. Sci. 26:164–166.

McCoy, C. J., Jr., E. J. Censky, and R. W. Van Devender. 1986. Distribution records for amphibians and reptiles in Belize, Central America. Herpetol. Rev. 17:28–29.

McCoy, C. J., Jr., and T. P. Maslin. 1962. A review of the teiid lizard *Cnemidophorus cozumelus* and the recognition of a new race, *Cnemidophorus cozumelus rodecki*. Copeia 1962: 620–627.

McDiarmid, R. W., and K. Adler. 1974. Notes on territorial and vocal behavior of Neotropical frogs of the genus *Centrolenella*. Herpetologica 30:75–78.

Meerman, J. C. 1992. The status of crocodiles in the eastern Corozal District. Occas. Pap. Belize Nat. Hist. Soc. 1:1–5.

———. 1992. A new snake for Belize. Occas. Pap. Belize Nat. Hist. Soc. 1:26–27.

———. 1993. Checklist of the reptiles and amphibians of the Shipstern Nature Reserve. Occas. Pap. Belize Nat. Hist. Soc. 2:65–69.

Mendelson, J. R., III. 1990. Notas sobre una colección de anfibios y reptiles de Pueblo Viejo, Alta Verapaz, Guatemala. Publ. Ocas. Fundación Interam. Invest. Trop. 3:1–18.

———. 1992. Frequency of tail breakage in *Coniophanes fissidens* (Serpentes: Colubridae). Herpetologica 48:448–455.

———. 1994. A new species of toad (Anura: Bufonidae) from the lowlands of eastern Guatemala. Occas. Pap. Mus. Nat. Hist. Univ. Kansas 166:1–21.

Meyer, J. R. *Symphimus mayae*, an addition to the herpetofauna of Belize. Occas. Pap. Belize Nat. Hist. Soc. (*in press*).

Meyer, J. R., and C. Farneti-Foster. 1996. A guide to the frogs and toads of Belize. Krieger Publ., Malabar, Fl. 80 pp.

Miller, C. M. 1997. Natural history notes: *Eumeces sumichrasti*, brood. Herpetol. Rev. 28:151–152.

Milstead, W. W. 1969. Studies on beach lizards in Veracruz, Mexico. Herpetologica 25:140–146.

Minton, S. A., Jr., and M. R. Minton. 1991. *Masticophis mentovarius* (neotropical whipsnake): Reproduction. Herpetol. Rev. 22:100–101.

Mittleman, M. B. 1949. Geographic variation in Marcy's garter snake, *Thamnophis marcianus* (Baird and Girard). Bull. Chicago Acad Sci. 8:235–249.

Moll, D. 1986. The distribution, status, and level of exploitation of the freshwater turtle *Dermatemys mawei* in Belize, Central America. Biol. Conserv. 35:87–96.

Moll, E. O., and H. M. Smith. 1967. Lizards in the diet of an American caecilian. Nat. Hist. Misc. Chicago Acad. Sci. 187:1–2.

Morelet, A. 1871. Travels in Central America. Leypoldt, Holt, and Williams, New York. 430 pp.

Myers, C. W. 1971. Central American lizards related to *Anolis pentaprion:* Two new species from the Cordillera de Talamanca. Am. Mus. Novit. 2471:1–40.

———. 1974. The systematics of *Rhadinaea* (Colubridae), a genus of New World snakes. Bull. Am. Mus. Nat. Hist. 153:1–262.

Neill, W. T. 1960. Nature and man in British Honduras. Maryland Nat. 30:2–14.

———. 1965. New and noteworthy amphibians and reptiles of British Honduras. Bull. Florida St. Mus. 9:77–130.

———. 1971. The Last of the Ruling Reptiles. Columbia Univ. Press, New York. 486 pp.

Neill, W. T., and E. R. Allen. 1959a. Studies on the amphibians and reptiles of British Honduras. Publ. Res. Div. Ross Allen's Rept. Inst. 2:1–76.

———. 1959b. The rediscovery of *Thamnophis praeocularis* (Bocourt) in British Honduras. Herpetologica 15:223–227.

———. 1959c. Additions to the British Honduras herpetofaunal list. Herpetologica 15:235–240.

———. 1960. Noteworthy snakes from British Honduras. Herpetologica 16:145–162.

———. 1961a. Further studies on the herpetology of British Honduras. Herpetologica 17:37–52.

———. 1961b. Colubrid snakes (*Tantilla, Thamnophis, Tropidodipsas*) from British Honduras and nearby areas. Herpetologica 17:90–98.

———. 1962. Reptiles of the Cambridge Expedition to British Honduras 1959–60. Herpetologica 18:79–91.

Nelson, C. E. 1972. *Gastrophryne elegans.* Cat. Am. Amph. Rept. 121.1–2.

———. 1972b. Systematic studies of the North American microhylid genus *Gastrophryne.* J. Herpetol. 6:111–137.

———. 1974. Further studies on the systematics of *Hypopachus* (Anura: Microhylidae). Herpetologica 30:250–274.

Nelson, C. E., and R. Altig. 1972. Tadpoles of the microhylids, *Gastrophryne elegans* and *G. usta.* Herpetologica 28:381–383.

Nussbaum, R. A. 1988. On the status of *Copeotyphlinus syntremus, Gymnopis oligozona,* and *Minascaecilia sartoria* (Gymnophiona, Caeciliidae): A comedy of errors. Copeia 1988:921–928.

Oliver, J. A. 1947. The seasonal incidence of snakes. Am. Mus. Novit. 1363:1–14.

———. 1948. The relationships and zoogeography of the genus *Thalerophis* Oliver. Bull. Am. Mus. Nat. Hist. 92:157–280.

Olson, R. E. 1986a. *Dipsas brevifacies.* Herpetol. Rev. 17:67.

———. 1986b. *Sibon sanniola.* Herpetol. Rev. 17:67.

Parker, H. W. 1927. A fer-de-lance's strange meal. Nat. Hist. 1(3):81–82.

Penner, J. 1973. Habitat preferences of *Sceloporus chrysostictus* and *Sceloporus cozumelae* in the vicinity of Progreso, Yucatán, Mexico. Bull. Maryland Herp. Soc. 9:6–7.

Pérez-Higareda, G. 1980a. Additions to and notes on the known snake fauna of the Estación de Biología Tropical "Los Tuxtlas," Veracruz, México. Bull. Maryland Herp. Soc. 16:23–26.

———. 1980b. Notes on nesting of *Crocodylus moreleti* in southern Veracruz, Mexico. Bull. Maryland Herp. Soc. 16:52–53.

———. 1981a. Additions to the knowledge of the amphibians of the Estación de Biología Tropical "Los Tuxtlas" (UNAM), Veracruz, Mexico. Bull. Maryland Herp. Soc. 17:61–63.

———. 1981b. Nesting and incubation times in *Corytophanes hernandezi.* Bull. Maryland Herp. Soc. 17:80–82.

Pérez-Higareda, G., A. Rangel-Rangel, D. Chiszar, and H. M. Smith. 1989. The courtship and behavior of Morelet's crocodile (*Crocodylus moreleti*) in southern Veracruz, Mexico. Bull. Chicago Herp. Soc. 24:131–132.

———. 1995. Growth of Morelet's crocodile (*Crocodylus moreletii*) during the first three years of life. Zoo Biol. 14:173–177.

Pérez-Higareda, G., and H. M. Smith. 1989. Termite nest incubation of the eggs of the Mexican colubrid snake, *Adelphicos quadrivirgatus.* Herp. Rev. 20:5–6.

Pérez-Higareda, G., H. M. Smith, and R. B. Smith. 1985. A new species of *Tantilla* from Veracruz, Mexico. J. Herpetol. 19:290–292.

Pérez-Higrareda, G., and R. C. Vogt. 1985. A new subspecies of arboreal lizard, genus *Laemanctus,* from the mountainous region of Los Tuxtlas, Veracruz, Mexico (Lacertilia, Iguanidae). Bull. Maryland Herp. Soc. 21: 139–144.

Pérez-Higareda, G., R. C. Vogt, and O. Flores-Villela. 1987. Lista anotada de los anfibios y reptiles de la región de Los Tuxtlas, Veracruz. Est. Biol. Trop. "Los Tuxtlas," Inst. Biol., Univ. Nac. Autón. Mexico. 23 pp.

Peters, J. A. 1953. Snakes and lizards from Quintana Roo, México. Lloydia 16: 227–232.

———. 1960. The snakes of the subfamily Dipsadinae. Misc. Publ. Mus. Zool. Univ. Michigan 114:1–243.

Platt, S. 1992. Belize: Morelet's crocodile studies. Crocodile Specialist Group Newsletter 11:7.

———. 1993. *Rhinoclemmys areolata* (furrowed wood turtle): Diet. Herp. Rev. 24:32.

Polisar, J. 1994. New legislation for the protection and management of *Dermatemys mawii* in Belize, Central America. Herp. Rev. 25:47–49.

Porras, L., J. R. McCranie, and L. D. Wilson. 1981. The systematics and distribution of the hognose viper *Bothrops nasuta* Bocourt (Serpentes: Viperidae). Tulane Stud. Zool. Bot. 22:85–108.

Pounds, J. A., and M. P. Fogden. 1996. Conservation of the golden toad: A brief history. Brit. Herpetol. Soc. Bull. 55:5–7.

Prichard, P. C. H. 1979. Encyclopedia of Turtles. T.F.H. Publications, Neptune, N. J.

Pyburn, W. F. 1963. Observations on the life history of the treefrog, *Phyllomedusa callidryas* (Cope). Texas J. Sci. 15:155–170.

———. 1966. Breeding activity, larvae and relationship of the treefrog *Hyla phaeota cyanosticta*. Southwest. Nat. 11:1–18.

———. 1967. Breeding and larval development of the hylid frog *Phrynohyas spilomma* in southern Veracruz, México. Herpetologica 23:184–194.

———. 1970. Breeding behavior of the leaffrogs *Phyllomedusa callidryas* and *Phyllomedusa dacnicolor* in Mexico. Copeia 1970:209–218.

Ramírez Velázquez, A. 1992. Los gecos: Cuijas, niños, tamagaces y salamanquesas. Cuader. Divul. Instit. Hist. Nat. (Tuxtla Gutiérrez, Chiapas, México) 2:1–25.

Rand, A. S. 1972. The temperatures of iguana nests and their relation to incubation optima and to nesting sites and season. Herpetologica 28:252–253.

Rand, A. S., and E. P. Ortleb. 1969. Defensive display in the colubrid snake *Pseustes poecilonotus shropshirei*. Herpetologica 25:46–48.

Ream, C. H. 1965. Notes on the behavior and egg laying of *Corytophanes cristatus*. Herpetologica 20:239–242.

Ross, C. A. 1987. *Crocodylus moreletii*. Cat. Am. Amph. Rept. 407.1–2.

——— (ed.). 1989. Crocodiles and Alligators. Facts on File, New York.

Ross, C. A., and F. D. Ross. 1974. Caudal scalation of Central American *Croc-*

odylus. Proc. Biol. Soc. Washington 87:231–234.

Rossman, D. A. 1963. The colubrid snake genus *Thamnophis:* A revision of the *sauritus* group. Bull. Florida St. Mus. 7:99–178.

———. 1970. *Thamnophis proximus*. Cat. Am. Amph. Rept. 98.1–3.

———. 1971. Systematics of the neotropical populations of *Thamnophis marcianus* (Serpentes: Colubridae). Occas. Pap. Mus. Zool. Louisiana St. Univ. 41:1–13.

Rossman, D. A., N. B. Ford, and R. A. Seigel. 1996. The Garter Snakes: Evolution and Ecology. Univ. Oklahoma Press, Norman. 332 pp.

Rossman, D. A., and G. C. Schaefer. 1974. Generic status of *Opheodrys mayae*, a colubrid snake endemic to the Yucatan Peninsula. Occas. Pap. Mus. Zool., Louisiana St. Univ. 45:1–12.

Rossman, D. A., and K. L. Williams. 1966. Defensive behavior of the South American colubrid snakes *Pseustes sulphureus* (Wagner) and *Spilotes pullatus* (Linnaeus). Proc. Louisiana Acad. Sci. 29:152–156.

Roze, J. 1982. New World coral snakes (Elapidae): A taxonomic and biological summary. Mem Inst. Butantan 46:305–338.

Ryan, M. J. 1985. The Túngara Frog: A Study in Sexual Selection and Communication. Univ. Chicago Press, Chicago. 230 pp.

Sapper, K. 1932. Klimakunde von Mittelamerika. Hand. Klimat., band 2, 74 pp.

Savage, J. M. 1966. An extraordinary new toad (*Bufo*) from Costa Rica. Rev. Biol. Trop. 14:156–167.

———. 1987. Systematics and distribution

of the Mexican and Central American rainfrogs of the *Eleutherodactylus gollmeri* group (Amphibia: Leptodactylidae). Fieldiana Zool. New Ser. 33:1–57.

Savage, J. M., and B. I. Crother. 1989. The status of *Pliocercus* and *Urotheca* (Serpentes: Colubridae), with a review of included species of coral snake mimics. Zool. J. Linn. Soc. 95:335–362.

Savage, J. M., and M. H. Wake. 1972. Geographic variation and systematics of the Middle American caecilians, genera *Dermophis* and *Gymnopis*. Copeia 1972:680–695.

Savitzky, A. H. 1981. Hinged teeth in snakes: An adaptation for swallowing hard-bodied prey. Science 212: 346–349.

Schmidt, K. P. 1924. Notes on Central American crocodiles. Publ. Field Mus. Nat. Hist., Zool Ser. 12:79–92.

———. 1936. Guatemalan salamanders of the genus *Oedipus*. Field Mus. Nat. Hist., Zool. Ser. 20:135–166.

———. 1941. The amphibians and reptiles of British Honduras. Field Mus. Nat. Hist., Zool. Ser. 22:475–510.

Schmidt, K. P., and E. W. Andrews. 1936. Notes on snakes from Yucatan. Field Mus. Nat. Hist., Zool. Ser. 20:167–187.

Schmidt, K. P., and A. S. Rand. 1957. Geographic variation in the Central American colubrine snake, *Ninia sebae*. Fieldiana Zool. 39:73–84.

Schultz, K. D. 1996. A monograph of the colubrid snakes of the genus *Elaphe* Fitzinger. Koeltz Scientific Books, Czech Republic. 439 pp.

Seib, R. L. 1980. Human envenomation from the bite of an aglyphous false coral snake *Pliocercus elapoides*

(Serpentes: Colubridae). Toxicon 18: 399–401.

———. 1984. Prey use in three syntopic neotropical racers. J. Herpetol. 18: 412–420.

———. 1985. Euryphagy in a tropical snake, *Coniophanes fissidens*. Biotropica 17:57–64.

Sexton, O. J. 1980. Comments on the reproductive cycle of *Anolis limifrons* (Sauria: Iguanidae) at Turrialba, Costa Rica. Caribbean J. Sci. 16:1–4.

Sexton, O. J., and K. M. Brown. 1977. The reproductive cycle of an iguanid lizard, *Anolis sagrei*, from Belize. J. Nat. Hist. 11:241–250.

Sexton, O. J., J. Bauman, and E. Ortlieb. 1972. Seasonal food habits of *Anolis limifrons*. Ecology 53:182–186.

Sexton, O. J., and H. Heatwole. 1965. Life history notes on some Panamanian snakes. Caribbean J. Sci. 5:39–43.

Sexton, O. J., E. P. Ortlieb, L. M. Hathaway, R. E. Ballinger, and P. Licht. 1971. Reproductive cycles of three species of anoline lizards from the Isthmus of Panama. Ecology 52:201–215.

Shattuck, G. C., et al. 1933. The Peninsula of Yucatán: Medical, Biological, Meteorological, and Sociological Studies. Carnegie Institute, Washington, D.C. 576 pp.

Shreve, B. 1957. Reptiles and amphibians from the Selva Lacandona. *In* R. A. Paynter (ed.), Biological Investigations in the Selva Lacandona, Chiapas, Mexico. Bull. Mus. Comp. Zool. 116:193–298.

Sites, J. W., Jr., and J. R. Dixon. 1982. Geographic variation in *Sceloporus variabilis* and its relationship to *S. teapensis* (Sauria: Iguanidae). Copeia 1982:12–27.

Slevin, J. R. 1939. Notes on a collection of reptiles and amphibians from Guatemala. I. Snakes. Proc. California Acad. Sci. 23:393–414.

———. 1942. Notes on a collection of reptiles and amphibians from Guatemala. II. Lizards. Proc. California Acad. Sci. (4)23:453–462.

Slowinski, J. B., and J. M. Savage. 1995. Urotomy in *Scaphiodontophis:* Evidence for the multiple tail break hypothesis in snakes. Herpetologica 51:338–341.

Smith, E. N. 1994. Biology of the snake fauna of the Caribbean rainforest of Guatemala. M.S. Thesis, University of Texas at Arlington. 138 pp.

Smith, E. N., and M. E. Acevedo. The northernmost distribution of *Corallus annulatus* (Boidae), with comments on its natural history. Southwest. Nat. 42:348–350.

Smith, H. M. 1938. Notes on reptiles and amphibians from Yucatan and Campeche, Mexico. Occas. Pap. Mus. Zool. Univ. Michigan 388:1–22.

———. 1939. The Mexican and Central American lizards of the genus *Sceloporus*. Field Mus. Nat. Hist., Zool. Ser. 26:1–397.

———. 1941. On the Mexican snakes of the genus *Pliocercus*. Proc. Biol. Soc. Washington 54:119–124.

———. 1942a. A résumé of Mexican snakes of the genus *Tantilla*. Zoologica 27:33–42.

———. 1942b. A review of the snake genus *Adelphicos*. Proc. Rochester Acad. Sci. 8:175–195.

———. 1942c. Additional notes on Mexican snakes of the genus *Pliocercus*. Proc. Biol. Soc. Washington 55:159–164.

———. 1944. Notes on a small collection of reptiles and amphibians from Tabasco, México. J. Washington Acad. Sci. 34:154–156.

———. 1965. Two new colubrid snakes from the United States and Mexico. J. Ohio Herpetol. Soc. 5:1–4.

Smith, H. M., and W. L. Burger. 1949. A new subspecies of *Anolis sagrei* from the Atlantic coast of tropical America. Anal. Inst. Biol. Mex. 20:407–410.

Smith, H. M., and D. Chiszar. 1996. Species-group taxa of the false coral snake, genus *Pliocercus*. Ramus Publ., Pottsville, Pa. 112 pp.

Smith, H. M., O. Flores-Villela, and D. Chiszar. 1993. The generic allocation of *Tantilla canula* (Reptilia: Serpentes). Bull. Maryland Herp. Soc. 29:126–129.

Smith, H. M., and T. H. Fritts. 1969. Cannibalism in the lizard *Sceloporus chrysostictus*. J. Herpetol. 3:182–183.

Smith, H. M., and H. W. Kerster 1955. New and noteworthy Mexican lizards of the genus *Anolis*. Herpetologica 11:193–201.

Smith, H. M., and L. E. Laufe. 1946. A summary of Mexican lizards of the genus *Ameiva*. Univ. Kansas Sci. Bull. 31:7–73.

Smith, H. M., and G. Pérez-Higareda. 1989. The distribution of the snake *Clelia scytalina* in Mexico. Bull. Chicago Herp. Soc. 24:8.

Smith, H. M., G. Pérez-Higareda, and D. Chiszar. 1993. A review of the members of the *Sceloporus variabilis* lizard complex. Bull. Maryland Herp. Soc. 29:85–125.

Smith, R. E. 1968. Studies on reproduction in Costa Rican *Ameiva festiva* and

Ameiva quadrilineata (Sauria: Tei-idae). Copeia 1968:236–239.

Smithe, F. B. 1966. The Birds of Tikal. Natural History Press, Garden City, N.Y. 350 pp.

Snyder, R. C. 1949. Bipedal locomotion of the lizard *Basiliscus basiliscus*. Copeia 1949:129–137.

Solórzano, A., and L. Cerdas. 1987. *Drymobius margaritiferus* (speckled racer): Reproduction. Herp. Rev. 18:75–76.

———. 1989. Reproductive biology and the distribution of the terciopelo, *Bothrops asper* Garman (Serpentes: Viperidae), in Costa Rica. Herpetologica 45:444–450.

Stafford, P. J. 1994a. Amphibians and reptiles of the Upper Raspaculo River Basin, Maya Mountains, Belize. British Herpetol. Soc. Bull. 47:23–29.

———. 1994b. *Gymnopis syntrema* (Cope): An addition to the herpetofauna of Belize. Caribbean J. Sci. 30:277–278.

Stanley, P. C. 1941. The forests of Guatemala. Tropical Woods 67:1–18.

Stanley, P. C., and J. A. Steyermark. 1945. The vegetation of Guatemala: A brief review. Pp. 275–278 *in* Plants and plant sciences in Latin America. Chronica Botanica, Waltham, Mass.

Starrett, P. H. 1960. Descriptions of tadpoles of Middle American frogs. Misc. Publ. Mus. Zool. Univ. Michigan 110:1–38.

Stebbins, R. C., and N. W. Cohen. 1995. A Natural History of Amphibians. Princeton Univ. Press, Princeton, N.J. 316 pp.

Stuart, G. E. 1992. Maya heartland under siege. Nat. Geogr. 182:95–107.

Stuart, L. C. 1934a. A contribution to a knowledge of the herpetological fauna of El Peten, Guatemala. Occas.

Pap. Mus. Zool. Univ. Michigan 292:1–18.

———. 1934b. Studies on neotropical Colubrinae. IV. An apparently new species of *Coluber* from Guatemala. Occas. Pap. Mus. Zool. Univ. Michigan 284:1–4.

———. 1935a. A contribution to a knowledge of the herpetology of a portion of the savanna region of central Petén, Guatemala. Misc. Publ. Mus. Zool. Univ. Michigan 29:1–56.

———. 1935b. A new *Anolis* from northern Central America. Occas. Pap. Mus. Zool. Univ. Michigan 310:1–4.

———. 1937. Some further notes on the amphibians and reptiles of the Peten forest of northern Guatemala. Copeia 1937:67–70.

———. 1940. Notes on the "*Lampropholis*" group of Middle American *Lygosoma* (Scincidae) with descriptions of two new forms. Occas. Pap. Mus. Zool. Univ. Michigan 421:1–16.

———. 1941. Studies of neotropical Colubrinae. VIII. A revison of the genus *Dryadophis* Stuart, 1939. Misc. Publ. Mus. Zool. Univ. Michigan 49:1–106.

———. 1942. Comments on the *undulata* group of *Ameiva* (Sauria). Proc. Biol. Soc. Washington 55:143–150.

———. 1943. Taxonomic and geographic comments on Guatemalan salamanders of the genus *Oedipus*. Misc. Publ. Mus. Zool. Univ. Michigan 56:1–33.

———. 1948. The amphibians and reptiles of Alta Verapaz, Guatemala. Misc. Publ. Mus. Zool. Univ. Michigan 69:1–109.

———. 1950. A geographic study of the

herpetofauna of Alta Verapaz, Guatemala. Contrib. Lab. Vert. Biol. Univ. Michigan 45:1–77.

———. 1954. Herpetofauna of the southeastern highlands of Guatemala. Contrib. Lab. Vert. Zool. Univ. Michigan 68:1–65.

———. 1955. A brief review of the Guatemalan lizards of the genus *Anolis*. Misc. Publ. Mus. Zool. Univ. Michigan 91:1–31.

———. 1958. A study of the herpetofauna of the Uaxactun-Tikal area of northern El Peten, Guatemala. Contrib. Lab. Vert. Biol. Univ. Michigan 75:1–30.

———. 1961. Some observations on the natural history of tadpoles of *Rhinophrynus dorsalis* Duméril and Bibron. Herpetologica 17:73–79.

———. 1964. Through rain, mud and dark of night from Poptun to Guatemala City. Zoologists at Large Contrib. No. 1. Privately printed. 12 pp.

———. 1970. A brief review of the races of *Sceloporus serrifer* Cope, with special reference to *Sceloporus serrifer prezygus* Smith. Herpetologica 26: 141–149.

Swanson, P. L. 1950. The iguana *Iguana iguana iguana* (L.). Herpetologica 6:187–193.

Taylor, E. H. 1935. A taxonomic study of the cosmopolitan scincoid lizards of the genus *Eumeces* with an account of the distribution and relationships of its species. Univ. Kansas Sci. Bull. 36:1–643.

Taylor, H. L., and C. R. Cooley. 1995a. A multivariate analysis of morphological variation among parthenogenetic teiid lizards of the *Cnemidophorus cozumela* complex. Herpetologica 51:67–76.

———. 1995b. Patterns of meristic variation among parthenogenetic teiid lizards (genus *Cnemidophorus*) of the Yucatán Peninsula and their progenitor species, *C. angusticeps* and *C. deppei*. J. Herpetol. 29: 583–592.

Trapido, H. 1944. The snakes of the genus *Storeria*. Am. Midl. Nat. 31:1–84.

Trueb, L. 1970. The evolutionary relationships of casque-headed treefrogs with co-ossified skulls (family Hylidae). Univ. Kansas Publ. Mus. Nat. Hist. 18:547–716.

Villa, J. 1970. Notas sobre la historia natural de la serpiente de los pantanos, *Tretanorhinus nigroluteus*. Rev. Biol. Tropical 17:97–104.

———. 1977. A symbiotic relationship between frog (Amphibia, Anura, Centrolenidae) and fly larvae (Drosophilidae). J. Herpetol. 11:317–322.

———. 1984. Biology of a neotropical glass frog, *Centrolenella fleischmanni* (Boettger), with special reference to its frogfly associates. Milwaukee Pub. Mus. Contrib. Biol. Geol. 55: 1–60.

Vitt, L. J., and P. A. Zani. 1996. Ecology of the lizard *Ameiva festiva* (Teiidae) in southeastern Nicaragua. J. Herpetol. 30:110–117.

Vogt, R. C. 1990. Reproductive parameters of *Trachemys scripta venusta* in southern Mexico. Pp. 162–168 *in* J. W. Gibbons (ed.), Life history and ecology of the slider turtle. Smithsonian Instit. Press, Washington, D.C.

Vogt, R. C., and O. Flores-Villela. 1992a. Effects of incubation temperature on sex determination in a community of neotropical freshwater turtles in southern Mexico. Herpetologica 48:265–270.

———. 1992b. Aspectos de la ecología de la tortuga blanca (*Dermatemys mawii*) en la reserva de la Biosfera Montes Azules. *In* Vásquez-Sánchez, M. A., and M. A. Ramos (eds.), Reserva de la Biosfera Montes Azules, Selva Lacandona: Investigación para su Conservación. Publ. Esp. Ecosfera 1: 221–231.

Vogt, R. C., and S. Guzman Guzman. 1988. Food partitioning in a neotropical freshwater turtle community. Copeia 1988:37–47.

Volpe, E. P., and S. M. Harvey. Hybridization and larval development in *Rana palmipes* Spix. Copeia 1958:197–207.

Wake, M. H. 1977. Fetal maintenance and its evolutionary significance in the Amphibia: Gymnophiona. J. Herpetol. 11:379–386.

———. 1995. The spermatogenic cycle of *Dermophis mexicanus* (Amphibia: Gymnophiona). J. Herpetol. 29:11–122.

Webb, R. G. 1958. The status of the Mexican lizards of the genus *Mabuya*. Univ. Kansas Sci. Bull. 38:1303–1313.

Wellman, J. 1963. A revision of snakes of the genus *Conophis* (family Colubridae, from Middle America). Univ. Kansas Publ. Mus. Nat. Hist. 15: 251–295.

Wells, K. D., and J. J. Schwartz. 1982. The effect of vegetation on the propagation of calls in the neotropical frog *Centrolenella fleischmanni*. Herpetologica 38:449–455.

Werler, J. E. 1951. Miscellaneous notes on the eggs and young of Texan and Mexican reptiles. Zoologica 36: 37–48.

Weyer, D. 1990. Snakes of Belize. Belize Audubon Society, Angelus Press, Belize. 54 pp.

Williams, K. L. 1988. Systematics and natural history of the American milksnake, *Lampropeltis triangulum*. 2nd, revised edition. Milwaukee Public Museum, Milwaukee. 176 pp.

Wilson, L. D. 1966a. The range of the Rio Grande racer in Mexico and the status of *Coluber oaxaca* (Jan). Herpetologica 22:42–47.

———. 1966b. *Dendrophidion vinitor*: An addition to the snake fauna of British Honduras. J. Ohio Herpetol. Soc. 5:103.

———. 1975. *Drymobius margaritiferus*. Cat. Am. Amph. Rept. 172.1–2.

———. 1978. *Coluber constrictor*. Cat. Am. Amph. Rept. 218.1–4.

———. 1982. A review of the colubrid snakes of the genus *Tantilla* of Central America. Milwaukee Pub. Mus. Contrib. Biol. Geol. 52:1–77.

———. 1983. A new species of *Tantilla* of the *taeniata* group from Chiapas, Mexico. J. Herpetol. 17:54–59.

———. 1987. *Tantilla schistosa*. Cat. Am. Amph. Rept. 409.1–2.

———. 1988a. *Tantilla canula*. Cat. Am. Amph. Rept. 434.1.

———. 1988b. *Amastridium veliferum*. Cat. Am. Amph. Rept. 449.1–3.

———. 1988c. *Tantilla moesta*. Cat. Am. Amph. Rept. 454.1.

———. 1988d. *Tantillita brevissima, T. lintoni*. Cat. Am. Amph. Rept. 455.1–2.

Wilson, L. D., J. R. McCranie, and K. L. Williams. 1985. Two new species of fringe-limbed hylid frogs from Nuclear Central America. Herpetologica 41:141–150.

Wilson, L. D., and J. R. Meyer. 1969. A review of the colubrid snake genus *Amastridium*. Bull. S. California Acad. Sci. 68:146–160.

———. 1971. A revision of the *taeniata* group of the colubrid snake genus *Tantilla*. Herpetologica 27:11–40.

———. 1972. The coral snake *Micrurus nigrocinctus* in Honduras (Serpentes: Elapidae). Bull. S. California Acad. Sci. 71:139–145.

———. 1985. The snakes of Honduras, 2nd edition. Milwaukee Public Museum, Milwaukee. WI. 150 pp.

Wright, J. W. 1993. Evolution of the lizards of the genus *Cnemidophorus*. Pp. 27–81 *in* J. W. Wright and L. J. Vitt (eds.), Biology of Whiptail Lizards (Genus *Cnemidophorus*). Oklahoma Mus. Nat. Hist., Norman.

Zug, G. R., S. B. Hedges, and S. Sunkel. 1979. Variation in reproductive parameters of three neotropical snakes, *Coniophanes fissidens, Dipsas catesbyi,* and *Imantodes cenchoa*. Smithson. Contrib. Zool. 300:1–20.

PHOTO CREDITS

David G. Barker (DGB): Figures 60, 94, 144, and 149.

Edmund D. Brodie Jr. (EDB): Figures 21, 39, 75, 137, 153, 160, and 166.

Jonathan A. Campbell (JAC): Figures 4–9, 15–17, 20, 22, 26, 29, 34–38, 40, 42, 46–48, 50, 53–54, 56, 58, 62, 66–71, 73, 76–79, 81–82, 85–86, 89–93, 95, 99–105, 107–108, 110–111, 113–114, 116–117, 120–121, 125, 130, 133–134, 136, 138, 140–141, 146, 150–152, 155–156, 165, 170, 172, 174–175, 181, 184, and 188–189.

Courtney Conway (CC): Figure 55.

William E. Duellman (WED): Figures 96–97, 112, and 124.

William W. Lamar (WWL): Figures 14, 19, 23–24, 28, 30–32, 43–45, 51, 57, 63–65, 80, 87, 106, 118, 129, 131, 135, 143, 145, 158–159, 161, 168, 171, 173, and 176–179.

Julian C. Lee (JCL): Figures 98, 109, 128, and 163.

Robert A. Lubeck (RAL): Figure 154.

Mark A. Nelson (MN): Figure 33.

Louis Porras (LP): Figure 185.

Peter Rockstroh (PR): Figure 162.

Eric N. Smith (ENS): Figures 18, 25, 41, 49, 59, 72, 74, 83–84, 88, 115, 122, 132, 139, 142, 147–148, 157, 164, 169, 180, 182–183, and 186–187.

Peter J. Stafford (PJS): Figure 126, 167.

Richard C. Vogt (RCV): Figures 27, 52, 61, 123, and 127.

John E. Werler (JEW): Figure 119.

INDEX

This index contains the scientific, English, and local names of species discussed in the book. References in boldface type indicate color illustrations